The International Congress on World Evangelization held in Lausanne, Switzerland, in 1974 was a milestone in the history of evangelicalism around the world. One of the factors (perhaps the most important one) that made a difference was the significant input that Lausanne I had from the Majority World especially on issues related to the social dimension of both the gospel and the mission of the church. I am very pleased to recommend this collective work as a wonderful demonstration that the seed that was planted at that historical gathering has been bearing and continues to bear fruit on a global scale.

C. René Padilla, author of Mission Between the Times: Essays on the Kingdom, *President Emeritus of the Kairos Foundation, and President of the Micah Network*

It may have taken half a century but at last it seems that evangelicals have grown past the struggle to re-unite what they should never have pushed asunder in the first place. If the Lausanne Covenant of 1974 provided a powerful mandate for recovering an integrated and holistic understanding of biblically authentic mission as intrinsically including both evangelism and social responsibility, then Cape Town 2010 ought to mark the consolidation of that recovery and enable us all to move forward alongside those parts of the world church that have always had such an understanding of the gospel and mission, unhampered by western dichotomizing. This comprehensive volume, rich in its range of content and of international voices, helpfully documents a century of debate and gathers together some of the major issues in it – theological and practical – through the authoritative reflections of some of those who have been most influential in the movement, and others who are poised to carry the message to their own generation. It is particularly encouraging that in this volume a third major issue of missional importance has been recognized and added to the two that Lausanne 1974 wrestled with – namely creation care in the name of Jesus Christ, the Lord of heaven and earth. "We remind ourselves that the Bible declares God's redemptive purpose for *creation* itself. Integral mission means discerning, proclaiming, and living out, the biblical truth that the gospel is God's good news, through the cross and resurrection of Jesus Christ, for individual persons, *and* for society, *and* for creation. All three are broken and suffering because of sin; all three are included in the redeeming love and mission of God; all three must be part of the comprehensive mission of God's people." *Cape Town Commitment*, Lausanne III, 2010.

Christopher J.H. Wright
International Director, Langham Partnership International
Author of The Mission of God *(IVP), and* The Mission of God's People *(Zondervan)*

For much of the last century Christian mission has been bifurcated between those have majored on evangelistic proclamation and those who have defined mission as embodying the values of the reign of God. This collection of essays will forcibly remind the former that the gospel in its fullness is a message of the transforming rule of God over all creation. Equally it will remind the latter that God's reign of justice will not come unless mission-minded churches introduce people to transforming encounters of repentance and faith. The contributors of these essays, coming as they do from all parts of the globe, provide ample testimony that for the majority of the world church today there is no contradiction between the gospel of grace and the gospel of justice.

Brian Stanley, Professor of World Christianity, University of Edinburgh

The broad perspectives shared in the book are insightful and thought-provoking, especially for those of us who come from a background where cultural and religious practices are so intertwined. We need to keep biblical witness sharp and we are helped here to do that. 'Lay missionaries' will find themselves grappling with the true meaning of the gospel, and thinking through new ways to present it to individuals and communities, within their context. This book brings out the need for continuous engagement, dialogue and theological reflections on biblical doctrine and practices.

Affy Adeleye, HIV and AIDS co-ordinator for IFES
in English and Portuguese-speaking Africa

This is a valuable sample of evangelical 'reflection on praxis' from men and women active in holistic mission as well as theological education in different parts of the world. The book offers different but complementary perspectives on the development of the concept of holistic or integral mission in Asia, Africa, Latin America and Europe. The Lausanne movement since 1974 contributed to match evangelical zeal for evangelism with realism and sensitivity to the pain and tragedy of the human condition of the poor who are the majority of the world. Some of the tensions within world evangelicalism that are part of this development point to a process of growth in acceptance of the fact that the Christian church today is a global reality. Acceptance and acknowledgement of that fact is indispensable for the continuation of Christian mission, and this book is an excellent contribution towards that kind of understanding.

Samuel Escobar, Chairman of Senior Advisory Committee for Lausanne 3,
presently teaching Missiology in Spain

'Holistic mission' has bread an extensive literature since it was adopted around 50 years ago as a new way of describing the evangelistic task to which God calls evangelical Christians. Many now prefer 'integral' but either adjective now describe what is probably the default evangelical understanding of mission. The beauty of this volume is that it brings together in one place contributions from many that have been key players in the development of the concept. For anyone who wants to find out about the origin, meaning and story of 'holistic mission' this is an ideal place to start. For those committed to the task it maps the challenges that we face if we are to fulfil the vision.

Dewi Hughes, Theological Adviser for Tearfund UK,
member of Lausanne Theology Working Group and author of
Power and Poverty: Divine and Human Rule in a World of Need, *IVP*

REGNUM EDINBURGH 2010 SERIES

Holistic Mission

God's Plan for God's People

REGNUM EDINBURGH 2010 SERIES

Series Preface

The Centenary of the World Missionary Conference of 1910, held in Edinburgh, was a suggestive moment for many people seeking direction for Christian mission in the 21st century. Several different constituencies within world Christianity have been holding significant events around 2010. Since 2005, an international group has worked collaboratively to develop an intercontinental and multi-denominational project, known as Edinburgh 2010, and based at New College, University of Edinburgh. This initiative has brought together representatives of twenty different global Christian bodies, representing all major Christian denominations and confessions, and many different strands of mission and church life, to mark the Centenary.

Essential to the work of the Edinburgh 1910 Conference, and of abiding value, were the findings of the eight think-tanks or 'commissions'. These inspired the idea of a new round of collaborative reflection on Christian mission – but now focused on nine themes identified as being key to mission in the 21st century. The study process has been polycentric, open-ended, and as inclusive as possible of the different genders, regions of the world, and theological and confessional perspectives in today's church. It has been overseen by the Study Process Monitoring Group: Miss Maria Aranzazu Aguado (Spain, The Vatican), Dr Daryl Balia (South Africa, Edinburgh 2010), Mrs Rosemary Dowsett (UK, World Evangelical Alliance), Dr Knud Jørgensen (Norway, Areopagos), Rev. John Kafwanka (Zambia, Anglican Communion), Rev. Dr Jooseop Keum (Korea, World Council of Churches), Dr Wonsuk Ma (Korea, Oxford Centre for Mission Studies), Rev. Dr Kenneth R. Ross (UK, Church of Scotland), Dr Petros Vassiliadis (Greece, Aristotle University of Thessalonikki), and coordinated by Dr Kirsteen Kim (UK, Edinburgh 2010).

These publications reflect the ethos of Edinburgh 2010 and will make a significant contribution to ongoing studies in mission. It should be clear that material published in this series will inevitably reflect a diverse range of views and positions. These will not necessarily represent those of the series' editors or of the Edinburgh 2010 General Council, but in publishing them the leadership of Edinburgh 2010 hopes to encourage conversation between Christians and collaboration in mission. All the series' volumes are commended for study and reflection in both church and academy.

Series Editors

REGNUM EDINBURGH 2010 SERIES

Holistic Mission

God's Plan for God's People

Edited by Brian Woolnough and Wonsuk Ma

A full listing of titles in this series appears at the end of this book

First published 2010 by Regnum Books International

Regnum is an imprint of the Oxford Centre for Mission Studies
St. Philip and St. James Church
Woodstock Road
Oxford OX2 6HR, UK
www.ocms.ac.uk/regnum

09 08 07 06 05 04 03 7 6 5 4 3 2 1

British Library Cataloguing in Publication Data
A catalogue record for this book is available from the British Library

ISBN: 978-1-506476-08-7

Typeset by South View Lodge Publishing

The publication of this title is made possible through the generous financial assistance of the Commission on Theological education of Evangelisches Missionwerk in Deutschland (EMW, Dr. Verena Grüter), Hamburg, Germany.

Distributed by 1517 Media in the US and Canada

Contents

Foreword ix
Preface and Acknowledgements xi
Abbreviations xiv

Part A: Introduction

Good News for the Poor – Setting the Scene
Brian Woolnough 3

Part B: What is Holistic Mission?

What if We Defined the Gospel the Way Jesus Did?
Ronald Sider 17
Mission as Transformation – Its Journey among Evangelicals since Lausanne I
Chris Sugden 31
From Fourfold Mission to Holistic Mission: Towards Edinburgh 2010
Esther Mombo 37
The Missionary Journey of the Son of God into the Far Country
Damon So 47

Part C: Holistic Mission, From 1910 to 2010

Precursors and Tensions in Holistic Mission: An Historical Overview
Al Tizon 61
The Emerging Church in Africa and Holistic Mission: Challenges and Opportunities
Nicta Lubaale 76
The Work of God as Holistic Mission: An Asian Perspective
Samuel Jayakumar 87
Holistic Mission in Latin America
Tito Paredes 102

Part D: Underlying Issues in Implementing Holistic Mission.

Holistic Mission: New Frontiers
Bryant Myers 119
Mission as Transformation and the Church
Vinay Samuel 128

The Local Church, Transforming Community
Tulo Raistrick 137
Christian NGOs and their Role in Holistic Mission
Glenn Miles and Ian De Villiers 149
Development as Holistic Mission
Deborah Ajulu 160
Confronting the Powers: The Church's Political Commitment
Melba Maggay 175
The Churches Involvement with National Politics
Martin Allaby 187
God's Good News for Women, and Gender Issues
Beulah Herbert 198
Storm Clouds and Mission: Creation Care and Environmental Crisis
Margot R Hodson 212

Part E: The Way Ahead With Holistic Mission

Implications for the Church of Tomorrow
Brian Woolnough 229

Bibliography 248
Index 262
Contributors 266
Conference Delegates 269

FOREWORD

One of the most important developments in contemporary Christian missiology is the recovery of a theology of mission in the late twentieth century that integrates faith and life, word and deed, proclamation and presence. This holistic understanding of Christian mission is deeply rooted in the biblical theology of the Judeo-Christian faith of the Old and New Testaments.

In the explosion of Christianity in the global south in the twentieth century the church has had to contend with sharp socio-political issues of poverty, greed, corruption, health, education, and human sin in all its manifestations. How does the gospel address the human condition in an age that historian Eric Hobsbawm (1994) describes as 'The Age of Extremes'?[1] Where is the good news for the poor?

Because the Christian gospel of the kingdom of God is universally transformative, strong, and holistic, it challenges the *status quo* everywhere it is proclaimed. In proclaiming this gospel our Lord in his earthly ministry, practiced and modeled a holistic approach to ministry. As the gospel writers recorded, he went throughout the towns and villages, "*teaching* in their synagogues, *preaching* the good news of the kingdom and *healing* every disease and sickness. When he saw the crowds, he had *compassion* on them, because they were harassed and helpless, like sheep without a shepherd" (Mat. 9:35-36). His ministry of teaching, preaching, healing, and compassion transformed human lives and restored human beings to the dignity of the *Imago Dei*. His gospel, expressed in word and deed, powerfully reconciled human beings to their creator in a living and vital relationship that not only impacted the individual but also families, communities and nations.

That historical understanding of the mission of the people of God as witnesses and participants in the holistic demonstration of God's love and mercy in the world, suffered a major blow in the first half of the twentieth century, in what David Moberg (1972) describes as *The Great Reversal*.[2] The Great Reversal, which was a huge retreat by sections of the church from a holistic and integral understanding of the gospel to an individualized, soul-saving mission, polarized and divided the church. The gospel of Christ was

---

[1] E.J. Hobsbawn, *Age of Extremes: The Short History of the Twentieth century 1914-1991* (London: Abacus, 1995)

[2] D.O. Moberg, *The Great Reversal: Evangelism versus Social Concern* (Philadelphia: Lippincott, 1972, 3rd edition 2010)

diminished as a consequence, and the workings of God's kingdom in the world not sufficiently understood.

The church today is still challenged to authenticate the gospel in contexts where colonialism has left a legacy of structural poverty, economic underdevelopment, and disempowered and marginalized peoples. Thank God that an authentic biblical understanding of Christian mission as holistic and integrated is being restored, and that mission thinkers and practitioners now universally embrace holistic ministry as the truly transformative Gospel.

This volume on holistic mission addresses this challenge in a dynamic and multi-faceted way through a variety of voices from different contexts. Many should find the collection of materials it contains useful, stimulating and rewarding. Above all, as I commend it to you, may it stir greater response and engagement in the spread of the gospel of the kingdom of God throughout the world.

Las G. Newman, PhD
Chair, Council of Trustees, Oxford Centre For Mission Studies
President, Caribbean Graduate School of Theology

PREFACE AND ACKNOWLEDGEMENTS

Holistic Mission, or integral mission as it is often called, was not a term used at the World Missionary Conference in Edinburgh 1910. Mission, though not formally defined, was understood to be carrying the gospel into all the non-Christian World. This would address the conversion of both the soul and the injustices of society. It was to be taking the gospel from the western Christian world to enlighten and civilise those living in the dark, non-Christian countries. Prior to the twentieth century the work of the church and the missionary societies had 'naturally' been holistic.

And yet, in those 100 years the world has changed. There has been the end of colonialisation, a growing criticism of paternalism, and the striking growth of Christianity in the majority world, with those 'non-Christian countries' now having become the centre of gravity of the Christian world. The west, especially Europe, has no longer a predominantly Christian culture, and the centres of thriving Christianity are now found in the south, in the majority world, in the countries of Africa, South America and Asia. And the paternalist attitudes, even the colonial, imperialistic attitudes, are no longer appropriate, certainly no longer acceptable to the majority world. Even the understanding of the gospel, what is God's good news, has changed for many – though not all – Christians. There has grown a polarisation within Christendom. Whereas many still do see the gospel as being essentially about personal salvation, others see the gospel primarily in terms of a 'social gospel'. We would argue that Christians should revert to the traditional and biblical position and see God's good news as being holistic, being concerned with transforming the whole of creation, the whole person, body, mind and spirit.

The kingdom of God is here on earth and we are to seek, as we pray so often in The Lord's Prayer, that, "His kingdom may come, his will be done, on earth as it is in heaven." And that implies justice, peace, health, and wholeness, shalom, on earth as it is in heaven. Hence the term Holistic Mission, which addresses all aspects of human and social life, and seeks not only to address problems of sin, the fundamental root of all injustices and poverty, in the individual, but also to address those problems at the community, national and inter-national level.

In this book we will consider how such changes have come about since Edinburgh 1910, not only in the west, but also in the majority world. It will consider different ways, and different organisations through which the holistic gospel is being delivered and the issues that each contain. It will consider the successes, the limitations and the opportunities for the future that each contain.

Back in 2009, the Oxford Centre for Mission Studies (OCMS) was in discussion with the leadership of Edinburgh 2010 to undertake a study process to look at holistic mission. An agreement was soon reached between the two parties. To illuminate these issues we have had a two pronged approach. We have collected together an eclectic group of expert practitioners, church leaders and theologians, all of whom have much experience and expertise in and commitment to holistic mission, and asked them to share their insights in one specific aspect. We have sought global insights from experts from Africa, Asia, South and North America, and the UK. The first 18 chapters of this book represent their input. Then we held a conference, a workshop, at OCMS in Oxford where we gathered together a group of similarly committed practitioners to wrestle with the questions relating to each of the six groups demonstrating holistic Christianity today: the individual Christians, the local churches, the denominations and church groupings, the Christian NGOs working in relief and development, the missionary societies, and the theological training institutions. The final chapter brings together these findings and suggests an agenda for the future. Though there has been some co-operation between the contributors, it should be stressed that the content of each chapter is the responsibility of the named author writing it.

The perspective of this book, and the tradition of the different contributors, are largely from the conservative, evangelical, Pentecostal, charismatic wing of the church. This limited scope is due to the fact that the development of the holistic mission movement in the twentieth century has been a corrective effort to challenge the board evangelical communities, particularly those growing rapidly in the global south, to expand their understanding of mission beyond proclamation. This global Christian grouping has grown rapidly since 1910, particularly in the global south, and has probably shifted more in relation to holistic mission than others. It is estimated to represent around one billion Christians, one half of Christendom.

We are enormously grateful to the many contributors who have helped us with this venture, to the many years of service in holistic mission they represent, and to the way that God has used them mightily to further his kingdom here on earth. Though it is invidious to single out any one contributor, many would want to join me in expressing particular gratitude to Professor Ronald Sider, who through his seminal book *Rich Christians in an Age of Hunger*, through his more recent writings, including his chapter in this book, and through his presence and lead address at the Oxford conference, have proved a real inspiration to so many. We are grateful too to the Commission on Theological Education of *Evangelisches Missionswerk in Deutschland* for helping to fund the publication of this book, and to *First Fruit Inc* who helped us also with other expenses related to the conference.

I personally would like to thank most warmly Deborah Lake, Kate Harris and Tony Gray at Regnum, who have supported and encouraged me mightily, both as a planning group and individually, through a period which has not been entirely uneventful! And, of course, we would wish to thank our great and mighty God, who has strengthened and inspired us, and in whose service we have purpose as we seek to share holistic mission with his people.

We commend this book to others, not as a perfect answer to the problems of delivering God's gospel to a needy world, but as a humble contribution to all of those who seek to walk forward in God's ways and in God's service. To all those who seek to answer and obey the question, "What would Jesus do?"

Editors
OCMS, August 2010

Abbreviations

ACK	Anglican Church of Kenya
AIC	African Independent (or Instituted, or Indigenous) Church
AIM	Africa Inland Mission
AIPCA	African Independent Pentecostal Church of Africa
ATP	Agriculture and Theology Project
BFBS	British and Foreign Bible Society
BMS	Baptist Missionary Society
CAFOD	Catholic Oversees Development Agency
CBO	Community Band Organisation
CCS	Church Community Services
CD	*Church Dogmatics* (of Karl Barth)
CDE	Centre for Development and Enterprise
CIM	China Inland Mission (Now OMF, Overseas Missionary Fellowship)
CLADE	Latin American Congress of Evangelism
CMS	Church Missionary Society
CNGO	Christian Non-Government Organisation
COME	Christian Outreach for Mission and Evangelism
COWE	Consultation on World Evangelism
CRES	Christian Rural and Environmental Studies
CRESR	Social Responsibility in Grand Rapids
CSI	Church of South Indians
CTD	Consultation on a Theology of Development
DAC	Development Assistance Committee
EAM	Evangelical Association of Malawi
ECI	Evangelical Church of India
EEN	Evangelical Environmental Network
EFICOR	Evangelical Fellowship of India Commission on Relief
EMC	Emmanuel Ministries, Calcutta
EPA	Economic Partnerships Agreement
FBO	Faith Based Organisation
FMPB	Friends Missionary Prayer Band
FTC	Federal Trade Commission
GAIN	Global Aid Network
HBI	Hindustan Bible Institute

HDI	Human Development Index
HDR	Human Development Report
HIV/AIDS	Human Immunodeficiency Virus/Acquired Immune Deficiency Syndrome
ICCO	InterChurch organization for development co-operation
IEM	Independent Evangelical Mission
IFAD	International Fund for Agricultural Development
IFES	International Fellowship of Evangelical Students
IMC	International Missionary Council
IMS	Indian Missionary Society
INERELA	International Network of Religious Leaders living with or personally affected by HIV and AIDS
INFEMIT	International Fellowship of Evangelical Mission Theologians
INGO	International Non-Government Organisation
IPCC	International Panel on Climate Change
JRI	Josh Ray Institution
KCS	Keeping Children Safe
LCWE	Lausanne Committee for World Evangelism
LDC	Less Developed Country
LMS	London Missionary Society
LTEG	Lausanne Theology and Education Group
LTF	Latin American Theological Fraternity
MDG	Millennium Development Goal
MFC	Mission Founded Churches
MSF	Mission Sans Frontiers
MTM	Mission as Transformation Movement
NCCP	National Centre for Children in Poverty
NGO	Non-Government Organisation
NIC	Newly Industrialised Countries
NICA	National Independent Church of Africa
NMS	National Missionary Society
NRSV	New Revised Standard Version
NT	New Testament
OAIC	Organisation of African Institutional Churches
OCMS	Oxford Centre for Mission Studies
OT	Old Testament
OVC	Orphans and Vulnerable Children
PCEC	Philippine Council of Evangelical Churches
PLWA	People Living with Aids
REAP	Rural Extension with Africa's Poor
SAPs	Structural Adjustment Programmes
SCM	Student Christian Movement
SLC	Simple Lifestyle Consultation
SSA	Sub-Sahara Africa
TEE	Theological Education by Extension

TTI	Theological Training Institutions
UMN	United Mission in Nepal
UNCTAD	United Nations Conference on Trade and Development
UNDP	United Nations Development Programme
UNEP	United Nations Environment Programme
WB	World Bank
WCC	World Council of Churches
WEF	World Evangelical Fellowship
WWF	World Wildlife Fund
ZOE	Zimbabwean Orphans Endeavours

Part A

Introduction

GOOD NEWS FOR THE POOR – SETTING THE SCENE

Brian Woolnough

Jesus, our exemplar as well as our Saviour, asserts that he came to earth "to bring good news to the poor…." (Is. 61:1 and Lk. 4:18). He commissioned his disciples to go out and "make disciples of all men…" (Matt. 28:19). His clearest, and strongest, message to his disciples was that they should care for those in need around them (eg Matt. 25:31-46, Lk. 16:19-31, Lk. 10:25-38). It is difficult not to recognise that the good news that God wants us to share with the world is holistic. The good news that Christians are to take to the world is indeed a holistic mission, catering for all the needs of the world; the spiritual, the emotional, the psychological and the physical. And yet much missionary work in the past has been far from holistic, directed either at conversion and church planting or at social work, rarely at both together. The growth of holistic mission in the twentieth century, especially in the latter half, has arguably been one of the most significant and most heartening in the history of the church's mission to the world.

In this volume we have sought to tell the story of how holistic mission has developed since Edinburgh 1910, to explore the meanings of holistic mission, to examine the underlying issues, and to consider the implications for the church as it looks towards the future. We have been fortunate in bringing together a group of authors, all of whom have been instrumental in the development of holistic mission through out their lives, all of whom have sought reflectively to share God's good news with the world.

A Personal Introduction

Perhaps I may be permitted to give a personal introduction to this theme, to explain why it is so important to me, a non-theologian. Over the last decade or so I have met in Asia and in Africa a different type of Christian. I had grown up in a typical western Christian context, from a Christian home, through sound university Christian Unions and good evangelical churches. Yes, I had been influenced as a young Christian by Ron Sider's book on *Rich Christians in an Age of Hunger,*[1] but essentially my Christianity was focussed on believing the 'right things' – we were 'justified by faith'. Then I went to India, and to Africa, primarily to see and share in something of the work of Tearfund's relief and

[1] R.J. Sider, *Rich Christians in an Age of Hunger* (London: Hodder and Stoughton, 1977).

development partners in those countries where I met Christians like the late Vijayan Pavamani in Emmanuel Ministries Calcutta (EMC). He was the most Christ-like man I had ever met – humble, gracious, able, and totally committed to serving the poor. For him, his life was devoted to sharing the love of God with others, the poor and needy, on the streets of Calcutta. And that love of God was expressed quite naturally in addressing their physical and emotional needs in the context of their spiritual needs. He, and others like him, gave themselves and the love of God to those in need, not as a means to the end of getting them 'converted', but simply because God is love, and they needed that unconditional love. Subsequently I have had the privilege of meeting many such Asian and African Christians for whom their Christianity is a holistic out-working of the love of God, addressing the material and spiritual needs of the poor and their communities, not as two separate parts of their lives, but as a single, holistic whole. Such examples of Christianity in practice have challenged my fragmented view of what I should believe and what I should do, and inspired me to revert to the old maxim, 'What would Jesus do?' This book will attempt to unpack just what that simple, but infinitely profound, question means for individuals, Christian organisations and the church.

Jesus on the Streets[2]

We saw Jesus on the streets of Calcutta and Mumbai.
He, and she, was Indian.
He treated the sick and dying.
He fed the hungry.
He took in and cared for the homeless.
He taught them the ways, and the joy, of the Lord.
He gave himself for the poor and the needy, and he gave them unconditional love.
He brought joy to the hopeless, beauty in brokenness, and radiant love into many a dark and joyless place.

What do we Mean by Holistic Mission?

Holism or Integration

Holistic mission is usually accepted as that mission which addresses the body, mind and spirit in human beings. It is not exclusively addressed to the spirit, aimed at conversion and personal discipleship, nor is it exclusively concerned with the social gospel, tending to care merely for people's physical welfare. In 1974, at the Lausanne Conference, the evangelical community lead by Billy Graham and the International Congress in World Evangelism, brought together 2,300 evangelical leaders from 150 countries. Lead by John Stott, after considerable debate, they produced a paper, 'The Lausanne Covenant', which

[2] From Brian Woolnough's *Life on the Streets: Reflections on Visits to India with Tearfund* (Abingdon, UK: Larkhill Publishers, 2001), 4.

made it acceptable, indeed compulsory, for the evangelicals to include the social element in their mission to the world. They wrote, under a heading of Christian Social Responsibility, of "...expressing penitence for our neglect (of social responsibility) and for having sometimes regarded evangelism and social concern as mutually exclusive." They affirmed that, "evangelism and socio-political involvement are both part of our Christian duty." Adding, for good measure, that "faith without works in dead."

This statement has become seminal in the development of the evangelical approach to addressing the needs of the world, and was used more recently by Micah Challenge[3] as the basis for their work. At the Oxford meeting in 2001, this group stated that integral mission (their term for holistic mission) is

> …the proclamation and demonstration of the gospel. It is not simply that evangelism and social involvement are to be done alongside each other. Rather, in integral mission our proclamation has social consequences as we call people to love and repentance in all areas of life. And our social involvement has evangelistic consequences as we bear witness to the transforming grace of Jesus Christ. If we ignore the world we betray the word of God which sends us out to serve the world. If we ignore the word of God we have nothing to bring to the world. Justice and justification by faith, worship and political action, the spiritual and the material, personal change and structural change belong together.

But such an approach, integrating the different aspects of mission into a single integrated whole, could be considered a distinctively, and uncommonly, western approach. Western thought patterns, based on Greek dualism, tend to consider different aspects of life as being distinct. A person consists of a mind, a body and a soul. Knowledge can be fragmented into science, religion, and psychology etc. Thus, when westerners want to consider all aspects of life together they have to gather together, to integrate, the component parts. But such an approach is quite different to the thought patterns of the early writers of the scripture, of many Africans, Asians and South Americans, indeed for most of the world apart from the west, and those who have been influenced by western thought patterns.

This alternative, this majority world thought pattern, starts with a holistic approach to life. It sees a person in a holistic way, as being one, which automatically and obviously consists of all aspects of life – body, mind and spirit. Knowledge inevitably includes both spiritual and physical dimensions. There is no need to bring together, to integrate, different distinct components into a single whole; they already exist in a holistic unity. In the bible too we see the holistic approach in the Hebrew of the Old Testament and the words and culture of Jesus, in comparison with the more dualistic Greek language and thought patterns of Paul.

It has been suggested, by Asian and African theologians, that for them there is no problem with holistic mission, with integral mission, as their whole approach is holistic – 'holistic mission is a western hang-up'. Perhaps so, and

---

[3] For the story of Micah Challenge see M. Hoek and J. Thacker, *Michah's Challenge* (Milton Keynes, UK: Paternoster, 2009).

certainly it is clear that western Christians can learn much from their more holistic southern brothers and sisters in the majority world.

It is interesting to consider why some speak of holistic mission and some integral mission. For most the terms are synonymous. Integral mission has been used by some, e.g. Micah Challenge, to distinguish it from the word holistic which has been high-jacked in the west by the New Age movement in such terms as holistic medicine.

We shall in this book use the term holistic mission, though in doing so would not want to infer any artificial distinction from integral mission.

The target and the practice of holistic mission

This still leaves un-answered what, in practice, we mean by holistic mission. Are we speaking purely of the spiritual life and the physical welfare of an individual? The salvation of the individual? Or are we seeing the individual as part of the local community? Again, the western approach often separates the individual from the community, whereas for many around the world the community is seen as the fundamental unit to which each person belongs.

Much holistic mission starts with the personal needs of the individual. Hospitals and medical clinics cater for the individuals' health cares. Schools and educational projects are directed at individuals' academic needs and personal welfare. Water and sanitation projects cater again for the health and general welfare of the individual as well as the community. Children at Risk projects, sex-trafficking, anti-drugs projects, fair trade, micro-finance, and the like are all aimed at abuses of human rights for the individual.

But many, if not all of such ills in society, could be seen as the results of wider injustices in the world. Hence the inclusion of battles for social justice as an integral part of holistic mission. Yes, the cause of most suffering can be traced back to sin, hence the need again to treat not just the symptom but to address the root cause through the Christian gospel of repentance, forgiveness and salvation. It is also the reason why many see holistic mission as including political action, in fighting social injustice in the contentious political arena. Those fighting social oppression in South America, civil rights battles in America, apartheid in South Africa, political corruption in Africa, the caste system in Asia, are all propagating an aspect of holistic mission.

Shalom

Currently, as a result of sin, the world is in a state of dis-harmony. Myers[4] describes four senses in which our relationships are broken: the relationship with God, the relationship with self, the relationship with others, and the relationship with the rest of creation. Holistic mission must seek to heal all of

---

[4] B.L. Myers, *Walking With the Poor: Principles and Practices of Transformational Development* (Maryknoll, NY: Orbis Books, 1999).

these broken relationships. The old Hebrew word *shalom,* meaning peace, completeness and welfare, is at the heart of holistic gospel. Thus not only does it propose a way of restoring our relationship with God, but also to mend individual psyches, to bring justice and peace to the political systems between peoples, and to heal our relationship with God's created environment.

This fourth aspect of holistic mission has come relatively lately to the Christian world. Yes, Christians have recognised the world and the planet that God created, and praised him for it. But the concept of stewardship of the world has more commonly been translated as subduing it, and using for the benefit of humankind. Only recently has it been recognised that the 'use' has often been 'abuse', and the benefit has often been to a minority of people and to the detriment of others, and that any benefit has often been very short term with long term benefits being very far from apparent. Selfish greed has often predominated action and lead to grave abuses of God's created world, of which resource depletion and global warming are but two of the more obvious aspects. It is good to see that aspect of holistic mission developing through *a Rocha* and other Christian environmental groupings. How sad that so much of this campaign has been lead by secular organisations, whilst Christians have only recently got involved through a more fundamental shalom approach, and that even now some Christians oppose such mission, believing that the destruction of the earth will hasten the coming of the kingdom.

The church in its different forms.

In discussing holistic mission in relation to the church we need to differentiate different ways that the church expresses itself. The church is the body of Christ, the company of the saints, and this may be expressed through church organisations, denominations and their missionary societies, through local churches, through Christian Non Governmental Organisations concentrating on relief and development (CNGOs), through Theological Training Institutions (TTI), and through individual Christians working among their own communities. In this book we will be considering each of these aspects as valid expressions of the church in delivering holistic mission.

Much of the church's missionary strategy has been about church growth, and remarkably successful this has been over the last century, especially in the majority world and through the Pentecostal and charismatic churches. Traditionally, especially with western missionary societies, this has meant taking the gospel, the word of God through the bible, explaining Christian theology and persuading the locals to accept and be converted. The preacher, the missionary, will speak about the love of God, especially through his sacrificial love in sending his Son to earth to save us, and so encourage the listener to accept this.

There is another way, perhaps characterised by St Francis of Assissi's maxim, 'Preach the gospel at all times, if necessary, use words.' This is at the heart of holistic mission. I spent some time in the slums around Delhi, seeing the work of ASHA, a CNGO committed to improving the health, the hygiene and the physical state of the slum communities there. They worked through the local residents, empowering them to help themselves. They were apparently loath to preach the Christian gospel explicitly, and yet among those communities lively and vibrant home church groups were springing up. The approach of ASHA was to enter the slum community, get to know them and their needs, to work together with them to share, to analyse and tackle their problems, to spend time with them, to eat with them, to work together and to pray together about their social and physical problems. Then when they spoke of the love of God, the community responded positively: 'Oh yes, we know about the love of your God, we have seen it in your actions.' This was incarnational mission, and though the 'churches' produced, often as house groups, looked very different from the church plants that would have arisen from conventional mission outreach, it was exciting and much more akin to the early churches as described in Acts. Similar church growth was seen in India, through the work of Discipleship Centre and EFICOR, following their involvement in Tsunami relief. Superficially they were concerned with rebuilding houses and boats, but in practice they were involved with rebuilding communities and holistic church growth.

It was only boats and house[5]

It was *only* boats and houses that the Tearfund partners brought to the stricken communities.
No! It was new found life. It was holistic transformation.

Lives rebuilt.
Communities restored,
Spirits revived.
Love rekindled.
Smiles returned.
Hope re-awakened.

Some call it holistic mission. God's good news for the poor, God's love in action.
Jesus, said "I am come that they might have life, and life to the full."

A recent prayer letter from Moldova, a very poor country in eastern Europe, tells of a growing church involved in evangelism and training, and providing hot meals for the elderly, visiting and supporting local prisons and orphanages, providing youth clubs, life-skills training, and a farm and agricultural association for local poor farmers – holistic indeed.

---

[5] From Brian Woolnough's *Life on the Streets, and by the Sea: Reflections on Visits to India with Tearfund* (Abingdon, UK: Larkhill Publishers, 2006), 26.

How Holistic Mission has Developed Through the Church Since 1910

Pre 1910

Prior to 1910, right from the beginnings of the church, God's good news reached out strongly to the poor. Right through the Old Testament times and through into the story of the early church in the New Testament there is a strong message that those in need should be cared for, 'there should be no poor among you' (Deut. 15:11). Indeed it has been calculated that there are over 2,000 references in the bible to God's concern for the poor and the oppressed, and his hatred of injustice. In Acts it was clear that the early church 'had all things in common and shared what they had with the poor' (Acts 4:32-35), and that when there was a famine in Jerusalem the Macedonian church saw it as their responsibility, and privilege, to collect money and send it to them in relief (2 Cor. 8:1-4).

The church throughout the centuries had great concern to care for those in need, especially, but not only, those who were fellow Christians. Schools and hospitals, and food supplies, were an integral part of the life of the churches and monastries from the earliest days through to the present – one thinks of the founding by the church of the great schools and colleges throughout the world and the centuries, and a similar commitment to the building of clinics and hospitals. Church leaders, including those of the evangelical persuasion, have been involved in the anti-slavery movement, with social and prison reform, the development of workers' rights, and the fight for civil rights (though it must be said that other church leaders, perhaps the majority, were also involved directly with the slave trade, with social and worker abuse, with gross industrial exploitation and ill-treatment of fellow human beings). In regard to mission, though much of the missionary movement of the nineteenth century was concerned primarily with evangelism, the missionaries were equally, and seamlessly, involved with social action; tackling the caste system in India, boycotting the products of slave labour, and providing education and medical care where needed. Clearly holistic mission has been central throughout the two millennium since Christ. The 1200 leaders of missionary societies and church mission boards who attended Edinburgh 1910 would also have seen their tasks as holistic.

1910 and beyond

And yet since 1910 we find an increasing split within Christendom, with one group following up the ecumenical tradition set up at Edinburgh, whilst another group wished to prioritise personal salvation. The former group stressed less the doctrinal distinctions and concentrated more on action, and the social gospel. This lead in 1948 to the establishment of the World Council of Churches. The latter grouping, the conservative evangelicals, wished to base their faith firmly on the authority of the scriptures, reacted against the liberal biblical criticism growing throughout Europe, and increasingly adopted a pre-millenial theology in which they saw society as irredeemably depraved. They argued that society could only be saved, and the kingdom of heaven brought in, by first tackling the fundamental problem of individual sin. With the growth of Pentecostalism and the prosperity gospel, and the charismatic movements within the other denominations, this increased emphasis on individualism, and the concentration on individual spirituality increased and lead many evangelicals to ignore the needs of their local society. By the mid 1950s and 1960s this split was strong, with the evangelicals having built up an intellectual rigour for their faith and 'sound evangelicals' rejecting the 'doctrine-free' WCC, with its strong associations with the social gospel. Even Christian students at universities had to choose between joining the SCM (the liberal Student Christian Movement) or the IVF (the conservative evangelical InterVarsity Fellowship). Ironically, it was the conservative evangelicals, with their claims to believe in the absolute authority of the bible, who were rejecting the thoroughly biblical message of holistic mission.

Then, throughout the world, there was great intellectual, cultural and social revolution. In the 1960s, every aspect of social, political and religious life was questioned and reshaped. With the civil rights movements in the States, the 'winds of change' sweeping through Africa, and cultural norms and authority being challenged, it is not surprising that the church and its long-held traditions should also be questioned.

Perhaps in our context the seminal event was the renewed discussion being held within the evangelical world about the nature of mission, the relationship between saving souls and the 'social gospel', which culminated in the Lausanne Conference of 1974. This concluded with the clear affirmation in the 5th section of the Lausanne Covenant that the full gospel should include both personal salvation and social responsibility for the fallen world. For many evangelicals, however, this call for Christian social responsibility seemed to have fallen on deaf ears. Perhaps much of the church, especially in the prosperous countries throughout the world, has been compromised by being too readily assimilated into the dominant, social and financial culture of the increasingly materialistic world.

Alongside this movement within the church was the birth and growth of the Christian Relief and Development organisation, which provided a vehicle for Christians to work out, and support, the needs of poor and suffering around the world. Often arising out of war and conflict situations, the media brought into the homes of the west the pictures and stories of the suffering refugees. Exposure and compassion to such needs following the second world war (Christian Aid), then in Korea in the 1950s (World Vision), in Bosnia and Biafra in the 1960s (Tearfund), Christian relief and development organisations were set up by Christians with a heart for the suffering and oppressed. Other such CNGOs around the world sprung up around that time and have been active ever since, e.g. CAFOD (1962), CORD (1967), EFICOR (1968), and MSF (1971). The media, with ever more graphic TV pictures of suffering around the world, in Ethiopia, Bangladesh, Argentina or India, alerted Christians to the enormous needs and diversity of the 'third world' and the Christian NGOs provided a channel for those concerns.

The existence and growth of the CNGOs provided both a channel for the western churches and also an excuse for the churches themselves to ignore their responsibility to the poor and oppressed around the world. But slowly the churches themselves became involved in such work, especially as the CNGOs increasingly started working with and through the local churches in the developing world. Christians in their home churches could start relating to their brothers and sisters in other countries, and share in the holistic gospel with them.

Of course, one hundred years ago at Edinburgh 1910 mission would almost entirely have been seen in terms of the church's missionary societies, with western churches sending teams of missionaries 'Carrying the gospel to all the non-Christian World.' Societies such as the Baptist Missionary Society (BMS), the Church Missionary Society (CMS) and the China Inland Mission (CIM) – though this was one of the the growing number of inter-denominational, faith based missions. In those days mission was very much about the 'transmission of faith', and in practice this meant making other people 'like us' and building and bringing 'foreigners' into church. Now, especially over the last few decades, missionary societies have changed their goals and methods. This has been partly as a result of a broader understanding of the gospel, partly through the growth of the indigenous Christian church in the developing world, and partly as a result of what was acceptable to other, non-Christian, countries. In Nepal, for instance the goal of the United Mission to Nepal (UMN), founded in 1954, was 'to strive to address the causes of poverty as it serves the people of Nepal in the name and in the spirit of Jesus Christ.', and quite explicitly did not involve itself with direct evangelism.

The CMS now hold to the five marks of mission as expressed by the Anglican Communion: To proclaim the good news of the kingdom, To teach, baptize and nurture new believers, To respond to human need by loving service, To seek to transform unjust structures of society, To strive to safeguard the integrity of creation and to sustain the life of the earth. This is a thoroughly holistic mission. Many other missionary societies have moved in the same direction.

The history of the different church missionary societies make fascinating reading, we would commend readers to the appropriate sites (often now available on the mission's websites). We would commend especially the work of David Kerr and Kenneth Ross,[6] and of Kenneth Hylson- Smith[7] 'To the ends of the earth – the globalisation of Christianity.' The growth of the church and the sending churches in America, in Korea and in Africa, and the way that they

---

[6] D.A. Kerr and K.R. Ross, *Edinburgh 2010: Mission Then and Now* (Oxford: Regnum Press, 2009).

[7] K. Hylsom-Smith, *To the Ends of the Earth: The Globalisation of Christianity* (Carlisle, UK: Paternoster, 2007).

are now sending missionaries around the world, has been dramatic, and would have been almost inconceivable in 1910.

Alongside the humanitarian work of the holistic gospel, with its self-evidently 'good' intent, was the more contentious and political issue of fighting injustice. It has been said that God has a bias to the poor. He certainly shows through-out his word his great love for the poor and the oppressed and his hatred of injustice. Unfortunately much of the Christian church seems to have had a bias to the rich and the powerful, and a record more often of being on the side of the oppressor than the oppressed. However, in South America, Christians were being challenged by liberation theology to fight for the oppressed.[8] Bishop Osca Romero lead this movement in San Salvador and suffered with his life. In the United States, the civil rights movement lead by Rev Martin Luther King brought rights to the blacks and Hispanics. In South Africa the fight against apartheid had many Christian leaders, Father Trevor Huddleston and Bishop Desmond Tuto to name but two, but here again there were many in the church who supported the *status quo* of apartheid. Indeed the Dutch Reformed Church explicitly advocated it, justified by their interpretation of the bible. Others in Africa, such as Bishop Gitari in Kenya, fought for justice with their political leaders. In the Philippines, the church lead was central in overthrowing the corrupt government of President Marcos in their people's revolution. In Europe the church was central in the over-throw of communism. In the UK, and around the world, the churches were central in getting debt relief and fair trade for many of the poorest countries, through campaigns like Jubilee 2000, and Make Poverty History. Such contentious political action seems a long way from the apparently apolitical stance of those missionaries of 1910, but it is an integral part of holistic mission. If we are to bring shalom to all aspects of God's suffering and disjointed world we must get involved here too.

Ecumenism through holistic mission

Edinburgh 1910 was important in bringing many church denominations together in working together in ecumenical structures. Through the subsequent century, the ecumenical movement between the denominations has waxed and waned. Despite many initiatives and much effort and good will, the separate denominations are still distinct and far from united in the eyes of the world.

However, there is one area where ecumenism develops quite naturally, and that is in holistic mission where churches work together in addressing the common needs of society. Over the years, where churches have shared a common concern for the physical, material and social needs of their communities, they more readily work together to fight poverty and injustice. Recently the churches have come together around issues such as Jubilee 2000,

---

[8] Evangelicals Rene Padilla and Samuel Escabor were highly influential in bringing such majority world concerns onto the Laussane agenda in 1974.

Making Poverty History, Stopping the Traffic (in sexual exploitation) and in fighting other social evils. I have recently experienced other graphic examples of such ecumenical action in Malawi, where all the churches are tackling the problem of HIV/AIDS and health deprivation in the rural areas, working together through the EAM; in Southern India, where Tearfund was working through the local CNGOs to tackle the Tsunami destruction, it was interesting to note the Roman Catholic priests working alongside the Salvation Army – both churches who have had a long and glorious tradition of caring for the poor in holistic mission through medical and educational care. In our own church in the UK, we find that we are working alongside other churches in the town in establishing a food-bank for the needy and destitute. Somehow, the finer points of denominational distinctions seem to be irrelevant when serving the poor.

Structure of the Book

In considering how holistic mission has developed over the last 100 years, and the issues currently underlying the role of holistic mission in the church of today and into the next century, we have structured this book around three main sections.

The first section deals with the nature of holistic mission. Ron Sider sets the scene in its biblical context and challenges us to define the gospel as Jesus did. Chris Sugden then considers mission as transformation, an important concept especially among evangelicals, and traces how this has developed among this constituency since the seminal Lausanne conference in 1970. Esther Mombo then considers from an African perspective how mission developed from the fourfold ministries of evangelism, education, health and industrial training, into a more holistic practice. She highlights, among other things, the significance of holistic mission to women. Damon So takes us back to the fundamentals of Christianity, the life of Jesus, and illustrates holistic mission as being embodied in that exemplary life, death and resurrection.

The next section describes how holistic mission has developed since Edinburgh 1910, across different parts of the world. One hundred years ago the issue of mission was discussed from a largely Euro-centric perspective. The global church now is completely different, with the strength and life of the church having moved further south, east and west. Al Tizon takes a largely western perspective. Nicta Lubaale describes how the emerging church in Africa has had fresh opportunities and challenges to face. Sam Jayakumar gives an Asian perspective, where poverty and oppression have been at the root of their religious systems, and where examples of particularly Indian Christian missionaries have demonstrated holistic mission well before it was fashionable in the west. Tito Paredes takes us to Latin America where, arguably, some of the most dramatic, certainly the most political, expressions of holistic mission have developed.

The third section considers the issues relating to holistic mission in the current days. Bryant Myers challenges us to think more deeply about what 'walking with the poor' means in practice, particularly in the training of Christian practitioners who can challenge the secular development workers to a fuller, genuinely Christian, remedy for the world's poor. Vinay Samuel and Tulu Raistrick, from their different perspectives, analyse how the local churches can transform their local community, and are in fact the key to the implementation of a full, holistic, gospel. Tulu comes from the perspective of Christian relief and development NGOs, a perspective developed by Glenn Miles with Ian de Villiers and Deborah Ajulu. Christian NGOs have been a central development over the last half of the twentieth century and have been a way that the church, as para-church, has propagated holistic mission. Now they are increasingly working through the local church.

One of the most contentious areas of holistic mission has been the involvement of the church with the political systems of the day. For many Christians, particularly evangelical Christians, political issues, fighting the injustices of society, have been quietly ignored. We have tackled this issue head-on through chapters by Melba Maggay and Martin Allaby. Melba argues the case for political involvement, Martin expands on some of the difficult practicalities.

Finally, two issues central to the meaning of holistic mission have been addressed. Though at the time of the first Edinburgh conference the role of women was being debated actively in the west through the suffragette movement, the dominant role of men in the church has remained an unsatisfactory and unresolved sore. This role of women, so active in the social leadership in the home and the community, and so central in holistic mission, is addressed by Beulah Herbert, and also Esther Mombo earlier. Finally, an area which did not appear on the agenda of Edinburgh 1910 relates to the way that Christians relate to the environment, how God's shalom includes his created earth – Margot Hodson, opens up this increasingly important area of holistic mission.

In conclusion, after the discussions in the contributing chapters and the workshop in Oxford, we will draw together the key areas relating to holistic mission which are relevant to the church today, and suggest some challenges and opportunities for the future.

We have deliberately sought to give a wide-ranging, perhaps eclectic, overview of holistic mission. We have deliberately brought together perspectives from theologians, from church leaders and from practitioners, and we have sought insights from around the world with global leaders from the UK, from Asia, from Africa and from southern and northern America. We have been privileged in being able to bring together such an authoritative group of writers, and trust that their joint insights will be illuminating and inspirational.

PART B

WHAT IS HOLISTIC MISSION?

WHAT IF WE DEFINED THE GOSPEL THE WAY THAT JESUS DID?

Ronald J. Sider[1]

Evangelicals have a problem. Many evangelicals today do not define the gospel the way Jesus did.

If you ask evangelicals what the gospel is, the answer of many is: "Forgiveness of sins." Or, if they have studied theology: "Justification by faith alone." Frequently, the impression is given that the core of Christian faith, the essence in comparison with which other things are less important, is forgiveness of sins.

There are two problems with this understanding. First, if the gospel is only the forgiveness of sins, then it is a one-way ticket to heaven and you can live like hell until you get there. (One can embrace the Good News of forgiveness and still go on living the same adulterous, racist, unjust life as before.) The second problem is that forgiveness of sins is simply not the primary way Jesus defined the gospel.

Unless Matthew, Mark, and Luke are totally wrong, all who want to preach and live like Jesus must define the gospel as the Good News of "the kingdom of God." This phrase (or Matthew's equivalent, the "kingdom of heaven") appears 122 times in the first three gospels – most of the time (92) on the lips of Jesus himself.

Jesus points to the kingdom as the purpose of his coming. Both his preaching and his miraculous healing are signs of the kingdom. And he sends out his disciples to announce the kingdom.

For Mark, the kingdom is the best summary of his entire gospel: "After John was put in prison, Jesus went into Galilee, proclaiming the Good News of God. 'The time has come,' he said. 'The kingdom of God is near. Repent and believe the Good News'" (Mk. 1:14-15). Jesus explicitly defines his own mission in these terms: "I must preach the Good News of the kingdom of God to the other towns also, because that is why I was sent" (Lk. 4:43).

Jesus' response to John the Baptist demonstrates that Jesus viewed his preaching and healing as signs of the kingdom. In Luke 7:18-28, John's disciples ask whether Jesus is the "one who was to come" – i.e. the long-

---

[1] This chapter is adapted from my 'What Is the Gospel?' *Transformation* 16 (1999), 31-34, and *Good News and Good Works: A Theology for the Whole Gospel* (Grand Rapids: Baker, 1999), chs 3 and 4.

expected Messiah who will usher in the Messianic kingdom of God. For his answer, Jesus points to his preaching, and his healing of the blind, the lame, and even the socially ostracized lepers. Later, in his argument with the Pharisees, he makes the same claim, insisting that his miraculous casting out of demons is visible proof that the kingdom has begun (Mt. 12:28).

When Jesus sends out his disciples, he commands them to preach and demonstrate the kingdom in the same way. "As you go," he commissions the twelve, "preach this message: 'The kingdom of heaven is near.' 'Heal the sick, raise the dead, cleanse those who have leprosy, drive out demons'" (Mt. 10:7-8). The Seventy-Two disciples receive the same instructions: "Heal the sick... and tell them, 'the kingdom of God is near you'" (Lk. 10:9).

If anything is clear in Jesus, it is that the announcement and demonstration of the kingdom are at the very core of his message and life.

It is surely astonishing that precisely those Christians who speak most often about their desire to be biblical and their passion for evangelism do not define the gospel the way Jesus did. That in itself would be problematic. But it is even more serious when we realize that understanding the gospel merely as forgiveness of sins rather than as the Good News of the kingdom of God tends to lead to more serious problems. It easily leads us to reduce salvation to an inner, spiritual relationship between the individual soul and God. It also helps promote the neglect of the social transformation (e.g. between Jew and Gentile in the early church) that is clearly part of what the New Testament means by salvation. In fact, a failure to define the gospel the way Jesus did easily leads to cheap grace and a neglect of social ministry.

An examination of the story of Zacchaeus (Lk. 19:2-10) illustrates the problem. Zacchaeus was a wicked tax collector using and abusing an unjust structure. (The Jewish people had very good reason for their intense dislike of Jewish tax collectors working for the Romans!) But when Zacchaeus meets Jesus, he returns everything taken unjustly and gives half of his goods to feed the poor. The story concludes with Jesus' words: "Today salvation has come to this house…." (NRSV)

When one examines this passage carefully, one discovers that there is not a word in the text on forgiveness of sins. That is not to suggest that Jesus did not forgive his sins. The rascal surely needed it. But that is not what the text talks about. The passage describes the new, transformed economic relationships that Zacchaeus began to live out with his neighbors after Zacchaeus meets Jesus. That is what the text highlights as the salvation that Jesus brought to Zacchaeus. If the gospel were merely forgiveness of sins, it would not make sense to ignore forgiveness completely in the text and then announce the arrival of salvation which is surely what we receive when we embrace the gospel. On the other hand, if the gospel is the good news of the kingdom, the Zacchaeus passage does make sense.

A careful examination of what Jesus meant by the gospel of the kingdom of God will clarify both our theology and Christian discipleship. Jesus came, claiming to be the long expected Messiah and announcing that the Messianic reign of God was breaking into history in a special way in his person and work. But what *was* the Messianic expectation?

There are two basic strands in the prophets' Messianic predictions: a vertical and a horizontal component.

Jeremiah 31:31-34 shows that right relationship with God was at the centre of the Messianic hope. In the Messianic time when God makes a new covenant with Israel and Judah, God promises to "forgive their wickedness and remember their sins no more" (v.34). With forgiveness goes inner transformation because God also pledges to "put my law in their minds and write it in their hearts" (v.33). A renewed vertical relationship with God was central to the Messianic hope.

Equally important was the ringing declaration that the Messiah would restore right relationships with neighbor. "In the last days" (the prophets' shorthand for the Messianic time), "they will beat their swords into plowshares and their spears into pruning hooks" (Isa. 2:4). The parallel passage in Micah also foresaw a productive, just economic order: "They shall all sit under their own vines and their own fig trees, and no one shall make them afraid" (Mic. 4:4; NRSV). Not just inner hearts or individual relationships with a few neighbors but the whole social order will be transformed (Isa. 42:1-4). The prophets had long taught that God was especially concerned for the poor, weak and marginalized. Therefore it is hardly surprising that justice for the poor was central to their vision of the Messianic society. Of the Messianic shoot from the stump of Jesse, the prophet predicted: "With righteousness he will judge the needy, with justice he will give decisions for the poor of the earth" (Isa. 11:4). The prophets even dared to hope for renewed relationships with the non-human creation (Isa. 11:8-9).

The early church declared Jesus to be the fulfillment of these breathtaking Messianic prophecies. Matthew 4:15-16 quotes Isaiah 9:1-2 in connection with the beginning of Jesus' proclamation of the coming of the Messianic kingdom. Paul refers to Isaiah 11:1 and 10 in Romans 15:12. In Luke 1:68-79, Zechariah announces that John the Baptist will prepare the way for Jesus, the Messiah. Quoting Isaiah 9:2, Zechariah points with eager anticipation to the Messiah who will "guide our feet into the way of peace" (Lk. 1:79). When the angels (Lk. 2:14) announce Jesus' birth with the choral shout "on earth, peace," they simply confirm the dawning fulfillment of the prophetic vision of Messianic *shalom*.

Shivers of excitement must have raced through first-century Jewish listeners when Jesus announced the ringing words: "'The time has come,' he said. 'The kingdom of God is near. Repent, and believe the Good News.'" Jesus meant two things: he meant that he was the long-expected Messiah, and he meant that the Messianic age was breaking into the present.

Jesus never said the kingdom was fully present. Rather, he taught that the Messianic kingdom is already present, but is not yet complete. The account of Jesus' argument with the Pharisees about his power to cast out demons demonstrates that the kingdom was already present. "If I drive out demons by the Spirit of God, then the kingdom has come upon you" (Mt. 12:28). Jesus uses a past tense. The kingdom has already begun here in Jesus' person and work. But the kingdom is not here in its fullness. That will happen at Christ's return.

As in the case of the prophets, there are two aspects to Jesus' announcement of the Messianic kingdom of God: a vertical and a horizontal.

Entering the Kingdom: The Vertical Aspect

Jesus' teaching differed sharply from that of his contemporaries. The Pharisees believed that the Messiah would come if all Jews would obey the law perfectly. The violent revolutionaries of the time thought that the Messiah would come if all Jews would join in armed rebellion against Roman imperialism.[2] Jesus' way was (and still is) radically different. The kingdom comes as sheer gift. We enter not by good deeds or social engineering, but only as we repent and accept God's forgiveness.

In parable after parable, Jesus underlined God's acceptance of sinners (e.g. Lk. 18:9-14). The merciful Father in heaven is like the father who forgives the prodigal son (Lk. 15:11-32). It is not the self-righteous Pharisee but the greedy, oppressive tax-collector agonizing over his wickedness whom God forgives (Lk. 18:9-14). Only as we come as humble children with no claims can we enter Christ's kingdom: "Unless you change and become like little children, you will never enter the kingdom of heaven" (Mt. 18:3). When we do, we experience the boundless, eager mercy of God: "Do not be afraid, little flock, for your Father has been pleased to *give* you the kingdom" (Lk. 12:32). That same understanding of God led Jesus to die as the ransom for our sins (Mt. 20:28). Central to any biblical understanding of the kingdom is that we enter it by sheer grace and divine forgiveness. The kingdom comes as gift.

The Horizontal Aspect

According to Jesus' message, however, that is only *half* of the meaning of the good news of the kingdom of God.

Jesus was not a lone ranger. He was not an isolated prophet. He went around summoning people to *follow* him. Jesus gathered together a circle of disciples. Jesus and his disciples formed a new community that began to live in a way that was a visible model of Jesus' Messianic teaching. The new reconciled relationships in Jesus' new community are also central to the meaning of the gospel of the kingdom.

Jesus' teaching on divorce reveals a key part of the basic logic of Jesus' kingdom teaching on discipleship. The Mosaic law had permitted divorce (for

---

[2] Edward Schweizer, *The Good News According to Matthew* (Atlanta: John Knox, 1975), 132; and John Piper, *Love Your Enemies* (Cambridge: Cambridge University Press, 1979), 40-41.

the husband) because of sin. But that was never the creator's desire. Now, as the Messianic kingdom breaks in decisively, divorce is forbidden except for one kind of situation. Now, by the power of the spirit, it is possible–not perfectly, to be sure, but in radical new ways–for Jesus' followers to live the way the creator intended. A sweeping new horizontal reconciliation between husband and wife, rich and poor is possible. Why? Because the Messianic kingdom is now breaking in and the Holy Spirit is being poured out. In the power of the Spirit, Jesus' new Messianic community lives dramatically differently from the world.

According to Jesus, we cannot separate a right relationship with God from a right relationship to neighbor. Jesus' repeated linkage of God's forgiveness and our forgiving others underlines the point. Jesus tells the parable of the unforgiving servant (Mt. 18:21-35) to answer Peter's question about how often he must forgive other brothers and sisters in the community. Peter thought seven times might do! Jesus said seventy times seven – i.e. indefinitely. That is the context for Jesus' powerful parable of the unforgiving servant: "The kingdom of heaven is like a king…" (v.23) who forgives a prominent servant millions of dollars. Incredibly, that same servant instantly turns around and callously tosses one of his own obscure servants into jail for a few dollars. Furious, the king commands prison and torture for the merciless rascal. Jesus ends the story with the disturbing words: "So my heavenly Father will also do to everyone of you if you do not forgive your brother or sister from your heart" (v.35, NRSV).

Again and again Jesus repeats this point. In the Lord's Prayer, we ask God to "forgive us our debts as we also have forgiven our debtors" (Mt. 6:12, NRSV). Immediately after the prayer, Jesus emphasizes the point in the strongest way: "If you forgive others their trespasses, your heavenly Father will also forgive you; but if you do not forgive others, neither will your Father forgive your trespasses" (vv.14-15, NRSV).

Jesus is *not* teaching that our good deeds earn God's favor. But the creator who made us for community has decided that divine forgiveness will not forever remain with those who violate community by withholding forgiveness from the offending neighbor.

Challenging Evils of the Status Quo

One important thing to note about the horizontal aspect of the gospel of the kingdom of God is that Jesus and his new Messianic community challenged the status quo at numerous points where it was wrong. Think for example of Jesus' teaching about rich and poor, the marginalized, women, political leaders, and the violent revolutionaries.

Rich and poor. Jesus shocked the rich with his words about sharing. He told the rich young man who came inquiring about eternal life (and, probably, membership in Jesus' new circle as well) that he would have to sell his vast holdings and give all his wealth to the poor. As the wealthy youth turned away sadly, Jesus added a comment that still jars all of us who are rich: "It is easier for a camel to go through the eye of a needle than for a rich man to enter the kingdom of God" (Lk. 18:18-25). When another wealthy person responded in obedient repentance, he gave half of his vast riches to the poor (Lk. 19:2-10). Jesus urged the rich to make loans to the poor, even if there was no reasonable hope of repayment (Lk. 6:34-35). Those who do not feed the hungry and clothe the naked, he said, go to hell (Mt. 25:31-46). Jesus offered a sweeping challenge to an uncaring wealthy establishment.

The other side of this challenge to the rich was a powerful identification with the poor. Born in a stable, introduced to the agony of refugees as a child, Jesus, the wandering teacher, had no house of his own (Mt. 8:20). The poor flocked to him. He fed and healed the needy.

It is especially important to understand Jesus' teaching that his Messianic kingdom is especially for the poor. "Blessed are you who are poor, for yours is the kingdom of God. Blessed are you who hunger now, for you will be satisfied" (Lk. 6:20-21).

When John the Baptist asked if he was the Messiah, Jesus pointed to the fact that he healed the sick and preached the gospel of the kingdom to the poor (Lk. 7:21-22). The inaugural address in the synagogue at Nazareth includes the same statement about preaching to the poor (Lk. 4:18). One simply does not understand Jesus' teaching on the kingdom unless one sees that he was especially concerned that the poor realize that the kingdom breaking into history was particularly good news for them. Our proclamation of the gospel is simply unbiblical unless we, like Jesus, focus special attention on the poor.

The heretical neglect of the poor by many affluent Christians is a flat rejection of the Lord of the church. If Jesus is the norm, then faithful Christian sharing of the gospel will make the poor *one* major priority in such a way that the poor in the world today are as convinced as the poor in Jesus' day that the gospel is fantastic news for them – precisely because Jesus' new kingdom community embraces the poor, welcomes them into their fellowship, and shares economically so that, in the words of Acts, "there is no poor among them."

Any announcement of the gospel that does not include Jesus' kind of concern for and emphasis on the poor is not the biblical gospel.

The marginalized. Jesus' special concern for the poor extended to all the marginalized, weak and socially ostracized. In sharp contrast to his contemporaries, Jesus demonstrated a special interest in the disabled, children, drunkards, prostitutes and lepers (cf. Lk. 7:32-50; 19:1-10). In Jesus' day, lepers experienced terrible ostracism (Lk. 17:12), living alone in awful poverty, shouting "unclean, unclean" lest anyone accidentally touch them. Jesus gently touched the lepers and miraculously healed them (Mk. 1:41).

From the Dead Sea Scrolls, we learn that the Essenes, a Jewish religious group of Jesus' day, actually *excluded* the disabled from the religious community. Jesus, by contrast, commands the members of his new Messianic community to invite *precisely* these people: "When you give a banquet, invite the poor, the crippled, the lame, the blind" (Lk. 14:13). In the parable of the

Great Banquet, Jesus repeats the lesson, teaching that his kingdom is for "the poor, the crippled, the blind, and the lame" (Lk. 14:21). Jesus was directly defying contemporary norms and social practices.

Women. Jesus' attitude toward women reflects the same sweeping challenge to the status quo. In Jesus' day, it was a scandal for a man to appear in public with a woman. A woman's word was considered useless in court. It was better to burn a copy of the Torah (the first five books of the Old Testament) than allow a woman to touch it.[3] Indeed, according to one first century statement, "If any man teach his daughter Torah, it is as though he taught her lechery." Women were excluded from most parts of the temple. Nor did they count in calculating the quorum needed for a meeting in the synagogue. A widely used prayer by Jewish males thanked God they were not Gentiles, slaves or women: "I thank Thee Lord, that Thou hast not made me a Gentile... Thou hast not made me a slave... Thou hast not made me a woman."

Jesus and his new community rejected centuries of male prejudice and treated women as equals. Jesus appeared with women in public (Jn. 4:27), and taught them theology (Lk. 10:38-42). He allowed a woman (Lk. 7:36-50) that everybody knew was a sinner to wash his feet with her tears, wipe them with her long hair, kiss and perfume them – all in public! When Mary abandoned her traditional role cooking food to listen to Jesus' theology lesson, Martha objected. But Jesus defended Mary (Lk. 10:38-42).

Jesus must also have upset men with his teaching on divorce. In the first century, Jewish men could easily get a divorce. Women did not have equal privileges. Contemporary thinkers would probably have eliminated this inequality by granting women equal privileges. But that was not Jesus' way. Jesus insisted that God wanted a man and a woman to live in life-long faithful covenant.

In its attitude toward women, the early church continued to live Jesus' Messianic challenge to the status quo. Messianic prophecy had foretold that in the last days, daughters and sons, women and men would prophesy (Joel 2:28). That happened in the early church. Women prophesied (Acts 21:9; I Cor. 11:5) and corrected the theology of men (Acts 18:24-26). Liberated from the restrictions of the synagogue, women participated enthusiastically in the early church's worship services. Paul joyously boasted that in Christ, there is "neither Jew nor Greek, slave nor free, male nor female" (Gal. 3:28).

One understands this incredible claim about early Christian community only when one remembers that Paul is probably referring explicitly to the common Jewish prayer quoted above where men thank God that they are *not* Gentiles, slaves, or women. What an astonishing upsetting of the status quo! Jesus and his new community of women and men were indeed an upside-down kingdom.

Rulers. Jesus must have infuriated Herod. When someone warned him that Herod wanted to kill him, Jesus shot back his response: "Go tell that fox" (Lk.

---

[3] See C.F.D. Moule, 'The Significance of the Message of the Resurrection for Faith in Jesus Christ,' *Studies in Biblical Theology* 8 (1968), 9.

13:32). In Jesus' day, that word meant about the same thing as the slang use of the word 'skunk' does today.

In Jesus' time as today, rulers enjoyed dominating their subjects. Jesus was bluntly descriptive: "You know that those who are regarded as rulers of the Gentiles lord it over them." Jesus' kingdom model for his new community is strikingly different: "Not so with you. Instead, whosoever wants to become great among you must be your servant, and whoever wants to be first must be slave of all. For even the Son of Man did not come to be served but to serve, and to give his life as a ransom for many" (Mk. 10:41-44).

Jesus points to the cross, where he dies as the substitute for our sins, as the model for servant leadership in his new community.

Violent revolutionaries. The zealots believed that the Messiah would come if the Jewish people would all rise up in armed rebellion against the Roman imperialists. But that was not Jesus' way. The way of the kingdom was love – even for enemies (Mt. 5:44).

"You have heard that it was said, 'Love your neighbor and hate your enemy.' But I tell you: Love your enemies, and pray for those who persecute you, that you may be children of your Father in heaven" (Mt. 5:43-45). In this passage, Jesus rejects the standard Jewish interpretation, which limited neighborly love to fellow Israelites. Instead, he condemns retaliation and vengeance and extends neighborly love to anyone in need, even oppressive Roman imperialists.

Jesus fits the humble, peaceful view of the Messiah that was described in Zechariah 9:9-10. The crowds shouted Messianic slogans as Jesus made his triumphal entry into Jerusalem (Lk. 19:38; Mt. 21:9). But the Messiah rides on a humble donkey, not a warhorse! Jesus' peaceful path to Messianic shalom was a radical alternative and direct challenge to the popular, religious revolutionaries of his day.

It is important to see that the religious establishment moved to destroy Jesus for two reasons: because of his radical socio-economic challenge to the status quo and because of his alleged blasphemy. It is quite understandable that the religious, economic, and political establishment viewed Jesus' attack on the status quo as highly threatening. They obviously had to change their values and actions fundamentally or get rid of this disturbing prophet. We simply misunderstand what led up to the cross if we miss the fact that Jesus' execution is, "the punishment of a man who threatens society by creating a new kind of community leading a radically new kind of life."[4]

Jesus' theological claims also infuriated them. When he claimed divine authority to forgive sins, they objected (Mk. 2:6-11). When he set his own authority above that of Moses, they were offended (Mt. 5:31-39). When he told the parable of the tenants who destroyed the master's vineyard and identified himself as the special Son sent by the Master (Lk. 20:9-18), they began looking for a way to arrest him (v.19). When he broke their rigid rules by healing on the

[4] John Howard Yoder, *The Politics of Jesus* (Grand Rapids: Eerdmans, 1972), 63.

Sabbath, they decided to destroy him (Mt. 12:9-14). When, at the trial, he acknowledged that he was "the Christ, the Son of the Blessed One," they tore their clothes and pronounced him a blasphemer (Mk. 14:62-64).

Blasphemer, social radical, and Messianic pretender. That was the charge. That is why the political and religious leadership conspired to kill him. When they forced Pilate to admit that Jesus' Messianic claims were a political threat to Rome (Jn. 19:12-13), Pilate agreed to crucify him. The inscription on the Cross (*King of the Jews*) shows that the alleged crime was Jesus' Messianic claim. Roman governors regularly crucified Jewish Messianic pretenders in the first century.

In fact, Pilate and the priestly aristocracy were right. Jesus was a threat to their unjust, oppressive, unfaithful power and system. Jesus came, claiming to be the Messiah of the Jewish people. He urged the whole society to accept God's radical forgiveness and begin living his new kingdom values. But to do that, they would have to adopt Jesus' radical challenge to the way they exercised power and leadership and the way they treated the poor and marginalized. Equally serious, they would have to accept Jesus as God's Messiah and only Son. They preferred to kill him.

According to Jesus, the gospel is the good news of the kingdom of God. The vertical aspect of this gospel assures us of unconditional divine forgiveness. The horizontal aspect proclaims the fantastic news that the kingdom is now taking visible, concrete shape because Jesus' new community is actually beginning to live according to Jesus' kingdom norms. As they love the whole person the way Jesus did, challenge society at the points of its sinful rebellion, and embrace and become the instruments of grace to transform broken people, Jesus' disciples become a visible sign of the kingdom which is already present and will come in its fullness at Christ's return.

How Then Do We Communicate the Gospel of the Kingdom?

By word and deed. Jesus preached and healed. He taught and modeled. The eternal word become flesh was the perfect combination of word and deed.

Matthew 9:35 summarizes Jesus' entire public ministry under the three headings of teaching, preaching and healing: "Jesus went through all the towns and villages, teaching in their synagogues, preaching the good news of the kingdom and healing every disease and sickness." When he sent out the twelve, Jesus gave them the same holistic commission, "to preach the kingdom of God and to heal the sick" (Lk. 9:2). Both words and wonders, both preaching and miracle, both gentle invitation and sharp confrontation, were central to Jesus' communication of the kingdom.

Jesus modeled what he taught. He not only announced the arrival of the Messianic time of justice and shalom for the poor and oppressed. He also fed the hungry and welcomed the socially ostracized into his new community. His diverse circle of men and women, rich and poor, crippled and well, was a visible demonstration of the kingdom he announced.

In fact, the reality of Jesus' new redeemed community was part of the gospel of the kingdom. To be sure, Jesus nowhere explicitly says that. Paul however does. Ephesians 3:1ff. explicitly states that the existence of the multi-ethnic church is part of the gospel. In Ephesians 2, Paul says Jew and Gentile are reconciled at the cross. Because both are accepted with God on exactly the same basis (namely unmerited forgiveness through Christ's cross), there is now one new reconciled humanity of believing Jews and Gentiles. Then in chapter 3, Paul talks about the mystery of the gospel which he preaches. What is it? Verse 6 defines it: "that is, the Gentiles have become fellow heirs, members of the same body, and sharers in the promise in Christ Jesus through the gospel" (NRSV). The new multi-ethnic church is part of the gospel.

The Early Church and the Kingdom

Most of Jesus' contemporaries, however, found it hard to believe that the carpenter's small circle of forgiven tax collectors, prostitutes, and fishermen was truly the beginning of the glorious Messianic kingdom promised by the prophets. Jesus' circle was too weak and insignificant. His teaching was too demanding and costly. His claims were too presumptuous if not indeed blasphemous.

To prove this was wrong, the religious and political leaders had him crucified. But then God raised him from the dead! The Resurrection proved to the discouraged disciples that Jesus was truly the Messiah and that his Messianic kingdom had begun. Pentecost confirmed it. As one reads Peter's sermon in Acts 2, one sees clearly that it was the raising of the crucified One and the pouring out of the Holy Spirit that convinced the early church that the Messianic age predicted by the prophets had truly begun (Acts 2:17ff.; 29ff.). Jewish Messianic hope had expected the giving of the Spirit when the Messiah came. The Messianic prophecy of Joel (Joel 2:28-29) came true at Pentecost, thus confirming Jesus' Messianic claim.

The New Testament uses two interesting words to express the early Christian belief that the Messianic age had truly begun even though it was not yet fully present. They are the words *aparche* (firstfruits) and *arrabon* (pledge or downpayment). In 1 Corinthians 15:20 and 23, Paul says that Jesus' resurrection is the firstfruits of the general resurrection that Jewish Messianic hope expected at the coming of the Messiah. In 2 Corinthians 1:22 and 5:5, Paul describes the Holy Spirit as a downpayment or guarantee (cf. also Rom. 8:23; Eph. 1:14).

The word 'firstfruits' is used in the Old Testament to talk about the early harvest festival that celebrated the first arrival of the new crops (see Ex. 23:16, 19; Deut. 26:2, 10). The full harvest was not yet present, but the beginnings of the harvest had already arrived. The presence of those firstfruits caused rejoicing for they were visible, tangible evidence that the full harvest would surely come. Jesus actually rose from the dead on precisely the day when, in Jewish worship, the first ripe sheaf of the harvest was presented to the Lord.

Arrabon (downpayment or guarantee) is a loan word from the Semitic. It comes from the arena of commerce and means a deposit that pays part of a total debt and gives a legal claim for the full repayment. It is a present tangible pledge that ratifies a contract.

These words were particularly suited to express the early Christian belief that Jesus' life, death, resurrection and Pentecost were visible, tangible evidence that the Messianic kingdom had begun. Like the firstfruits of the harvest, the Messianic age had truly dawned. The early Christians had already tasted the powers of the age to come (Heb. 6:5). Therefore, in spite of the powerful evidence that the Old Age was still very active, the early Christians were certain that the fullness of the Messianic kingdom would surely arrive in God's good time.

The Cosmic Dimensions of the Kingdom

It is crucial to understand that the kingdom expectations of the New Testament are all-encompassing. The dawning kingdom that Christ will complete at his return does not pertain only to the soul or only to the church or only to individuals. It relates to persons and social structures, indeed even to the non-human creation.

It was the present reality of the already dawning Messianic kingdom that anchored this breathtaking cosmic hope of the early Christians. They dared to believe that the crucified and risen carpenter was the key to history. They dared to believe that at his return he would complete his victory over every rule and authority, even death itself (I Cor. 15-20-26), and bring all things into subjection to God. They even believed that "the Creation itself will be liberated from its bondage to decay and brought into the glorious freedom of the children of God" (Rom. 8:21). Even though they were an almost infinitesimally insignificant minority in a powerful pagan empire, they dared to proclaim that God would reconcile all things in heaven and on earth through the cross of this Jewish carpenter (Col. 1:15-20). They dared to hope for that cosmic completion of the kingdom that Jesus announced precisely because the life, death, and resurrection of Jesus, plus Pentecost, were solid, tangible evidence that the Messianic reign had already begun.

The Difference it Makes

Defining the gospel as the Good News of the kingdom rather than merely the Good News of forgiveness or the Good News of personal salvation matters a great deal. For one thing, people who confess Jesus as the way, the truth, and the life ought to be careful not to abandon his central teaching! For another, understanding the central Christian message as the gospel of the kingdom provides a comprehensive, wholistic framework that helps us avoid both cheap grace and a narrow, one-sided understanding of mission.

Jesus' kingdom is clearly wholistic. Thank God that it *does* bring forgiveness with God and personal, inner sanctification in the power of the Spirit. But it also challenges and changes the social order. The kingdom impacts soul and body, individual and society. The church properly communicates the Good News of Jesus' kingdom by word and deed: by proclamation, miracles, acts of mercy and justice, and living out the gospel as a winsome example to others. The Good News of the kingdom precludes an inward-looking preoccupation with the church. Howard Snyder puts it pointedly: "Church people think about how to get people into the church; kingdom people think about how to get the church into the world. Church people worry that the world might change the church; kingdom people work to see the church change the world."[5]

The church, to be sure, is important. Indeed so important that Jesus' new redeemed community is part of the Good News. God wants the church to be a little miniature now of the coming kingdom. For that reason, it should, like Jesus' first community, be a disturbing challenge to every kind of evil rather than a comfortable club of conformity to the world. The church has learned the awesome secret of God's cosmic design to restore the whole creation to wholeness. Therefore Christians go forth into the world both to lead people to faith in Christ and also to erect signs of the coming kingdom within the broken kingdoms of the world, confident that the Messiah will one day return to complete the victory over the kingdom of darkness. We can now see more clearly how much difference it makes when we define the gospel the way Jesus did; i.e. not *merely* as forgiveness of sins, but that and more. Jesus' gospel includes the fact that the Messianic reign has in fact begun and there is now a reconciled and reconciling community whose visible life is a sign of the kingdom that has already begun and will some day arrive in its fullness.

I want to underline seven differences – in addition to the important concern that surely Christians ought to define Jesus' central teaching the way Jesus himself did.

1. If the gospel is not just forgiveness of sins, but the Good News of the kingdom of God, we cannot separate a reconciled relationship with God and a reconciled relationship with brothers and sisters in Christ's body. I am not saying that the two relationships are identical – they are distinct. But they are also *inseparable*. We cannot continue in reconciled relationship with God if we refuse to be reconciled to other members of Christ's body. The gospel of the kingdom protects us from an unbiblical, individualistic spiritualism (and cheap grace)[6] that reduces salvation just to the forgiveness of the individual soul.

2. If the gospel is not just forgiveness, but the Good News of the kingdom of God, we are better able to understand that reconciled social and economic relationships in the body of Christ are one part of salvation. That is what the stories of Zaccheus and the early church show us so clearly. Economic

---

[5] Howard Snyder, *Liberating the Church* (Downers Grove, IL: Inter-Varsity, 1983), 11.

[6] See my *The Scandal of the Evangelical Conscience* (Grand Rapids: Baker, 2005), ch. 3.

sharing and racial reconciliation in the body of Christ are not some optional things that we can choose if we feel like it. They are essential parts of what it means to embrace the gospel. When the church fails to live that way, the church is a visible denial of Jesus' proclamation that the Messianic kingdom has already begun.

3. If the gospel is not just forgiveness, but the Good News of the kingdom of God, we understand more clearly that ministering to both the physical and spiritual needs of people is not some optional possibility, but essential to the gospel. In the Messianic time, the prophets promised, the Messiah would bring reconciled relationships with God and neighbor. Both spiritual and material needs would be met. Jesus the Messiah came, announcing and demonstrating his dawning kingdom by his words and deeds. Both his preaching and his healing were evidence that the kingdom was arriving. Tenderly ministering to the material needs of people in the name of Jesus is essential if we are to be faithful to the gospel of the kingdom.

4. If the gospel is not just forgiveness but the Good News of the kingdom, we see more vividly that the Christian community, if it is faithful, will always challenge what is wrong in the status quo. Jesus' Messianic community can never comfortably fit into any fallen society. Guided by the vision of the dawning kingdom and empowered by the Holy Spirit, the faithful church will always be a loving critic, a counter-cultural community. They will treasure what is good in their society and challenge what is broken, precisely because they know the creator of all is also the Redeemer who desires that Satan's inroads into this good creation be rolled back.

5. If the gospel is not just forgiveness of sins, but the Good News of the kingdom of God, then any sharing of the gospel that does not include a significant concern for the poor is unbiblical. That is not to say, however, either that God cares more about the poor than the rich or that every evangelistic effort must include a word or action empowering the poor.

God cares equally about everyone. Unfortunately, almost all comfortable people care more about themselves than about the needy and marginalized. God has an equal concern that every person accept Christ and enjoy the wholeness intended by the creator. Since sinful persons regularly neglect or oppress the poor, God's people will regularly appear to be on the side of the poor precisely because they share God's equal concern for everyone.

Concern for the poor does not need to find explicit expression in every evangelistic act. But every extended sharing of the gospel by a congregation or mission agency must make it as clear as Jesus did that the gospel is for the poor and that part of the Good News they share is that there is now a new Christian community where human dignity, social empowerment and economic justice for the least and poorest are being modeled and promoted in the power of the Spirit. Anything less is a denial of Jesus' gospel.

6. If the gospel is not just forgiveness, but the Good News of the kingdom of God, we perceive more clearly that there must always be a sharp distinction between the church and the world. One of the greatest temptations

of Christians over the centuries has been to slowly conform to surrounding society rather than live in faithfulness to Jesus' kingdom norms. Because we are not just forgiven but are also being sanctified by the power of the Spirit, Christians can and should live reconciled lives that make Christians stand out in stark contrast to the broken world around them. In the early church, Jews and Gentiles, slaves and masters, men and women were reconciled – not completely, to be sure, but in such powerful ways that their pagan neighbors saw the radical change and were astonished. In amazement their neighbors asked why they were so different. In response, the early Christians told them about Jesus. Today, the church looks so much like the world that neighbors seldom ask such questions. So we lose the opportunity for evangelism.

A clear distinction between the church and the world is crucial in a second way too. The fact that the reign of God becomes visible in the church in a way that it does not in the larger world does not mean that social change in the larger society is irrelevant. It just means we do not expect as much reconciliation in the world as in the church. Two things follow: first, our first task is to make sure the church is really Jesus' new reconciled community. Just doing that has a great impact on society. Second, we also work to improve the larger society. Some day Jesus will come back and the kingdoms of this world will become the kingdom of our Lord. Therefore we work now to nudge society in the direction of that coming wholeness, justice, and reconciliation because we know it will come fully at Christ's return.

7. Finally, if the gospel is not just forgiveness, but the Good News of the kingdom of God, we cannot share the gospel adequately just by preaching. We have to live it, too. Words and deeds must go together.

I am absolutely convinced that this full biblical gospel is what our broken world needs. It certainly needs the fantastic news of forgiveness. But it also longs to hear and see the amazing truth that right now there is a reconciled and reconciling community that broken people can enter and be loved and nurtured toward wholeness. If even a quarter of the world's Christians would both preach and live Jesus' full gospel of the kingdom, we would see revival and church growth on a scale never before seen. In addition, the world would become a better place. I pray that the church will embrace Jesus' whole gospel of the kingdom of God.

Mission as Transformation – Its Journey among Evangelicals since Lausanne 1

Chris Sugden

The Development in Thinking That Produced Mission as Transformation

The theology and missiology of transformation was developed through an interrogation of scripture in the light of the realities of mission. At its heart was an understanding of the nature of humanity as persons in community and a confession that central to addressing issues of poverty is the gospel of Jesus Christ – which brings a new identity to people as sons and daughters of God. This new identity gives them a new vision of who the God who created them means them to be, and can empower them to be.

There was also an understanding that at the heart of the tension between revelation as the source of Christian truth and the context as setting the agenda for Christian action, is the realisation that the revelation of God in Christ was given in a particular context, the context of the poor – whether that was the Hebrew slaves escaping Egypt or the people of the land among whom Jesus ministered – so the context of the poor took priority in exegeting the meaning of the gospel. What the good news of the kingdom means to those who receive it is to determine its meaning for everyone, and thus deliver the church's message and ministry from being taken over and determined by those with power and wealth.

Meanwhile in society in the '70s and '80s there was great cultural awareness of issues of poverty and injustice. It was the era of the civil rights movement and its successors and various expressions. So people coming into the church were already sensitized to issues of addressing poverty and injustice. Increasingly the role of the church was to show how this concern related to the Christian faith, rather than the Christian faith being the *fons et origo* of the concern for social and personal transformation. Often this was in very general terms of love and justice; but mission as transformation rooted it deeper in the nature of the kingdom of God, the nature of human persons as stewards and moral beings, the atonement of Jesus addressing sin, evil and fate, and the work of the Holy Spirit empowering people and communities to move in the direction of the hope God provides. As we shall see at the end, these different theological rootings lead either to a capitulation to the secular human rights agenda, or to rediscovering the role of the church as God's primary agent of change.

The development of the theology and missiology of transformation was not a debate between evangelicals and liberals. It was a debate within evangelicalism – between people who shared common convictions, namely that people should come to know Christ, believe in his atoning death and live the life of his resurrection in the power of the Spirit, based on the supremacy of the scriptures in determining doctrine and practice in the life of the church. In this debate within the evangelical family, the question was whether according to the determinative biblical sources Christian mission is wholistic in essence and nature. It was an interrogation of biblical teaching – what does the bible teach about mission – rather than an evaluation of the bible.

Those proposing the theology and mission of transformation were recovering themes in the bible which had been neglected by the whole evangelical family, themselves included.

These themes were the place of the poor in the proclamation and demonstration of the good news: what did good news to the poor really mean, the definition of the good news as good news of the kingdom of God, and that the good news had to do with redeeming and reconciling the whole of the world.

Once these biblical themes were investigated in depth, the inevitable question had to be faced: how did these square with existing understandings of evangelical mission practice, which was suspicious of anything to do with the poor and with social involvement? In those pre-1989 days of the contest between western capitalism and various species of Marxism, any sympathy with changing social structures or going beyond the relief of distress was under suspicion in some parts of evangelicalism.

People used a number of theological categories and traditions to attack the evangelical legitimacy of those who were making the case for wholistic mission: these included the metaphorical interpretation of biblical passages such as release to the captives, and a residual dualism of the priority of eternal salvation over present well-being. The battle was not for bible but for biblical teaching.

The concern for holistic mission also focused on mission done in context. This led to an increasing appreciation of biblically informed social analysis and of the role of the context in helping us to understand scripture and our mission, and in particular how to understand poverty and why people are poor, what change takes place and how, and what change really is. As a result, many people who were convinced of the biblical case for holistic mission regarded that case as closed. They concentrated their efforts on social research of the impact of holistic mission for example through micro-enterprise development, through addressing AIDS, and through comparison with the development work of other non-Christian religious communities. One question we need to ask is whether we should be encouraging new study of biblical material in the area of holistic mission.

Mission as transformation was the recovery of the wholeness – whole persons and whole communities. We should not forget that the consultation track at which mission as transformation was formulated was part of a wider consultation entitled 'I will build my church'. We identified with the Lausanne Covenant because it raised the concept of wholistic mission – our contribution was to insist that when we say whole, this is what wholeness is. Mission as transformation was able to tie together the whole gospel (including gospel to the poor), the whole church (which included communities of believers), and the kingdom of God (which enabled us to recover the point that it is life, not just a message or beliefs).

Implications of the Gospel for Social Action

The heart of the debate was the nature of the gospel itself. Did the gospel have necessary implications for action in the social sphere?

The answer of mission as transformation was that it did.

Developments over the last 20 years have drawn out the assumptions and implications of these statements and clarified their purpose. Thus in 1999 one of the original framers, Vinay Samuel, wrote: "Transformation is to enable God's vision of society to be actualized in all relationships, social, economic and spiritual, so that God's will may be reflected in human society and his love be experienced by all communities, especially the poor."[1]

This clarification, that transformation was about a vision of society where God's will was done and his love experienced, was prompted because many organizations adopted and used transformation to describe any and every form of mission and involvement with poor people, from welfare based development backed by a spiritual message, to plain economic growth without any spiritual input at all.

Everybody began to use the language of transformation – but why do they not get the concepts? Is it that the people who are uncertain about identifying the person and work of the Holy Spirit are more word-oriented and so still unwholistic? The role of the Pentecostals in the development of mission as transformation should not be neglected. Early material on wholistic mission was produced by Rene Padilla, Samuel Escobar and their colleagues in the Latin American Theological Fraternity, where Pentecostals addressed the challenges of Liberation Theology and Marxist social analysis with their own Holy Spirit informed practice and experience of social and community change.

In October 2002, Samuel clarified the concept of transformation further: "Mission is individuals coming to Christ, challenging corrupt and sinful systems, structures and cultures and enabling individuals and communities to experience God's transforming power."[2]

Transformation is here located not by specifying any outputs, but by identifying Christian action against sin and God's power as a transforming power. In developing and understanding transformation as our Christian

---

[1] V. Samuel and C. Sugden (eds), *Mission as Transformation* (Oxford: Regnum, 1999).

[2] V. Samuel, 'Mission as Transformation', *Transformation* 19:4 (2002).

understanding of development, it is important that we flesh out and express what the people of God have always understood through the bible as the nature of their discipleship and mission. Our task is expressing discipleship and mission in relation to the tasks and challenges of ministry with and for the poor.

Vinay Samuel's work in discussing transformation since 1983 focused on a number of constants:

(1) Transformation is focused on persons;

(2) Transformation is about the development of personhood in community and thus the building of communities;

(3) Transformation is through the action of communities and community institutions. Through communities we create the public good and attack evil systems.

Elaborating on these three dimensions:

Transformation is focused on persons: on reorienting their relationships and empowering their choices, to develop their character.

Transformation is:

- about bodies in time and space and therefore in relation to others; personhood is both our-selves and ourselves in relationships;
- about the development of the self: the substance of the person expressed in the choices we make in relating, receiving and understanding people and situations;
- about understanding the role that has been entrusted to us;
- about the ability to make moral choices, living up to convictions, codes of conduct, standards and guidelines;
- the integrity of a person's belief and actions: that which holds one together and expresses truth, faithfulness and dependability;
- the ability to be other-regarding: showing love in sacrifice, compassion, acceptance of difference and inclusion;
- the ability to resist wrong-doing: with strong ethical resistance but also being able to forgive, heal and rebuild;
- reconciling and renewing: recognizing that you yourself also have to be cleansed, renewed and reconciled;
- the development of creativity and stewardship: seizing the opportunity, building and taking responsibility;
- the reality of worship: in worshipping and turning to God in prayer we are truly fulfilled and flourish.

As we grow in personhood we become the place where Christ makes his dwelling in the Spirit. As we relate to people so that Christ may be formed in them, whether through adult literacy, or medical work, the Holy Spirit works through us for them.

Such process takes place in communities in covenant relationships. This means that to be sustainable, transformational development needs to be related to the church.

It is to be observed that development work is well accepted by evangelicals – who does not support some development or relief project? Such involvement is not seen as inimical to the gospel but rather an important expression of Christian love and discipleship.

However all is not well. While World Vision has placed the role of the churches as central to its development strategy and engaged deliberately with churches, even this can be for the pragmatic reason that where the poor are, the church is and remains. But many Christian and even evangelical development agencies are either critical of the church, or wish to remodel the church in their own image as centres of development, or see their own work as the essential addition to the work of churches to enable them to be wholistic.

This poses the challenge to us – what is it about the very nature of discipleship and the Christian community that should of itself arise out of gospel resources and address all the deformation of sin expressed in the experience of poverty and injustice?

The challenges in the next decade will be that campaigners against poverty and injustice will suggest that the church is inimical as an institution to addressing these issues: because of its stance (among some) on women in church leadership; because of its stance on the priority of marriage; because of its stance against what are seen as fundamental and absolute human rights in the area of sexuality. Many evangelicals will therefore distance themselves from the institutional church and its message in order to play their role in the struggle for human rights against poverty and injustice. This will be to their own detriment, and also to the detriment of the church.

The Challenge for Today

So what is the challenge that faces us today in the same way it faced us in the '70s and '80s? It is that those who have accepted the form of the development of transformation have elided its concerns with the prevailing human rights agendas of secular society. A general rooting of social concern in a non-specific appeal to the justice and love of God generally leads to elision with, and submersion by, a secular human rights agenda in the name of justice. Just as those who we confronted in the seventies had a false anthropology (change the individual through the gospel and you change society), so those we confront today similarly have a false anthropology (the human is constituted by a series of rights which emerge from the need to work for an equal and just society). These rights are self-authenticating, universal and absolute. The church is to be evaluated and found wanting in relation to them.

What we need to develop is a theology of human community, and therefore a theology of redeemed community in the church, rooted in the gospel foundations of the kingdom of God and the death and resurrection of Jesus. Seen in the light of the Christian proclamation of transformation, the problem with the development and justice movement is that it is too narrow in its definition of injustice or human potential. We are created for life in God's new heaven and earth. To be carried off by an early or unjust death is a great injustice in view of the purposes of God. The church is entrusted with the news about and the reality of the defeat of death. It must challenge the development and justice movement about its truncated view of life. In the light of the Christian proclamation of God's work in destroying death itself, the conception of the work of development appears to be too narrow.

Much relief and development work ignores or avoids the issue of death. In fact, the relief of natural disasters is embraced by agencies primarily with reference to caring for the survivors and trying to ensure that such a disaster does not happen again, which it often will. What answer has an aid agency to the mother who has lost three young children to hunger or disease, the person living with AIDS, the victim of famine? That such things should never happen again – that it will be better for our grandchildren? This partial approach is seen most clearly in the responses to AIDS. There is little investment in terminal care. Investment is primarily in prevention (and treatment at the early stage in richer countries). It is here that Christians raise a key concern and can give a major witness.

So in the light of the resurrection, the scope of the secular concern in relief and development work is too narrow, its notion of injustice is too restricted. An example of the wholistic concern the church provides is given in this testimony from a student of an MA programme in HIV/AIDS counseling in Nairobi Kenya, set up in partnership between St Pauls Limuru and OCMS.

> When we first saw her, she was thin, and almost unconscious. We started on a feeding programme with soft fluids for her. She slowly got a bit stronger but had pains all over, having lain in bed for long, hungry and sick. Feeding with food and God's word and being there just to listen and comfort her was all we provided. When I finally got a doctor to see her, he advised us to feed her because that was all she required. She received Christ and developed a will to live which was not there before. We visited and had fellowship in her house on a Sunday. The daughter by then had been given the fare to go to fetch the grandparents. She peacefully went to be with the Lord on Tuesday the following week. Base group members contributed to her burial and all felt the loss. We now have to think about the daughter.

It is such ministry that our missiology and theology must undergird, encourage and support.

FROM FOURFOLD MISSION TO HOLISTIC MISSION: TOWARDS EDINBURGH 2010

Esther Mombo

Introduction

The mission agencies of the eighteenth and nineteenth century left Europe to the continent of Africa with a four fold mission strategy which included evangelism, education, health, and industrial training. This fourfold mission strategy was to preach the gospel and deal with the social evils of the continent at the time. The mission of the church was practiced within this context and it yielded good results including producing the leadership for the churches in Africa. While this form of mission was ideal, it was identified with colonialism with its negative impacts of race, class, age, and gender issues that were not tackled by the church. These are the issues that holistic missions have to interrogate in order for the gospel to be holistic. In this chapter therefore, I will briefly look at the impact of the fourfold mission strategy, and then offer aspects of a holistic mission which will make the church in Africa an institution that is able to serve all its members in a holistic manner.

The word 'mission' comes out of the Latin word *missio* meaning 'a sending', with reference to what an individual or group wants to do or is convinced to do. We need to distinguish between 'mission' (singular) and 'missions' (plural). While the first term refers to the *missio dei* (God's Mission), i.e. God's involvement with the world, the latter term refers to particular forms related to specific times, places, or needs of participation in the *missio dei.* Ultimately mission remains indefinable as it should never be limited by our narrow confines. The most we can attempt is to formulate some approximations of what God's mission is all about for our times and the realities that persist today in our context. These are the harsh realities that compel us to reformulate our response to God's presence in the world in the local context in which our church exists to witness to and proclaim God's liberating presence.

Thus our mission in this world is our response to God's continuous interventions in our times and to participate in the process of extending God's reign. It focuses on the Christian church and the Christian community for whom Christ is the supreme revealer and the revelation of God. Jesus' way of life is the model that the church is called to follow. God's mission is an ongoing process of God's self revelation, of the active liberating presence of God in the world. We as Christians understand God's self communication in Jesus Christ as the basis for God's mission. Through Christ, God invites all people to participate in this process to live out the liberating love and presence of God in our own contexts.

Historically the church has interpreted and been involved in the mission of God in different ways. In the eighteenth and nineteenth centuries the churches of Europe and America were involved in what was understood as a fourfold mission. In the fourfold mission, agencies supported by the church sent out missionaries to do mission among people other than their own. Their mission policy and ideology in the fourfold mission was based on the understanding that the others did not know, thus they needed information and technology to be able to know. It is in this context, for instance, that Bishop Tucker on his way to Uganda in 1928 passed through western Kenya and remarked that,

> Can nothing be done for Kavirondo? If only Christians at home could see us, surrounded by swarms of these ignorant people, and unable to promise them teachers, they could surely have pity on us and them, and provide the men and means of this vast field and most blessed and Christ like work.[1]

Such kinds of observation and others similarly led the mission agencies to prepare for a fourfold mission. This mission strategy composed of evangelism, education, medical work and industrial training. Evangelism was aimed at conversion. One missionary observed that,

> Our aim, first and always, is the definite, positive salvation of the individual and coupled with this, to help these destitute people to become strong and self-reliant, and to cause them not to be satisfied with a coat of grease and clay or a filthy piece of skin, and to live in a miserable hut, swarming with vermin, but to long to be superior in every way to their present heathen condition. While the mission was organised primarily to give the gospel to the African people those in charge soon felt that industrial work must be used as one of the means to this end.[2]

Even if education, industrial and medical work could contribute in changing the lifestyle of the people that were being evangelized, it was not enough unless they had obtained what the missionaries defined as 'positive salvation of the individual'. This is something that the missionaries themselves understood, and in order to realize it they prohibited what they found questionable in most traditional practices of the African people, be it in social life and or spiritual life.

As well as evangelism, education was key in the mission of the church. The aim of education was two-fold. Firstly to teach the Africans to read the bible, and secondly to give basic skills of writing and doing simple arithmetic to give basic literacy and numeracy. There were two levels of education such that the general education was for all to be readers of the bible especially, but elite education was along class and gender lines. Elite education was offered to sons

---

[1] Alfred Tucker, *Eighteen Years in Uganda* (London: Edward Arnold, 1908), 102.

[2] Edna H. Chilson, *Ambassador for the King* (Wichita, KS, 1943), 40.

of chiefs believed to take over from their fathers as chiefs. For men, education meant going to work as a clerk in a colonial system. The women on the other hand were being trained to be good wives for educated men. Most women were taught in domestic work along the lines of home and family life. Their education was not meant for outside employment but raising families, hence the stress of aspects of raising Christian families.

Together with education, medical work was also part and parcel of mission for the mission agencies during this early period. Medical work also played a significant part in the establishment of mission work. Medical work was important initially for two reasons. Firstly, to challenge the traditional healers and their methods of doing medicine. This, for most missionaries at the time, was regarded as superstition.

> The native method of doctoring consists of certain ceremonies to appease evil spirits. This may include the killing of an animal, tying pieces of flesh on the neck or wrists of the patient; or worse still, rubbing the vilest filth into the sore.[3]

As well as challenging the traditional healing methods, medical work became another contact place for evangelism. Writing about a mission hospital in 1918 Elisha Blackburn, serving as a Quaker missionary, observed that,

> Those who come for hospital treatment come in contact with Christian teaching and have opportunity to observe the lives of Christian people. As we shall recall what an important part the healing of disease had in the ministry of our master and how often it was the precursor of the salvation of the recipient, we may be sure that medical service rendered to the people will be instrumental in winning some to Christianity.[4]

Through medical work, missionaries were able to learn about some of the practices of the African people and to challenge them, for instance about female circumcision. This was not an easy thing to confront, as it had deep roots in the patriarchal structures of most African societies and especially those that practiced it.

The other form of mission was through industrial training. It was to teach practical skills to the men in the communities in order to improve their lifestyle. The missionaries were attempting to bring about an outward change since the spiritual transformation would be reflected in a change of lifestyle:

> While we expect God to transform the inner man, we believe he is looking for us to transform the outer man, and as he by the Holy Spirit raises the spiritual so we by manual training propose to raise the outer, thus bringing the whole being to a higher plan. [5]

The above forms of mission helped the mission agencies to introduce and establish mission stations within a given area. Thus Christianity was spread to members in different parts of Africa. Christianity was identified with

[3] *African Record* 7 (January-March, 1911), 7.

[4] *Twenty-Five Years in East Africa: A Description of the Field Work of Friends African Mission* (Richmond, IN: American Friends Board of Mission, 1925).

[5] *African Record* 2 (April- July, 1907), 6.

development, a move from African ways of life to western ways. The western ways, inculcated into the minds of both young and old transformed the African people, making them carriers of the gospel more than the missionaries themselves. The mission of God included challenging that which seen as not affirming life.

Challenges of Fourfold Mission Forms of Missions

Mission activities linked to colonial expansion

While mission work impacted people's lives and changed communities by introducing a new faith and a Euro-American culture, which had positive impact on the peoples of Africa, it has been observed that mission in some places was later associated with colonisation.

> The perspective of many in the third world was that missionaries with their commercial and governmental friends (the interests of the trading companies and the colonial powers) were supportive of the agenda to 'colonize, Christianize, exploit, westernize and civilize' the people. However, much good work was also done by missionaries: the starting of schools, health centres, hospitals and helping to address social ills. They encouraged a spirit of caring, sharing and service that was well received and many missionaries were pioneers in this essentially 'service'-orientated concern for the people they met. Very soon the work of the mission agencies separated in the traditional role of evangelism, church planting and the running of local churches from the maintenance of educational, training and health centres and welfare concerns. They were complementary, but different.[6]

The Kikuyu saying *'Gutire muthungu na Mubea'* (meaning there is no difference between a European and a missionary) captures the link between missionary work and colonialism. The phrase arose from the fact that the presence of both missionary and colonialism portrayed racial discrimination, land deprivation and other social injustices.[7]

The link between mission and colonialism meant that the local people reacted in different ways. Politically many countries worked towards their freedom through liberation wars. Some of the mission agencies were implicated as supporting and others not. The reaction of the churches included the creation of independent churches. Barret has observed that these churches arose as a result of three failures, namely:

---

[6] Mukari Daleep, 'Christian Development Agencies and Mission: A Christian Aid Perspective', *Connections* 1, vol. 7 (2003), 22-24.

[7] E.N. Wanyoike, *An African Pastor* (Nairobi, East Africa Publishing House, 1974), 176. Others who have discussed the topic on the link between missionary and colonial expansion putting it in historical context include Brian Stanley, *The Bible and the Flag, Protestant Missions and British Imperialism in the Nineteenth and Twentieth Centuries* (Leicester: Apollos, 1990).

1. Failure to practice love as understanding which led to a disastrous absence of the scriptural quality of brotherly love.
2. Failure to understand Africanism sufficiently well to differentiate the good elements in it from the bad.
3. Failure to discern the existence of any links between traditional society and biblical faith.[8]

These churches were largely founded by people who had been to mission schools and were members of the mission churches. The founders of these churches tried to integrate biblical faith and African realities, especially the spiritual realities. The translation of the bible was one of the driving forces to the creation of the independent churches. Through reading the bible in their own languages, those who founded the African Instituted Churches challenged what they saw as western culture, by interpreting the bible to themselves. They integrated the African culture and the bible rather than accept the dualistic approach that seemed to have been introduced by the missionaries. There was a difference between the Christians in the main mission churches and those of the African Independent Churches. The former appeared to have problems integrating the Christian faith with their cultural context while the latter were able to integrate Christianity and culture better.

Mission from Europe to Africa

As well as being associated with colonization, mission was understood as coming from Europe to Africa. Maluleke has captured this point in the following words

> Christian mission was something that the west did to Africa and not as a reciprocal or even an intra-African activity. In this way mission was something that Whites did to Blacks and never *vice versa*. It was also something that men did to women and seldom, if ever, the other way round. Therefore, theologically, Christian mission was the mission of the (western) church as it sought to multiply itself and its sphere of influence in the world, especially since that influence was under attack in the west itself. In this sense the church was mission and mission was the church. This could explain the fact of extreme western Protestant denominationalism.

This had a number of implications for the African church but two are worth mentioning. First it was that mission was an imported thing brought by others, and those who received mission were in a state of helplessness. This was reflected in the language used about mission work and the image painted of those to whom mission was done. Those to whom mission was done were identified with a state of need and could not do anything for themselves. They lacked initiative and innovation and could only depend on what was brought to them in the material, social and moral spheres. This attitude was inculcated in

---

[8] David B. Barrett, *Schism and Renewal in Africa: An Analysis of Six Thousand Contemporary Religious Movements* (Oxford: OUP, 1968), 156-157.

the minds of the first converts and it led to a dependency syndrome, materially and also ideologically.

Second, western Protestant denominationalism found a breeding ground among the different ethnic communities of Africa. In order to deal with mission rivalries, a spheres of influence policy was adopted and in most cases Protestant mission agencies divided themselves along ethnic lines. Mission expansion was identified with denominational expansion, in which the teachings of a denomination were over and above the mission of the church. This historical mistake has continued to impact on the African church in all ways but especially in the election of their leaders. Thus, in some instances, ethnicity is over and above other qualifications required of a leader. In recent years, denominationalism appears to have strengthened negative aspects of ethnicity in regard to the unequal power relationships and sharing of material wealth. Even though spheres of influence contributed a great deal in the establishing and expansion of Christianity, its impact today is still felt at the level of ethnic tensions due to a failure to separate mission from denominationalism.

Mission appendage of the church

As well as mission being something done by some on others, the fourfold mission methodology supported the assumption that church and mission are two separate things, and church is not part of mission. As Maluleke observes,

> Mission was, the activities of a missionary organization and thus, by extension, the mission of the sending church. If churches did not delegate mission work to voluntary mission organizations they formed almost-autonomous mission departments to handle all matters of mission. Some did this on their own, while others came together as churches to form such mission organizations. Mission became a specialised activity, outsourceable by home and abroad.[9]

The impact of this was that it created a dependent syndrome so that all mission work was to be done by a missionary or missionary agency. Financial dependence became paramount for most of the churches leading to unequal relationships between and among those who served within the church. This reduced initiative and innovation among those who became Christians and chose to serve the church. The unequal relationships and dependency syndrome led some local churches to call for a moratorium on missionaries in the 1970s. In his speech on this John Gatu observed the following:

> We in the third world must liberate ourselves from the bondage of western dependency by refusing anything that renders impotent the development of our spiritual resources which in turn make it impossible for the church in the third world to engage in the mission of God in their own areas…The gospel will then have a deeper and a more far reaching effect than our mission Christianity.[10]

---

[9] Tinyiko Sam Maluleke, 'Christian Mission in Africa in the Twenty-First Century' (a conference paper).

[10] Cited in Eliot Kendal, *The End of an Era: Africa and the Missionary* (London: SPCK,

The call for a moratorium was not aimed at sending the missionaries away or ending links with those who were sending missionaries, but a call to an end of the patronising spirit which seemed to exist in mission agencies and had reduced initiative and the creativity of members from being involved in mission in their own context. It was also a way of redefining mission, not as something done by some to others. For example, it was seen as the powerful doing it for the weak, or those who have giving to those who do not have. Mission was not portrayed as being a partnership in a sharing the gifts of God by the people of God. Mission was not confined, under the moratorium, to a group of individuals, but among all the people of God wherever they were and whatever their circumstances.

Holistic Mission: Towards Edinburgh 2010

The purpose of God's mission in our world is to bring life in all its fullness. Then there will be a harmonious interaction, interdependence and intra-dependence between God, the world and human beings. Life in all its fullness can be experienced only when there is transformation, which manifests God's presence and reign where love, equality and peace with justice are experienced and affirmed in all realms of our lives, affirming diversity. Thus integral development focussing on the overall development of human beings and the entire natural world, that includes the whole of creation, is very important.

Holistic mission challenges first the geographical understanding of mission, which seemed to locate the centre of mission as being in Europe or America, what was understood as the north. It is in this context that mission was linked to colonial expansion. The north/south paradigm for mission has been challenged in various writing, both Christian and non-Christian. For instance M. Nazirali wrote a book entitled *From Everywhere to Everywhere*, in which he challenged the one-way traffic of mission movement emanating from one source.[11] Similar ideas have been put across by Ngugi in his book *Moving the Centre,* where he has argued that if there is going to be freedom for people between nations and within nations, there is a need to move the centre from its assumed location in the west to a multiplicity of centres. This would deal with issues of race and gender so that those who have been in the receiving end become participants or subjects rather than objects.[12] There is a sense in which the north/south paradigm of mission had to do with power, both politically and economically. Holistic mission is a call to share the good news of Jesus Christ which involves a passion to challenge those things that deny life in its fullness – things based on power and hierarchy such as race, class, and gender, inequalities which continue to render most of the world's population useless. In this case mission

---

1978), 87.

[11] Michael Nazir-Ali, *From Every Where to Everywhere: A Worldview of Christian Mission* (London: Harper Collins, 1990).

[12] Ngugi Wa Thiongo, *Moving the Centre: The Struggle for Cultural Freedom* (London: Heinemann, 1993).

encompasses all that Jesus stood for and did as reflected in his own ministry. This is reflected in the words of the scriptures, "Jesus went throughout Galilee, teaching in their synagogues, preaching the good news of the kingdom and healing every disease and sickness among the people" (Mt. 4:23).

As well as challenging the notions of geography and power, holistic mission also challenges the language of mission. The language of mission within the geographical expansion described mission in terms of the activities done on others, or of what was exported to the mission field. Mission was measured and quantified on the basis of the number of mission stations and the number of converts and the status of the converted. For those who were involved in mission, numbers increased their financial and moral support from the sending church or agency. Geographical expansion and the amount of mission activity was not a true reflection of the growth of the Christian faith, which has remained as superficial among many of those that profess the faith. The presence for example of gender inequality, ethnic tensions, and massive poverty, especially among women, questions the nature and depth of the Christian faith. Holistic mission is reflected not only in numbers but also in the quality of life of the people. The mission of God is about life in abundance, and in cases where life is threatened in all its totality the affirmation of life is one of the goals of mission.

David Bosch in his book of mission theology notes that mission is the responsibility of all the disciples of Christ. They should be participating in Jesus with a mission of liberating love and doing this as part of a community. Mission means beginning with people, being with people, and feeling the pain of the people.[13] This brings to light those who are involved in mission but have not yet been recognized as doing so.

Women as Carriers of Mission

Among the pitfalls of the fourfold mission strategy was the implication that mission was done by some to others, who were objects of mission. From the analysis above it clear that mission is the involvement of all in sharing God's love with all. For centuries the reality of the church's life and activities everywhere has been of women playing a silent role as carriers of God's mission in varying capacities. Beginning with Jesus' ministry, women, mostly unnamed, visibly supported Jesus, caring for his daily needs and following him in his ministry. Jesus recognized them by allowing them to touch him and listen to his teaching, thus breaking with the custom of his day.

Women were present at the founding of the church and they supported the work of the apostles while spreading the good news of God's love. Paul mentions women in Romans 16 as co-workers in the mission and ministry of the early church. It is true to say that the church would not have grown to where

[13] David Bosch, *Transforming Mission: Paradigm Shifts in Theology of Mission* (Maryknoll, NY: Orbis Books, 1993).

it is without the support, contributions and transmission of faith by women. The role of women as mothers, teachers, evangelists, and bible women has been important in mission. The areas that women have excelled in have been in providing pastoral care, creating educational opportunities and being there to provide comfort and assistance. This has been done whilst working in their families, in neighborhood social centres, when visiting the sick or comforting the mourning. Mission in the style of Christ takes women to places which would have otherwise remained hidden corners.

Despite the involvement of women in mission, they continue to struggle and suffer much under oppression and dehumanization in their homes, work places and the churches in which they serve faithfully. In dealing with some of these issue the Ecumenical Decade of Churches in Solidarity with Women (1988-1998) noted the following:

> In 1988 the Ecumenical Decade of Churches in Solidarity with Women was launched. It was aimed at empowering women to challenge oppressive structures in the global community, their churches and communities. To affirm through shared leadership and decision making theology and spirituality the decisive contributions of women in churches and communities; to give visibility to women's perspectives and actions in the work and struggle for justice, peace and integrity of creation… to encourage the churches to take actions in solidarity with women.[14]

Even if the churches welcomed this, and national and international conferences have been held on the same subject, the role of women as carriers of mission is yet to be fully appreciated. The ideology of patriarchy is alive in the church, and women have remained on the periphery – and that is where most of the church would wish to have them remain. While women are involved in mission in areas that are most needy, the church seems to be silent on issues that affect women both in the church and society. These issues include social, economic, religious and or political perspectives. In the HIV/AIDS era, women have taken on more pastoral responsibilities to help the infected and affected live better lives. Yet the church appears not to deal with areas that impact on women themselves when it comes to HIV/AIDS, especially in the area of sexuality and marriage. These issues have been highlighted by various groups, but especially the circle of Concerned African Women Theologians who have done research and written on the plight of women in the era of HIV/AIDS.[15]

---

[14] Letters, *A Report of Visits to the Churches During the Ecumenical Decade – Churches in Solidarity with Women* (Geneva: WCC, 1997).

[15] I.A. Phiri, B. Haddad and M. Masenya (eds.) *African Women, HIV/AIDS and Faith Communities* (Pietmaritzburg: Cluster, 2003); *Grant Me Justice: HIV/AIDS and Gender Readings of the Bible* (Pietmaritzburg: Cluster, 2004); M.A. Oduyoye and E. Amoah (eds.), *People of Faith and the Challenge of HIV/AIDS* (Ibadan: Sefer, 2004); E. Amoah, D. Akintunde and D. Akoto (eds.), *Cultural Practices and HIV/AIDS: African Women's Voice* (Inbadan: Sefer, 2005); A.I. Phiri and S. Nadar (eds), *African Women, Religion and Health: Essays in Honor of Mercy Amba Ewudziwa Oduyoye* (Maryknoll: Orbis,

Holistic mission for women means bringing to light that which affects them most and enables them to continue doing mission as the disciples of Christ. This will include providing space for women to study where they have been excluded, to participate in leadership which has been exclusively male, and to explore different ways of doing mission to all.

Conclusion

From the foregoing, we have noted how the fourfold mission strategy provided room for the growth of the church within the context of the time. This mission strategy had its challenges largely because it was identified with colonialism and expansion. Using the available resources and language of the time, mission was interpreted as meaning something that is done by some to others, limiting its activities and potential. But God's mission is not limited to one part of the world – God's mission is for all God's people in any given context. This chapter has shown that holistic mission brings the wholeness of mission to the people of God regardless of their gender, race, ethnicity and class. Edinburgh 2010 is a call to correct the past and move forward to the next century with courage and hope.

2006); T. Hinga, A. Kubai and H. Nyanga (eds.), *HIV/AIDS, Women and Religion in Africa* (Nairobi: University of Nairobi, 2008).

THE MISSIONARY JOURNEY OF THE SON OF GOD INTO THE FAR COUNTRY

Damon So

Introduction

This chapter proposes that the church's mission is significantly shaped by her view of Jesus Christ. A holistic view of Jesus held by the church will tend to produce holistic mission engagement, while a partial picture of Jesus Christ will produce partial or non-holistic mission engagement. The pattern is that churches which focus on the atoning death of Jesus with relative less attention paid to his life and ministry, and resurrection, tend to lean towards a more 'spiritual' gospel with less emphasis on the physical and social aspects of human needs. Churches which pay relatively little attention to the atoning death of Jesus could lean towards a more 'social' gospel. In a general sense, these two types of churches correspond to the conservative and the liberal wings respectively. However, the sharp division in this general statement may have been blunted in the last few decades since the debates on holistic mission from Lausanne 74 (or earlier) onward have brought greater awareness to conservative churches of the need to care for the whole person and the whole community as they engage themselves in mission work amongst them.

This chapter attempts to provide a sound theological basis for holistic mission engagement, with some special and useful reference to Karl Barth's work in *Church Dogmatics* (*CD*). The title of this chapter is an adaptation of the title of a subsection in Karl Barth's *Church Dogmatics* IV.1, 'The Way of the Son of God into the Far Country'. In this subsection, Barth speaks of the journey of the Son of God from exaltation and glory into the sphere of sinful and needy humanity. Because of the distance between the God of holiness and humanity in sin, the journey of the Son of God is a journey into a distant or far country. The important point is that the Son of God did take this long missionary journey so that needy humanity can be saved and reconciled to God. Barth's choice of this title was based on the parable of the prodigal son where the rebellious son went into a far country. But here in the case of the Son of God, his journey into the far country is to meet with sinners and bring them back to the Father. His unitary theme of Jesus' identification with needy humanity throughout his birth, life, death and resurrection is a helpful remedy to the partial pictures of Jesus Christ briefly mentioned above. The church in the twenty-first century will do well to pay attention to this influential theologian of the twentieth century and find correctives from him which will have far reaching effects on her mission engagement in the world. Furthermore, a theology of holistic mission developed from this unitary theme emphasised by Barth is not a light theology supported by a few texts here and there from the scripture; it will be a substantial and robust theology on which the church's practical actions of mission engagement can be built.

The Divinity and the Condescension of the Son of God

Barth in his *Church Dogmatics* frequently wrote about the divine grace poured out to sinful and needy humanity in Jesus Christ. The journey of the Son of God began from above, from outside, i.e. from God. The journey from the side of God into humanity was a journey 'into the far country' because this far country is "the evil society of this being which is not God and against God" (*CD* IV.1, 158). Barth therefore reminds us of the state of humanity visited by the Son of God – sinful, undeserving, against God. It is important not to lose sight of this fact for it illuminates the scale and extent of the Son's downward journey of condescension. It also illuminates the scale of God's grace, his free action, in his coming down to us in Jesus Christ.

Barth put great emphasis on the divinity of Jesus Christ, in sharp contrast to the 'low' view of Jesus Christ in liberal Protestantism. He strongly maintains that when the Son of God became man in his condescending journey, he did not lose his divinity. Barth does not explain how the two aspects of the divinity and humanity of Jesus Christ can possibly be held together in his one person. He does not argue for such a possibility inductively from some prior principles. For Barth, the actual existence of Jesus in these two aspects witnesses to the possibility. The possibility is inferred from the actuality. In the final analysis, the fact that this possibility exists and was actualised in the person of Jesus was due to the freedom of God.[1]

The Birth of Jesus

> The Lucan narrative of the childhood of Jesus mentions no less than three times that the first resting place of Jesus was a crib [manger], because his parents could find no room in the inn. The narrative in Matthew tells of the shadow of death which immediately fell on him: of Herod, who sought his life; of the flight into Egypt and the slaughter of the innocents in Bethlehem. ... There is unmistakable reference to the suspicion which surrounded his birth (Mt. 1:19). (*CD* IV.1, 165)

With this short summary of Jesus' birth, Barth highlights the extent to which the Son of God was willing to go into the far country. The circumstances of his

[1] George Hunsinger, 'Karl Barth's Christology', in John Webster (ed.), *The Cambridge Companion to Karl Barth* (Cambridge: Cambridge University Press, 2000), 133.

birth in a stable, the lowliness of the family into which he was born,[2] and the political persecution which he faced soon after his birth all witness to the fact that the Son of God willed to journey to be amongst poor and needy humanity – he chose to identify with humanity in its physical and political need. This act of identification is quite unmistakeable. At the point of his entry into the far country (the world), the Son of God was already making a clear statement of his solidarity with all those who suffer because of their lack of physical provision and their oppression under political persecution – the arbitrary and unjust use of political power. The compassionate heart of God was already revealed through his Son at his birth.

His Identification with Israel/Humanity

The theme of the identification of the Son of God with humanity continues from the birth of Jesus, through his baptism into his temptations in the wilderness. In particular, his identification with Israel can be seen quite clearly in the following. If (i) the infant Jesus' exile to Egypt and return in Matthew 2 is read in conjunction with (ii) his baptism in the Jordan, followed by (iii) the forty days of temptation in the desert, it only takes a small step of imagination to see that Matthew is drawing a parallel between Jesus and Israel, which (i) was brought out of the exile in Egypt, (ii) crossed the Red Sea and (iii) spent forty years in the wilderness before entering Canaan. In particular, Matthew in 2:15 uses Hosea 11:1 – "Out of Egypt I called my son," which refers to Israel as God's son – as an Israel-Jesus typology and sees Jesus as the fulfilment of Israel. Jesus' identification with Israel can be further confirmed by Matthew 8:17 – 'He took up our infirmities and carried our diseases.' This theme of identification with Israel is also found in other parts of the New Testament.[3] The old Israel had failed to obey God and fulfil his righteousness and mission to the nations. She was put into exile. Jesus, by representing Israel, or being the true Israel, fulfils God's righteousness, saves the people from their sins (Mt. 1:21) and ends their exile (Mt. 1:17). In Jesus Christ, Israel is truly liberated from their sins and exile in foreign territory.

According to Barth, Jesus expressed his identification with sinful Israel/humanity in a public manner – in his baptism. For Barth, Jesus' baptism symbolised the eventual death of Jesus in which his solidarity/identification with sinners reached its climax.

---

[2] When Joseph and Mary consecrated Jesus to God in the temple, they were only able to afford a pair of doves. See Lk. 2:22-24.

[3] Moule found applied to Jesus in the New Testament as a whole "a great convergence of Israel-titles and other collectives... Servant of Yahweh, Son of Man, Zechariah martyr, rejected-but-vindicated stone, cornerstone, foundation stone, stumbling-stone, temple.... This marks him as, in the estimate of Christians, the climax of the pattern of true covenant-relationship.... Thus, to a unique degree, Jesus is seen as the goal, the convergence-point, of God's plan for Israel, his covenant-promise." C.F.D. Moule, 'Fulfilment-Words in the New Testament', *New Testament Studies* 14 (1974), 300-1.

> His first public appearance is that of a penitent in *unreserved solidarity with other penitents* who confess themselves to be such in the baptism of John, and can look only for the remission of their sins in the coming judgment (Mt. 3:15) – *a clear anticipation of the story of the passion,* towards which the narrative in all the Evangelists hastens with a momentum recognisable from the very first, and at the climax of which Jesus is crucified between two thieves (Mt. 27:38). (*CD* IV.1, 165, italics mine)

In his baptism, Jesus identifies himself with sinful Israel/humanity; he stands amongst sinful men as one of them even though he is without sin. His baptism is a symbol or prefiguration of his death and this can be substantiated in the following. The Old Testament teaches that without the shedding of blood there is no forgiveness of sin. Jesus in identifying with sinful humanity and in seeking their cleansing will have to pay the price for their forgiveness, which is the shedding of his own blood. This is confirmed by the missionary statement that his Father speaks to him in his baptism, "This is my Son, whom I love, with him I am well pleased." The second half of the statement comes from Isaiah 42 about the servant whose suffering is made explicit in Isaiah 53. Jesus' baptism is therefore a symbolic preview of his death. But more than this, his baptism signifies his commitment to "fulfil all righteousness" from beginning to end (Mt. 3:15), i.e. to fully obey his Father in his whole *life* unto *death. His baptism is therefore an outward expression of his commitment and dedication to identify with needy humanity throughout his whole life and death according to the good and perfect will of his Father.* Here Jesus is making a public statement of his intention to finish the long journey into the depth of the far country of needy humanity. At his baptism, he has already set his heart to obey his Father from the beginning to the very end. But his commitment to obey his Father is soon put to the test in the wilderness.

Barth interprets Jesus' temptations in the wilderness as a test of his fidelity to the commitment he made in his baptism – solidarity with humanity according to his Father's will.

Jesus' resistance to these temptations thus means that he wills not to use his power for his own convenience and for building an earthly kingdom for his own gain. He is determined not to amass wealth or power for himself. Rather, he chooses to remain in a state of lowliness; in a spirit of humility (Mt. 11:29) he wills to stand in solidarity with people of lowliness and need. He does not commit himself to the kingdom of this world but he is committed to the kingdom of his Father for which he will have to suffer unto death in order to save the people from their sins (Mt. 1:21). The temptation episodes show that Jesus does not waver in his solidarity with and steadfast love for Israel/humanity, that he determines to keep this course of obedience to his Father to the end.[4]

Barth likewise links Jesus' temptation in the Garden of Gethsemane with his baptism at Jordan (and his temptations in the wilderness).

---

[4] See Damon W.K. So, *The Forgotten Jesus and the Trinity You Never Knew* (Eugene, OR: Wipf and Stock, 2010), 123-35 for more detailed discussions.

> [I]n this prayer of Jesus there took place quite simply the completion of the penitence and obedience which he had begun to render at Jordan and which he had maintained in the wilderness. Had not his whole resistancc in that temptation, the No which he had victoriously opposed to it, aimed at the different but no less victorious Yes which he said to the will of God in this hour? (*CD* IV.1, 272)

Jesus' words of prayer to his Father – 'Yet not as I will, but as you will.' – show his resolute will to complete the missionary journey from Jordan, to persevere in this solidarity with man and to maintain the unity and consonance of will with his Father to the end.

Jesus' Public Ministry: His Manifesto and His Work Amongst Needy Humanity

At the beginning of his public ministry, he was invited to speak in the synagogue in his home town, Nazareth. There, he stood to read the prophetic passage from Isaiah 61:1-2 in the power of the Holy Spirit:

> The Spirit of the Lord is on me;
> because he has anointed me,
> to preach good news to the poor.
> He has sent me to proclaim freedom for the prisoners
> and recovery of sight for the blind, to release the oppressed,
> to proclaim the year of the Lord's favour. (Lk. 4:18-19)

Jesus is certain of his own identity before God as his Son. He experiences his Father's presence through the Spirit as a fact, he knows the missionary journey his Father has for him, now he proclaims publicly in unequivocal terms where his journey into the far country of needy humanity will take him. He will go to those who are poor, who are imprisoned and crying for help, who are oppressed and longing to be liberated, who are blind and yearning to see, who are dispossessed, disenfranchised and waiting for comfort and justice. He will go and proclaim the good news to them, he will give them his unsearchable riches, he will liberate and comfort them, he will give them sight and pour out the abundant grace of God into their lives because the time of God's favour has arrived. These are monumental tasks in themselves, but they are even more so as they are the work of the coming Spirit-filled Messiah. Jesus, knowing that he is the fulfilment of this prophecy and he is the Messiah sent from God (or anointed by God), boldly claims that this Scripture has been fulfilled before the very eyes of his audience. He does not shirk from this claim, he does not run away from it, he does not make this claim with any hesitancy or embarrassment, he does not dilute it or apologise for it, he plainly and straightforwardly claims these monumental tasks (of the Messiah) as the very work that his Father has sent/anointed him to do. Such is the power of his proclamation and such is the grace of his words that the people of his native Nazareth were amazed at him.

Jesus' utterance here can be understood as his manifesto for his coming ministry, as the blueprint for his Messianic work. He knows his identification with needy humanity will be of such a depth that he will live amongst the poor and needy, he will move amongst them as one of them, he will share their joys and their sorrows, he will have compassion for them and he will bring the healing love of God to them.

> Jesus went through all the towns and villages, teaching in their synagogues, preaching the good news of the kingdom and healing every disease and sickness. When he [Jesus] saw the crowds, he had compassion on them, because they were harassed and helpless, like sheep without a shepherd (Mt. 9:35-36).

Concerning Jesus' compassion for the people, Barth expounds on this inner dimension of Jesus to some considerable depth (*CD* IV.2, 184, see also *CD* IV.3, 774 and *CD* III.2, 211).

"He took it [their misery] from them and laid it on himself... He himself suffered it in their place... Jesus had made it his own" (*CD* IV.2, 184). These sentences in *CD* IV.2 are reminiscent of the theme of Jesus' identification and solidarity with men, which Barth expounds at length in 'The Lord as Servant' in *CD* IV.1, where the culmination of this solidarity is Jesus' atoning death. Here Barth brilliantly makes the observation that Jesus identifies with men not only in his coming as man and dying for men, not only in his baptism, not only in his physical presence and ministering to the needy people, but also in his fellowship with them in his (*inner*) life and emotion, in his sharing with them of their grief and sufferings, such that his solidarity with them is a true, comprehensive, holistic and integrated one. He is not one whose presence is only in outward form and whose inner thought is aloof, uncaring and alienated from the people, but he is one who stands in the midst of the people and stands in oneness with them even in their miseries and emotions. Barth's observation here throws light on the understanding of Jesus' unity with humanity – he is not merely *with us* and *for us* in his death alone. He is already *with us* and *for us* in his life, which is of a piece with his being *with us* and *for us* in his death on the cross. From the beginning to the end of his missionary journey, Jesus Christ is *with us* and *for us* not only in his ministry of words and actions, but also in his thoughts and feelings for us.[5]

Jesus' missionary journey of compassion and identification with needy humanity is not without its obstacles. The revolutionary nature of the unconditional love which he teaches (Mt. 5:43-48; Lk. 6:27-31) and fulfils brings him into severe confrontation with the religious leaders. Barth writes about the revolutionary nature of Jesus' work and lifestyle (*CD* IV.2, 179-80).

We need to take careful note here that in his ministry, Jesus identified himself *both* with sinners, i.e. those who were *spiritually* poor, and those who were *physically* poor and unwell. Jesus, in his compassion and in his freedom

---

[5] For further elaboration of God's love for humanity by Barth, see Damon W.K. So, *Jesus' Revelation of His Father: A Narrative-Conceptual Study of the Trinity with Special Reference to Karl Barth* (Milton Keynes: Paternoster, 2006), 135-8.

as the Lord, moves amongst sinners and eats with them, touches the untouchables and heals the leper, applauds the faith of a gentile centurion and announces that the kingdom of God has come to people such as him (Mt. 8:5-13). He heals the sick on the Sabbath, speaks to women in public, welcomes prostitutes into his company and embraces children in his arms. He allows his disciples to eat with unwashed hands and pick ears of corn on Sabbath. His radicalism is revealed when he will not let the barriers of race, gender, age, ritual cleanliness, time and even sin bar the people from the unconditional love of God.[6] His journey into the far country, into needy humanity, will not be impeded or cut short by these legalistic/ritualistic boundaries and barriers. Rather, with the characteristic supreme authority of God (which he himself rightly owns), he confronts these boundaries and barriers in the power and freedom of the Spirit, breaks and transcends them in the most public and fearless manner. As Barth has written, "[W]e do not really know Jesus (the Jesus of the New Testament) if we do not know him as… this *revolutionary*" (*CD* IV.2, 180). In his freedom, his Lordship and the radicalism of God, Jesus releases the captives, set the prisoners free and concretely proclaims by his authoritative words and actions the year of the Lord's favour, the coming of the kingdom of God to man. But the religious leadership, which treasures the legalistic/ritualistic boundaries and barriers, sees Jesus as the dangerous radical who breaks and teaches against the Torah and thereby draws people away from God. To them, Jesus is the nation's enemy who in leading people away from God is ultimately obstructing the coming of God's kingdom. To them, removing Jesus and his dangerous influence on the people is a responsible service to God.

As we have seen, in his public ministry Jesus identified himself both with the spiritually poor and the physically poor. As he abolished the boundaries and barriers which impeded people from receiving the grace and blessings from God, he did not then set up a new boundary between the physical needs and the spiritual needs of a person, and then only care for one side of the person's need. This kind of artificial boundary and barrier was totally alien to Jesus' thinking and actions. He preached the good news of the kingdom to the spiritually poor, cast out demons from those thus possessed, and healed the sicknesses of those who were physically unwell. He did all these out of his compassion for them. It will be absurd to say that he had compassion only for those who are spiritually poor, i.e. he did not really care for those who are suffering physically. It will be equally absurd to say that he had compassion only for those who are physically poor, i.e. he did not really care for those who are suffering spiritually. Jesus in his compassion did not discriminate between these two aspects of human needs. He saw people holistically and cared for them holistically. The church will do well to take heed of the way he saw people and draw near to them in his undiscriminating love.

---

[6] For further treatment of Jesus' radicalism and his transcending of these barriers, see So, *Jesus' Revelation of His Father*, 113-24 and So, *The Forgotten Jesus and the Trinity You Never Knew*, 59-100.

His Journey into Jerusalem, His Death and His Resurrection

Jesus' entry into Jerusalem is another crucial stage of his fateful journey into the far country. He is not unaware of the danger from the religious leaders in Jerusalem. He knows that his entry into Jerusalem will mean his death, which he has already repeatedly made known to his disciples. He could have chosen to return to Galilee instead of making this ill-fated entry into Jerusalem. He could have saved himself from the coming suffering and pain. But Jesus, knowing his Father's love for him and his Father's will for him to complete this journey into the ultimate depth and end of the far country, publicly, courageously and triumphantly enters Jerusalem. He begins to openly lay claim to his Messiahship by this symbolic act of riding on a donkey which was prophesied in Zechariah 9:19 concerning the Messiah. His claim seems to have been understood by some who shouted, 'Hosanna to the Son of David!' But his gentleness and non-violence, symbolised by the donkey rather than a war horse, might not have been appreciated by them.[7] The king and Messiah will fulfil his missionary journey not by a show of military power but by a humiliating death, in accordance with his Father's will and his own commitment which he has made in his baptism and maintained throughout his ministry. His action of purifying the temple – by overturning the tables of the money changers and the benches of those selling doves (Mt. 21:12-13) – further strengthens his claim to Messiahship.[8] Jesus' confrontation with the religious leadership has already reached a state of high tension in Galilee. Inevitably, the tension and confrontation between Jesus and the religious leaders escalates after his entry into Jerusalem through his public claims and 'outrageous' actions in the temple.

There could only be one outcome from the revolutionary nature of Jesus' teachings and from his radical fulfilment of his own teaching. His solidarity with the needy, the poor, the marginalised, the unclean, the sinners, the excluded gentiles – to whom he expresses his Father's love in an undiscriminating and unconditional manner (Mt. 5:43-48) – could not be accommodated by the old wineskin of the old order. The new wine of the kingdom of God is bound to burst the old wineskin. Jesus declared that the temple (referring to his body) would be destroyed and he would raise it in three days, meaning that the old order with all its weaknesses and sinfulness will be put away through the destruction of his own body, and humanity would be raised to new life in him in three days. This declaration could only be interpreted by the religious leaders as a threat to their whole way of life – religious, social, national and personal. With such a declaration supported so powerfully by his teaching and lifestyle, he could not be tolerated by the

[7] Richard France, *The Gospel According to Matthew: An Introduction and Commentary* (Leicester: Inter-Varsity Press, 1985/7), 298-9.

[8] France, *The Gospel According to Matthew*, 300. Jewish expectations included the belief, based on the visions of Ezek. 40-48, and focused by Zech 6:12-13, that the Messiah would renew and purify the temple. See also B. Gärtner, *The Temple and the Community* (Cambridge: Cambridge University Press, 1965), 105-11.

religious leaders, who viewed their plotting and actions to remove Jesus as a service to their nation and to God.

Jesus' death on the cross is the climax of his missionary journey into the far country; it is also the climax of his identification with needy and sinful humanity. When one considers his passion and death – the manner of his suffering, the manner of his self-denial and self-sacrifice, the manner of his enduring the taunts, hatred, ugly violence and painful injuries inflicted by evil men without retaliation, the manner of his drinking this cup from his Father and experiencing his abandonment, the manner of his giving himself willingly into the hands of evil men for the sake of their forgiveness and salvation – it must be seen as the climax, fulfilment, coronation and culmination of his life and ministry (as Barth has correctly observed in *CD* IV.2, 252). And his passion and death is the climax of Jesus' revelation of the unconditional divine love of himself and of his Father. It is also the climax of his missionary journey into the far country in which his identification with sinful humanity plumbs its utmost depth and reaches its ultimate height. It is because of Jesus' complete identification with us from the beginning of his life to the end that he is able and worthy to be our substitute and representative on the cross, that he can truly die for us and take the consequence of our sins in our place. As Barth has put it:

> [I]n the suffering and death of Jesus Christ it has come to pass that in his own person he has made an end of us as sinners and therefore of sin itself by going to death as the One who took our place as sinners. In his person he has delivered up us sinners and sin itself to destruction. (*CD* IV.1, 253)

Barth's interpretation of atonement hinges critically on Jesus' identification with sinful and needy humanity, hence his subsection on 'The Way of the Son of God into the Far Country' in *CD* IV.1.

Jesus Christ has faithfully and obediently finished his journey into the far country, into the depth of human sorrows and sufferings, into the unfathomable depth of alienation from his Father, into the darkness and dereliction reserved for sinful humanity. But this journey by the Son of God into the far country is not the end of the gospel story because it is followed by the home-coming of the Son of God, which is his resurrection from the dead by the power of the Holy Spirit. In this home-coming of his, he brings along his brothers and sisters, now cleansed and renewed, from the far country to the home of his Father who has been longing and waiting for their return from the far away land of rebellion and self-indulgence; his Father embraces them and kisses them in his compassionate love. The home-coming of the Son of God inaugurates a new humanity which has been made possible by his birth, life, ministry, death and resurrection. This new humanity in Christ, empowered by the Holy Spirit, calls upon God as Father and continues the witness in the world to the Father, Son and Holy Spirit in its new life of unconditional love and radical self-giving, until the Son returns to bring the new humanity into the new heaven and new earth, into the new Jerusalem.

Conclusions

Barth has provided a way for us to see Jesus' life and his death as a unity – through the theme of Jesus' identification with needy humanity in his missionary journey into the far country. It is when we interpret his death from the perspective (prospectively) of his life of identification with humanity that we fully appreciate his death in the place of humanity. And it is when we interpret his life from the perspective (retrospectively) of his death that we fully appreciate the full extent of his intention of identification with humanity in his life. To fully appreciate how Jesus Christ is *with us* and *for us*, we need to know him in his life as well as in his death. His deep sense of commitment to us becomes more apparent, and impinges on us more strongly, if we understand that commitment as one which undergirded his long and consistent journey from heaven.[9]

The whole missionary journey of the Son of God from the place of glory and exaltation into the far country reveals to us the heart of God, his heart to be *with us* and *for us* from the beginning to the end. As Barth has said, "Even the strongest 'with us' is not enough to describe what Jesus Christ is in relation to us. No one and nothing in the order of creation can be 'for us' in the strict sense, in the way in which Jesus Christ is 'for us' in the order of reconciliation" (*CD* IV.1, 229). By the grace of the living Spirit, the church will do well to grasp the profound sense of Jesus being *with us* and *for us*, so that she will in turn learn to follow Christ to be *with* those and *for* those who are needy and crying.

The discussion above traced through different phases of Jesus' life, ministry and death, and saw how Jesus identified with needy humanity both in the physical and the spiritual sense. At certain phases, his identification with the physically poor is evident, e.g. his birth and his ministry, while at other phases his identification with the spiritually poor is in clear view, e.g. his baptism, his temptations in the wilderness and Gethsemane, his ministry and his death in Jerusalem. Even in his death, there is a strong sense of his identification with those who are physically and unjustly oppressed. One has to conclude that his identification with needy humanity is a *holistic* one if we think of Jesus Christ in his *whole* journey from heaven, via Bethlehem, Egypt, Nazareth, the Jordan and Galilee to Jerusalem.

However, the holistic view of Jesus Christ in his whole missionary journey of being *with us* and *for us* is not always grasped by the church. N.T. Wright has made the following observation:

> The Reformers had very thorough answers to the question 'why did Jesus die?'; they did not have nearly such good answers to the question 'why did Jesus live?'... It would not, then, be much of a caricature to say that orthodoxy, as represented by much popular preaching and writing, has had no clear idea of the purpose of Jesus' ministry. For many conservative theologians it would have been

---

[9] See So, *The Forgotten Jesus and the Trinity You Never Knew*, 101-84 for an extended presentation of this long journey.

> sufficient if Jesus had been born of a virgin, lived a sinless life, died a sacrificial death, and risen again three days later. ... His ministry and his death are thus loosely connected.[10]

The liberals' comparative reticence about Jesus' death (and the gravity of sin therein) and their contentment to speak about his life form the other extreme. The dichotomy between the conservatives' emphasis on the death of Christ and the liberals' emphasis on the life of Christ is an unnecessary and unbiblical one.[11] But this dichotomy has grave consequences for the mission of the church. The liberals who are contented with speaking about Jesus' life tend towards imitating Jesus in social action which is good in itself but by no means the whole gospel. The conservatives have the tendency to neglect the important value of Jesus' life and ministry and his identification with needy humanity in this phase of his earthly existence, where he heals the sick, feeds the hungry and stands with the poor and the socially marginalised. The conservatives' neglect of Jesus' life could lead to a purely spiritualised gospel with weak implications for physical restoration, socio-political transformation and liberation from injustice. The kind of picture of Jesus that the church sees correlates with the kind of action she takes. A non-holistic picture of Jesus correlates to non-holistic actions by the church. But if the *holistic* picture of Jesus Christ in his dynamic radical teachings, his revolutionary actions and his sacrificial death is held firmly by the church as suggested above – using the *unitary* theme of his identification with needy humanity in his *whole* journey into the far country, this vision of Jesus Christ in his compassion for the poor and in his passion for sinners motivates the church to be compassionate and self-giving as the Lord is, and both the physical and spiritual elements of the whole gospel will be firmly kept in view, exercised and fulfilled.

As has been mentioned above, Jesus viewed a person *holistically*. He did not set up a boundary within a person and care for one aspect of the person only. This is totally contradictory to his undiscriminating love shown to the people which broke all boundaries and barriers. This kind of dualistic view of a person has more to do with ancient Greek thinking than biblical perspective. The church must follow her Lord in a *holistic* understanding of a person in her mission in the world. *To summarise, a holistic view of Jesus Christ in his long journey to the far country coupled with a holistic view of humanity form the firm basis for holistic mission.* Strictly speaking, a holistic view of Jesus will involve looking into his fundamental relationship with his Father through the Spirit but this trinitarian perspective on Jesus cannot be treated here in a short chapter and is the subject of a longer presentation in So, *The Forgotten Jesus and the Trinity You Never Knew*.

To conclude, in view of the possible non-holistic pictures of Jesus, different wings of the church have to seriously examine themselves on the kind of

---

[10] N.T. Wright, *Jesus and the Victory of God* (London: SPCK, 1996). See Wright's other comments to the same effect on 14-15.

[11] For an analysis of this dichotomy, see So, *Jesus' Revelation of His Father*, 161-2.

picture of Jesus that they hold and proclaim, and ask themselves whether the picture they hold is a one-sided one or a holistic one. If the church truly opens her mind and heart to the *whole* gospel story of Jesus Christ, his emphatic identification with needy people from the beginning of his life (his birth) to the end of his life (his death) would be unmistakeable to her. If Jesus Christ, as the divine Lord and head of the church, so emphatically went into the far country and identified himself with needy and sinful humanity – that he stands on the side of the physically poor, *and* he is with sinners and for sinners – how could the church not follow her Lord and Saviour by going into the far country, identifying with the physically poor and needy, reaching out to the spiritually blind and captives of this world, with the committed intention of bringing them back to the Father in a home-coming journey of liberation, healing, forgiveness, recovery of sight, freedom, jubilation, thanksgiving and praise?

Part C

Holistic Mission, From 1910 to 2010

Precursors and Tensions in Holistic Mission: An Historical Overview

Al Tizon

'Holistic mission' has become a household phrase of sorts among evangelical missiologists and missionaries. In the words of Rene Padilla, "It is now widely accepted that the church's mission is intrinsically holistic...."[1] But how did it get there? This is an important question, especially in light of the evangelism-only theology of mission that pervaded evangelicalism for the greater part of the twentieth century.

Few would argue that the International Congress on World Evangelization in 1974 held in Lausanne, Switzerland, marks the first serious attempt to correct this shortsightedness. To begin, however, with Lausanne '74 to understand the historical development of evangelical holistic mission would overlook some key precursors that led to the social vision articulated at the Congress. The first part of this chapter identifies these precursors or roots.

Major tensions emerged at Lausanne '74 and shortly thereafter concerning the place that social concern should occupy in the mission of the church. As uncomfortable and painful as these tensions were, they proved to be, in the hands of God, the impetus for a fuller development of evangelical holistic mission. The second part of this chapter analyzes each of these tensions.

Roots of Evangelical Holistic Mission: Pre-Lausanne 1974

Lausanne '74 championed the practice of evangelism; how could it not, being an international congress on world evangelization? However, many were confounded at the prominence given to social responsibility at the same congress. But should they have been, given certain developments within the evangelical communion that pointed toward a more favorable spirit toward social concern? What were these developments? Such a question begs a preliminary one: What occurred in the history of Protestant mission that led to the marginalization of evangelical social concern in the first place?

---

[1] C. Rene Padilla, 'Holistic Mission', in John Corrie (ed.), *Dictionary of Mission Theology* (Downers Grove, IL: IVP, 2007), 162.

Evangelism vs. social concern

The historical development of the relationship between evangelism and social concern constitutes the first root of evangelical holistic mission. Most mission historians agree that the battle between evangelism and social concern is a twentieth century phenomenon. Before it erupted in the 1920s, evangelicals engaged society as part and parcel of their practice of faith. William Carey, 'the father of modern missions', exemplifies the historic seamlessness between evangelistic aspirations and social reform.[2] In addition to preaching and planting churches in India, Carey spoke out against the caste system, protested slavery in Britain, organized a boycott against sugar imports from West Indian plantations cultivated by slaves, taught agriculture, and built systems of higher education. He conducted these activities in concert with his evangelistic efforts.

At least two undeniable factors led to what sociologist David Moberg has identified as the 'Great Reversal',[3] referring to the move of evangelicals from spearheading social reform in the eighteenth and nineteenth centuries to retreating almost totally from mainstream society. A strong reaction to the increasing sway of liberal theological developments, which included an emphasis on social concern, constitutes the first factor. Evangelicals, primarily in North America, began to steer away from social concern when they perceived the social gospel movement as eclipsing personal evangelism.[4]

The second undeniable culprit was the shift from a predominantly post-millennial to a pre-millennial eschatology. This shift had a devastating effect upon the social involvement of evangelicals, as dispensational pre-millennialists preached the irredeemable depravity of society. Men and women trapped on board the sinking ship of society described human existence, and offering the lifeboat of Christ to the doomed (evangelism) defined the mission of the church. By the late 1920s, to be evangelical meant, for most, identification with pre-millennial fundamentalism that reactively erased social responsibility from the missionary agenda. By then, writes David J. Bosch, "All forms of progressive social involvement had disappeared. The 'Great Reversal' had been completed."[5]

The polarization between fundamentalists and modernists occurred primarily in North America but diffused throughout the world by means of the west-to-east, north-to-south missionary movement during the first half of the twentieth

---

[2] David J. Bosch, 'In Search of New Evangelical Understanding', in Bruce J. Nicholls (ed), *In Word and Deed: Evangelism and Social Responsibility* (Grand Rapids, MI: Eerdmans, 1986), 68.

[3] David O. Moberg, *The Great Reversal: Evangelism Versus Social Concern* (Philadelphia, PA and New York: J.B. Lippincott, 1972), 30-34. Credit for the term should ultimately go to historian Timothy L. Smith, as Moberg himself acknowledges (11, 30). Moberg, however, expands upon the phenomenon from a sociological perspective and deserves the credit for popularizing it.

[4] For relatively recent treatments on the social gospel movement, see Christopher H. Evans, *The Social Gospel Today* (Louisville, KY: Westminster/John Knox, 2001).

[5] Bosch, 'In Search', 70-71.

century. Bong Rin Ro says it succinctly when he writes, "The establishment of the Protestant church in the Third World was basically the fruit of Protestant mission from the west ... [And] both the western model of the liberal social gospel and the model of ... evangelical soul saving ... have been copied in the Third World."[6] This divide within Protestantism did not intensify as heatedly in the non-western world as it did in North America. However, we cannot deny the influence of the Great Reversal upon evangelical churches worldwide.

The evangelism-social concern debate expressed itself in Protestant missions amidst a larger debate over the ultimate meaning of mission between evangelicals and ecumenical Protestants (or 'ecumenicals'). The publication of *Re-Thinking Missions* by William Hocking in 1932 ignited the debate. The 'shocking Hocking Report', as it came to be called, summarized a two year project carried out by the Layman's Foreign Missions Inquiry in the early 1930s. The report challenged what were then basic Protestant tenets, such as the uniqueness of Christianity among the religions of the world and the necessity of preaching personal conversion to Christ.[7] The report declared that the purpose of mission was not to convert people, but to seek religious cooperation toward a better world. Needless to say, evangelicals strongly opposed the findings of the report, thus widening the polarization between evangelicals and ecumenicals around the world.

If the Hocking Report deepened the missionary evangelical-ecumenical polarity in the 1930s up through the 1950s, then disconcerting developments within the WCC took the rift to unprecedented heights in the early 1960s through to the mid-1970s. Beginning with the official merger of the International Missionary Council (IMC) and the WCC in 1961 at New Delhi, evangelicals began to give strong expression to their growing sense of alienation from the WCC.

By the mid-1960s, evangelicals poised themselves to launch their own international missionary conferences. In 1966, they met together not once, but twice – in Wheaton, Illinois USA and Berlin, Germany respectively – as a 'counter-World Council of Churches movement'.[8] Many identify the fourth WCC Assembly in Uppsala, Sweden in 1968 as the proverbial straw that broke the camel's back. 'The great debate', as Roger Hedlund terms it, over the meaning of mission finally came to a head in Uppsala. Hedlund writes, "Two basic theologies – two ideologies – were in conflict.... On the one side were the

---

[6] Bong Rin Ro, 'The Perspectives of Church History from New Testament Times to 1960', in Bruce J. Nicholls (ed.), *In Word and Deed: Evangelism and Social Responsibility* (Grand Rapids, Mich: Eerdmans, 1986), 34.

[7] William E. Hocking, *Rethinking Missions* (New York and London: Harper & Brothers, 1932), 3-78.

[8] Efiong S. Utuk, 'From Wheaton to Lausanne', in James A Scherer and Stephen B. Bevans (eds.), *New Directions in Mission and Evangelization 2: Theological Foundations,* (Maryknoll, NY: Orbis, 1994), 101.

advocates of mission as humanization, on the other side... [those concerned] with... the evangelization of the lost...."[9]

Although evangelicals demonstrated amazing unity in the two world gatherings in 1966, largely held together by a common distrust of the WCC, the differences regarding how they viewed the relationship between evangelism and social concern eventually came to the surface. The voices of the 'new evangelicals' increased in volume and intensity, the most influential belonging to a young theologian named Carl F.H. Henry, challenging the fundamentalist monopoly on mission. In 1947, Henry jolted the evangelical world with the classic publication, *The Uneasy Conscience of Modern Fundamentalism*, wherein he tactfully accused fundamentalists of not proclaiming the whole gospel. He wrote, "Fundamentalism in revolting against the Social Gospel... also... revolt[ed] against the Christian social imperative."[10] Such a statement may seem benign now, but in 1947 it had enough potency to have started a re-awakening of the evangelical social conscience in America and beyond. Henry continued to lead the charge to call God's people to re-engage society for the sake of the gospel. In a later publication, he labeled the evangelism-only posture as part of an unbiblical 'fundamentalist reduction'.[11] Henry led the way in propagating this new kind of evangelicalism (which was not so much 'new' as it was a harking back to the pre-Great Reversal days). The reaffirmation of Christian social responsibility, which held a prominent place in the new evangelicalism, made its presence felt in the 1966 gatherings primarily by the likes of Henry, Horace Fenton (then director of the Latin American Mission) and an itinerant evangelist named Billy Graham. These and other speakers at the two congresses made it clear, however, while reaffirming social responsibility, that evangelism must continue to hold a primary place in authentic biblical mission. They assured the evangelical constituency that their understanding of social concern did not and must not eclipse the primary task of world evangelization.

Such prioritizing made many evangelicals from the two thirds world feel increasingly uneasy, and they gradually began to voice their discomfort at different gatherings. Padilla notes that the new concern for social problems shown at the 1966 Wheaton Congress "was by no means unrelated to the presence of a good number of participants from the two thirds world."[12] While gratified that their brothers and sisters from the west increasingly challenged

---

[9] Roger Hedlund, *Roots of the Great Debate in Mission* (Bangalore, India: Theological Book Trust, 1997), 229. Hedlund's perspective is decidedly evangelical. For balance, see T.V. Philip, *Edinburgh to Salvador: Twentieth Century Ecumenical Missiology* (Delhi, India: ISPCK; Tiruvalla, India: CSS, 1999), 97-131.

[10] Carl F.H. Henry, *The Uneasy Conscience of Modern Fundamentalism* (Grand Rapids, Mich: Eerdmans, 1947), 32.

[11] Carl F.H. Henry, *Evangelical Responsibility in Contemporary Theology* (Grand Rapids, MI: Eerdmans, 1957), 33.

[12] C. Rene Padilla, 'Evangelism and Social Responsibility: From Wheaton '66 to Wheaton '83', *Transformation* 2:3 (April/June 1985), 28.

the 'fundamentalist reduction', two thirds world evangelicals continued to press the international missionary community to investigate further the integral place of social concern in the mission of the church.

A group of 'young evangelicals' from North America joined their brothers and sisters in the two thirds world and began expressing a similar kind of discomfort with what they interpreted as weak token affirmations of Christian social concern in the context of the volatile 1960s.[13] They called the nation to self-critique in general and the church to a rediscovery of its prophetic ministry in particular. Their historic meeting in Chicago in 1973 produced the Chicago Declaration, which articulated a gospel-inspired commitment to compassion and justice, alongside the crucial, non-negotiable work of evangelism.[14]

Meanwhile, the fundamentalist spirit remained strong as did the Henry-ian version of the new evangelicalism. These persuasions continued to exert themselves at all of the aforementioned conferences, promoting their respective views. So during the period between 1966 and 1973, we can identify three broad groupings that outlined the diversity of missionary social ethics among evangelicals: (1) the fundamentalists, who maintained the primacy of evangelism largely at the expense of social concern as a continued reaction against the 'apostate ecumenical movement', (2) the new or moderate evangelicals, who, while maintaining the primacy of evangelism, called for a return to an historic, socially-engaged evangelicalism, and (3) the younger, radical evangelicals who called for an uncompromising socio-political commitment to biblical compassion and justice as integral to the gospel. Viewing it in one-two-three terms like this might give the impression of progressive development, as if the 'young radicals' phased out the 'moderates' who phased out the 'fundamentalists'. But missionary convictions die hard; these three strands not only continue to exist today, they also each have spawned variations of themselves, making evangelical missionary social ethics a very diverse and complex phenomenon.

Evangelical relief and development ministries after World War Two

Alongside the historical root of the evangelism-social concern debate grew a lesser root that also significantly determined the nature of holistic mission. Calling it 'lesser' simply means that it originated from, and therefore depended upon, the larger root of the evangelism-social concern debate. This particular tension – created by the inconsistency between practice and theology among evangelicals – warrants special attention because it was precisely the attempted efforts to address this inconsistency that led to the affirmation of social concern at Lausanne '74.

---

[13] Richard Quebedeaux, *The Young Evangelicals* (New York: Harper and Row, 1974), 99-134.

[14] Ronald J. Sider, 'An Historic Moment for Biblical Social Concern', in Ronald J. Sider (ed.), *The Chicago Declaration* (Carol Stream, IL: Creation House, 1974), 29-31.

Despite the North American 'fundamentalist reduction' that dominated the global evangelical missionary community, evangelicals continued to practice works of social uplift in the service of the gospel around the world. David M. Howard, who has chronicled the history of the World Evangelical Fellowship (WEF), states confidently that WEF leaders "have always understood the obligation of Christians to reach out in love to those in need and give a cup of cold water."[15] The disappearance of a social ethic during 'the dark ages of evangelicalism' failed to eliminate missionary social action.[16] It did, however, greatly diminish in the 1920s and '30s due to the pressures generated by the fundamentalist-modernist controversy.[17]

The inconsistency between missionary social practice and the lack of a social ethic increasingly distressed the more evangelical thoughtful. Did not continued social involvement betray the stand against the theology of the social gospel? If the social gospel was to be rejected, how could evangelicals justify their ongoing humanitarian work? This became an increasingly important question as the post-World War Two period marked a significant increase in evangelical humanitarian ministries.

However, the consequences of the fundamentalist-modernist debacle lingered on, as a cloud of suspicion loomed over evangelicals who were involved in social ministries. The suspicion led to accusations that ranged from accommodating the Social Gospel to sympathizing with dangerous leftist groups. Even many of the evangelicals, who were engaged in social ministries, saw their work as secondary to the 'real' work of the gospel of evangelism and church planting.

The frustration caused by the inconsistency between maturing social practice and a lack of a social ethic to warrant it came to bursting point; something had to give. Amid this frustration, evangelical mission scholars and development practitioners finally woke up to their inevitable need for one another, and Lausanne '74 proved timely for such collaboration.[18]

This root of evangelical growth in a practical theology of development grew out of, and alongside, the larger root of the evangelism-social concern debate. If the working out of the evangelism-social concern debate constituted the theological root, then the theologically-groundless growth of relief and development ministries among evangelicals constituted the practical root.

---

[15] David M. Howard, *The Dream That Would Not Die: The Birth and Growth of the World Evangelical Fellowship, 1846-1986* (Exeter, UK: Paternoster, 1986), 189.

[16] Athol Gill, 'Christian Social Responsibility', in C. Rene Padilla (ed.), *The New Face of Evangelicalism: An International Symposium on the Lausanne Covenant* (Downers Grove, IL: InterVarsity, 1976), 93.

[17] Linda Smith, 'Recent Historical Perspectives of the Evangelical Tradition', in Edgar J. Elliston (ed.), *Christian Relief and Development: Developing Workers for Effective Ministry* (Dallas, TX: Word, 1989), 25-26.

[18] Vinay Samuel and Chris Sugden, 'Introduction', in Vinay Samuel and Chris Sugden (eds.), *The Church in Response to Human Need* (Oxford: Regnum; Grand Rapids, MI: Eerdmans, 1987), ix.

Together these two roots eventually sprouted a type of mission theology that demanded both proclamation and demonstration, i.e. a holistic approach.

Internal Tensions: Lausanne 1974 to Wheaton 1983

What was the social vision forged at Lausanne '74 and articulated in the Lausanne Covenant? Billy Graham, the inspirational figurehead and catalyst of Lausanne '74, listed four hopes in his opening address at the Congress, the third of which pertains directly to the social question.[19] He announced at the outset, "I trust we can state… the relationship between evangelism and social responsibility… [which] disturbs many believers. Perhaps Lausanne can help to clarify it'.[20] This opening statement demonstrates that by the time of Lausanne '74, thanks to the factors discussed earlier, Graham and many others came prepared to settle this issue.

Lausanne '74 clearly recognized and affirmed social concern as essential to the task of world evangelization by making it an integral part of the Covenant. It was primarily Article 5 entitled 'Christian Social Responsibility', which basically synthesized the papers presented at the Congress by Rene Padilla, Samuel Escobar and Carl Henry, that articulates Lausanne's social vision most clearly.[21] Klaus Bockmuehl's detailed interpretation of the nine 'verbs of action' contained in the Article further developed its missionary implications.[22] At least two overall themes emerge from his analysis: (1) To act prophetically in society, denouncing injustices and calling governments to repentance, and (2) To demonstrate and promote the righteousness of the kingdom of God for and among the oppressed.

The Covenant's clear affirmation of social concern did not go unchallenged at the Congress. Many conservatives saw it as a distraction from the original Lausanne vision of 'cross-cultural evangelism'. Others to the right of the conservatives went even further and accused Lausanne's stated social vision as being the old Social Gospel in evangelical clothing.[23] For those left of centre,

---

[19] Billy Graham, 'Why Lausanne?' in James D. Douglas (ed.), *Let the Earth Hear His Voice: International Congress on World Evangelization* (Minneapolis, MN: World Wide Publications, 1975), 34.

[20] Graham, 'Why Lausanne?', 34.

[21] Klaus Bockmuehl, *Evangelicals and Social Ethics*, trans. David T. Priestly (Downers Grove, IL: InterVarsity, 1979), 8-12. These papers to which Bockmuehl refers are available in James D. Douglas (ed), *Let the Earth His Voice* (Minneapolis, MN: World Wide Publications, 1976), the official reference volume of Lausanne I. Padilla's address entitled 'Evangelism and the World' (116-146) and Escobar's 'Evangelism and Man's Search for Freedom, Justice, and Fulfillment' (303-326) were both plenary papers, while Henry's address 'Christian Personal and Social Ethics in Relation to Racism, Poverty, War, and Other Problems' (1163-1182) provided a foundation for the sessions of a special committee on ethics.

[22] Bockmuehl, *Evangelicals and Social Ethics*, 17ff.

[23] See Valdir R. Steuernagel, 'The Theology of Mission in Its Relation to Social Responsibility within the Lausanne Movement' (ThD thesis, Lutheran School of

however, the affirmation of socio-political involvement in the Covenant did not go far enough. They claimed that even though Article 5 repented of past negligence and affirmed the inseparable relationship of social responsibility to evangelism, it did not define that relationship. Moreover, social concern still felt like an appendage to the 'real work' of the gospel.[24]

So a group of about two hundred people at the Congress formed an ad hoc committee to discuss the shortcomings of the Covenant's social affirmation in light of the implications of radical discipleship. They drafted an official response to Lausanne aptly titled "Theology [and] Implications of Radical Discipleship".[25] Divided into four main parts, the document challenged the Congress to declare more overtly the place of social concern in the mission of the church by affirming the comprehensive scope of the gospel of the kingdom of God.[26] "[The gospel]," the paper read, "is Good News of liberation, of restoration, of wholeness, and of salvation that is personal, social, global and cosmic."[27] The Statement on Radical Discipleship repudiated the dichotomy between evangelism and social concern, challenged the language of the primacy of evangelism, and broadened the scope of God's salvific work in the world, all the while remaining wholly committed to biblical authority and world evangelization.

Although the Statement did not end up as part of the Covenant, convener John Stott presented it at the end of the Congress along with the final draft of the Covenant, thus giving it prominence.[28] Moreover, almost 500 people, approximately a quarter of the number of official delegates, signed it before leaving the Congress. So between the Covenant's affirmation of socio-political involvement and the inclusion of the Statement on Radical Discipleship among the official papers of the Congress, the status of social concern enjoyed a new level of validation that it had not experienced since the days before the fundamentalist-modernist debacle.

The broadness of the Lausanne social vision allowed for diversity in interpretation, and at the outset, this broadness served as a valuable point of evangelical unity. Valdir Steuernagel sees it "as a sign of strength and of a rare

---

Theology at Chicago, 1988), 151-156; Hedlund, *Roots of the Great Debate*, 294-299; and Padilla 'Evangelism and Social Responsibility', 29, to know who had problems with the Covenant's social affirmation. The list included Peter Wagner, Ralph Winter, Donald McGavran, Arthur Johnston, and Peter Beyerhaus. Hedlund mentions these individuals sympathetically from a 'church growth' perspective, which he shares, while Padilla discusses them from a radical evangelical perspective. Steuernagel attempts a more objective discussion, although he falls decidedly on the radical evangelical side.

[24] Chris Sugden, 'Evangelicals and Wholistic Evangelism', in Vinay Samuel and Albrecht Hauser (eds.), *Proclaiming Christ in Christ's Way: Studies in Integral Evangelism* (Oxford, UK: Regnum, 1989), 33.

[25] 'Theology [and] Implications of Radical Discipleship', in James D. Douglas (ed.), *Let the Earth His Voice* (Minneapolis; MN: World Wide Publications, 1975), 1294-1296.

[26] 'Theology and Implications of Radical Discipleship', 1294-1296.

[27] 'Theology and Implications of Radical Discipleship', 1294.

[28] Sugden, 'Wholistic Evangelism', 34.

and delicate moment of consensus. One step backwards", he posits, "and Lausanne would have lost the radical discipleship group; one step forward and it would have lost the conservative evangelicals."[29]

But as much as its broadness proved valuable in the beginning, it eventually needed sharpening if socio-ethical thinking and practice had a future on the evangelical missionary agenda. Predictably, evangelicals went about interpreting and developing the Lausanne social vision according to their respective schools of thought. And as proponents of these various schools encountered one another at conferences, as well as on the mission field, an unprecedented level of tension intensified within the post-Lausanne evangelical missionary community.

Indeed an understanding of holistic mission emerged out of very real tensions between 1974 and 1983. The Covenant's affirmation of social concern, as well as the prominence of the Statement on Radical Discipleship, led some to believe that what we now call holistic mission would find its way into the evangelical mainstream sooner rather than later. But its acceptance today was by no means instant. In the decade that followed Lausanne '74 a theological battle ensued as to who would dictate the course of evangelical mission; it brought to the fore the different agendas of evangelicals corresponding to the various schools of thought. At least three overlapping tensions related to socio-political involvement define the contours of the battle.

Narrow view vs. broad view

Narrow and broad views of the nature of mission characterized the first tension, which intensified as early as the first meeting in 1975 of the Lausanne Continuation Committee in Mexico City.[30] Meeting with the purpose of clarifying its role in continuing the efforts begun at Lausanne, conservative evangelicals fought for singling out and focusing on evangelism, while others pleaded that all facets of the agreed-upon Covenant be taken seriously, especially the church's social responsibility. After a week of intense deliberations, the committee tried to take into account both the narrow and the broad by concluding that its purpose was to further the total biblical mission of the church, recognizing that "in this mission of sacrificial service, evangelism is primary," and that our particular concern must be the evangelization of the 2.7 billion unreached people of our world.[31]

A year later, the committee convened again in Atlanta, henceforth calling itself the Lausanne Committee for World Evangelization (LCWE). There it formed four working groups, one which the LCWE named the Lausanne Theology and Education Group (LTEG).[32] Mandated "to promote theological

---

[29] Steuernagel, 'The Theology of Mission', 156.

[30] Steuernagel, 'The Theology of Mission', 173-179.

[31] Leighton Ford cited in Steuernagel, 'The Theology of Mission', 174.

[32] 'Historical Background of the Lausanne Committee', in Billy Graham Center Archives, www.wheaton.edu/bgc/archives/GUIDES/046.HTM#3 (accessed 2 April

reflection on issues related to world evangelization and, in particular, to explore the implications of the Lausanne Covenant", the LTEG sponsored or co-sponsored four consultations between 1977 and 1982.[33] As social responsibility continued to be a 'hot potato', two out of the four consultations dealt with various aspects of evangelical social concern: the 1980 International Consultation on Simple Lifestyle in London (SLC) and the 1982 Consultation on the Relationship between Evangelism and Social Responsibility in Grand Rapids, MI (CRESR).

The SLC in London sought to grasp both the theological and practical meaning of a conviction expressed in Article 9 of the Lausanne Covenant. After expressing shock by world poverty, Article 9 reads, "Those of us who live in affluent circumstances accept our duty to develop a simple lifestyle in order to contribute to both relief and evangelism."[34] In an attempt to take this conviction seriously, participants of the SLC synthesized their findings in a statement they simply called 'The Commitment', which made the necessary and unavoidable connection between personal lifestyle and a world of dire poverty.[35]

Some of the leaders of the LCWE expressed grave concern over the consultation's findings.[36] They accused it of being imbalanced in the selection of participants and therefore imbalanced in theological orientation, leaning on the side of the radical. Moreover, drafters of 'The Commitment' did not adequately connect the theme of simple lifestyle to the singular focus of world evangelization. These concerns aggravated the conservative constituency, which interpreted the SLC's findings as the continued and deliberate 'torpedoing' of the specific task of world evangelization, a 'torpedoing' that began at Lausanne '74.[37]

Undoubtedly, this dissatisfaction strengthened the resolve of the LCWE to reassert its narrower agenda at the 1980 Consultation on World Evangelization in Pattaya, Thailand (COWE) – just three months after the SLC in London. The facilitators of COWE towed the hard line of single-focus evangelism and structured the consultation accordingly around the church growth concept of unreached people groups. Church growth strategist Peter Wagner applauded the fact that COWE upheld 'the functional definition of evangelism agreed upon by the LCWE', which read:

2003).

[33] Ford cited in Steuernagel, 'The Theology of Mission', 179-180.

[34] 'The Lausanne Covenant', in John R.W. Stott (ed.), *Making Christ Known: Historic Mission Documents from the Lausanne Movement, 1974-1989* (Grand Rapids, MI; Cambridge: Eerdmans, 1996), 34. The drafting committee of the Covenant consisted of five members: John Stott, Samuel Escobar, James Douglas, Leighton Ford, and Hudson Armerding.

[35] 'The Commitment', in Ronald J. Sider (ed.), *Lifestyle in the Eighties: An Evangelical Commitment to Simple Lifestyle* (Philadelphia, PA: Westminster, 1982), 13-19.

[36] Steuernagel, 'The Theology of Mission', 185-186.

[37] C. Peter Wagner, 'Lausanne Twelve Months Later', *Christianity Today*, 4 July 1975, 961-963.

> The *nature* of world evangelization is the communication of the Good News. The *purpose* is to give individuals and groups a valid opportunity to [hear]. The *goal* is the persuading of men and women to accept Jesus Christ as Lord and Savior.[38]

Wagner praised COWE's steadfast maintenance of this kind of evangelization over and against the "dangerous tendency" espoused by "advocates of holistic evangelism."[39] These 'advocates of holistic evangelism' considered this limited vision at COWE as a deplorable step backward. They criticized the LCWE of not being true to the broad, holistic vision of the Covenant and of reducing evangelization once again to the verbal proclamation of the gospel. Samuel and Sugden lament that COWE "seemed... painfully unaware of all the developments in the Lausanne movement in seeking to communicate the whole gospel to the whole world. The years of slow growth in sensitivity to the social dimensions of the gospel and to the contexts in which it was proclaimed, seemed to be wiped out."[40]

Those who concurred with such sentiments joined forces and drafted a Statement of Concerns that nearly one third of COWE delegates signed at the end of the consultation. This statement basically challenged the LCWE to look at the world in terms of social, economic, and political institutions in addition to the category of unreached people groups and to provide guidance for justice to Christians living in oppressed lands and for abetting oppressive regimes. The plea not to isolate verbal proclamation from the total demands of the gospel drove the signers of the Statement of Concerns to challenge the LCWE to take more seriously the social dimensions of the missionary task. The statement demanded that the LCWE reaffirm its commitment to all aspects of the Covenant, encourage study and action in fulfillment of Lausanne's commitment to socio-political involvement, convene a world congress on social responsibility, and give guidelines for evangelicals living in oppressive situations.[41]

The chairman of the LCWE, Leighton Ford, took their concerns seriously enough to call a meeting between the LCWE and representatives of the 'concerned group' – namely, Orlando Costas, Vinay Samuel, and Ron Sider.[42] Tension no doubt filled the meeting. But as a result, claims Costas, the official final version of the Thailand Statement, drafted by Stott, "did address... some of the issues that we were raising."[43]

---

[38] C. Peter Wagner, 'Lausanne's Consultation on World Evangelization: A Personal Assessment', *TSF Bulletin* 4:1 (October 1980), 3.

[39] Wagner, 'Lausanne's Consultation', 3.

[40] Samuel and Sugden cited in Steuernagel, 'The Theology of Mission', 196-197.

[41] 'Statement of Concerns', in Rene Padilla and Chris Sugden (eds.), *Texts on Evangelical Social Ethics, 1974-1983* (Nottingham, UK: Grove Books, 1985), 24-25.

[42] Orlando Costas, 'Report on Thailand '80', *TSF Bulletin* 4:1 (October 1980), 5.

[43] Costas, 'Report on Thailand '80', 5.

Costas, however, describes the subsequent formal response of the LCWE to the Statement of Concerns as "cool and disappointing."[44] Its overall response consisted, first of all, of denying the charge that the LCWE undermined the comprehensive scope of the Covenant; second, that plans were already underway for a consultation on the relationship between evangelism and social responsibility; and third, that it was not the place of the LCWE to give guidelines for evangelicals in oppressed and discriminatory lands. The disappointment of the signers of the Statement of Concerns was palpable. Costas wrote, "[The response] made us wonder how committed indeed was the LCWE to the whole of the Lausanne Covenant."[45]

The tension between the narrow and broad views of evangelization came to a head at Pattaya, and the narrow view won the official battle. By the end of 1980, Steuernagel rightly observes that "the evangelical family was more divided than [ever]. While the SLC was interpreted as speaking too much the language of the 'radical evangelicals', COWE was being criticized not only because it had excluded 'social responsibility'... but also because it was embracing [too narrow] a definition and strategy of evangelization.[46]

Prioritization vs. holism

The narrowness or broadness of mission characterized the first tension; the relationship between social concern and evangelism in that mission described the second tension. These obviously interrelate, but whereas different answers to the question, 'Is social responsibility included at all in the task of world evangelization?' created the first tension, struggling with, 'If social responsibility, then where does it fit into the overall scheme of that task?' created the second tension. Few missiologists at that point would have disputed that social responsibility has some role to play (in light of Article 5 of the Covenant), but how important a role with reference to evangelism? While conservatives maintained the primacy of evangelism, radicals questioned the very language of prioritization.

If any hope existed to find some level of consensus on the social question, it hinged upon the 1982 Consultation on the Relationship between Evangelism and Social Responsibility in Grand Rapids, MI (CRESR). Steuernagel's description of the CRESR as "the most carefully planned, sensitive, feared, and threatening consultation ever held by the LCWE" underscores what was at stake – namely, unity or another tragic split of the worldwide evangelical family.[47] The CRESR gathered fifty evangelicals from around the world to

---

[44] Orlando Costas, 'Proclaiming Christ in the Two Thirds World', in Vinay Samuel and Chris Sugden (eds), *Sharing Jesus in the Two Thirds World* (Grand Rapids, MI: Eerdmans, 1984), 3.
[45] Costas, 'Proclaiming Christ', 3.
[46] Steuernagel, 'The Theology of Mission', 18.
[47] Steuernagel, 'The Theology of Mission', 199.

understand better the relationship between evangelism and social responsibility in biblical, historical, and missiological perspectives.

For a full week, the delegates presented papers and responded to each other with openness and respect as well as with honesty and intensity, in what turned out to be, according to the CRESR chairpersons Bong Rin Ro and Gottfried Osei-Mensah, "a model of how Christians should approach a... divisive issue".[48] The CRESR produced a seven-chapter, sixty-four-page document entitled 'The Grand Rapids Report on Evangelism and Social Responsibility: an Evangelical Commitment'.[49]

The strength of the report relied on the fact that it did not arrive at any one conclusion concerning the relationship; instead it offered a range of possibilities that it considered faithful to biblical and historic Christianity. According to the report, social action can be understood as: (1) a *consequence of* evangelism – one of the principle aims of a changed life is to serve others; (2) a *bridge to* evangelism – with no need of manipulation, good deeds naturally create opportunities to share the gospel; and (3) a *partner with* evangelism – the church must witness Christ in the world by both word and deed.[50] Due to this range of valid views, delegates for the most part reached an important level of consensus on the subject.

As important a level of consensus as the CRESR reached, however, it still operated under a false North American-nurtured dualism between body and soul and between social and spiritual, thus separating two vital realities from each other and then falsely asking which one has priority over the other.[51] Many evangelicals desired to do away completely with the falsity of this unbiblical dualism, to begin to train their thinking and therefore their doing in more non-dualistic, i.e. holistic, terms. For the most part, at least early on, those who adhered to these holistic notions remained somewhat marginalized from the mainstream of the Lausanne movement.

First world theology vs. two thirds world theology

The third notable tension between evangelicals in the decade after Lausanne had to do with power shifts in theology and mission. Lausanne opened the door for two thirds world evangelicals to take seriously their respective contexts for informing their view of God, worship, church, and mission. As evangelicals in these parts of the world began to assert themselves, tension emerged between western and non-western mission theologians.

---

[48] Bong Rin Ro and Gottfried Osei-Mensah, 'Preface', in Bruce J. Nicholls (ed.), *Word and Deed: Evangelism and Social Responsibility* (Grand Rapids, MI: Eerdmans, 1986), 7.

[49] 'The Grand Rapids Report', in John R.W. Stott (ed.), *Making Christ Known*, 167-210.

[50] 'The Grand Rapids Report', *Making Christ Known*, 181-182. Italics mine.

[51] Mark Lau Branson, 'Striving for Obedience, Haunted by Dualism', *TSF Bulletin* 6:1 (September/October 1982), 11.

Two thirds world evangelicals did not wait for the LCWE to 'see the light' of holism. In spite of the hesitancy of institutional evangelicalism, evangelicals who were profoundly touched by Lausanne's broader vision began to initiate local movements. Indeed some of the most significant fruit of the post-Lausanne period resulted not so much from activities emanating from LCWE headquarters but from "local, national or regional initiatives."[52]

Consistent with these local initiatives, a second movement began with a discussion among many of the same people who signed the Statement of Concerns at Pattaya. In their disappointment for the way COWE went, they "resolved to meet again as a two thirds world consultation."[53] Making good on their promise, the first consultation – framed and organized for the first time by theologians of evangelical conviction from the two thirds world – convened in 1982 at Bangkok to discuss Christology. This gathering led to the formation of the International Fellowship of Evangelical Mission Theologians in 1987 (INFEMIT).

A third movement among many of these same evangelicals began as they considered the implications of the gospel to the growing practice of development. A significant meeting occurred in September 1978 between five concerned evangelicals who proposed a long-term biblical and theological reflection process on development.[54] From that brainstorming and planning session, another meeting convened with theologians and practitioners in April 1979 where the participants determined the need for a consultation on a theology of development. Hence in March 1980, a consultation of that title, sponsored by WEF's Theological Commission, convened (just a week before and in the same location as the SLC). The Consultation on a Theology of Development (CTD) not only forged ahead with exploring the meaning of evangelical socio-political involvement, it also steered evangelical thinking in the decisive direction of holistic community development.

The CTD appointed a steering committee to continue reflecting upon the theme of development since the consultation only scratched the surface of this vital practice. This steering committee committed itself to a three year study process that culminated at the Consultation on the Church in Response to Human Need in 1983 held in Wheaton, Illinois, USA. More than culminating the particular study process on development, however, Wheaton '83 served as a significant marker for the theological maturation of holistic mission thinking among many evangelicals after Lausanne.

At this consultation, the word 'transformation' was adopted to convey the large vision of God's redemption, which includes socio-political structures and the human heart and everything in between. Samuel and Sugden offered the

---

[52] Steuernagel, 'The Theology of Mission', 170-171.

[53] Sugden, 'Wholistic Evangelism', 38.

[54] Ronald J. Sider, 'Introduction', in Ronald J. Sider (ed.), *Evangelicals and Development: Toward a Theology of Social Change* (Exeter, UK: Paternoster, 1981), 107. The 'five concerned evangelicals' were Wayne Bragg, Bruce Nicholls, John Robinson, Vinay Samuel and Ronald Sider.

following definition of transformation in 1999: "Transformation is to enable God's vision of society to be actualized in all relationships, social, economic and spiritual, so that God's will be reflected in human society and his love be experienced by all communities, especially the poor".[55]

Ever since the holistic missionary movement took on the name 'transformation,' its proponents have steadily advanced their agenda throughout the world, urging churches and mission agencies to refuse to understand evangelization without liberation, a change of heart without a change of social structures, vertical reconciliation (between God and people) without horizontal reconciliation (between people and people), and church planting without community building. Although the degree of integration between these dimensions of mission continues to vary, holistic mission has found its way in the mainstream consciousness and practice of evangelicals around the world.

---

[55] Vinay Samuel and Chris Sugden in Chris Sugden, 'Transformational Development: Current State of Understanding and Practice', *Transformation* 20.2 (April 2003), 71.

THE EMERGING CHURCH IN AFRICA AND HOLISTIC MISSION: CHALLENGES AND OPPORTUNITIES

Nicta Lubaale

Introduction

Holistic mission is given many understandings, from linking the gospel with social services to linking the gospel with social justice and to being a prophetic voice in various realities that require change. This chapter explores the nature of holistic mission in a group of churches in Africa I refer to as 'emerging church', but which are also called African Independent, African Instituted, and African indigenous churches. I will be looking at three categories of emerging church: the 'nationalist' churches and the Spiritual churches (which by and large emerged in the colonial period), and the newer Pentecostal churches. The Pentecostal churches I will be referring to are those which fall in the category of community-based churches and I will be using this term to refer to all the other churches because the given definition fits all of them. All these churches have their own distinct ways of doing mission but they have two common traits. They are engaged in community building in sectors of society that are largely excluded from the benefits of the formal economy, and they are in most cases led by people who are as vulnerable to poverty as their followers.

Initiatives in Holistic Mission by the Founding Generation of AICs

The emergence of the African Independent or African Instituted Churches (AICs) in the early twentieth century was a response to what the founders of these churches saw as the political, cultural, spiritual, and to a certain extent, economic challenges the colonial era. To understand the holistic mission of the AICs during this era, one has to look at the different values and actions of the various categories of AICs.

Key to the founding of these churches was the availability of the scriptures in local languages. This has enabled Africans to understand the place of the Holy Spirit in their lives both as individuals and as community. The consequent integration of the work of the Holy Spirit in the mission of the AICs has helped local communities to contextualize Christianity in the local realities and to bring security in the lives of those who have abandoned their traditional beliefs for a new faith.

In colonial Kenya, the working of the Holy Spirit in the emerging churches brought about the integration of a discourse of liberation in their mission in two distinct ways. The Nationalist churches like the African Independent Pentecostal Church of Africa (AIPCA) and the National Independent Church of Africa (NICA)[1] understood their mission during the colonial era as one of liberation from colonial domination in politics and culture, and getting back their land which had been taken by the foreign commercial farmers. The struggle for liberation became part of their liturgy and hymnology. They also went ahead to establish their own educational system – which reflected their emphasis on African cultural values. It is this understanding of mission that led the AIPCA to participate in the Mau Mau struggle for the independence of Kenya from 1952 onwards.

The Roho or Spiritual churches[2] on the other hand expressed their understanding of liberation principally through ministries of the Holy Spirit. They brought drums into the church. They introduced Christian prophets into the community of faith, reflecting the reality that the Spirit of God can speak to local communities in their own languages. Even women were empowered by the Spirit to prophesy, and their voice gained space in the worship and in the life of local communities. Peasants, plantation workers, and factory workers were empowered after being filled with the Holy Spirit to start creating new communities of Christians who developed a spirituality that engaged with the emerging reality of colonialism. The Roho churches distrusted the use of money in church, expressing in this way their desire to separate themselves from the overarching power of the emerging capitalist economy which was so different from the economy of reciprocity that they had known. They may not have had all it takes to understand the newly emerging economy based on market values, but they made a clear moral statement: you cannot use money to commodify life and then use it in church.

To the Roho churches, holistic mission also meant the integration of the Christian faith in the African worldview. It was the Holy Spirit's presence in the lives of the people and the community that enabled them to overcome the evil that had always kept them in fear. They started facing issues like witchcraft, the fear of spirits and other areas of African traditional belief systems which had not been adequately handled by the Mission Founded Churches (MFCs). These churches also participated in the political struggles, but in a way a little different from that of the nationalist churches. They acted through prayer, prophecy against the colonial domination, and the development of radically different liturgies to the liturgies of the MFCs. Two of the innovations of the Spirit churches were the re-definition of priesthood, making it accessible to the common people, and the transformation of the worship space into a place where the day-to-day struggles, hope uncertainties and

---

[1] These are the post-colonial names given to two denominations that emerged from the church that was known as the African Independent Pentecostal Church in the colonial period.

[2] *Roho Mtakatifu* is Swahili for 'Holy Spirit', often shortened to *Roho*, or 'Spirit'.

success of ordinary people are shared. On the political front the churches drew on the empowerment of the Holy Spirit to reject what they understood to be structures of economic and political domination. The refusal to use money in the church, the refusal to wear ties and suits by some churches and the use of their own flags (Padwick,) reflects the attempts by the Roho churches to develop a spirituality on which their mission to create moral communities – acting as counter communities to the colonial society – was based. Part of the mission of the church was to assert local citizenship – the power and right of ordinary people to act at the local level to control the spiritual and moral and hence the material development of their communities – rejecting in the process the model of development that was being imposed on them from the north, which had few moral foundations in African life.

The challenge Roho and Nationalist churches are faced with is that they challenged a number of practices in the local cultures but did not go far enough to understand the gospel of Jesus Christ in certain areas. The place of women in society is one of those areas. Their closeness to African culture is resourceful but has also been a barrier because these churches easily relate to the Old Testament when it comes to relations between men and women.

For the Roho churches – especially in the rural areas – their understanding of wholeness goes beyond individual wellbeing. So there is a constant search for what has gone wrong in the community whenever there are unwanted situations like sickness, deaths whose cause cannot be explained, drought and any other calamities. This search will always end up identifying spiritual causes which require repentance, forgiveness, correction of those who have gone wrong, casting out evil spirits and some other processes which can heal in individuals and communities. This understanding of wholeness and wellbeing however ignores the structural causes to the suffering of individuals and communities. The contradiction is that these churches had a clearer understanding of structural issues during the colonial era – and that is why they came up with initiative mentioned earlier in this chapter. They also retain an understanding of just systems in relation to the moral economy at the micro level, where all are expected to use part of their resources for the well being of the community, but all this is not linked to the process of building just systems at the national and international levels.

The Case of Community-Based Pentecostal Churches

The more recent emergence of newer forms of Pentecostalism on the continent brings another dimension into the mission of the church. Although this movement is attracting people who are demographically diverse – young and old, male and female, rich and poor (Boadi, 2005: 173)[3] – and in consequence

[3] Adelaide Maame Akwa Boadi, 'Engaging Partriachy: Pentecostal Gender Ideology and Practice in Nigeria' in Chima J. Korieh and Ugo G. Nwokeji (eds.), *Religion, History and Politics in Nigeria: Essays in Honour of Ogbu U. Kalu* (Lanham, MD: University

is producing a rich and ever-expanding variety of different models of church, the focus of this chapter will be on the Pentecostal churches that have been called community based (CDE, 2008:15).[4]

In many ways, these community-based Pentecostal churches are close to the Roho churches in their understanding and practice of mission. Mission is based on the empowerment that comes with the baptism of the Holy Spirit and the gifts that believers receive after this experience. Like the Roho churches, these Pentecostal churches depend on the gifts of the Holy Spirit for ministries such as healing and deliverance from demonic oppression. Many of the missioners in these churches have not had any formal theological education. The new Pentecostal churches are largely independent – in that they are not linked by denominational ties – but they have local, national, and regional networks. The Pentecostal churches have been clearer in the demands of the gospel of Jesus Christ on some areas where many of the older AICs did not pay adequate attention. The place of women and young people in the mission of the church is an area of great strength. They are also clearer in dealing with the cultural values and attitudes that prevent women from being in senior leadership in the church. So bringing the demands of Jesus Christ, the bible, together with the understanding of the place of the Holy Spirit, is bringing a new dimension of mission at the grassroots.

In contrast to the nationalist and Roho churches, however, the lack of a clear history of political and social struggles among the new Pentecostals limits their participation in the public space. It leaves them without an adequate tradition to engage with contemporary issues from the position of social justice. The resources which they use to empower themselves in the form of sermons on TV and FM radio stations, and books and magazines, focus rather on individual effort through faith, prayer and giving. All these are strengthened by sermons that stress the role of personal achievement. It is these resources which enable the missioners to participate in the contemporary environment with skill but at the same time uproots them from the concrete realities of their mission environment. Because their discourse is wanting in the area of social justice, in their engagement with these realities they can use only spiritual tools.

The other challenge for the Pentecostal churches is their understanding of prosperity and how it relates to coming out of poverty. Naturally prosperity is desired by many. Even in the African traditional religion people go to mediums to get guidance on how to prosper or thrive in their businesses, careers, marriages and other areas of life. However preaching of prosperity in the community-based Pentecostal churches becomes unbalanced when giving, tithing, faith and overcoming spiritual barriers like curses in the lives of individuals, families and communities, are understood as the only keys to prosperity. The failure to include socio-political causes of poverty in this understanding of well-being holds back the leadership and members of these

---

Press of America, 2005), 172-186.

[4] *Dormant Capital: Pentecostalism and its Potential and Social Economic Role* (Johannesburg: Centre for Development and Enterprise, 2008).

churches from engaging with the broader issues that keep masses of people in poverty.

Challenges Faced by Emerging Churches from Outside

The struggle to affirm their own methodology of doing mission

Below is an interaction between students from mainline churches, a lecturer from St. Paul's University, Limuru, and pastors from Roho and Pentecostal churches at Tafakari centre in the large informal settlement of Kibera, in which I participated.

> *Student*: You Pentecostals are always looking for money because of the way you propagate the prosperity gospel.
> *A Pentecostal pastor from Kibera*: If you want money, you go to the city centre and plant a church in a place where you can attract people who have money.
> *A pastor from a mainline church in Kibera*: We have also started singing in our worship services the choruses you sing.
> *A pastor from a small Pentecostal church in Kibera*: That is fine but for us these choruses are sung on a daily basis. They are part of us throughout the week. So make sure that you are not limiting them to the confines the church walls.
> *Student*: Our churches do ministry in these places [meaning the informal urban settlements] by reaching out with services and food donations.
> *Pastor from a Roho church*: You do ministry by reaching out. For us we live here and work with the people through their difficulties on a daily basis.
> *A lecturer*: You've said that Roho churches can raise their voices in public through raising the flag. You've said that it is at the foot of the flag that the evils that hurt the community are named and thrown out. What if they name people living with HIV as part of the evil?
> *Author's response*: It's at the foot of the flag that the church should name stigma, discrimination against people living with HIV, and the marginalization of women as issues that harm the community.

This brief discussion brings to the surface a number of issues in the way we understand mission. The participants from the mainline churches seem to come from a position of power, the pastors from the independent churches have to counteract the stereotypes developed by others, and finally the need for constructive engagement between different church traditions on mission for us all to benefit.

The lack of appropriate processes to mobilize and engage the emerging churches

The emerging church is lagging behind because of the lack of scholarship about the place of Spirit-led churches in the public space and the lack of appropriate resources for education. As a result, these churches either try to copy what the mainline churches are doing – hence failing because they do not have similar structures and opportunities of access to financial resources – or they copy what the evangelical churches do in North America – hence ending up with a strong voice that only emerges in seasons when there are moral issues in the public discourse.

In the case of Roho churches and the nationalist churches their invisibility in the public space is also partly due to:

- their failure to build on the resources in their histories of struggle during the colonial era and a subsequent shift from reading the scriptures in the context of both political and social realities to that of social realities only;
- their weak institutional frameworks especially at national levels;
- their historical and continuing exclusion from the public media;
- the trust that the Independent churches had in the pre-independence nationalist movements, and which was carried forward into the post-colonial governments, has consequently blunted their ability to speak prophetically into the contemporary issues that face Africa.

Engaging with the values of the global development industry

A faith-based response to any issue should be the action that comes out of the interaction of people's faith with their realities. It is people's faith that gives them the ideological framework for understanding and explaining their realities. Kurt Alan Ver Beek who defines spirituality "as a relationship with the supernatural or spiritual which provides meaning and a basis for personal and communal reflection" affirms this fact.[5] The international development discourse, however, does not fully recognize faith and spirituality as a basic and fundamental resource in development. Indeed, the development industry is often driven and managed in a way that makes Africa a participant in the jargon and themes that are continuously generated elsewhere – as a result of the analysis of situations but also as a way of establishing control. The values behind this discourse are suspicious of faith and look at it as a barrier to achieving development objectives. The end result has been their appreciation of the physical infrastructure and the human resources of the church only, and not their belief systems. As a result churches tend to apportion their mission resources to provide a framework for the non-faith-based development agencies to work with, and they hold back from using their faith resources and in consequence deny themselves the opportunity of developing and building on their belief systems. The tragedy is that many Christian agencies in Europe and the rest of the north had also been caught up in the secularization going on in their midst and had started designing programs for the developing countries in a way that focused only on the structures of the churches, leaving out the real

---

[5] Kurt Allan Beek, 'Spirituality: a development taboo', *Development in Practice* 10:1 (2000), 31-43 http://www.informaworld.com/smpp/content~db=all?content=10.1080/09614520052484.

resources of faith. It is only recently that many of these agencies are beginning to recognize the value of faith in the lives of people in developing countries. Initiatives by Christian Aid and ICCO are an example.

Limiting the search and understanding of justice and human dignity to the context of small communities

In most parts of Africa people have learnt to build social support systems on which they rely to face the difficulties of poverty and exclusion from the formal economy and their lack of access to basic social services. These support systems are in form of women's groups, farmers' groups, youth groups, and various church ministry groups, and operate on the values of reciprocity and a moral economy. The mission of the congregations of community-based churches is built on similar values. These communities of support have with time become an alternative (Mwaura, 2009) to a contracted state that is not well established in the lives of the people because of its failure to provide basic social services to many. In these circumstances the Christian faith and mission of the churches is to bring harmony and to continuously rebuild lives that are broken by their exclusion from the formal economy and their lack of access to basic social services. The songs, the testimonies, the prophecies, the sermons in the churches and the day to day conversations of their members reflect this reality. People can share their problems in relation to poverty but they rarely refer to themselves as the poor when they are on their own. Rather, they are apostles, prophets, pastors and evangelists. In the fellowships and other groups where the people at the margins meet, all the issues that affect them are shared. The fellowship or church service becomes a space of collective lamentation or collective celebration. This is the space where those who are battered by poverty and other forms of hardship look for support. It is a space where those who live in indignity find dignity. It is a space where those who do not have a voice in the public space – which is controlled by politicians and the visible civil society organizations – find space for their voice. Here people share their hardships, dreams, visions, songs, success and information on any economic opportunities. Unfortunately this also results in ordinary citizens withdrawing from laying a claim on the public and governmental structures and institutions that are responsible for providing essential social services and the defense of their rights, and instead they seek mutual support and comfort in spiritual fellowship, in 'a place to feel at home' in the midst of a harsh world.

What it Will Take for the Emerging Church to Play a Greater Role in the Public Arena?

Transform claims making

The prophetic voice of the community-based churches should be linked to claims making. Spector and Kitsuse[6] define 'claims making' as a form of interaction, a demand made by one party to another that something be done about some putative condition. A claim implies that a claimant has a right at least to be heard. In the context of the emerging churches, claims making is made on a daily basis, only that the claims made are directed to God in prayer – on the basis of the scriptures where promises have been made for a good and prosperous life, to members of the congregation where there is a right to be cared, and to community groups. In these churches claims are rarely directed to the political and economic structures of this world. This could mean that claims making in this context is directed to where people actually expect they can get some measure of justice. People at this level participate in shaping the structures-fellowships, ministry groups etc. – in a way that makes them responsive to their needs. So there is a heavy engagement in building just communities in the mission of the community based churches. What the missioners need to do is to study the scriptures in a fresh way and understand that God stands with the weak and has made a claim on the larger political and socio-economic structures that are responsible for keeping people in indignity. The day this will be internalized in the understanding of God who demands for righteousness as well as justice will be the time to see a fresh wave of revival deeply rooted in the voice of the Spirit for a just world.

Recovery of the prophetic voice for the older AICs

For some of the Spirit churches like the Roho churches in Kenya, one way ahead is through the recovery and updating of the vision of the founders. The founders spoke truth to the colonial structures and developed liturgical and hymnal resources that supported their mission. There are enormous resources in the theology of these AICs. What is required here is the updating of these visions to make them relevant to the contemporary environment where Africa has to deal with poor governance at the local, national, and international levels

Illuminating reality and transforming existing theologies

What affects the churches at the margins is a partial understanding of reality. For the OAIC the development of appropriate mobilization and training processes has been critical in mobilizing the member churches to expand their

[6] Malcolm Spector and John I. Kitsuse, *Constructing Social Problems* (New Brunswick, NJ: Transaction Publishers, 1987).

understanding of mission to include critical issues like HIV and AIDS in their mission.

"Now I know the reason why cotton farming has disappeared." This is a statement by Eliazaro Onyando – a peasant farmer who is also a bishop from an African Independent Church in rural Kenya in conversation with the author. He made this remark after a two-day interdenominational workshop on the on-going Economic Partnerships Agreements (EPAs) between the European Union and African states. Cotton farming which was one of the major economic activities in his community collapsed over 25 years ago. It was in that workshop that the impact of agricultural subsidies in developed countries was explained in very simple terms. Bishop Onyando had lived with and felt the reality of loss of income due to the collapse of the cotton industry, yet he didn't understand the cause. Onyando has since then developed an interest in trade policies.

Another clear example where churches in Africa faced a challenge in their response is the HIV and AIDS pandemic. Since the mode of transmission is mainly through sex, initially most churches held the view that AIDS was a result of sin – hence looking at it as a judgment from God. The churches' reading of scriptures in this context was selective and geared towards affirming the negative understanding of the reality of HIV and AIDS in the community. As a result the churches – especially those at the margins of society which act as safety nets for the poor – held back their resourcefulness from supporting the people living with HIV. To respond to this challenge the OAIC transformed its mobilization program from simply giving scientific facts about HIV to the analysis of the theological, cultural, political and economic issues. This process helped the church leaders to root their reading of the bible in the social realities of the communities they serve. One of the major revelations was the vulnerability of women because of the power relations at family level, in the church, and in the wider society. As a result women and young people started making a claim on the governance structures of the churches and the church leaders started listening to the voices of women and young people who wanted them to allocate more of their resources to HIV and AIDS programs. The OAIC terms these processes as laboratories for developing the capacity for civic engagement among the churches and community groups.

This process requires opening up the scriptures, reflecting on the language used in church and outside church and enabling people to acquire the knowledge and skills they need to participate effectively in the public space to address injustices that are keeping people in indignity. Corwin Smidt says that where as citizens do not need become policy experts to fulfill their civic responsibilities, lacking knowledge on the specific issues they want to address impairs their participation. [7]

---

[7] Corwin E. Smidt et al, *Pews, Prayers: Participation and Civic Responsibility in America* (Washington, DC: George Town University Press, 2008).

Expand the understanding of the role of the Holy Spirit in society

Healing, seeing into the future, identifying and overcoming what harms the community (especially evil spirits) – these practices clearly manifest belief in a God who heals and builds the community, a God who is known to be present in their midst. Wilhelmina Kalu[8] refers to this role as the calling of a Christian "to discern the spirits that are at work in communities, families and individual lives and confront them with the power of the spirit, the water of the word and the blood of Jesus." It is this calling that should be expanded to include discernment in the area of social justice, to the causes of social inequalities, unjust international policies, and the plunder of national resources by the political and business elite from both Africa and beyond. It is this that will liberate the mission of the Spirit-led churches.

For such transformation to take place, the Spirit-led churches have to overcome the fear of losing the Spirit. In an Urban Missions conference held in Nairobi in 2009, one Pentecostal pastor from an informal settlement asked his colleague – who was involved in multiple community projects – how he gets involved in studying for a degree in a theological college, leads a church, initiates and gives oversight to an expanding income generating project without losing the Holy Spirit. Such an understanding of the work of the Holy Spirit is limiting and calls for engagement through theological reflection. It is time for the Spirit-led churches to re-read the Apostle Paul in I Thessalonians 5:19, "do not quench the Spirit." This scripture is used in relation to allowing the Holy Spirit to speak, rebuke, correct, guide, and exhort the church. But the Spirit's voice must also not be quenched from speaking into the social, political and economic issues that affect Africa.

This Spirit of God must also be allowed to speak to issues that have not been handled at family and local community levels. It is at this level of society that the impact of poverty is reflected in the gender and generational inequalities. The empowerment and liberation of the Spirit has to be felt and experienced by the women of Africa who are the majority in the church

Conclusion

In social contexts where many people are living in deprivation, holistic mission is not an option. There is no line between what is termed as the gospel – the proclaimed word – and the social gospel. Such demarcations are created by Christians writing or speaking from a middle or upper class context. Missioners in contexts of deprivation and exclusion from the benefits of the formal economy and basic social services develop mission approaches that are born out of their faith's interaction with the realities the communities they are part of. They may not understand fully each and every issue, but they have the

[8] Wilhemina Kalu, 'Soul Care in Nigeria: Constructing Pentecostal Models in Pastoral and Counseling', in Chima J. Korieh and Ugo G. Nwokeji (eds.), *Religion, History and Politics in Nigeria: Essays in Honour of Ogbu U. Kalu.*

ability to learn from and engage with their belief systems and to transform their methods of doing mission. This process leads to a continuous review of the beliefs, and a consequent expansion of the frameworks of action which in turn transforms mission. This doesn't mean that the missioners at the margins of society are adequate in themselves. The fact that they are immersed in the realities of the excluded and to a great extent are themselves the excluded, means that they need accompaniment for them to be able reflect objectively on their calling and the actions that come out of it.

THE WORK OF GOD AS HOLISTIC MISSION: AN ASIAN PERSPECTIVE

Samuel Jayakumar

Introduction

The purpose of this chapter is to describe the work of God as holistic mission as carried out by the church in Asia. During the last 100 years, the church in Asian countries has grown in quality as well as in quantity. Asian churches have contributed a great deal to developing indigenous leaders, articulating wholesome theologies, establishing various types of missions and ministries, as well as training institutions.

The impact of the modern missionary movement was so pervasive that it continued through the first half of the twentieth century. Some of the eminent leaders, such as V.S. Azariah and others, played an important role in shaping the mission of the church. The next half of the century witnessed a tremendous growth of cross-cultural missions, congregations, organizations for relief and rehabilitation, as well as seminaries. Christians in Asia got involved in various new forms of ministries as the situations demanded. In a number of ways churches contributed to nation building, correcting injustice and social oppressions.

To illustrate holistic mission since Edinburgh 1910, as understood and practised by the Asian church, I have drawn lessons, first, from the Dornakal mission (a single great movement of this era among the Dalits headed by V.S. Azariah) and secondly, I refer to two remarkable evangelical movements of this century, namely Friends Missionary Prayer Band (FMPB) and Evangelical Church of India (ECI), being singularly influenced by the teaching of D. A. McGavran, who was a missionary in India for about thirty years. Finally I describe the Pentecostals' contributions to holism.

Holistic Mission – A Christian Heritage that Overflows

The gospel of Christ has always been *holistic* and never been un-holistic. The four gospels present a holistic transformation of individuals, families and communities. The command of Jesus was to *preach the gospel, heal the sick and drive out the demons (social evils).* The early apostles and their followers were committed to holistic transformation in the contexts they served. The early church was sympathetic towards the slaves and prisoners and often worked for their deliverance by paying their ransom. The early Christians took care of the poor, the destitute, orphans and widows. During medieval times the monks offered a dedicated service to common people, especially to poor peasants and victims of barbarians.

As Ralph Winter has pointed out, the European and American evangelical awakenings of the seventeenth and eighteenth centuries were characterized by a broad dual social / personal, earthly / heavenly spectrum of concern, ranging from foreign missions to changing the legal structure of society and even war. This period was significantly characterized by evangelicals in a position of civil leadership. For the most part the nineteenth century missionaries were committed to combining evangelism and social concern. They worked within the window of awareness that made the transformation of society feasible – something which was within their grasp. They could readily believe not only in a profound transformation of individuals, but also in a wide range of different aspects of social transformation and God-glorification.[1]

However, on the one hand, since the turn of the twentieth century there has been a growing undue polarization over the meaning of Christian mission. Since the Edinburgh Missionary Conference, the traditional models of missions have come under severe criticism, especially, throughout the latter half of the century. Also from Edinburgh came two major streams of the modern missionary movement: the first was evangelical and the second ecumenical. After Edinburgh, theological changes quickly swept the whole world, weakening evangelistic fervour, especially among the youth. Furthermore the two world wars caused further hindrance and discouragement to the world-wide church.

On the other hand, there was a brighter side, with challenges for gospel engagement. Asians, including national leaders like M.K. Gandhi, were ready to accept all the Christian humanitarian services in the field of education and healthcare as well as Jesus' teachings and ethics but not willing to confess that Jesus Christ is Lord. However, the 'good works' carried out by missionaries and Christians have always been understood to be an expression of their love and obedience to the Lord Jesus Christ. The underlying motivation, of course, was their obligation to proclaim the salvation of God through faith in Jesus Christ. Asians have by and large been willing to receive the former, but many have rejected the need for the latter – as the upper castes in particular would say, "We have our own saviours."[2]

---

[1] Ralph Winter, 'The Future of Evangelicals in Mission', *Mission Frontiers* (September-October, 2007), 5-7.

[2] Graham Houghton, 'The Foundation Laid by Christian Missionaries', in Bishop M. Ezra Sargunam (ed.), *Christian Contribution to Nation Building* (Chennai: Mission Educational Books, 2006), 2. M.K. Gandhi equated this name with the Hindu god Rama and the prophet Muhammad by saying that, "Iswar Allah dere nam, sabku sannadhe de bahavan", that is, "there is only one God whom Hindus call Rama, the Muslims call Allah and the Christians call Jesus." Gandhi and many other great Indians such as Radha

As Graham Houghton maintains, the Christian community has felt that it has contributed to the building of the nation. This because any encounter with Jesus, for those who have decided to follow him have precipitated a personal and social transformation. The outcomes have been an effective cause of upward social mobility which has changed lives, benefited families, neighbourhoods, villages and entire ethnic / caste communities. It needs to be added that this is particularly the case among the poor and the disenfranchised, namely those who today are classified as backward classes and *dalits* i.e. the oppressed.[3]

Although Gandhi was a convert to modernity in terms of the education that he acquired and his exposure to western ideas, he did not cultivate cultural openness, whereas his contemporary V.S. Azariah more positively recognized Christian faith not as a cultural contradiction but as a fulfilling of the imperfect native culture. He was of the opinion that the Christian gospel was a refinement of the culture of natives to enable them to live a civilized life, free from the negative and oppressive aspects of their culture such as ignorance, illiteracy, spirit worship, immorality and other traditional practices.[4]

The gospel of Christ confronts the culture of poverty to bring about transformation. India is known the world over for its ancient culture and belief systems as well as for its poverty. All these elements are quite inter-related with each other. So much so that poverty is very much linked with culture and religion. Traditionally, Indian belief systems have always determined Indians' lifestyle. For the majority of Indians, life has been one of negation rather than affirmation. Rightly or wrongly, Indian sages chose to renounce the world and run away from all the goodness of life rather than face the challenges of it. These ascetics lived off alms, in abject poverty and want. Although modernity and western culture have affected our Indian belief systems and cultures, poverty is still regarded as the outward sign of 'spirituality' for the *swamijis* and *mahatmas.* While these *swamijis* and *mahatmas* adopt this type of austere and simple life, theirs and the message of the priestly class to the masses, the poor and the oppressed is a little different. They say that they are poor, untouchable and handicapped because of their *karma* – retribution of the sins they have carried with them into this birth. The belief in '*karma janmanthra*' destroys the spirit of enterprise and the inner urge for development and growth. Any belief system that doesn't liberate the people from the shackles of poverty and misery, but rather compels them to accept the sufferings as their fate, needs to be jettisoned.[5]

Krishnan were reluctant to acknowledge the uniqueness of this name, whereas they were ready to attribute the title 'Lord' to religious leaders such as Ramakrishna Paramahamsa and Vivekananda. But they would not call Jesus 'Lord'.

[3] Graham Houghton, *The Foundation Laid by Christian Missionaries*, 2.

[4] V.S. Azariah, 'The Bishop's Letter', *Dornakal Diocesan Magazine,* 1934, 4. S. Harper, *Azariah and Indian Christianity during the Late Years of Raj* (D.Phil Thesis, University of Oxford, 1991), 249f.

[5] M. Ezra Sargunam, 'Culture as an Element of Development' (unpublished paper,

Even so, at the turn of the twentieth century, Christian mission in Asian countries such as India among the poor and outcaste communities was the envisioning of a new society. This was humanly speaking very odd for the Indian church. In reality Indian Christians were hoping against hope, because the church still had to work in a society that was deeply religious, deeply caste-ridden, the lower castes of which were terribly oppressed. The Christian task was still a battle against sati (burning of widows), untouchability, child marriage, temple prostitution, infanticide, slavery, illiteracy, oppression of women, children, etc. Nevertheless, a new society was taking shape before their very eyes as the church worked towards it.

From the inception of the modern missionary movement, Christian mission and social transformation of the poor and oppressed are always inseparable. The Asian Christian leaders believed that the gospel of Christ was not only the power of God for salvation but also the power of God for socio-economic and political liberation.[6] They saw conversion to Christ as much related to "the prospect (or envisioning) of India's regeneration."[7] Against this backdrop let us examine the kind of mission carried out by Asian national leaders such as V.S. Azariah and his successors

The Dornakal Mission: A Case Study on Holistic Mission Practised Among the Dalits

V.S. Azariah was a champion of ecumenism among the younger churches of south India. Along with a few other Indian Christians, he founded the first indigenous missionary society, the Indian Missionary Society (IMS) of Tirunelveli, in 1903, and the National Missionary Society (NMS) in 1905. Azariah had great zeal for missionary activities combining evangelism and social concerns.

He was modern India's most successful leader of the Dalits and of non-Brahmin conversion movements to the gospel of Christ during the early twentieth century. His evangelistic work among the Telugus resulted in enormous growth of Christian congregations. He was consecrated Bishop of Dornakal in 1912, the first Indian to become a Bishop of the Anglican Church of India. He contended that churches had to become missionary churches.

By the year 1928 his diocese contained 158,000 Christians. All the pastoral work was organized under a system of pastorates which were grouped into district church councils. While the Indian clergymen were directly responsible to the Bishop, the Indian lay workers were responsible to their own clergy. Accordingly, each of the out-caste villages had its own corporate church life with independent activities – village schools, morning and evening prayer in each village, bible study and classes for catechumens.

October 13-14, 1999).

[6] V.S. Azariah, *Dornakal Diocesan Magazine* 13:4 (April, 1936), 3-4.

[7] R.D. Paul, *Chosen Vessels* (Madras: CLS, 1961), 145ff.

The work in Dornakal had general and liberal support from foreign money. Azariah and his associates, year after year, wrote numerous letters and traveled to many countries to promote the work among the oppressed classes. He evolved an elaborate network through which parishes in England were linked to Christian villages in Dornakal. Azariah insisted that older churches around the world whom God had blessed with wealth must give, and must give with abandon and cheerfully for the work of God among the poor and the oppressed communities.

From the beginning, Azariah had the conviction that the gospel of Jesus Christ was meant for the poor and the oppressed, and when it was preached to them it evoked their response. As he loved the rural poor and rural congregations, he understood their problems and needs so that he could serve them effectively in many ways.

> The church in India, therefore, is essentially a village church. Its problems are village problems, its education needs to be adapted to the conditions of village life and its leaders must be men and women able and willing to live and work among village folk. And it is the church of the poor. This has often been cast back in its teeth as a reproach.[8]

The Dalits were struggling hard with Christian discipline and character formation. As the first generation of converts were from illiterate and poverty stricken groups, their understanding and knowledge was very limited. They often had to endure persecution from the Brahmins and caste Hindus, and spiritual and moral achievement was imperfect. However, Christian teachings had been accepted as a challenge by the Dalits so that they were continually helped with their all-round advancement.

Azariah, like his missionary predecessors, regarded the gospel of Christ as a social religion and Christian conversion as an instrument of social change. He showed a harmony between evangelism and social action. He understood the church as not only an agent of evangelism but also the bearer of civilization. He wrote, "where Christianity goes, education, civilization, and habits of cleanliness in body, dress, and food, in speech and conduct, are the concomitant results."[9]

Azariah and his co-workers accepted social change as "the very essence of the gospel of Christ and therefore an integral part of the Christian message." They asserted that "its sure sanction was Jesus Christ himself."[10]

Azariah maintained that rural uplift and awakening of outcaste villagers was effected through Christian education. He wrote,

---

[8] V.S. Azariah and H. Whitehead, *Christ in the Indian Villages* (London, SCM, 1930), 18.

[9] V.S. Azariah, 'The Church in Rural India', *Dornakal Diocesan Magazine* 5:10 (October 1928), 3-4.

[10] V.S. Azariah, 'Rural Reconstruction', *Dornakal Diocesan Magazine* 7:8 (August, 1930), 16.

> Through Christianity too illiteracy is being chased out of rural India. It was well known that the first thing done for a village which desires to join the Christian church is to send a resident teacher there to instruct the village in the Christian Faith and open a school for their children. The teacher and his wife – if he has one – are truly the introducers of Light and Learning.[11]

He often asserted that. "to teach, teach, teach" is one of the needs of the hour.[12] According to Azariah, the education of a single girl means the uplifting of the whole family. He rightly understood that in India among the poor and the oppressed the success of the male education depended on women's education. Azariah encouraged the education of girls and women. He made elaborate arrangements to promote adult literacy and education among illiterate women.[13]

The purpose of education among the outcaste Christians of Dornakal was to empower as well as enlighten the Dalit converts so that they might be restored to personal awareness. Moreover, he wanted the education given to them to prepare them for life, believing that thus trained, Christians would become centres of light wherever they were. Hence he maintained,

> Any education given to such people must, we believe, include education to prepare them for life. Our aim then is to produce through this school a new generation of men – men who will not be ashamed of manual labour, men who will be willing to go back to the village with knowledge of some handicraft, and settle down there to earn an honest livelihood and to become centres of light, in their turn, creating a sturdy, self-respecting rural Christian manhood.[14]

Christian education greatly awakened the Dalits' consciousness of the injustice and deceit caused by the caste Hindus. Azariah's co-workers reported that the young adults who learnt to read and write, generally at night schools, in due course began to question their Hindu masters about their 'debts' and became aware in many cases of how they had been deceived.[15] Azariah observed that Dalit Christians "on account of integrity, command higher field wages; that Christian labourers are in demand for transplantation and harvesting because they do not require close supervision."[16]

Azariah understood education as something that belongs to the Judeo-Christian tradition. Furthermore, Azariah's concept of education was very much value based. It was offered as an instrument to correct, to direct, to change and to transform the lives of the Dalits. Education offered by the mission was useful to them in their day-to-day living. It prepared them to take up jobs and earn their livelihood. It provided them with strong self-awareness

---

[11] V.S. Azariah, 'Church in Rural India', *Dornakal Diocesan Magazine* 5:10 (October 1928), 4.

[12] V.S. Azariah, 'A Charge Delivered to the Clergy of the Diocese of Dornakal' (November, 14, 1923), 9-10.

[13] V.S. Azariah, 'The Bishop's Letter', *Dornakal Diocesan Magazine* 6:1 (January,1932), 12f.

[14] V.S. Azariah, *SPG-DL,* India II, (February 27, 1930), 2.

[15] A.F.R. Bird, *Telugu Mission,* SPG – R, 1922, 7.

[16] V.S. Azariah, *The Church in Rural Inida*, 5.

which in turn established their sense of individuality. It assisted them to be careful with their wages and to maintain their health and hygiene.[17]

The first generation Dalit Christians of south India confessed that, "Christianity has brought us fellowship and brotherhood. It has treated us with respect, and it has given us self-respect. It has never despised us because of our lowly origin, but on the contrary has held us as individuals who are valuable before God and man as any man of any origin."[18]

The need then of Dalits was not a false hope or even a positive feeling, but faith and confidence in a tangible personal God, the Saviour who removes guilt, both real and false, such as *karma.* Proclamation of the gospel provided the poor and the oppressed with a general confidence that life is meaningful and that it was possible to change one's quality of life by one's efforts. Bishop Picket came up with a similar conclusion after undertaking a thorough study of Dalit conversion movements:

> The depressed classes in India are desperately poor. But their chief economic need is not financial; it is an antidote to the poisonous ideas that have made them incapable of struggling successfully with their environment. As severe as is the physical oppression to which they are continuously subjected, the depressed classes could not have been reduced by its operation alone to the low state in which they have lived for centuries. Much more devastating than physical oppression has been the psychological oppression inflicted by the Hindu doctrines of karma and rebirth, which have taught them that they are a degraded, worthless people suffering just retribution for sins committed in earlier lives. It is, then, a true instinct that makes the depressed classes respond more eagerly to the preaching of the Christian gospel than to any direct ministry to their social and economic ills. The concepts that the Christian gospel gives them of themselves and of God in relation to their sufferings and sins are worth incomparably more to them than any direct social or economic service the church could offer.[19]

The experiences of Indian leaders, who are involved in community development among the poor, concur with this view. V. Mangalwadi wrote that,

> Perhaps the most devastating effect of the centuries of poverty and oppression is total loss of self- respect, self-confidence, trust in others and hope for any change. … Poverty is not their main problem. The lack of hope (for a better future), lack of faith (in man, government or God) and lack of initiative (born out of dehumanizing oppression and loss of self-confidence) are paralyzing mental / cultural factors which prevent them from any action towards freedom and development.[20]

---

[17] V.S. Azariah, 'Bishop's Letter' *Dornakal Diocesan Magazine* 7:6 (June, 1930), 2-3.

[18] V.S. Azariah, 'Open Letter to Our Country Men…', *Indian Witness* (September 17, 1936), 598.

[19] J.W. Picket, *Christ's Way to India's Heart* (Lucknow: Lucknow Publising, 1938), 173.

[20] V. Mangalwadi, 'A Theology of Power in the Context of Social Development', *TRACI Journal*, April, 1981, 15.

Evangelical Legacy of Holistic Mission Continues Through Evangelism and Church Growth Movements

The foreign mission in the Indian sub-continent (including the countries such as Pakistan, Bangladesh, Sri Lanka, Burma, Nepal, etc) began to end following the exit of the British in 1947. By the early 1960s all missionaries who required visas had been withdrawn. However, the native Christians for the most part continued the legacy of the missionaries combining evangelism and social concern – churches continued with medical, educational and other philanthropic enterprises. But the primary motivation for mission in India was the spread of the gospel and the growth of churches.

For evangelicals in the 1950s and '60s, although Christian mission was the mission of saving the souls, it never lost sight of human misery. Missions and ministries that were started with soul winning and church planting could not ignore social concerns such as community development – involving themselves in health care, poverty alleviation programmes, providing drinking water, opening up schools and orphanages, and other rehabilitation activities. For example, the Evangelical Church of India (ECI), Friends Missionary Prayer Band (FMPB), Indian Evangelical Mission (IEM), Indian Missionary Society (IMS), National Missionary Society (NMS) as well as many other missions and ministries, while they speak of evangelism as their priority, in practice they have been holistic – in mission that combines evangelism and social concern.

Here we may refer to two outstanding missionary statesmen of the twentieth century, J.R. Mott and D.A. McGavran who made great impact on the minds of the Asian Christian lay leaders, especially in India. Mott's ideas of mission originally come from the Enlightenment,[21] being influenced by the popular evangelist D.L. Moody, whereas McGavran's ideas emerged from his three decades of missionary work in India. Both persons insisted on implementing the Great Commission. Mott wrote about implementing the Commission in this generation and created a sense of urgency among evangelical Christians. He maintained that,

> If the gospel is to be preached to all… it obviously must be done while they are living. The evangelization of the world in this generation, therefore, means the preaching of the gospel to those who are now living. To us who are responsible for preaching the gospel it means in our lifetime; to those to whom it is to be preached it means in their lifetime. The unevangelized for whom we as Christians are responsible live in this generation; and the Christians whose duty it is to

---

[21] Being affected by the liberalism of Enlightenment and the Victorian discourse of social development, the missionaries were anxious to see a visible Christian social order. In Britain evangelical belief was that the regenerative power of the Gospel would drive a society along basically the same path of socio-economic and political progress. This is perhaps one of the reasons why Mott wanted to see the evangelization of the world in this generation. For details see Brian Stanley, *The Bible and the Flag: Protestant Missions and British Imperialism in the 19th and 20th Centuries* (Leicester: Apollos, 1990), 173. David Hempton, 'Evangelicalism and Reform', in J. Wolffe (ed.), *Evangelical Faith and Public Zeal* (London: SPCK, 1995), 17ff.

present Christ to them live in this generation. The phrase 'in this generation', therefore, strictly speaking has a different meaning for each person. In the last analysis, if the world is to be evangelized in this or any generation it will be because a sufficient number of individual Christians recognize and assume their personal obligation to the undertaking.[22]

After about approximately 50 years, in the 1960s and '70s, Mott's slogan, the 'evangelization of the world in this generation' came alive in some circles in south India. The slogan created urgency, especially among the Tamil Christians, and paved the way to a further thinking of what will happen to the people who are unevangelized. Indian lay Christian leaders and evangelists began categorically to preach that the unevangelized are lost. Indian missions such as the Friends Missionary Prayer Band were founded on this premise.[23] The lay leaders were very successful in recruiting hundreds of young men and women as well as forming prayer groups for prayerful support for cross-cultural missions in the northern parts of India. Indeed mission was understood in terms of *rescuing* people who would be otherwise lost.

The same idea of the "loss of the unevangelized" was introduced among the seminary students. For instance, Hindustan Bible Institute (HBI), founded in the city of Madras (now Chennai) by an upper caste Hindu convert by name Paul Gupta, instilled this doctrine into the minds of young boys and girls and prepared them for cross-cultural missions. During the 1960s and '70s almost all the graduates of HBI went to northern parts of India as missionaries.[24] Like HBI, many bible schools were founded especially in the city of Madras, professing to train young people for cross-cultural missions in north India. These seminaries were meant for only equipping the people of God to fulfil the Great Commission. They did not train 'parish priests' because that was not their goal.[25] They were committed only to training 'harvesters' for harvesting. Consequently, these schools did not see theological education in India as primarily for the ministry of the church. For them the urgency of the evangelistic task should determine the nature and purpose of seminary training and not the ministerial needs of the church.[26]

---

[22] John R. Mott, *The Evangelization of the World in This Generation* (New York: SVM, 1900), 3, 6-7, 15-16, 105, 109, 115, 116-117.

[23] The FMPB is indigenous both in its finance and personnel. Membership is restricted to Christian Indians. FMPB is a sodality body, serving as an arm of the church to plant churches across the country. Therefore FMPB is not a church, it is a non-denominational, a trans-denominational and a non-sectarian society. The mission works with the goal of doing saturation evangelism among 300 people groups. The organization wants to place 2,500 cross-cultural missionaries among these many people groups during the next few years.

[24] Files maintained by the Student Missionary Secretaries provide this information.

[25] The tradition of bible school movement is related to the modern missionary movement. Bible schools are primarily meant for preparing non-ordained missionaries and to train lay-people for witness. See B. Ott, 'Mission Oriented Theological Education', *Transformation* 18:2 (April, 2001), 75f.

[26] This is still one of the weakness of this type of seminaries. For details see Gnana Robinson's criticisms after a many years of existence of such seminaries in the city of

The revival that was going on in Tamil Nadu was further fueled by the ideas of McGavran who spent much of his life trying to overcome social barriers to Christian conversion. [27] He promoted aggressive evangelism among the responsive people groups. Asian evangelicals were challenged by his slogan "win the winnable while they are winnable." He often critiqued the World Council of Churches for their omission of a clear statement on the priority of the Great Commission as the heart of their theology of missions. During the late 1960s and early 1970s in a response to Uppsala's draft document on mission McGavran wrote, "Do not betray the two billion." He insisted on the importance of the evangelization of non-Christians, baptizing them and making them disciples.

> This is a time to emphasize discipling, not to turn from it. This is not a time to betray the two billion but to reconcile as many as possible of them to God in the church of Jesus Christ. For the peace of the world, for justice between (peoples) and nations, for advance in learning, for breaking down hostilities between peoples, for the spiritual health of countless individuals and the corporate welfare of (humankind) *this is a time to disciple nations, baptizing them in the name of the Father, Son and Holy Spirit and teaching them whatsoever our Lord has commanded us.*[28]

It is note-worthy that the ideas of Mott and McGavran spread in India in the early 1960s and '70s when secular theologies were popular in the west. The whole idea of that period was that the world will be secular. At the same time in south India there was much revival among lay Christian leaders. [29] Consequently they reacted very strongly to the secular and liberal theologies, but appropriated any teaching that was conservative and orthodox.

McGavran's thinking greatly influenced the evangelical churches especially. Many evangelical missions and ministries adopted the church planting approach to mission and still cherish this singular aim. Their mission is nothing but pioneer evangelism and planting churches. This is the way most of the missionaries understand and practice mission. Consequently, they continue to carry on their work of preaching the gospel and conversion of people to Christ. Some of these missions are very successful and have led thousands of people to Christ and formed hundreds of new congregations. For instance, the

---

Madras. Gnana Robinson, 'Theological Education in India Today', *NCC Review* 115:4 (April, 1995), 292-293.

[27] In the recent decades Christians in some parts of India in particular, and in south Asian countries such as Singapore, Indonesia and Nepal in general have been experiencing a new vitality, life and vision. S.P. Athiyal, 'Southern Asia', in J.M. Philips, and R.T. Coote (eds.), *Toward the 21st Century in Christian Mission* (Grand Rapids: Eerdmans, 1993), 61-62. But liberal circles in India, especially among theologians such as M.M. Thomas, were equating humanization with evangelism. After Bangkok, the WCC emphasis strengthened the secular liberation movements in line with emerging Latin American Liberation theologies.

[28] A. Glasser and D.A. McGavran, *The Conciliar Evangelical Debate* (Waco: Word Books, 1972), 233-234.

[29] Most of the indigenous missions were founded during this period.

Evangelical Church of India (ECI) within the span of last 40 years planted over 2,500 churches across the country and paved the way for three new dioceses and the consecration of two additional bishops.[30] The ECI has established a large number of schools, children's homes, and relief and rehabilitation structures. In a unique manner it address social injustice through its body, Social Justice Movement of India, an arm of ECI. The ECI bishops, particularly Ezra Sargunam, have easy access to the top leadership of the Indian state and central governments to address social evils. He himself was the Chairman of the State Minority Commission and held several other positions whilst bishop.

Similarly, the Friends Missionary Prayer Band has had a phenomenal growth of congregations, especially in north India, and has laid the foundation of three new dioceses in the Church of north India. The FMPB grew out of the evangelistic concern in 1958 of a group of young people belonging to the diocese of Tirunelveli, south India. Bands of concerned Christians were formed to pray for the unevangelized. The field work of the mission began in 1967 when the first missionary was sent to one of the hill tribes in south India. In 1972 the vision was enlarged to include the 11 states of north India. A target was set to send 440 missionaries to the 220 districts of these 11 states by 1982. The goal was steadily realized. At present FMPB has over 1,100 cross-cultural missionaries serving all over India. It has won 4,000,000 people for Christ; founded 60 homes for children; erected 900 church buildings; prepared 1,100 local evangelists; translated bible into 13 languages; and reached 240 people groups. Further the mission has established about 5,500 worshiping communities/congregations and still hundreds of smaller congregations are emerging among the tribals. Evangelism, church planting, bible translation and social uplift are the main ministries of the organization. It works in 23 Indian States based in 260 mission fields. FMPB is a missionary movement of Christian Indians to present the gospel of Jesus Christ personally to every person of India, particularly to those who have never heard the gospel.[31]

For the most part Asian indigenous missions and ministries adopted holistic mission practice. For example, both FMPB and ECI partnered with NGOs such as EFICOR, World Vision, CASA, Compassion, etc to minister to their poor and oppressed believers. Roger Hedlund explains such partnerships for uplifting the tribal communities such as Malto.

> The experience of the Malto people in Jharkand is an impressive story of social and spiritual redemption. Decimated by malnutrition, tuberculosis, goiter, jaundice, cholera, malaria and various water-born diseases, the Malto people also were exploited by rapacious money lenders. Addiction to alcohol and other substances was a further degrading influence. This dehumanized tribe had

---

[30] Recently two dioceses, Delhi and Chennai, have been formed. Rev. Dr. Jagthri Mashi and Rev. Dr. Sundar Singh are the consecrated bishops for these two dioceses. The third one will be the formation of Andhara diocese and the fourth one will be the Delhi Diocese. Ar present Rev. Richard Howel is the Bishop's Commissary for Delhi ECI.

[31] Cf. Vinay Samuel and Chris Sugden (eds.), *Mission as Transformation* (Oxford: Regnum, 1999), xv1.

> declined from one million to less than 70,000 during the past 40 years and was moving toward extinction. Into this context of human despair, missionaries of the Friends Missionary Prayer Band and other social development workers came to live and serve. Despite opposition by vested interests, community development is underway, and the Maltos are no longer a population in decline. From the work of the FMPB among the Malto people of North Bihar has arisen an entire new diocese. Previously illiterate, oppressed and exploited, and decimated by rampant diseases today the downward trend has ended. The Maltos are receiving rudimentary education, learning basic norms of health and hygiene, resulting in a new sense of human dignity. Today the Malto people find their self-identity in Christianity...[32]

Like the evangelicals, the Pentecostals and charismatic leaders had been using the *rescue model* in many parts of Asia. Great crowds follow leaders who offer salvation for their souls. Their slogans are, "believe the gospel of Jesus Christ, you can be saved today, you shall be saved today." They have vowed "to plunder hell, to populate heaven."[33] However, many Charismatic and Pentecostal leaders who were known for "winning the souls", also opened orphanages and old-age homes in Asian countries.[34]

Among the Pentecostals, as we shall see below, the use of the *rescue model* has given birth to prosperity and blessing theologies (or health and wealth gospel) in Asia. Jesus saves people from sin, sickness and Satan. Blessings and prosperity are available through Jesus Christ who has triumphed over Satan. The Messianic signs of "the blind see, the deaf hear, the cripple walk, the dead are raised" are once again repeated now in front of their eyes. Jesus *rescues* people from all sorts of sorrows and troubles.[35]

The Pentecostals and Holism

In Asia Pentecostals are challenging the mission practitioners to understand holism not only in terms of evangelism and social concern, but in terms of evangelism, social concern, and signs and wonders. Peter Kuzmic writes, "the whole gospel... is in word, deed, and sign."[36] In his book *By Word, Work and*

---

[32] Roger E Hedlund, 'The Witness of New Christian Movements in India' (paper presented at the IAMS assembly, Malaysia 2004).

[33] Read 'Plundering Hell to Populate Heaven', in *Missionaries* (London: BBC Books, 1990), 100ff.

[34] In India a number of orphanages, children's homes and old age homes are run by evangelical and Pentecostal missions and ministries. See Rebeccah Samuel Shah (ed.), *Handbook on Christian Missions and Ministries* (Oxford: OCMS, 1998).

[35] The rescue model seems to be based on compassion. For details see Michael Bergunder, 'Ministry of Compassion: D.G.S. Dhinakaran, Christian Healer-Prophet from Tamil Nadu', in Roger Hedlund (ed.), *Christianity Is Indian: The Emergence of an Indigenous Christianity* (Delhi: ISPCK, 2000), 158-174.

[36] Peter Kuzmic, 'Pentecostals Respond to Marxism', in Murray W. Dempster, Byron D. Klaus, and Douglas Petersen (eds.), *Called and Empowered: Global Mission in Pentecostal Perspective* (Peabody, MA: Hendrickson, 1991), 160.

Wonder, McAlpine defines holism this way: "the Christian community is to be a sign of the kingdom, in which evangelism, social action and the Spirit are present and inseparably related." For the most part, it is because of the contributions of Pentecostals that definitions for holism are increasingly reflecting the work of the God in terms of signs and wonders.[37]

An OCMS Alumni, Ida Samuel, a development worker who works among the villages of Erode district, south India, says that, "non-Christians are coming to know Christ only when they experience miracles in their lives. People accept the gospel in order to get rid of their problems, sufferings, incurable diseases, etc. When some one is miraculously healed in a family, then the whole family embraces Christ." She writes that, "we carry on our ministry through preaching the word, by doing social work, and expecting miracles – wonders from God." During the twentieth century often Pentecostals have challenged the churches and Christians everywhere to understand our task not only in terms of evangelism and social concern, but in terms of evangelism, social concern, and signs and wonders. *The Jesus Miracle Ministry* combines all these three. We are committed to the whole gospel which is in word, deed, and sign."[38]

An emerging trend in Asian church growth is due to rise of mega-churches in cities. In fact the world is witnessing a mega-church movement. Mega-churches are changing the global makeup of Christianity to the extent that some scholars are characterizing them as the harbingers of 'The Next Christendom' and the 'African Century of Christianity'. Asia has the largest mega-church in the world, in South Korea (the Yoido Full Gospel Church), and many other mega-churches have sprung up in China, Malaysia, India, Indonesia and Singapore. The Asian mega-church movement is largely Pentecostal, growing mainly in secularized and urbanized societies that allow religious freedom.[39]

According to Bryant Myers, at present about 70 percent of evangelical Christians live in non-Christian World. During recent years there has been a phenomenal increase of independent, non-denominational Christians from 10 to 20 percent, most in the global south. "These Christians of the global south, including mega-church movement, are changing the face of Christianity with local insights and interpretations, sending missionaries abroad themselves and challenging Christians of the world to reconsider old paradigms."[40] In the light of the above development, the church is understood as a 'pilgrim community'. Church is no more a civilizing or westernizing agent, but an agent of spiritual and social transformation – transforming all of life for all of the people of God. Also, due to the above two reasons, being motivated by the kingdom, independent congregations including mega-churches are showing interest in advocacy, dealing with poverty and other social evils.[41]

---

[37] Thomas H. McAlpine, *By Word, Work and Wonder* (Monrovia: MARC, 1995), 2.

[38] Ida Samuel, 'Jesus Miracle Ministry News Letter' (April, 2010), 2.

[39] S. Gramby-Sobukwe and Tim Hoiland, 'The Rise of Mega Church', *Transformation* 26:2 (April, 2009). 105-106.

[40] Quoted by S. Gramby-Sobukwe and Tim Hoiland, 'The Rise of Mega Church', 106.

[41] S. Gramby-Sobukwe and Tim Hoiland, 'The Rise of Mega Church', 106.

In south India mega-churches are becoming a phenomena in cities such as Chennai and Bangalore. For the most part mega-churches are neo-Pentecostal and now focus on preaching about blessings. Consciously these independent preachers are developing new hermeunitics that are contextual and for the most part acceptable, because in the post-modern context there is no doctrinal meta-narrative that could bind them. They are free to develop exegesis according to the context so that they are contextual hermeneutics. In this, the bible is treated as an 'answer book' for day-to-day needs such as deliverance from poverty, sickness, financial debts, etc. For them the bible is a 'success book'. "If you want to be successful then you have to find your success from the bible." Also, the bible is considered as the new covenant – a will / testament / agreement / contract given to believers. Sermons are preached under topics such as, 'Who you are in Christ?'; 'Who you are and what do you have?'; 'You are born to reign'; 'You are justified'; 'You are righteous'; 'You are free from sin'; 'God is on your side'; 'The laws / principles of increase'; 'Living under open heaven'; 'You are more than conquerors', etc.

Philip Jenkins in his recent book *The New Faces of Christianity: Believing the Bible in the Global South*, provides an extended discussion about the so-called 'prosperity theology' which has become a fascinating teaching and preaching model among the two-third world Christians, especially in Asian and African churches. Jenkins does not reject the relevance of prosperity preaching nor consider it as pure materialism. On the contrary he argues that prosperity teaching must be understood in "the wider context of extreme poverty, a world in which it seems impossible to survive without miracles." As a result it is difficult for the rich Christians to comprehend its relevance. Jenkins states that "the prosperity gospel is an inevitable by – product of a church containing so many of the very poorest."[42] Indeed some Asian prosperity preachers such as Sam P. Chelladurai, a distinguished senior pastor of the Apostolic Fellowship Tabernacle (AFT), a mega-church in Chennai, provide new hope for the poor and the sick. They offer sound financial management, enable people to live a Christ-like life and help nurturing Christian families.

Conclusion

There is no doubt that at present many of the Asian missions and ministries are holistic in their practice, although some of the native missionaries of Indian missions who are involved in cross-cultural evangelism and church planting continue to see mission as 'rescuing souls' for heaven. They often try to provide a scriptural basis for what they are doing. Mission is seen as a matter of winning the lost souls, reaching the unreached, evangelizing the unevangelized.

The rescue model often works well with those who understand salvation in terms of personal and individualistic terms. But those who use it do not get the

---

[42] Philip Jenkins, *The New Faces of Christianity: Believing the Bible in the Global South* (New York: Oxford University Press, 2006), 95, 97.

maximum out of it when their interests limit the power of the gospel of Christ. It can never affect the forces and situations. So the rescue model is not complete in itself, if it does not lead to holistic mission practice. However, at present, for the most part, Asian missions are partnering with NGOs so that their practice becomes holistic.

The chief purpose of Edinburgh 1910 was to prepare the church for the final onslaught on the powers of darkness – poverty, social evils, violence and injustice – that reigned supreme in the non-western world. The Asian church has done well to some extent, but not exceptionally.

HOLISTIC MISSION IN LATIN AMERICA

Tito Paredes

Introduction

When in June of 1910 the World Missionary Conference took place, it was primarily a western missionary gathering with very few Asian Christians present and one African. From Latin America there was no representation from evangelical churches or from the Protestant missionary societies who had already been working in these lands for many years. According to Bryan Stanley, one of the specialists on Edinburgh 1910, this was due to Anglican politics.[1] Furthermore Stanley says:

> It was a condition of the participation in the conference of leading Anglo-Catholics (notably Bishops Charles Gore, Edward Talbot, and H. H. Montgomery) that the conference and its preparatory commissions should be concerned only with missionary efforts among non-Christians, and not with Protestant missions in Roman Catholic territories such as Latin America.[2]

During Edinburgh 2010, the library of New College of the University of Edinburgh had an exhibition on important documents and letters of Edinburgh 1910, including a letter that discusses the request of the Anglican representation not to include Latin American delegates in the 1910 gathering.[3]

In contrast, at Edinburgh 2010 there were 16 Latin Americans, plus representatives of African as well as of Asian Christians. In 1910 the centre of gravity of Christianity was Europe and North America, so Edinburgh 1910 reflected such situation. In 2010 this centre of gravity had shifted to the south. Yet Edinburgh 2010, despite the efforts made to be more inclusive did not significantly provide the space to hear the church in the global south. A delegate from the south stated, what many of us present felt, that not only was the physical representation from the south important, but its agenda and concerns as well. This will have to wait for another significant world gathering to take place, where this will have to be worked at intentionally!

---

[1] Personal communication on 11 June 2010 at the Library of New College, University of Edinburgh.

[2] Brian Stanley, 'Twentieth-Century World Christianity: A Perspective from the History of Missions', 4, n.13. From an unpublished manuscript.

[3] I visited and saw the letter on 11 June 2010.

From the perspective of holistic mission, and with 100 years of looking back, we may conclude that Edinburgh 1910, at least for Latin Americans, meant exclusion and the exertion of power and political manoeuvring to implement this exclusion. This exclusion meant closing the ayes to at least 100 (1810-1910) years of Protestant presence in Latin America that in significant ways was a holistic presence.

By 1910, the presence of evangelical Latin American churches was already a reality. During the colonial period (1492-1810) this presence was more sporadic, although nonetheless significant as many of them died or suffered persecution from the Inquisition for their Protestant faith.[4]

The witness of holistic mission among evangelicals in Latin America, since the beginning of our political independence from Spain, has taken place within a very turbulent changing context. During our first 100 years of independence (1810-1910) we see a holistic approach that includes bible colportage, tacit support for our independence from Spain, promotion of education and the firm establishment of historical and nondenominational evangelical churches – all fruit of the work of western missionary societies and key converts (1810-1910). During the last one hundred years (1910-2010) we see a continuation of this holistic vision and mission that continues to focus and expand in the area of education, struggle for religious liberty, health, bible translation, social responsibility and socio-political involvement. The latter part of the twentieth century, particularly the last 60 years, has witnessed the phenomenal numerical growth of Protestantism as well as an acute debate over the non-holistic reading of the bible and the imposition of this by many mission societies and theological traditions of the global north.

In this chapter we will reflect on some aspects of this holistic witness in the last 200 years, with special emphasis on the last 50 years within a context of socio-political turmoil in which the evangelical churches have been challenged to respond to the critical context of our continent.

Holistic Mission and the Nineteenth Century Missionary Movements (1810-1910)

The socio-political and religious context

In 1910, while preparations were taking place for the historic Edinburgh conference, several countries in Latin America were preparing to celebrate 100 years of political independence from Spain. This was a partial independence limited to the Mestizo-Creole, Spanish and Portuguese speaking population. In many ways no real transformation took place as our history after independence is filled with a constant struggle among many strongmen to attain power and

[4] Tomas Gutierrez Sanchez, *Los Evangélicos en Perú y América Latina: ensayos sobre su historia* (Cehila: Ediciones AHP, 1997).

hold on to it. The aristocratic Hispanic or Portuguese elite continued to rule our nations seeking their own interests rather than working for the well being of the majorities of poor people, particularly the indigenous populations who, though they fought against the Spaniards, saw little or no change for them after independence from Spain. The need for a more complete holistic liberation was the order of the day. It is in this context that the new socio-political movements emerged, including Marxism and its various expressions such as the social democratic movements.

As mentioned before, after the independence of our nations, the Roman Catholic Church, which had lost prestige for not supporting the struggle against Spain, began to regain its influence and accommodated to the new situation. During this period many of our constitutions, such as the ones of Peru, Bolivia, and Ecuador, did not permit the free public exercise of Protestant worship. It is in this context that the struggle for religious freedom, civil marriage and burial rights for non-Catholics became part of the agenda.[5]

In this struggle for religious freedom the Protestant leaders, both Latin American and missionaries, engaged the socio-political leaders, and authorities of liberal and social democratic persuasion, who became natural allies in these efforts. This alliance was able to secure a degree of religious freedom and the recognition of civil marriages and public cemeteries for burials of non-Catholics. Further research is necessary on the issue of the relationships of evangelicals with political movements and government authorities. There are lessons that can be learned from such actions, particularly when one considers that the Protestant community in the first half of the nineteenth century was very small and yet made significant inroads in these struggles for justice and holistic expressions of the gospel. This is particularly important as in 2010 the number of evangelicals in Latin America is significant and politicians seek them to secure their votes, and many pastors and leaders have been elected to important positions such as the congress and city hall – and yet on the whole with little transformational impact.

Holistic mission colportage work and education (1810-1910)

Within the context of our wars of liberation against Spain, the first significant Protestant efforts in Latin America had to do with the distribution of the bible and the introduction of education for our people who, under Spanish colonial rule, had been deprived of this opportunity. In several South American countries, the colportage and educational work of Diego Thomson, a Scottish Baptist pastor, was very significant.

---

[5] Juan Fonseca, 'Secularización y Tolerancia: cementerios, muerte y protestantismo en el Perú (1890–1930)', in Pablo Moreno (ed.) *Protestantismo y Vida Cotidiana en América Latina: un estudio desde la cotidianidad de los sujetos* (Cehila: Fundación Universitaria Seminario Teológico Bautista Internacional, Cali, Colombia, 2007), 57-80.

This early contribution of Protestantism to our new republics by James Thomson was made possible by the invitation of the new authorities who had been winning independence from Spain. Diego Thomson,[6] who represented the British and Foreign Bible Society (BFBS) and also the British and Foreign School Society (BFSS) introduced the Lancasterian system of education.[7] In Argentina he did this at the invitation of the city hall authorities of Buenos Aires in 1819, where he was named Director of Education, establishing several schools.[8] In the case of Chile he was invited by liberator O'Higgins and carried out similar educational work. In 1922, he was granted Chilean citizenship as a way to honor and thank him for his services to the nation.[9] In Peru he was one of the first educational authorities who worked for Liberator San Martin in establishing the Lancasterian system of education. A government decree by San Martin on 6 July 1922, authorized Thomson to implement this educational project as a government official. Since then, 6 July is an official holiday known as teacher's day in Peru. Few are aware of its Protestant origins. Diego Thomson "worked in Argentina (1818-1821), Peru (1822-1824), Gran Colombia (1824-1825) and Mexico (1826-1830; 1842-1844)."[10]

Thomson was one of the first Protestant figures who fulfilled the role of public servant under the new republics. His holistic vision of the gospel helped him see the importance of bible distribution, education and support for independence from Spain. His own participation and relationship with the new authorities made him an icon of holistic vision and mission early in our independent history.[11] His concern for the poor and marginalized included his translation efforts of the New Testament to Quechua and Aymara.[12]

> Thomson's successful work and acceptance as a Protestant educator by a predominantly Catholic population was due not only to his winsome character and ability of making friends; it was also due to the fact that Thomson collaborated closely with Catholic priests, and even more important, he had an official backing from the liberators.
>
> As the new Republics began to establish themselves their new leaders became conservatives and furthermore the church, which during independence times had lost influence, regained it again. As a result we see for a number of years of

---

[6] J.B.A. Kessler, Jr., 'Early Protestant Efforts in Peru and Chile', in *A Study of the Older Protestant Missions and Churches in Peru and Chile: with special reference to the problems of division, nationalism and native ministry* (Oosterbaan & Le Cointre N.V., Goes, 1967), 19-23.

[7] Pablo Alberto Deiros, *Historia del Cristianismo en América Latina* (Buenos Aires, Argentina: Publicado por Fraternidad Teológica Latinoamericana, 1992), 640.

[8] Deiros, *Historia del Cristianismo*, 641.

[9] Deiros, *Historia del Cristianismo*, 642.

[10] Tomás Gutierrez Sanchez, *Los Evangélicos en Perú y América Latina: ensayos sobre su historia* (Cehila: Ediciones AHP, 1997), 16.

[11] Diego Thompson supported a law of religious liberty proposed by San martin but disregarded by the first congress of Peru.

[12] Conversation with Bill Mitchell in Edinburgh on 5 June 2010.

> conservatism toward political as well as religious ideas which affected the activity of Protestants, bible sellers and pastors.
> In general during times of increased social conflict between liberals and conservatives, Protestants on the whole aligned themselves with the liberal cause; thus we have a pattern of Protestant tolerance when liberals were in power and repression when conservatives had control.
> Nonetheless Thomson's personality and previous work prepared the way for the future permanent establishment of Protestantism in Peru which took place many years later, not without its struggles and confrontation with the conservative Catholic clergy that was determined to stop the introduction of Protestantism in Peru and Ecuador.[13]

The life and work of James Thomson, along with his Latin American colleagues and supporters, incarnates in many ways the vision and mission of a holistic way of living out and communicating the gospel: concern for God's scriptures to be available to all peoples (including the indigenous populations of the Andes); concern that all peoples, not just the privileged elite had access to education; an ecumenical spirit, with concern to present the God of the bible and not necessarily a Protestant form of Christianity; the ability to work with and dialogue with the political leaders of the day in a context of war against Spain; concern for the liberation of our republics from the bondage from Spain. All these actions and attitudes manifest a concern and praxis for justice and freedom underpinned by the truth of the gospel for all peoples.

Holistic mission: the continuation of colportage work, education, numerical growth and persecution of evangelicals

Francisco Penzzotti and the permanent establishment of Protestantism in Peru: 1884-1915[14]

> Between 1884-1886 Francisco Penzotti made two extensive and successful trips selling bibles. The first trip started in Montevideo – Uruguay, continued through Argentina, Bolivia, southern Peru (Tacna area) and Chile. The second trip began in Buenos Aires, continued throughout some Brazilian ports, England and on the way back touched on the Antilles, Venezuela, Colombia, Ecuador, Peru and south on to Argentina.[15]

[13] Ruben Paredes, 'The Protestant Movement in Ecuador and Peru: A Comparative Socio-Anthropological Study of the Establishment and Diffusion of Protestantism in Two Central Highland Regions' (a PhD dissertation, University of California, Los Angeles, 1980), 113-115 ('Antecedents to the Permanent Establishment of Protestantism in Peru and Ecuador: An Overview–Colonial Times to 1884').

[14] Paredes, 'The Protestant Movement in Ecuador and Peru' , 119-125 ('The Permanent Establishment of Protestantism: 1884-1915').

[15] Paredes, 'The Protestant Movement in Ecuador and Peru, 119.

Resulting from this successful trip was the appointment in 1887 of Francisco Penzotti as agent for the American Bible Society in their plans of bible distribution for Latin America. These plans included the establishment of an agency in Peru which would serve Chile, Ecuador, Peru and Bolivia.

Penzotti and his family arrived in Callao in July 1888. He established residency at Callao and immediately began to work. As soon as he found a meeting place where he could preach he began knocking on doors trying to sell bibles, reading and explaining scriptures to those interested, while at the same time inviting them to come to the services at the meeting place.

The first gathering of Penzotti included his own family and another couple named Noriega. The next Sunday four people came; the subsequent one, 10 people, eventually 30, 40, 50, 60, 70 and 80, etc. The meeting place became inadequate to hold all the interested people. Penzotti was forced to find another place which they themselves fixed up due to dilapidation.[16]

Such was the interest of the people that soon the Sunday gatherings grew to over 300 people. During this time the English-speaking Protestant church was closed for lack of a pastor and no services were held. Penzotti was able to secure the use of this building for a while for the Sunday gatherings. However, the Catholic clergy began strong opposition towards Penzotti and some people threatened to blow up the English-speaking church. Under such circumstances the English-speaking commission in charge of the building deprived Penzotti of the use of it. Penzotti had to return to his smaller building for the Sunday gatherings.[17]

Penzotti refers to the genuineness of the conversion experience of the people. In one of the gatherings in which they were inaugurating a new auditorium, a revival took place where men and women, old and young, stood up and with tears in their eyes and openly testified about their conversions. Before his first years were up, Penzotti had a great many converts and six bible colporteurs who helped him in bible distribution around Lima and in the interior of the country.

According to Kessler,

> An important feature of Penzotti's work was that at once he started to train his converts in the work of evangelism sending them out two by two on Sunday afternoons to evangelize the town. ...At the end of his first year in Peru Penzotti had trained six of his converts as colporteurs and in the year 1889, 110 places in Peru were visited and the astonishing total of 7,000 bibles or portions had been sold.[18]

Bahamonde evaluates the missionary impact of Penzotti in the following manner:[19]

---

[16] F. Penzotti, 'Apuntes Autobiografía y Notas del Rev. F. Penzotti en Centro y Sud America', in Daniel Hall's *Llanos y Montañas* (London, 1913), cited in Paredes, 'The Protestant Movement in Ecuador and Peru', 120.

[17] Paredes, 'The Protestant Movement in Ecuador and Peru', 120.

[18] J. B.A. Kessler, Jr., 'The Establishment of Protestant in Peru', 33.

[19] Kessler, 'The Establishment of Protestant in Peru', 33; Paredes, 'The Protestant

> Due to the great impact done by the preaching and colportage work of Penzotti and the international scandal brought about by his famous imprisonment in 'casa matas' the missionary zeal from overseas on behalf of Peru was stirred up and it motivated the mission societies to initiate the missionary occupation of our country. Very soon independent societies began to establish themselves like that of Charles H. Bright in 1893, J.L. Jarret and F.J. Peters in Cusco (1895), of Mr. A.R. Stark of the Regions Beyond Missionary Union in Trujillo (1898). Between 1889 and 1900 the first works of the Seventh Day Adventists and of the independent Baptists were established.

In this manner, then, the permanent establishment of the Protestant movement in Peru was initiated. Penzotti's influence on behalf of Protestantism was also felt in Ecuador and other South American countries.

Struggle for religious freedom[20]

Undoubtedly the acquittal of Penzotti and his release from prison was a boost for the spread and acceptance of Protestantism in South America. However, at the time the constitutions of Ecuador, Peru and Bolivia did not guarantee freedom of worship and continued to uphold Catholicism as the official and protected religion at the exclusion of any other. This struggle continued to be part of the agenda of holistic mission for evangelicals for many years.

The establishment of the Methodist Church[21]

After Penzotti's release from the Casa Matas prison in 1892, it was recognized that he needed rest and a change of activity and location due to his failing health caused by his imprisonment.[22] Dr. Thomas Wood, who had been working as a missionary in Argentina and Uruguay for about 21 years, was appointed as the first resident missionary of the Methodist Episcopal Church in Lima to follow up Penzotti's work. Wood also came as a volunteer of the American Bible Society. He arrived in Lima in July of 1891.[23]

In January 1892[24] Wood received the assistance of Noriega, a Peruvian convert of Penzotti's, in the starting of Protestant services in Lima. In bible distribution he received the help of Adolfo Vasquez, another Penzotti convert.

Upon arrival Wood took up the responsibility for the Callao congregation started by Penzotti and on January 27, 1892 began Protestant services in Malambo, Lima, at the house of Manuel Noriega. Thirty-nine attended the first

---

Movement in Ecuador and Peru' 125 ('The Permanent Establishment of Protestantism: 1884-1915')

[20] Paredes, 'The Protestant Movement in Ecuador and Peru', 126.

[21] Paredes, 'The Protestant Movement in Ecuador and Peru', 130.

[22] J. Ritchie, 'El Renacimiento' (1936), 10.

[23] Ritchie, 'El Renacimiento', 10.

[24] Kessler, 'The Establishment of Protestant in Peru', 37-38.

meeting.[25] After meeting 30 times in this place, due to a growth in numbers, it was necessary to find a new place, a task which was not easy as people were still hesitant of renting their buildings for Protestant services. Finally, after a difficult search, a foreign resident rented a building to the Protestants on Plateros Street, where services were inaugurated on May 11, 1892. The meetings were conducted behind closed doors.

As the members of the Lima congregation augmented, some antagonism against it was expressed. Stoning the building and antagonism towards individual members were not uncommon. One night, for example, in the midst of the service, a military authority walked in, stopped the preaching of Dr. Wood and dismissed the congregation. Dr. Wood was arrested and later released under the excuse that it was a mistake.[26]

The arrival of Woods to Peru signaled the beginning of a marked educational contribution to the country by Protestantism. Education in Peru was still a luxury commodity in the nineteenth century, mainly available to the children of the rulers and powerful. The establishment of Protestant run schools not only contributed to the educational needs of the country but also contributed to break down the barriers of prejudice and hostility towards Protestants in general.

Between 1891 and 1900, the Methodists, under the leadership of Thomas Woods, established three elementary schools, a high school and two other educational centres in Callao and Lima. In 1899, a technical commercial school was also founded. Later, the Methodists established other schools in the interior highlands of Peru.

Penzotti's style of Protestant propagation and the circumstances that surrounded his stay in Peru were somewhat different from those of Wood, his replacement. Penzotti had to fight for the recognition of Protestantism as a legitimate endeavor within Peru; his emphasis was bible distribution and evangelization. In contrast, Woods, although by no means opposed, chose to place the emphasis on education. Other missionaries, Peruvian as well as foreign, placed the emphasis on direct 'preselecting' thus complementing this educational approach.

Woods wrote about his educational work:[27]

> No other form of effort approaches it in effectiveness for stopping the mouth of the enemies, breaking down prejudices and gaining popular sympathy. The bible opens more doors but the school work opens more hearts.

Both Penzotti and Woods are expressions of a holistic mission carried out by evangelicals early in the nineteenth century that continued into the next century.

---

[25] R. Algorta, 'El Renacimiento', *Enero* (1936), 10, cited in Paredes, 'The Protestant Movement in Ecuador and Peru', 131.

[26] *Ibid.*

[27] Kessler, 'The Establishment of Protestant in Peru',, 38.

Holistic Mission Within The Last 100 Years (1910-2010): Education, Numerical Expansion, Persecution, and Development of Some Tensions Between Holistic and Non Holistic Readings of Mission

Six years after Edinburgh 1910, The Latin America Missionary Congress took place in Panama in 1916. In a way it was a response to the exclusion of Latin America from the Edinburgh 1910 congress. A Latin American Cooperation Committee was formed for organizing the congress.[28] According to Escobar, the Panama gathering was, "decisive for the future of the evangelical work and its results were felt in various agreements of missionary cooperation, studies of the reality of the continent and various plans to work together."[29] After Panama, this committee organized two other gatherings: One in Montevideo in 1925 and another one in Havana in 1929.[30] Other congresses took place in the following decades.[31]

During the fifties we observe a polarization of the evangelical movement which reflects the polarization of the global north. The churches that are closely connected with the ecumenical movement related to the World Council of Churches (WCC) and the churches and movements related more to the traditions of the World Evangelical Alliance and Lausanne movement in the global north. Out of this polarization emerged a Latin American evangelical response associated with the Latin American Theological Fraternity and at the global level with the International Fellowship of Mission Theologians (INFEMIT). We will return to this later but for now continue examining twentieth century holistic witness in the first part of the century.

The Methodist contribution to education in Peru and many other countries has been quite significant. The Free Church of Scotland, through its Saint Andrew's school in Lima, has also made a valuable contribution. John A. MacKay was its founder and headmaster at a time of socio-political turmoil. He was in Latin America between 1916-1932.[32] He decided to enter the University of San Marcos in Lima and get his doctorate as a way to incarnate himself in the context of Latin America where he wrote his thesis on the Spanish philosopher Don Miguel de Unamuno.[33] In this process he became friends with leading political figures and socio-political actors of Peru, several of whom he recruited to teach at his school – among them Victor Raul Haya de la Torre,

---

[28] Samuel Escobar, 'El avance evangélico en América Latina', in *La Fe Evangélica y las teologías de la Liberación* (Casa Bautista de Publicaciones, 1987), 49-50.

[29] Escobar, 'El avance evangélico en América Latina', 50.

[30] Escobar, 'El avance evangélico en América Latina', 50.

[31] Escobar, 'El avance evangélico en América Latina', 49-63.

[32] Samuel Escobar, 'El Legado Misionero de Juan A. Mackay', in *El Otro Cristo Español* (Edición Especial de 1992, Casa Unida de Publicaciones S.A. de C.V: [CUPSA], México y Asociación de Ediciones La Aurora, Argentina y Ediciones Semilla, Guatemala. Tercera Edición, 1991. Edición Especial de Celebración de Bodas de Diamante del Colegio San Andrés (antes Anglo-Peruano). Impreso en Perú, Noviembre 1991), 20.

[33] Escobar, 'El Legado Misionero de Juan A. Mackay', 21.

founder of the social democratic party APRA, the party of the current president of Peru, Alan Garcia Perez (2006-2011).

John A. Mackay became an iconic figure of holistic vision, mission and ecumenism. His vision was to provide education of excellence to the general population of Peru that did not have this opportunity. He also wanted to mix with leaders for Peru who had high ethical standards.

In 1929 the government of Peru, due to pressure from the Roman Catholic bishop, decreed the closure of all schools that did not conform to Catholic teaching in the area of religion. The Saint Andrew's school authorities thought they would have to close the school as they were not going to accept such imposition. This was an occasion in which the school, then called Colegio Anglo-Peruano, had to mobilize not only prayer but influential contacts both in Peru and overseas such as British and US authorities, to put pressure on Peru not to touch the evangelical schools.[34] Fortunately through the intercession of a history teacher in the school, who happened to be the nephew of the president, the school was not affected.[35] This determination to pray as well as act gives us another example of holistic mission with a commitment to high quality education, without compromising Christian convictions. It also shows the socio-political involvement and advocacy displayed which is very much needed today.

The socio-political and religious context: liberation theologies and evangelical holistic mission

The 1950s and '60s witnessed after World War II the emergence of greater polarization between the forces that wanted to maintain the status quo and the forces that were pushing for revolutionary change. Let's remember that independence from Spain did not translate into an effective transformation, but for many it only meant a change of hands with the continuation of injustices of the colonial regime and in some cases worse, particularly for the indigenous populations. This need for more radical change was expressed through the emergence of socio-political movements and political parties. We also see this desire for change within certain sectors in the Catholic Church, as well as the evangelical churches. The socio-political movements inspired by Marx grew, and we also see some of this influence in the religious field with the rise of the theologies of liberation within Catholicism and the church and society movement (ISAL) within Protestantism.

> The decade of the 1960s witnesses the tension between two political projects that are contradictory and antagonic: the Developmental Project with its democratic and capitalist character with a strong economics base and the revolutionary

---

[34] John M. Macpherson, 'School and Nation: Roots Entwining', in *At the Roots of a Nation: The Story of Colegio San Andrés, a Christian School in Lima, Peru* (Edinburgh: Knox Press, 1993), 4-6.

[35] Macpherson, 'School and Nation', 4-6.

> violent liberation project with its Marxist-Leninist origins adapted to the special circumstances of Latin America.[36]

The failure of the developmental project to bring justice and transformation to our people increased the revolutionary fervour of Christians and non-Christians alike. Some Christians opted for joining the guerrilla movements in the continent and others opted for non-violent participation through traditional as well as new emerging socio-political movements. The theologies of liberation, influenced by Marxism, are expressions of this panorama. Within the Protestant circles the Church and Society movement (ISAL),[37] with its ties to the ecumenical movement, and the holistic evangelical mission movement generated by the Latin American Theological Fraternity (LTF), are part of this very dynamic context.

In the praxis of evangelicals since the nineteenth century we see dimensions of holistic mission in action. What was needed was a theological articulation and deepening of said practice. The theologies of liberation, with their articulation and praxis, were a challenge to evangelicals! One of the strong barriers to "examine everything and retain what is good" was the strong influence of conservative mission societies, greatly influenced by a narrow dispensationalism. An anti-communist and anti-intellectual attitude, coupled with a spiritualist, dichotomist vision of the gospel, was very resistant to dialogue with liberation theologies and our critical context. This theological influence was described by Padilla in the following terms:

> Very early in the history of the church, the Christian message was fixed in philosophical categories and the historical dimension of the revelation moved to a secondary place in respect to the dogma.[38].

We need to recognize that in the two thirds world evangelicals are still strongly influenced by this expression of western theology. Recognizing its valuable contributions, we can agree with Padilla that in many aspects this theology reflects:

> ...the rationalist epistemology, individualism, pragmatism, materialism, and atomization of reality...[39]

Liberation theologies had no problem dialoguing and incorporating social science theories in their analysis of Latin American socio-political reality. Often they borrowed the methodological approach and theories of Marxism to articulate their thinking. This was particularly bothersome for many

---

[36] Pablo Alberto Deiros, *Historia del Cristianismo en América Latina* (Buenos Aires, Argentina: Fraternidad Teológica Latinoamericana, 1992), 530 (my translation).

[37] Tomas Gutierrez Sanchez, *Desafíos a la Fe Cristiana: una Perspectiva Evangélica* (Lima, Perú: Ediciones AHP, 2002).

[38] C. Rene Padilla, 'Hacia una Cristología Evangélica Contextual', *Boletín Teológico* 30 (June, 1987). My translation.

[39] C. Rene Padilla, 'La contextualización del evangelio', in *Misión Integral: Ensayos sobre el Reino y la Iglesia* (Buenos Aires: Nueva Creación, 1986), 202, n. 24. My translation.

evangelicals. Nonetheless, evangelicals connected with the LTF were keen to take up the challenge of examining our Latin context as well as the articulation of liberation theologies. Samuel Escobar and Emilio Antonio Nuñez, among others, have written on these themes from an evangelical stance.[40]

After the take over of China by Mao, many western missionaries were deployed to Latin America. In USA and other western countries, a climate of anti-communism was a growing phenomenon. A number of missionaries who arrived in Latin America came with a strong anti-communist attitude, prioritizing 'soul winning' over social action. This wave of missionaries had a considerable influence preaching and teaching against a holistic communication and expression of the gospel. For a number of years this anti-holistic attitude and practice was the predominant mood among many evangelicals in Latin America.

At a worldwide level we see a great concern among US evangelicals to activate interest for the evangelization of the world, particularly as it was perceived that the influence of theological liberalism was growing in WCC circles. Fruit of this concern was the Berlin Congress of World Evangelization in 1966 and the regional congresses such as the CLADE I (Latin American Congress of Evangelization) held in Bogota, Colombia, in 1969.

It was in CLADE I that the concern for holistic mission was put on the agenda. Samuel Escobar gave a historic speech that many consider the shout for independence and liberation of theological tutelage on the question of holistic mission, until then dominated by many conservative mission agencies working in our continent. It is in this gathering where the Latin American Theological Fraternity (LTF) was conceived and a year later, 1970, born in Cochabamba, Bolivia. The LTF has been since its inception one of the leading movements within evangelical Latin American Christianity that has promoted holistic mission and vision with different emphases during its lifetime. Historian Sidney Rooy expresses this in the following terms:

> A mass Protestant conference of Latin American leaders was held in October of 1969 in Bogotá. One of the 25 speeches, given by Samuel Escobar, was on the 'Social Responsibility of the Christian'. He touched a responsive chord among many of those present, bringing to the surface the underlying existent tensions between those who called for soul salvation as the primary task of the church and those who sought a more integral kingdom-oriented vision of evangelism. In spontaneous conversations a group decided to call for a meeting the following year in Cochabamba, Bolivia, to discuss the authority of the Scriptures and their interpretation in the evangelistic calling of the church. There the Fraternidad Teológica Latinoamericana (FTL) was born, and a broad representation of Latin American leaders were invited to participate.[41]

---

[40] Samuel Escobar, *La Fe Evangélica y las Teologías de la Liberación* (Casa Bautista de Publicaciones, USA, Primera Edición. Nuñez, Emilio Antonio, 1988); *Teología de la Liberación: una perspectiva evangélica* (Miami, FL: Editorial Caribe, tercera edición).

[41] Sidney Rooy, 'Our story', taken from English section of the www.ftl-al.org, June 2010.

The Objectives of the LTF are:[42]

- To promote reflection on the gospel and on its significance for human beings within Latin American society. Towards this end, the FTL stimulates the development of an evangelical thinking that is attentive to the questions of life within a Latin American context. The FTL recognizes the normative character of the bible as the written Word of God and seeks to listen, under the Holy Spirit's direction, to the biblical message in relation to the relativities of our concrete situations.
- To create a framework for dialogue among thinkers who confess Jesus Christ as Lord and Saviour and who are willing to reflect biblically in order to communicate the gospel within Latin American cultures.
- To contribute to the life and mission of the evangelical churches in Latin America, without attempting to speak for them or assuming the position of being their spokesperson in the Latin American continent.[43]

Holistic mission, the indigenous churches and movements in Latin America

> The political independence of most Latin American countries from Spain and Portugal did not translate into significant socio-political benefits for the indigenous peoples. Conditions for them continued the same and in some cases worsened. In a sense, they still await their liberation, and have become conscious that unless they themselves take the initiative and leadership to claim their basic human rights as full citizens in their own countries, non-indigenous peoples will not willingly share power with them. As a result we have a confrontation between the indigenous peoples and the non-indigenous ruling elites that are not willing to share the power they already hold.[44]

Protestant Christianity did not receive acceptance among the ruling. For them, being Latin American and Roman Catholic was the same. Just as in colonial times one could not conceive a different way of being a human being, so in our continent until recently, being Latin American has been a synonym of being Roman Catholic. As a result, the Protestant gospel received wide acceptance among the lower classes and among the indigenous groups. One interesting phenomenon that took place among indigenous populations that were converted to Protestant Christianity was its holistic way of expressing the gospel, in spite of non-holistic teaching either by expatriate missionaries or Spanish speaking pastors. The holistic worldview of the indigenous population shaped its understanding and praxis of the gospel. This was expressed in the

---

[42] *Journal of Latin American Theology: Christian Reflection from the Latino South* (2007), Vol.2, n.2, Ediciones Kairos.

[43] For recent activities and chapters of the LTF see the web page: www.ftl-al.org.

[44] Ruben Paredes, 'Indigenous Peoples', in John Corrie (ed.), *Dictionary of Mission Theology: Evangelical Foundations* (Downers Grove: Inter-Varsity Press, 2007), 188.

integration of the sacred and profane, individual and group, natural and supernatural, among other things. Indigenous worldviews, such as African and Asian worldviews, have a holistic primal dimension that may be seen as the substructure of biblical Christianity. It is these realities that offer great potential for alternative ways of articulating and doing theology that is holistic and biblical.

> Indigenous people have great contributions to make to the universal church, particularly in expressing practical solidarity with other needy human beings, also in their relationship to creation and the integration of the sacred and secular. An ecological sensitivity and integration of the whole of life are practical contributions and consequences of indigenous people's holistic view of the gospel and mission.[45]

The challenges for the future in holistic mission in Latin America

In the last 200 years most of our relationships, influences and dialogue have been north-south. These have been relationships that have brought much blessing to our continent, for which we are very grateful. However, they have also been, to say the least, relationships of dependence, tension and confrontation. Likewise, they have caused much pain and challenge. Similar situations, and perhaps more dramatic, have been the experiences of our brothers and sisters from Africa and Asia. There are many things we have in common with one another, and also many that are only peculiar to each of our contexts. There is so much we can learn from each other and resonate with one another. The challenge for holistic mission today lies in the learning and understanding of holistic mission that our God has been doing in the churches and peoples of the global south, where we find the new centre of gravity of Christianity. It is our praxis and reflexion as people of God in the global south, in the midst of struggle for survival and justice, that we offer to God and the churches of the world as evidence of the transforming power of the gospel.

The Challenge for the Christians in the global north lies in whether they are open to hear and receive this rich life and experience of the global south to enrich their lives.

Conclusion

As we can see in the 100 years previous to Edinburgh 1910, evangelical Christianity, although in terms of numbers insignificant, was able to have a very significant impact in the lives of our emerging nations in several of our countries through the labours of bible colporteurs in the area of education. An iconic figure in this is Diego Thomson. His work also sought to bring persons and families to conversion to Jesus Christ, although not necessarily to evangelical churches at first.

---

[45] Paredes, 'Indigenous Peoples', 189-190.

During this time we also see the permanent establishment of evangelical Christianity through the formation of local churches where the new converts gathered. As evangelical Christianity gained influence and especially many converts, the Catholic Church became concerned and made every effort to stop their influence – persecution of evangelicals followed. Evangelical work through education expanded to the area of health and so other areas of holistic witness grew.

The insertion of Latin American evangelical Christianity in the global evangelical community affected its agenda, often responding to problems and themes not relevant to our situation, for example: what has priority, evangelism or social action? the individual or the group? inerrancy of scripture, etc. This distraction was made more acute in the light of the need for transformation of our unjust relationships and structures, rampant poverty and very unequal distribution of resources. Latin America is one of the most unequal continents in the world. In response to this critical situation, the theologies of liberation emerged in their Catholic and Protestant versions, which were then catalysts for the emergence of what might be called the holistic evangelical movement associated with the Latin American Theological Fraternity, founded in Bolivia in 1970. A few years later this holistic thinking and praxis begun to be articulated in the historic congress of Lausanne 74, where members of the LTF such as Rene Padilla and Samuel Escobar played a significant part, speaking in plenaries as well as participating in the draft of the Lausanne Covenant.

The challenge for us in Latin America remains, paraphrasing the CLADE III motto, "To live and take the whole gospel to all peoples (cultures) from and in Latin America." May this be so in the power and sovereignty of our God the Father, Son and Holy Spirit.

PART D

UNDERLYING ISSUES IN IMPLEMENTING HOLISTIC MISSION

HOLISTIC MISSION: NEW FRONTIERS[1]

Bryant L. Myers

The purpose of this chapter is to look briefly at the journey of evangelicals toward an integrated way of thinking about and practicing holistic mission. A look backward is then joined with a look around us today with the intention of sketching out what may be useful frontiers for further action, research, theological reflection and study. This is done in the spirit of recognizing that a new generation of young evangelicals, deeply called to ministries of social action and Christian witness, are emerging all over the world and they need to be encouraged to take over the conversation and extend its frontiers.

Where are We Coming From?

In the 1920s, American evangelicals took a holiday from history when it came to social action. Deeply wounded by the modernist-fundamentalist controversy, our conservative forbearers retreated behind the fundamentals of the faith and the singular importance of evangelism, and stayed in a defensive posture for almost 50 years.

In 1952, Carl H. Henry, the seminal conservative evangelical theologian of his era, stirred the waters when he wrote *The Uneasy Conscience of Fundamentalism*, in which he recalled the evangelical involvement with social issues at home and on the mission field throughout the nineteenth century (Henry 1947). Henry wondered if losing sight of the social side of the gospel of Jesus Christ might have been an unintended consequence of the "battle for the faith" in the 1920s.

It took almost another quarter century before this question was raised again during the emergence of the Lausanne movement and its inaugural meeting in Lausanne in 1974. As the Lausanne Covenant (Stott 1975) – still the most widely accepted contemporary affirmation of evangelical beliefs – was being drafted, some courageous brothers from the south insisted that no statement of evangelical belief could be complete if it did not include a gospel call for action on behalf of the poor and the oppressed. Today we stand indebted to Samuel Escobar, René Padilla and others for reminding evangelicals who we really are.

[1] A version of this chapter was presented at the Transformational Development Conference, hosted by Food for the Hungry, Eastern College and George Fox College in Portland, OR, August 14-26, 2008.

During the 1980s, a new, but related, disagreement emerged. It was agreed that social action and concerns for justice reflected a biblical understanding of Christian ministry. But were evangelism and social action equally important? Wasn't evangelism primary?

In the early 1980s, meetings under the Lausanne umbrella were held in Grand Rapids (Nicholls 1986) and at Wheaton College (Sine 1983; Samuel 1987). Discussions ranged over issues relating to justice, social action, eschatology, and the importance of reaching the unreached. Evangelism and social action were described as two sides of the same gospel coin or two wings on the gospel bird.

New questions emerged. Is development – a construct of the west – the right word for evangelicals to use or not? Is holism spelled with a 'w' or an 'h,' and so on. In the midst of this discussion, Wayne Bragg of the Wheaton Hunger Center introduced a new word: transformation. The gospel was about change – material, social and spiritual change – and the biblical word was transformation. The word stuck.

By the early 1990s, a strong movement of evangelical social action emerged that grew increasingly self-confident. A variety of labels emerged: holistic mission, wholistic development, integral development and transformational development. Evangelical agencies like Food for the Hungry, World Relief, World Vision, World Concern and many others moved forward to the next question: What does transformational development look like in practice? How does one do it well?

During the 1990s, this was the question that evangelical relief and development agencies and practitioners met to talk about. Ted Yamamori, myself, and others organized meetings where practitioners shared case studies in holistic mission. This was done in Africa, Latin America, and Asia; there was also a meeting on holistic ministry in the cities. The World Vision/MARC series on holistic ministry were a result of these ongoing conversations (Yamamori et al., 1995, 1996, 1997, 1998).

Today, the issue of social action or evangelism among evangelicals is largely a historical footnote. Over half of the incoming masters students to the School of Intercultural Studies at Fuller Theological Seminary in 2007 enrolled to study children-at-risk, international development and urban studies. Allen Hertske has documented the growing engagement of contemporary evangelicals with human rights and advocacy work (Hertzke 2004). Ron Sider has made the cover of *Christianity Today*. Operation Blessing is an outgrowth of Pat Robertson's ministry. Campus Crusade has its Global Aid Network (GAiN). Small evangelical missions are simply getting on with transformational development, like Mission Moving Mountains and their discipleship for transformation training programs.

This brief and oversimplified overview of the evangelical conversation on holistic mission sets the stage to examine the new frontiers of thinking about and doing holistic mission in 2010 and beyond. This essay will examine contemporary evangelical social action, its understanding of transformational development, and make some suggestions about what remains to be done. Where are today's frontiers?

We need to begin by noting what has not happened. No new volumes of case studies have been published in the last ten years. There are very few new books on transformational development. There are very few serious program evaluations that are genuinely holistic. There is very little, if any, serious research by Christian practitioners – very few PhD studies, and almost no academic research into transformational development. There is very little new theological reflection; we are resting on the excellent work done in the 1980s. There is no new ecclesiology, and yet the question of the relationship between the Christian relief and development agency and local churches remains unclear. The bottom line is this: for the last twenty years, evangelical holistic mission activists have acted. They've gone out and done transformational development. Doing is good. But there is more to doing than just acting.

Recovering From Modernity

As the conversations of the 1980s came to a close, some of us realized that we had been arguing about evangelism and social action without understanding the root cause of the problem – the pervasive impact of the modern worldview on evangelical theology and practice. Modernity, the long-standing and dominating outcome of the Enlightenment, had distorted our theological conversation. Modernity's separation of the spiritual from the material was the root of our argument about evangelism or social action (Myers 1998). We realized that if our worldview was genuinely Christian, we would have less trouble with the idea that loving God and loving neighbor are missional outcomes of the same Christian gospel.

The problem was that once we agreed on the gospel validity of both evangelism and social action, we evangelicals stopped working conceptually and theologically for the most part. Yet we lived then, and continue to live now, in a world in which the modern worldview still is the dominant interpretive construct for development theory and practice.

Some will say that the world is post-modern now, so this is old news. In the areas of popular culture, cultural and critical studies and the social sciences, this is true. But in the world of poverty eradication and development, the institutions and the thinking are still modern in nature and practice. From the World Bank to USAID to Action Aid, poverty is still a problem to be solved and the solution is to be found in human ingenuity, generosity, and skilled technical practice.

While this continuing preoccupation with the material is understandable for secular agencies, it is an indictment of us as Christians, whether we are academics or practitioners. Once the false argument about evangelism or social action ended, we should have moved with vigor and diligence to thinking through a genuinely biblical way to frame our theory and especially our practice of transformational development. Many of the frontiers in what follows are actions Christian development folks should have been working on for the last twenty years.

There are at least five specific examples of this unfinished work of recovering from modernity.

First, we need to be more intentional and deliberate in the formation *of holistic practitioners*. Holism is a state of mind, not a program. Holism is a way of thinking and seeing the world. We need practitioners who have been trained to overcome their captivity to a two-tiered modern worldview, which is a product of their professional education or culture or both. We need practitioners who use the bible and theology, along with their understanding of spirituality, to infuse and shape their transformational development theory and practice. Holistic practitioners must be trained to think theologically about their work and especially their actions – *acting* theologically is an important skill. We need holistic practitioners who have been enabled to practice a spirituality that strengthens them for the journey.

Second, we need to do a better job at figuring out *where local churches fit into the work of transformational development* on the ground. For too long, Christian development agencies worked in the material realm – their work did not look all that different from their secular counterparts – while ignoring the local churches on the grounds that churches are not development agencies, but the caretakers of spiritual matters for local Christian souls. This is a false and unhelpful dichotomy that reflects a modern worldview (Myers 2000).

Yet the local churches are the body of Christ, present before agencies come and present long after they leave. We need a new development ecclesiology that helps us understand local churches as being both the caretakers of local Christians, and also as one expression of God's activity in the form of civil society. In many parts of the world, and in the inner cities of the United States, local churches are often the only functioning civil society there is. Christian agencies must recover from their pride and professionalism and find a way to become part of the Christian community on the ground. Agencies must figure out how to become engaging, supporting and empowering partners of local churches, with each discovering and respecting their respective roles in God's work of transformation.

Third, we need to *recover the Christian account for why development technology is effective.* The modern worldview places God in the spiritual realm and technology and science in the realm of the 'real world'. Technology explains itself by pointing to its effectiveness. This is an echo of the modern, not Christian worldview. When we find water in the desert, there are reasons that are deeper and more Christian than just effective hydrology and soil science. Vaccinations that protect children from disease are illustrations of God's grace, as well as testimonies to effective science.

We've forgotten where the science came from. Part of the science story is that the world was created by an order-making God. We've forgotten that the reason we can figure science out in the first place is that we are made in the image of this God, and are hence rational order-recognizing humans, who are thus able to figure out how things work in God's world.

Before the Enlightenment, God was part of the explanation for technology. We need to recover that story and reclaim it. This will require that theologians leave their quiet, comfortable places and join agencies living with and among the poor. This will require theologians who are willing to admit their former captivity to the modern worldview.

Fourth, we need to create a biblical and theologically informed *Christian understanding of macro-development.* The stage is currently dominated by the predominantly modern frame of Jeffrey Sachs and his *End of Poverty* (Sachs 2005), the more post-modern frame of William Easterly and his *White Man's Burden* (Easterly 2006), and the more eclectic and pragmatic package of solutions offered by Paul Collier in *The Bottom Billion* (Collier 2007). These offerings provide approaches for the eradication of poverty that are secular and materialistic, resting on the assumption that human beings can save themselves.

Surely if we overcame the limitations of the dichotomy between the spiritual and the material, Christians might be able to give a more complete account of both why there is poverty in the world and why human beings can create wealth. We should be able to propose a conceptual framework for human development that accounts for both the ability of human beings to create and improve creation, and an account for why human beings also act unjustly and selfishly. Further, the biblical framework provides an account for the eventual restoration of the world to its originally intended condition.

Fifth, and related to number four, is the need to provide *a deep and nuanced response to globalization.* This deep-seated historical change process is a fact of life that is rapidly changing the world in which we live, and has been doing so since the late nineteenth century. It is both creating wealth and poverty, and is the dominant contextual factor within which all of us are doing our transformational development work.

Max Stackhouse has reflected deeply on globalization in an eight-year study process involving scholars from all over the world at Princeton's Center for Theological Inquiry. In the fourth volume in his series on God and globalization, Stackhouse (2007) concludes that God is not surprised by globalization. Globalization must be seen as a historical process reflecting both grace and the fall, of things that are for life and things that degrade life. Stackhouse reminds us that God has made a covenant with human beings that is still in play and that the death, resurrection and coming again of Jesus is the final say. Stackhouse concludes "… that the vision of that end is the New Jerusalem, a cosmopolitan and complex urban civilization into which all the peoples of the earth can bring their gifts. This is the key to a theology of history and thus to the dynamics of globalization." (2007:32)

Stackhouse further argues that the conversation about globalization reflects a modernity that ignores the religious and theological. This results in two serious weaknesses. First, it ignores the simple fact that "certain influences from the classic Christian traditions of theology and ethics are at least partly responsible for the patterns and deeper dynamics that are driving globalization" (2007:35). Second, it ignores the importance of religious ideas and ethics in shaping societies and cultures – which is modernity's fatal flaw. Modernity cannot provide a moral or ethical architecture to shape and guide globalization.

Stackhouse calls Christians, along with those of the other major faith traditions, to contribute to the shaping of globalization in the form of what he calls public theology. "It is the duty of public theology to provide a reasonable proposal with regard to the moral and spiritual architecture and the inner guidance systems of civilizations." (2007:84).

One contribution we can make is to the global conversation on what constitutes true human development, and to a holistic and grounded view of what poverty is and the keys to its eradication. Our challenge is to think biblically and theologically to provide an account that seamlessly integrates the spiritual and material with the biblical story of God's transformation project in human history that ends in the New Jerusalem.

In terms of items four and five above, it is time that Christians emerge from their captivity to the two-tiered modern worldview, thus limiting themselves to focus on things spiritual, and, as a consequence, leave the material world of globalization, macro-development theory, and development technology to the secular world and its thin and ultimately unsatisfactory account for improving the human condition.

Other Challenges that Need Attention

There are five other challenges that require our attention as transformational development practitioners.

First, we need to *develop transformational organizations*. If transformational development is a biblical process of social change that is good enough to practice among the poor, then we should practice it in our organizational lives as well. Our organizational development process must echo our understanding and practice of transformational development. We must learn to listen to and trust those who are on the frontline of ministry – those who actually know the poor. We must seek the same better future, and use the same process of change – on ourselves and our partners – that we use among the poor. We must let the voices of the poor drive our organizations and find ways to encourage our donors to understand and value this as an issue of ethical importance.

Second, we need to *integrate advocacy and public policy into our practice* of transformational development. Many Christian relief and development agencies have been doing transformational development long enough that the need for local advocacy and policy work is becoming inescapable. Local community-based organizations (CBOs) have been formed and are maturing. All the initial poverty responses are in play. Communities are used to problem solving and planning solutions. The inadequacies of local and regional government services are obvious, and communities have growing confidence in their voice and power as citizens. Thus training in engaging with local institutions and making policy needs known is becoming unavoidable. Developing good citizenship and working for good governance must become part of transformational development practice.

Third, we need to *professionalize without secularizing*. We need to be just as good in a technical sense as any secular practitioner. We need to hire professionals in sustainable agriculture, education, microfinance, water and sanitation, community psychology, participatory methods for empowerment and the like. But we must also understand that the places one goes to get such training operate out of the modern, secular worldview. God is no longer needed as part of the explanation for why soil scientists and hydrologists can find water in the desert. We need to help these professionals recompose their technical stories so that the poor get both the benefit of current technology, and yet avoid the secularizing nature of what technology alone has done to us in the west.

Fourth, we need to *demonstrate that we are doing good work*. We need to believe enough in our transformational development theory and practice to be willing to subject it to serious scrutiny. We need to do the research and the impact evaluations that show that our approach is in fact superior because it does all that the secular agencies can do in the material realm, and much more that a secular approach cannot get to.

This means that we need to articulate the outcomes of transformational development. What are they? How can they be measured? If the goals of transformational development are changed people and changed relationships, then what are the indicators that this is the case and do these indicators reflect a biblical or secular worldview?

But there's more. Evaluation must not just limit its focus to outcomes and impacts, as important as these are to our accountability to donors and the poor. There are other important questions that need attention. For example, do our practices, especially our technical practices, reflect a biblical or modern worldview? Do we understand that God is part of the explanation for our transformational development? What might we learn if we asked our beneficiaries why fewer children were dying, or how they explained finding water in the desert, or how their agricultural production had increased? Would they talk about God, creation and grace as the explanation for effective technology? Or would they explain the positive change in terms of witchcraft or the marvels of western science? Does God get credit at the end of the day?

This means that agencies need to find donors who are willing to pay for serious research and substantive evaluations. This means Christian social scientists need to be willing to redirect their preoccupations with western issues toward a career doing the research that helps improve and refine our practice of transformational development, so that we can demonstrate the superior power of a holistic framework of action that seamlessly relates the material, social and spiritual.

Finally, we need to engage the *secular development world with confidence*, instead of timidly sitting down at the table unconsciously apologizing for the fact that we are Christian. It is true that NGO coordinating committees and UN and secular development conversations are both western and secular in their nature. It is also true that they view Christian practitioners and agencies with suspicion. It is also true that sometimes we deserve this treatment.

But the secular development conversation is changing. In the last ten years, a shift has begun in terms of its thinking about religion and development. At first, there was recognition that religion or faith might be useful for development, an instrumental approach. Then, a slow awareness began to grow of the seemingly obvious fact that most of the poor with whom they work have deeply held religious beliefs and practices.

With Amartya Sen and his seminal book, *Development as Freedom,* the human wellbeing/human capability movement emerged as a dominant voice and included a validation of the role of religion as a source of values without which any development frame seeking human well being was impoverished (Sen 1999). Building on and extending Sen, community psychologist, Isaac Prilleltensky, added the psychological dimension to an understanding of what Prilleltensky calls human wellness and has inserted 'meaning and spirituality' into his wellness frame (Prilleltensky 2003).

Most recently, UK secular development studies researchers, Deneulin and Bano, have taken the brave step of calling for the secular development community to 'rewrite its script' when it comes to what they now call 'religion in development'. (Deneulin and Bano 2009). Deneulin and Bano wonder if it is time for a secular-religious dialogue on their common development concerns for the poor, social justice and seeking human well being.

In metaphorical terms, the secular development folk have just discovered the theological front yard of the religious traditions. They have wandered in and are intrigued by some of the plants and trees they find there. Rather than retreating behind the door of our house, fearful that these secular folks do not understand the content, rationality or revelation behind our development theology and practice, we need to go out and welcome them in. We need to recover our confidence as Christians, lost in face of the overwhelming coercive power of early modernity, and believe again that we have something to offer to the development conversations at the end of the day.

A Final Word

My final word is to the coming generation of practitioners who seek to pursue transformational development as a career, to the coming generation of theologians who wish to do their theology from below. Those of us who have been part of the evangelical conversation since the 1970s need you to take up the responsibility for this conversation. We need young holistic practitioners who can think and act theologically. We need mission agency and Christian NGO leaders who understand the importance of being authentically holistic and who can lead truly transformational organizations. We need researchers, PhD students, and professors who are willing to make this transformational development theory and practice their professional focus in life. The church needs to get better and better in terms of its understanding and practice of this thing we call transformational development.

Why? Because there are too many poor people in God's world. Because the poor deserve the best news we can share with them. Because God expects us to do as he did in creation: do good work. Because the gospel demands it.

Mission as Transformation and the Church

Vinay. K. Samuel

Introduction

The understanding and expression of Christian mission as transformation developed among evangelicals since the first Lausanne Conference on World Evangelization in 1974. A mission movement of theological, missiological reflection and practice evolved around that way of understanding and engaging in mission.

This chapter attempts to explore the impact of the mission as transformation movement on Christian institutions, particularly churches. It will study how local churches and denominations committed to a biblically faithful theology responded to this understanding of mission and the energy of the movement around it. It will suggest that the mission as transformation movement (MTM) had little impact on churches in the area of motivating and shaping the church's engagement with the world, and the cultures in which they existed and operated. This is particularly true of non-western churches. A weak engagement with the world means there is little evidence of the transforming power of the gospel in changing cultures and society.

The chapter will suggest an agenda for the future.

The Turn To The World

In exploring the impact of mission as transformation on Christian institutions/churches, we need to examine the central aspect of transformational mission: engagement with the world. Dr. Rene Padilla prepared a paper for Lausanne 74 and titled it 'Evangelism and the World'. [1] In this seminal and influential study he drew out the biblical perspective of the 'world' and asserted that "the world is claimed by the gospel," not abandoned by it. In my view this identified the 'turn to the world' that began among evangelicals concerned about relating the gospel to addressing poverty and bringing social change. The key leaders of this turn were Latin American evangelical leaders like Rene Padilla, Samuel Escobar and Orlando Costas.

---

[1] R. Padilla, 'Evangelism and the World', *Lausanne 1974 Documents* (www.lausanne.org).

Much of the Evangelism of the 1950s and '60s was shaped by a fixed gaze on heaven which in practice meant, "This world is not my home, I am just a passing through," words from a popular song sung at most evangelical gatherings, at least in the non-western world. It is not that evangelicals turned away from the world, but their relationship to the world was to declare the gospel to people – individuals and communities. The world was seen primarily as a world of human persons – with common features and needs. The need for salvation was universal and that need was addressed through proclaiming a universal gospel.

Many evangelicals did not take serious note of the cultures in which humans are embedded. The gospel is declared to people with a universal, need but their identities and worldviews are shaped by the cultures in which they live. These cultures have institutions, customs, traditions, artefacts, social systems and moral frameworks that regulate people's lives and from which they draw their meaning.

The mission as transformation movement, while affirming the necessity of proclaiming the good news of Christ's kingdom, the need to invite people to accept Christ's Lordship and become citizens of heaven, also stressed that believers continued to be part of the world in which they lived and must relate their faith to its culture.

Mission as Transformation and Churches

The understanding of transformational mission as addressing the spiritual, social and economic needs of persons and communities gained wide acceptance in the past three decades.[2] Its impact on churches is not significant. The wider acceptance of 'wholistic mission' would encourage and possibly enlarge existing social ministries of churches, but had little effect on motivating and enabling churches to engage with the cultures of which they are a part. They declare the truth to the world but are weak in engaging the world with the truth, believing their main mission task is to declare the truth.

Many non-Roman Catholic churches in the non-western world are committed to biblical authority and are evangelical in mission commitments. Yet in the areas of action for culture change their record is poor. Democracy is more than a political system. It is founded on values of equality, justice and rights of all persons. A study done by Freedom House, Washington D.C., U.S.A. of 24 democratizing countries in Africa (between 1972-2009) found that only in 6 countries did the church play a leading role in advocacy and action for democracy and human rights. More often than not it was the Roman Catholic Church which was at the forefront of action. In 8 countries evangelicals were implicated in anti-democratic activities. Dr. Tim Shah, in a paper presented at Yale University in March 2010, concludes from the study that, "the church

[2] Al Tizon shows this in his doctoral thesis, *Transformation after Lausanne* (Oxford: Regnum, 2008).

lacked institutional independence from power and did not have incentive or capacity to resist power; it lacked a theology of power."[3]

In Kenya, which I have some personal knowledge of, there is widespread acceptance of the understanding of mission as transformation promoted by courageous church leaders like Archbishop David Gitari.[4] The failure of the church to prevent the widespread ethnic violence in 2008-2009 and to engage vigorously with it during the upheaval demonstrated that deeply held ethnic animosities were not dealt with at any depth by churches which have experienced significant church growth. The lessons of Rwandan genocide, where enthusiastic church life did not translate into dealing with ethnic prejudice, appeared to have little influence.

Similar judgements can be made of churches in Asia.[5] There are always exceptions, but the gap between the acceptance of the rhetoric of mission as transformation and the practice of it by churches is still wide.

It is not just in the sphere of politics but also in areas of marriage, family life, gender relationships, human sexuality, corruption and economic performance that the record of the churches' engagement with the world, with the culture in which the church lives and operates, is weak. There is no lack of declaration about what the bible teaches about these areas of society, but little evidence of engaging with the systems, institutions, cultural drives of the world.

Mission as Transformation and Cultural Institutions

In his recent book *To Change the World: The Irony, Tragedy and Possibility of Christianity in the Late Modern World*[6] James Davison Hunter assesses the impact of evangelical action to change culture in the United States of America. He concludes that in spite of significant numbers, financial resources and vigorous engagement to change American culture to reflect Christian values and truths, the result is a failure to bring such change. It is a controversial conclusion and has produced a lively debate, but the polls do show the increasing spread of anti-biblical values in public life. Biblical values are increasingly labelled as oppressive and bigoted.

Hunter's key insight is that evangelicals have a view of culture, "that fails to take into account the nature of culture in its complexity and the factors that give it strength and resilience over time." In my view, this is also true of

---

[3] T. Shah, 'The Political Witness of African Churches: Separating Sheep from the Goats' (Paper presented at the Workshop on Church and Society in Africa, Yale University, World Christianity Initiative, March 27, 2010).

[4] Gideon Githega, *The Church as the Bulwark Against Authoritarianism* (Oxford: Regnum, 2002).

[5] D. Lumsdaine, *Evangelical Christianity and Democracy in Asia* (New York: Oxford University Press, 2009).

[6] J.D. Hunter, *To Change the World: The Irony, Tragedy and Possibility of Christianity in the Late Modern World* (New York: Oxford University Press, 2010), 18-31.

evangelicals in the non-western world. Hunter asserts that institutions are fundamental to cultural change as they produce, distribute and administer culture. He writes, "constituted by powerful ideals, truths and narratives, patterns of behaviours and relationship, social organisation and a wide range of resources, institutions are a social reality that are larger than the sum total of individuals that make them up." Today media institutions exert enormous influence on peoples' social and moral formation.

As institutions and networks are the more powerful instruments of change, it is important to examine the acceptance and role of the movement in Christian institutions, particularly the church.

Mission as Transformation and Mission Institutions

Mission Institutions that rapidly adopted the understanding of mission as transformation were evangelical relief and development agencies. In the 1970s and into the mid 1980s there was some resistance from the leadership of evangelical development agencies and significant push back from evangelical mission societies. Not being indigenous institutions but cross-cultural ones makes their relationship to the cultures in which they operate provisional rather than permanent, and can lead to resistance to a missiology that sees culture change as essential.

Evangelical relief and development agencies soon saw that the mission theology that best justified and strengthened their work in relief and development was the understanding of mission as transformation. World Vision International drew on the reflection of MTM networks and developed its own theology and understanding of transformational development. The appointment of one of the non-western founding architects of mission as transformation as President of one of the leading western evangelical development agencies confirms that MTM found its most effective home in evangelical development organisations.

Meanwhile, historic mission organisations primarily engaged in cross cultural mission were slow to receive and adopt transformational mission perspectives. Emerging missions, particularly from the non-western world, used the language of transformation but gave it their own content. Most of them have little place for engaging with the world. They combined evangelism with response to social and economic need among poor communities and regarded it as transformational mission. Church planting continued as the main and sometimes the only end of mission. In the past two decades historic western evangelical mission agencies were not uncomfortable with the language of mission as transformation, but their practice is largely to support proclamation of the gospel and church planting.

Transformational Mission and Mission Institutions: An Analysis

Two models of Christian engagement with the world shaped MTM in its formation. One was the model of cultural transformation, i.e. shaping society according to Christian values. John Stackhouse in his book *Making the Best of it*[7] identifies it as the model promoted by Kyperian Calvinism and Pope John Paul II. The other model is 'Holy Distinctiveness'. Stackhouse describes it as Christian community living in contradiction to the rest of society and offering an alternative way of life. John Yoder and Stanley Heurwas are leading scholars and activists of this view.

The movement of mission as transformation incorporated both models in an often uneasy tension. Several streams developed. One drew on an older tradition of the Christian mind, championed so ably by John Gresham Machen in the early twentieth century and later by John Stott. It affirmed the primacy of changing minds and hearts to bring culture change. Chuck Colson is the prominent contemporary leader of this approach in the United States. The consultation on 'The Churches' Response to Human Need' (Wheaton 1983) popularized evangelical engagement to address poverty, developing responses like emergency relief, community development, enterprise solutions to poverty, advocacy for national debt relief, fair trade and greater flow of aid from rich to poor nations. Relief and development efforts defined engagement with the world in this stream.

Another stream that developed is the gospel and culture track. This track focused on enculturation of the gospel in cultures and developing culturally appropriate and contextual tools and strategies for evangelism. There was little interest in cultural change except in that part of the movement that developed in the west under the leadership of Leslie Newbegin. James Hunter's assessment applies to this movement in the west. Its achievements in culture engagement are not substantial, certainly not in the United Kingdom. In the non-western world the stress was on cultural translation, rather than on cultural transformation, with the conviction that cultural translation will inevitably lead to culture change.

Prof. Lamin Sanneh's work[8] showed that the translation of the bible into indigenous languages of Africa resulted in preservation and recovery of cultures threatened by insensitive forces of modernity unleashed by colonial powers. Sanneh also contends that it provided the basis for dealing with the forces of modernity and building modern societies and states. However, it is also true that while strongly affirming the translatability of the gospel to every indigenous culture churches have failed to resist cultural forces that are manifestly unjust and oppressive. Fuelled by cultural prejudices and stereotypes, such movements have destabilized and even destroyed families and

[7] J. Stackhouse, *Making the Best of It: Following Christ in the Real World* (New York: Oxford University Press, 2008), 5.

[8] L. Sanneh, *Translating the Message: The Missionary Impact on Culture* (Maryknoll, NY: Orbis,1989).

communities. Churches may have fought colonial oppression in several nations but have been found incapable of initiating cultural transformation in those contexts. Corrupt governance, caste, tribal and ethnic conflict and varieties of social oppression continue to be deeply embedded in cultures and exert dominating influence. The rhetoric of recovering, protecting and promoting traditional cultural identities often masks the unwillingness of the church to engage in cultural transformation. There are exceptions to this picture but the overall reality is one of failure to engage.

One of the key assumptions of MTM is the agency attributed to individuals and faith communities. It is assumed that as primary agents of transformation, individuals and communities would be empowered by a wholistic understanding of mission, by a piety shaped by biblical discipleship and the experience of spiritual empowerment by the Holy Spirit. That empowerment would lead to engaging the world and initiating transformation. The critically important role of cultural institutions in culture change was not taken into consideration. In the recent past reflections on power from a biblical and missiological perspective suggests a greater awareness of the role of institutions and cultural systems of power. In time it is hoped this will translate to mission strategy and action.

The implicit ecclesiologies of MTM are another possible cause for its inability to impact the church. A long tradition among the evangelicals sees mission as the bloodstream of the church. 'The church exists by mission' is stressed. This defines the church in mission terms. In practice it means that any group in mission is an ecclesial entity. The church as God's chosen kingdom presence in the world, the body of the Lord Jesus Christ living its life in the world institutionally, its life ordered by a revealed faith, guarded by a community of obedient disciples, is God's primary agent for claiming the world for Christ. Such a view of the church did not have a significant influence on MTM. The church is the institution that is called to be in the world and not of it. It prays daily "Your kingdom come on earth as in heaven", lives out its life seeking God's will for the world. It engages with the world to see God's will come, in however provisional fashion and awaits its consummation.

Another key understanding that shaped MTM is the view that social transformation is effected from bottom up. Most mission action for social change was invested in empowering the poor.[9] Theological basis for such a view was the missiological conviction of the preferential option for the poor. It was based on biblical themes of God's relationship to the poor but was also shaped by a social analytical framework of centre and periphery. Space does not permit an extended analysis of this approach theologically, but the following may be noted. In spite of four decades of significant engagement in empowering the poor by many religious and non-religious actors, large scale social transformation has eluded us, though there are some fine examples of

---

[9] *Transformation: An International Journal of Holistic Mission Studies*, Oxford.

localized social change. It is also worth noting that eminent development scholars happen to be arriving at similar conclusions.

The priority to empower the poor at the heart of MTM facilitates the development of movements and networks for social change. It does not develop institutions from bottom up as institutions are generally created from the top. The theology and strategy of MTM did not see the significance of institutions and found the institutional nature of churches irrelevant and often an impediment to mission action. Churches, particularly large bodies like church denominations, have a strong institutional character. They are led by leaders but run by bureaucracies whose default position is maintaining and growing the institution's activities by competent and effective management of its assets and resources. Bureaucracies are wary of movements and do not know how to provide space for movements and harness their energy. It is here the role of networks, particularly the networks of elites is critical. Elites know how to harness networks and movements and embed them in institutions. It means adding a top down dimension to the bottom up one if MTM is to be embedded in church institutions and become a resource to churches. Our ecclesiologies should embrace both – bottom up and top down.

The experience of major evangelical relief and development agencies illustrates the above contention. In the past two decades these agencies have turned to elites from the corporate world of business and government to fill their senior executive positions replacing seminary / bible college trained leaders (based on the untested assumption that business leaders can pick up theology quicker than seminary trained leaders can pick up institutional leadership and management skills!). This is not just the corporatization of evangelical development agencies but also recognition that elites are trained and equipped to operate in networks and run institutions which engage with the world. They are also essential to build substantial institutions which scale up rapidly and become a presence that the world notices and is open to engage with.

Church bureaucracies are a different matter particularly in the non-western world. They are often a mirror image of their government bureaucracies with all the attendant weaknesses.

Mission as Transformation and churches: An Agenda for the Future

The main home today of MTM is the evangelical relief and development organization. The movement needs to be more deeply involved in churches, particularly church denominations in the rapidly growing churches of the global south. That will enable it to deepen and mature to meet the challenges of fast changing societies.

There is need to develop theologies of culture that are biblically faithful and draw on the significant research on culture available to us today. James Hunter writes "Culture is first and foremost a normative order by which we comprehend others, the larger world and ourselves and through which we individually and collectively order our experience." He asserts "Culture is a system of truth claims and moral obligations."[10] A biblically faithful approach and understanding of culture must be developed in the non-western world. Significant work is being done in the west but much of it is not translatable to non-western contexts yet.

South Africa illustrates the urgency of the need. The strong drive to recover and privilege African traditions and traditional customs in church life is driving individuals, local churches and denominations to perform traditional ceremonies and engage in traditional social practices without adequately interrogating them against biblical norms. Any suggestion that such an interrogation is necessary is often dismissed as a western neo-colonial opinion. In the past two years of my involvement in South Africa, I am surprised to find even biblically faithful Christians intimidated by this aggressive cultural agenda and reluctant to challenge it. It is encouraging to see a different picture in Nigeria. The challenge needs to be strengthened by carefully thought through biblical and theological reflection.

There is need to develop biblical approaches to understanding institutions. Institutions use cultural capital as power and a key component of dealing with institutions is through developing theologies of power. A biblical understanding of social order that is sensitive to the way social order developed and is being shaped in the non-western world is a critical need.

Another need is to revisit the implicit social analysis in mission as transformation theologies. Terms like agency, empowerment, participation, freedom, capability, equity, and rights are at the heart of approaches to social change [11] and are used regularly by those reflecting on mission as transformation. Much of the analysis assumes that systems and institutions are part of the oppressive centre and see change coming only from the periphery.

Most churches in the non-western world rarely see themselves as part of the periphery. They eagerly seek to relate to the centre, align with it and do not have the tools to influence it, even if they have the will. The elites who belong to these churches are part of the centre and are not discipled and equipped to address the centre with kingdom values and convictions. We need to move from the ideological cage of received social analysis and examine our societies and cultures afresh.

John Stackhouse[12] asserts that in engaging with the world we need to recover Christian Realism. He suggests Christian realism means learning about the world from the world, i.e. take its self description seriously and not just look at the world through what the bible says about it. We must ensure a biblically

---

[10] J. D. Hunter, *To Change the World: The Irony, Tragedy and Possibility of Christianity in the Late Modern World* (New York: Oxford University Press, 2010), 33.

[11] S. Alkire, *Valuing Freedoms: Sen's Capability Approach and Poverty Reduction* (New York: Oxford University Press, 2002).

[12] J. Stackhouse, *Making the Best of It: Following Christ in the Real World* (New York: Oxford University Press, 2008), 5.

informed mind and worldview but develop an epistemic humility to understand how the world describes itself, aware that cultures are rapidly changing.

We must also be aware that the evil one blinds people to the real state of their situation and God is active in all cultures and biblical revelation provides us tools to identify God's providential action in cultures.

Conclusion

The church, particularly in the non-western world, is still largely faithful to the authority and teaching of the bible. It is committed to the uniqueness of Christ and the necessity of sharing the gospel. It needs to turn much more to the world; to the cultures in which it is placed and engage with them. The missiological resources of MTM are an essential resource for such engagement.

THE LOCAL CHURCH, TRANSFORMING COMMUNITY

Tulo Raistrick

Introduction: the local church at the heart of holistic mission

In 2001, 140 evangelical social action practitioners, church leaders and theologians came together in Oxford, England, to discuss holistic mission, or what they termed, integral mission. This meeting launched the Micah Network and approved a declaration – the Micah Declaration on Integral Mission – that placed the local church at the heart of what it means to do holistic mission. They declared:

> God by his grace has given local churches the task of integral mission. The future of integral mission is in planting and enabling local churches to transform the communities of which they are part. Churches as caring and inclusive communities are at the heart of what it means to do integral mission.[1]

The proceedings of the Oxford meeting were edited by Tim Chester and published in a book entitled *Justice, Mercy and Humility: Integral Mission and the poor.* In unpacking the declaration, Rene Padilla stated that:

> One of the greatest challenges we Christians have at the threshold of the third millennium is the articulation and practical implementation of an ecclesiology that views the local church, and particularly the church of the poor, as the primary agent of holistic mission.[2]

In his introduction, Tim Chester wrote that,

> At the heart of integral mission is the local church… The New Testament does not describe development projects or, for that matter, evangelistic initiatives. Its focus is on Christian communities, which are to be distinctive, caring and inclusive. Integral mission is about the church being the church. There can be no sustainable Christian development that is distinctly Christian without sustainable Christian communities. This means that often the planting of churches that are committed to the inclusion of the poor must be at the heart of integral mission.[3]

---

[1] 'The Micah Declaration on Integral Mission' (September 2001). See http://www.micahnetwork.org/en/integral-mission/micah-declaration.

[2] Tim Chester (ed.), *Justice, Mercy and Humility: Integral Mission and the Poor* (Carlisle, UK: Paternoster Press, 2002), 8.

[3] Chester, *Justice, Mercy and Humility*, 7-8.

And in the same volume Donald Mtetemala, who was then the Anglican Archbishop of Tanzania, stated that "the future for integral mission must be in the enabling of local churches so that they can serve as instruments to transform the communities around them."[4]

But why this emphasis on the local church? What is it about the *ecclesia*, the local gathering of Christian believers, that makes it so fundamental to holistic mission? Why is the local church, and not inspired individuals, or Christian para-church organisations, or the universal body of Christ, the heart of holistic mission?

The role of the local church in transforming relationships

Holistic mission is fundamentally about restoring relationships – with oneself, with others, with God and with creation. Indeed, broken relationships are at the root of poverty, for poverty is the result of a social and structural legacy of broken relationships with God, damaged understanding of self, unjust relationships between people, and exploitative relationships with the environment. The local church is at the heart of transforming these relationships.

Transforming relationships with others

The local church is called to be a caring, inclusive and distinctive community of reconciliation reaching out in love to the world. Jesus Christ, through his death and resurrection, brought into being communities of disciples that love and care for each other and that together love and care for the society where they are placed. They are communities of healing and restoration. It is in and through the communal living of Jesus' disciples in the power of the Holy Spirit that powerless, broken and vulnerable people are made whole. They are welcomed into a community of love and care.

The underlying values base of the local church is grounded in love for God and love for one's neighbour, with a very strong ethic of sacrificial love and compassionate service of others. The local church may struggle at times to live up to this, but we should be wary of being unduly sceptical. Research conducted by George Barna in the USA found that those who expressed and lived out a strong commitment to biblical discipleship lived lives differently from the prevailing culture. They were twice as likely to help people in need as those with little or no faith.[5]

The local church offers the opportunity for people to meet and worship together across social, cultural and economic divides, and to be enriched and transformed as a result. The rich are often challenged to re-evaluate their wealth

[4] Chester, *Justice, Mercy and Humility*, 145.

[5] Ronald J. Sider, *The Scandal of the Evangelical Conscience: Why Are Christians Living Just Like the Rest of the World?* (Grand Rapids: Baker Books, 2005), 128.

in the light of their poorer brothers and sisters in faith, and to offer up their resources and skills for the good of others. The poor are affirmed as they discover they too are not without assets, assets of faith and resilience that others can learn and gain from.

The local church is a profound context for holistic mission because it is made up of people, drawn together by faith, that have to work at living together and loving one another on a daily basis. They are not paid to be together, nor can they live in abstract isolation from one another. The local church brings people together to work at restoring relationship, people who are like the community from which they come, but people who are at the same time being transformed by the Holy Spirit into God's people. The church, in modelling reconciliation and community, creates a foretaste of the heavenly community. "When it is at its best, the church is a sign, a witness to the kingdom of God breaking into the world."[6] Just as Israel was meant to model to the world what human society should be under God so the church is now called to do the same. "The church does not claim to possess all truth and righteousness, but rather to point the world to the truly righteous one who is the truth, namely, Jesus Christ. And in that process of directing the world to Jesus Christ, the church herself is drawn into a deeper understanding of, and obedience to, the same Jesus."[7]

The local church also points to an important aspect of relationships. It is a body that reflects both the local and yet globally interconnected nature of our existence. We are connected to those we have never met, our actions have consequences on those thousands of miles away, through, for example, how we shop, how we treat the environment, and how we respond to government international policies. The local church expresses this in a profound and deeper way, for it gathers together local believers as part of the one, worldwide body of the church. We are one family, one people, with a responsibility of care and love for one another, whether next door or on a different continent.

Transforming relationships with God

For mission to be holistic, relationships with God need to be part of the focus of transformation. But how we make this our focus is of crucial importance. 1 Peter 3:15 encourages us to "always be prepared to give an answer to everyone who asks you to give a reason for the hope that you have." Commenting on this verse, Jim Wallis noted that all too often "evangelism becomes a special activity awkwardly conducted… instead of being a simple testimony rising out of a community whose life together invites questions from the surrounding society. When the life of the church no longer raises questions, evangelism degenerates."[8]

---

[6] Bryant L. Myers, *Walking with the Poor: Principles and Practices of Transformational Development* (Maryknoll, NYT: Orbis Books, 1999), 37-8.

[7] Howard Peskett and Vinoth Ramachandra, *The Message of Mission* (Leicester: IVP, 2003), 197.

[8] Jim Wallis, *A Call to Conversion* (Tring: Lion, 1981), 29.

It is the local church that can best provide the context in which questions are raised, and the context in which the gospel can be understood. It is true for everyone that actions are always witnessing to something, they are always subject to interpretation and to people attaching a meaning or explanation to them. As Myers points out, "we are always witnesses to something. The only question is to what or to whom? ... When water is found in a desert, or children live who would normally die, an explanation is demanded by the community."[9] Rooting holistic mission in the life of the local church means that the community are far more likely to interpret the action as connected to faith. After all, the main difference between the local believers and their neighbours is that of belief. It also means that there are local believers on hand to answer the questions raised and to explain their actions in language and idioms much more earthed in the local context. The community are more likely to connect Christian action to Christian faith; the acting Christians are more likely to be able to respond to questions prompted by their acts in ways that the community can understand and relate to. The local church thus provides a rich context within which relationship with God can be explored and restored. Thus the local church provides the context within which both Christian compassion and proclamation can be understood.

In addition, as compared with other development actors, the spiritual dynamic comes much more naturally to the local church. They are a people, first and foremost, drawn together by their faith in God and desire to worship him. Out of this springs their motivation to serve others, to pray, to witness. Faith in Christ is the essence of who they are. As a result, it is difficult for them to separate the 'spiritual' from the 'physical' in their service within the community, much to the frustration of secular donors! The one naturally permeates the other, leading to a much more holistic approach to mission. It is the local church that prays for and supports the sick, that buries the dead with dignity and purpose, and that cares for the bereaved, especially the widowed and orphaned. Separating the physical from the spiritual becomes impossible.

Transforming relationship with, and understanding of, self

Francis Njoroge, co-author of Umoja and a pioneer in envisioning and equipping local churches to mobilise their communities in addressing poverty, speaks with communities about "poverty being in the mind, not in the pocket."[10] It is a phrase that gets repeated by communities in many parts of Africa where he has worked, for it resonates with their experience. Part of the dynamic of poverty is that it robs people of hope – and with that self-esteem, self-worth and initiative. In turn, the loss of those attitudes leads to a downward

---

[9] Myers, *Walking with the Poor*, 207.

[10] *Umoja* is a series of training guides published by Tearfund to facilitate church and community mobilisation. For more information, see http://tilz.tearfund.org/Churches/Umoja.

spiral into yet deeper poverty. As people begin to see their lives in fatalistic terms, their ability and desire to work for positive change becomes less.

Local churches can play a key role in turning around such mistaken views of worth, giving people an understanding of their true identity as valued people, made in God's image with gifts, skills, character and resources that can be used for good and that are rooted in hope for the future. The local church is uniquely placed to bring about such a radical and holistic understanding of self because it proclaims the gospel message rooted within a local community of faith.

The gospel transforms understanding of self for it communicates hope and provides meaning for life. In proclaiming a message of liberation for those whose daily experience is one of slavery to poverty and slavery to the powerful, the gospel provides a foretaste of the full and true liberation that will be their's in life to come. In proclaiming a message of grace to those who experience exclusion on grounds of status, education, wealth, ethnicity, age or gender, the gospel that is open to all is an amazing message of acceptance, love, dignity and worth. In proclaiming a message of the incarnate, crucified and risen Lord to those who experience overwhelming despair and suffering, the gospel is a message of God's presence and ultimate victory. The gospel is life-giving, not only in terms of its eternal implications, but also in the here and now. In discovering God's love in the midst of suffering and despair, people discover that life is worth living, and will often keep alive when without hope they would die. Research has found that having a reason to live amongst those with AIDS can make a huge positive contribution to their health, physically and emotionally.[11]

It is the local church that ensures that the gospel is not communicated as some disembodied truth, but is rooted within the context of the community and the issues it faces. It is a community that is rooted in local history and culture, and yet able, in the light of the gospel, to stand back and challenge. Indeed, this is familiar territory for the local church, which is often the only institution in many communities that is actively wrestling with issues of values and worldview change. And in doing so it provides a community of support and encouragement to those who then do seek change.

Kathy Galloway brings an interesting sociological perspective on the role the local church can play in bringing about such values and worldview change:

> Local churches have a strong symbolic framework which is part of its ongoing life. Week by week, church members meet, remind themselves who they are, take an audit of their personal and corporate failures and achievements, assume responsibility for their failures (confession), are released from being defined by their failures, give thanks for good things, intentionally call to mind the needs and suffering of others, and commit themselves in caring ways for the realisation of

---

[11] Stan Nussbaum (ed.), *The Contribution of Christian Congregations to the Battle with HIV/AIDS at the Community Level: A seven-country research report prepared for the Summer Mission Briefing at the Oxford Centre for Mission Studies 7-9 June 2005* (Oxford: Global Mapping International, 2003), 25.

> the vision... Many secular organisations would be desperate for these rich historical, practical and symbolic resources which are a part of any church.[12]

Transforming relationships with creation

The local church is well placed to transform people's fourth axis of relationship – that with Creation. In transforming relationships with self, others and God, important foundations are laid for an approach to the environment that is sustainable, just and caring. The local church is in a place to encourage good stewardship of resources, to challenge exploitative use of the environment, to value and celebrate the beauty of the created world. In doing so, it helps people re-discover one of God's original purposes for humankind – the caring and tending of the world he has made.[13]

The local church as the long-term presence, catalyst and sustainer of holistic mission

The local church helps to transform relationships. It is central to holistic mission for other reasons too.

It is a long term presence in the community

Development and mission agencies need to regularly remind themselves that in many parts of the world the local church is already present as a transformed and transformative community living among the poor, for they usually are the poor too, already being used by God in his purposes of restoration and transformation, long before the external agencies arrive. The local church is also likely to remain in the community much longer. A Kenyan colleague living in the UK said to me: "Whenever I return to my home village, I can never be sure that the NGO (non-governmental agency) will still be there, but I know the church will always be there."

Local churches are present in some of the most difficult and isolated contexts, often in places few others can get to. In northern Uganda, for example, where more than 90 per cent of the population have been displaced, the local church is one of the few community structures which still functions – even in displacement camps.[14] And in Burma, when Cyclone Nargis hit in May 2008 with such devastating effect, it was 4,500 local churches who provided emergency supplies to tens of thousands of survivors in the immediate

---

[12] Kathy Galloway, *Starting Where We Are: Liberation Theology in Practice* (Glasgow: Wild Goose Publications, 1998), 15.

[13] Gen. 1:26-8.

[14] Seren Boyd, *In the Thick of It: Why the Church is an Essential Partner for Sustainable Development in the World's Poorest Countries* (London: Tearfund, 2009), 12.

aftermath. In contrast, it took weeks for some foreign aid workers to reach the worst-hit areas.[15]

The local church is present 24 hours a day, every day. It is part of the community. As the Archbishop of York put it: "The church does not drive in to places of strife in the morning and leave before the lights go down. The church remains as part of the community and where there is hurt, the church shares that hurt, is part of it and is hence uniquely placed to be part of the solution."[16]

It is able to organise and mobilise people for change

In many parts of the world, local churches are one of the most functional structures in their communities, used to bringing people together regularly, communicating and educating, sharing common ideals, raising internal resources, and encouraging people to work collectively. "Churches, even on a small scale, are used to making things happen."[17]

They also have the ability to mobilise large numbers of people. The underlying values base of the local church is grounded in love for God and love for one's neighbour, with a strong ethic of sacrificial love and compassionate service of others. This translates into a willingness to actively engage with the poor and marginalised. In Zimbabwe, for example, over 20,000 local churches run at least one HIV and AIDS related programme.[18] In Namibia, 87% of churches had initiated some kind of response to HIV and AIDS.[19] And in Wales, a recent audit found that more than 42,000 volunteers from different faith groups did 80,000 hours' community work each week. More than 98 per cent of these faith groups were Christian.[20]

And once church members are mobilised their work tends to be marked by dedication, persistence, loyalty and compassion.[21] Their hope in a better future gives them the energy to work for a better present, and because it is faith, rather than external resources, that tend to be their primary motivation for action, they will find ways of continuing to care and serve those in need in their community even when funds dry up.

---

[15] Boyd, *In the Thick of It*, 12.

[16] Archbishop of York Dr John Sentamu, Westminster Central Hall, London, 11 September 2008 quoted in Boyd, *In the Thick of It*, 7.

[17] Galloway, *Starting Where We Are*, 15.

[18] Nussbaum, *The Contribution of Christian Congregations to the Battle with HIV/AIDS*, 32.

[19] A Bowerman and M Amuyunzu-Nyamongom, *The Christian Distinctiveness in the Response to HIV and AIDS in Africa: Lessons for Action* (London: Tearfund, 2006).

[20] Gweini, *Faith in Wales: Counting for Communities* (Evangelical Alliance Wales, 2008), 6.

[21] Nussbaum, *The Contribution of Christian Congregations to the Battle with HIV/AIDS*, 53.

It is what makes any form of transformation both Christian and sustainable

If in holistic mission, we long to see lives transformed physically, spiritually, economically and socially, and relationships of all kind restored, we cannot hope for such change to be sustainable without the presence of a healthy, vibrant local church. As Bryant Myers puts it:

> A church full of life and love, working for the good of the community in which God has placed it, is the proper end of mission. Transformational development that does not work towards such a church is neither sustainable nor Christian... Any vision of a better human future that is Christian must include a vibrant, growing, living Christian community that is eagerly and joyfully serving God and the community. It is impossible to imagine a transforming community without a transforming church in its midst.[22]

Challenging Questions and Contexts

Recognising the central role of the local church in holistic mission, however, raises significant questions. What about the many churches who fail to live up to the ideals of holistic mission? What about the church's unease with dealing with issues of stigma around HIV? What about disaster contexts, and contexts where the local church is not present at all? What role can the local church play in speaking up for justice? What about the role of Christian NGOs?

Churches that fail to live up to the ideals of holistic mission

Churches struggle with living out holistic mission around the world. For those who are evangelical the challenge is often one of dualistic thinking. They want to separate the spiritual and physical aspects of life with the church's role seen as working exclusively in the spiritual realm. Issues of personal holiness and evangelism are focussed on, and involvement in social and community issues are seen as a distraction or of being of secondary importance. This, however, is changing, and there is a growing consensus reflected in the Lausanne Movement and the World Evangelical Fellowship that it is a holistic gospel that needs to be lived and preached.

How churches reach out to their communities raises further issues. Often churches adopt paternalistic welfare models, doing things *for* communities, rather than *with* them, treating people as passive recipients of their compassion rather than as co-workers involved in a common task. Such approaches may help meet immediate need, but in the long-term may simply reinforce dependency. Such paternalism is strengthened by the autocratic style of many church leaders, who may view themselves as the ultimate authority within the church on all matters. Such attitudes make participation in decision-making and empowerment through shared action very difficult. However, where senior church leaders model facilitative and servant-hearted leadership, remarkable

[22] Myers, *Walking with the Poor*, 39, 115.

change begins to happen. The Pentecostal Assemblies of God in Uganda, for example, is witnessing extraordinary change in their communities as church pastors begin to adopt the facilitative attitudes and approach of their senior leaders. Change can also happen from the bottom-up, as local churches' own empowerment challenges district and national level hierarchical church structures.

Churches that struggle with stigma and discrimination

Around the issue of HIV and AIDS, local churches have sometimes been guilty of feeding stigma by portraying HIV as the wages of sexual sin and, at worst, shunning HIV-affected people. Yet, as we have already seen, the local church is at the forefront of the fight against AIDS in many parts of the world through its care programmes. Increasingly, it is beginning to play an important role in ending stigma, as church members extend the hand of friendship and support to those, both within and beyond the church, affected by HIV. Church leaders are proving powerful advocates for change by promoting acceptance and showing true leadership by, for example, taking an HIV test, and by being open about their status if they are HIV positive.[23]

Churches in disaster contexts

When natural disasters or conflict-based disasters occur in a community, significant challenges can arise for local churches. They themselves will be significantly affected by the disaster, and as they seek to respond, they risk being overwhelmed both by the pastoral demands of supporting the bereaved and traumatised and burying the dead, and meeting the physical needs of the community through helping to distribute food or health supplies.

However, local churches can still be key in ensuring a holistic response in such contexts. Before disasters occur, they can play an essential role in gathering data and informing people. For example, local churches played an important role in providing information about the southern Africa crisis of 2002-3, and in Zimbabwe during 2008-9, the government's suppression of information meant that the church was one of the few institutions capable of gathering and passing on information to national levels. During disasters, churches are well placed to provide the relational support – prayer, pastoral care, hospitality, acknowledgement and care of people's inner hurt and grief – that is often lacking in NGO and INGO interventions. NGOs and INGOs often don't have the time to meet the pastoral and social needs of beneficiaries, and thus, the local church can play a very important complementary role in helping

[23] For example, INERELA+, the International Network of Religious Leaders living with or personally affected by HIV and AIDS, is having a huge impact by enabling church pastors who are HIV+ to share their stories and challenge stigma through conversation and discussion with other church leaders.

to make situations "more human", softening much of the inevitably harsh aspects of relief responses. This humane touch cannot be regarded as a luxury, but as being a critical element in the physical as well as emotional and spiritual well-being of traumatised communities. In northern Uganda, for example, local churches have offered hospitality, prayer support and a listening service to many internally displaced people.

Contexts where there is no church

There are some contexts where due to persecution or cultural resistance, there is no formal church. There may be scattered individual believers, but there are few opportunities for gathering together. There are other contexts where it may be legal for churches to exist, but not for them to reach out, whether in service or proclamation, to non-Christians. In such contexts, holistic mission of any kind is very difficult. However, the long-term goal of seeing sustainable Christian communities established who can be free to fully express the holistic nature of the gospel is one that many indigenous believers and staff of international Christian NGOs share and work towards.

Churches speaking up for justice

Many local churches are often reticent in speaking up for justice, advocating on behalf of the poor and marginalised. Sometimes this is due to their feelings of vulnerability in contexts of political or religious oppression, sometimes because of a theological understanding of submission to those in authority that avoids challenging political powers, and sometimes because the church is itself compromised and unwilling to speak out.

However, local churches can play a crucial role in this key aspect of holistic mission. They have the ability to exert influence on local issues and local power-brokers. In Zambia, for example, local churches were encouraged to challenge the provision of services at local government level, and succeeded in lobbying MPs to get essential roads constructed. They have the ability to bring injustices to light. During the Sudan government's illegal bombing raids of the south in the early 2000s, local churches reported on bombing incidents through their church structures up to national level. The information gathered was regarded as more accurate and reliable than even that of the CIA, and provided the basis for the concerted lobbying that led to UN resolutions on Sudan that helped to enforce a more effective cease-fire. And they can mobilise others. In one community in Tanzania, the local church helped the community to identify that one of the causes of their village's poverty was the corrupt village head-man, who had misappropriated the community's development fund. The community promptly went down to the man's house, and refused to leave until he delivered on promises to pay the community back!

The role of Christian NGOs

Viewing the local church as central to holistic mission does not mean that there is no place for the Christian NGO. Christian NGOs play a crucial role. They bring unique experience and expertise to bear on specific areas of Christian discipleship and development, often with dedicated staff who have capacity to develop and bring to fruition major projects and initiatives. They can work in a concerted way across a number of communities, and can advocate and bring about change at a regional or national level, in a way that certainly individual local churches, working in isolation from one another, could not achieve. And they can be focused on specific issues, channelling passion, energy and vision into addressing one specific issue or seizing one particular opportunity.

The challenge for local churches and NGOs alike is to build relationships of mutuality, where the local church is respected and valued for its relationships, local knowledge, faith, commitment, and the context it provides of worship, discipleship and mission, and where Christian NGOs are respected and valued for their experience, expertise, capacity and focus. Too often the relationship is lop-sided towards those with the financial and material resources (usually the NGO), and away from those who bring other strengths. A process of valuing all that God has entrusted us with – including, but not limiting it to, financial or material resources – is a first step in building confidence and respect in the work of holistic mission.

A model of local church holistic mission

This chapter has explored in broad terms the central place of the local church in holistic mission. How the church expresses this role will vary from church to church and context to context.

One way that it is expressing this role in many parts of the world and becoming more holistic in its outlook and practice is through an approach known as church and community mobilisation. A local church begins to study the bible together, seeing what it has to say to each member. Studies explore in particular the role of the church in caring for the poor and marginalised, and also look at the resources that God has given them as a church. The act of group bible study can be a radical and dynamic act in itself. For many church members, discussing and applying the bible for themselves, rather than being taught in a top-down, didactic manner from the pulpit, can be a liberating experience, and one that places the power of God's word literally into the hands of ordinary people. Through bible studies church members begin to discover that in listening to God's word and listening to one another, profound new insights are gained and vision and energy is released. Confidence is gained, and people begin to believe that just as Jesus used the meagre resources of one young boy's five loaves and two fish to feed the multitudes, so he can use their resources too.

Once enthused and energised, the local church begins the process of listening to the community. In many rural communities, this happens by bringing the whole community together. By discussion, reflection, challenge and analysis, the community as a whole are helped to identify the issues and needs in their community, and what resources they themselves already have. All too frequently, the church is known for proclaiming answers, and often to questions the community is not asking. Radically, as churches begin to listen to their communities, and ask them what they think and what could be done together, the relationship dynamic dramatically changes. The church comes to value and appreciate the community; the community begins to see the church as a caring community, motivated by love, and not driven by a need to swell its numbers and income. In North Sudan, for example, a church that had been prohibited from building a church building for years began listening to, and working with, the community. The local Imam was so impressed by the unconditional nature of the Christians' love that he personally lobbied the government until permission was granted for a new church building! Relationships also improve in other ways too. As community members begin to listen to one another, they come to appreciate and value one another more. Respect for women and other often excluded and marginalised groups are heard and valued.

Listening and analysis lead to the work of imagining a better future and planning for action. Change comes to be seen as possible. Fatalistic attitudes are left behind as churches and communities begin to use their resources to do such things as build classrooms and health clinics, start income generation projects, improve water access, and increase food production. Confidence grows to challenge injustice at local and district levels. Confidence also grows to work with others as equals, not dependents. In Nazareth in Ethiopia, for example, churches and communities lobbied successfully to ensure that all subsequent NGO interventions in their community should be focused on promoting self-reliance, not hand-outs.

This approach of church and community mobilisation is having a profound impact on churches and communities all over the world, and is a great example of why the local church is so central to the work of holistic mission. The local church is present and sustainable, and fundamentally it provides the context where relationships with God, others and self can be restored, the heart of holistic mission.

Christian NGOs and Their Role in Holistic Mission

Glenn Miles and Ian de Villiers

That part of Christianity that serves the poor with dedication and without distinction has been a feature that has attracted impartial observers over centuries as well as allowing the church to practice its mandate to a transformational holistic mission. This chapter sets out to understand further how that service to the poor has been developed through Christian non-governmental organisations (CNGOs) in recent years, and how these Christian NGOs have and are playing critical roles both in development and providing exemplary models of holistic mission. Having recognised this, we go on to consider the many issues that face Christian NGOs today as they stand at an interface between secular development agendas and Christian mission. Christian mission asks questions of CNGOs as to whether they are simply picking up the secular development agenda with some kind of religious face; secular development asks – at its extreme – if CNGOs are Trojan horses for proselytism, or perhaps neo-colonialism, or if CNGO work is 'all heart and no head'. Finally we look at how Christian NGOs can face the challenges of the future, looking particularly at how they can maintain Christian identities, and continue to build their legitimacy, capacities and accountability.

Holistic mission itself is discussed carefully in other chapters in this book and elsewhere[1] and so we do not further explore this except some specific aspects necessary to the question. The foundation we build on is that Christians are called to express God's love to all his Creation – physically, socially, and spiritually.

The Identity of CNGOs

Some very early roots in the development of CNGOs occur in early Acts, when the seven were chosen to administer and look after the widows. Roman commentator Tertullian noted the openness of Christians to the poor and marginalised of the day; by the third century after Christ and Marcus Aurelius' time (Bremmer 2007), Christian responses were clearly not just to Christians but also serving plague victims without discrimination. Since then the number

---

[1] According to the 'Integral Mission Declaration' (which can be found in full at http://www.micahnetwork.org/en/integral-mission/micah-declaration).

of CNGOs has mushroomed. Three recent phases could include, first, the development of health and education programmes that preceded or followed global colonisation, second, a wave after the second world and Korean wars (notably the foundation of probably the largest of the CNGOs, World Vision), and third, another in the 1990s, due to the AIDS epidemic; altogether there are several thousand CNGOs today – International Bulletin of Mission Research (2010) reckoned on 28000 Christian 'service agencies' (not including foreign missions). CNGOs have a remarkably distinguished track record as well as a huge reach, as these several thousand agencies have natural partners in the 5 million church congregations spread across the world, as will be explored below.

A CNGO just like any other NGO, or, in fact, any development agency is concerned with social goals external to itself (compared with a business, that has a goal to make profit for itself). Whilst that is essential to the altruistic nature of serving the poor and is one of the key attractions to other agencies of development, it also means that CNGOs have a perpetual problem of legitimacy because they take this trusteeship, a responsibility for fixing other people's problems, without always having been asked to do so. The question is whether they are intent on creating people and communities "who see themselves as stewards of creation and do not live for themselves but for others; persons who are willing to fulfil their God-given vocation in the world and to receive and to give love; persons who 'hunger and thirst for justice' and who are 'peacemakers' (Mt. 5:6, 9)" (Padilla 2005, 16). Foster (2004) makes a distinction between a community-based organisation (CBO) and an NGO; the CBO is a local organisation different from an NGO in that it does not employ staff. An NGO may typically be responsible to a wider group than either a congregation or CBO; both may receive external funding. In practice, CNGOs take on many sizes and forms: some are focused on training and capacity building for local partners, some are catalysed by mission agencies; others are branches of large international NGOs; some are national or local, set up by a pastor or a group from a church. They range from purely volunteer staff and tiny budgets to having thousands of staff with billion dollar budgets. Their challenges are very different in relation to their degrees of legitimacy, accountability, and technical, financial and people capacity.

Woolnough (2008) helpfully suggests four distinctives of CNGOS, including first, an aim that includes spiritual transformation as well as physical, emotional or economic change; second, partnership with local churches and Christians; third, a recognition that 'our battles are spiritual battles'; and fourth, that in serving the poor, 'we will listen to the poor'. The aim to include spiritual transformation is problematic, for reasons outlined below, which means that many CNGOs are unable to have it as a stated aim of their work, and certainly not as project goals. However, recognizing the Christian understanding of people as having a spiritual nature remains. The potential of partnerships with congregations is a point of interest for secular development agencies, craving the reach of those five million congregations. Listening to the poor certainly should be a feature of Christian NGOs as they responsibly act on their trusteeship of social goals for those poor. This has been increasingly recognized too in the secular agenda, following Robert Chambers and others' work in recent years, with participation – at the least a nominal listening to the poor – firmly integrated into development policies and practices. Woolnough's third goal, recognizing poverty as being part of a spiritual battle, is again not unique to a Christian understanding of poverty, but a Christian framing will provide distinct tools in addressing that. Thus how a CNGO approaches its work will be distinctive, recognizing the spiritual as well as the material both in its practices as well as its goals; it justifies that CNGOs have a valid and necessary role within holistic mission.

Inappropriate proselytism remains, sadly but realistically, a headline issue for CNGOs, with secular and other religious agencies seeing CNGO work as a means of proselytism and related fears of that. Morally, there are three dangers: first, of discrimination in acts of service; second, of making 'rice Christians' and third the potential of spiritual abuse of vulnerable people. Nearly all CNGOs do not discriminate against people of other faiths meaning that any distribution of resources will not be biased towards Christians or against people of other faiths. On the other hand, some secular organizations are convinced that we continue to 'force vulnerable people' e.g. children to believe in an alien religion against their will. Although some organizations do still push their own agenda, it is increasingly understood and even stipulated in policy and procedures of many CNGOs that coerced conversion is not wanted. It is understood that providing things conditionally does not lead to true acceptance of our values. As such a number of organizations working with children have included in their child protection policy a section on 'spiritual abuse' which is put alongside policy on physical, emotional and sexual abuse. It states that children will not be abused spiritually, meaning that they will be given the choice about being involved in Christian meetings in the organization and if they hold to another religious belief will not be discriminated against if they wish to worship in that way.

However, as may be expected by Christian development, conversion certainly does happen. It usually comes about where there is a relationship of trust, where the person is modelling a way of life that is appealing to the person who is receiving it and they are in a position where they can choose to accept or reject it. Whilst explaining this to observers may be difficult, Christians in CNGOs recognise it as a common phenomenon and it fits our understanding of holistic mission. This in no way gives license to those who tragically exploit positions of trust compared with relationships of trust, and points to the need to be utterly careful in relationships characterised by power asymmetries; it also shows how spiritually the local church, representative of the population, may enjoy a legitimacy in more overtly spiritual or prophetic work in the community than external NGOs, although again, the outsider dare not ignore local, deep power asymmetries that contribute to oppression.

Myers explains the question (more broadly) by suggesting that the critical role of acts of service is to provoke questions. If the practise undertaken in achieving the social or developmental goals of holistic mission is good enough, then there is likely to be a natural response of questioning the motive. At this point the church must be able to answer 'because...'. The signs of the kingdom point to the king. Many times poor and vulnerable will seek to enter into new relationship with that king. It may, of course, not be the community or individual experiencing some kind of transformation that asks the question, and in fact the NGO may never see the question being asked. However, if peace and justice – in their broad senses – are being wrought, these are powerful signs of the kingdom both to earthly and spiritual powers.

To be able to do this kind of work that is Christian at its core but can forego explicitly spiritual goals, CNGOs need to find more fundamental ways of practising their Christianity. James (2004) in a study for the Swedish Mission Council wrote of creating 'space for grace'. He observes that many CNGOs are in fact essentially secular in their working and most importantly, in their beliefs about how change happens. In fact, he argues, what CNGOs need to do is sort out their theology and affirm that God is actually the bringer of 'good change'[2]: this is how they achieve Woolnough's first distinctive of spiritual transformation.

This follows an understanding of spirituality (eg Samuel 1996) that is about recognising Christ's Lordship both over the CNGO itself and the people and community it seeks to serve (which, of course, means that God can bring about 'good change' through agents whether or not they identify themselves with Christian motivation). This spirituality provides meaning, is life-giving, gives connection, and relates to people's internal experiences (James 2004); in Samuel's Christian theological framing, it is eschatological, empowering, redemptive, and reconciling. Each of these ideas could be explored much further, of course; the point here is that a CNGO's understanding of itself can depend upon its spirituality. A clearly articulated spirituality pushes the CNGOs aims and values to allow what James calls 'space for grace': they allow God to act in and through that agency. The goals, that may be thoroughly comprehensible to a secular audience, become servants to a God-centred vision of transformational development.

CNGOs and Good Practice: Legitimacy, Capacity and Accountability

This section looks at some examples of how CNGOs are engaged in good development practice, and considers the development of legitimacy, capacity and accountability that make that more predictable and sustainable. In thinking about accountability, results and practices (or actions) count. Above it was seen

[2] Chambers (1975) suggested this as a practical (if very incomplete) understanding of development.

how the actions of a CNGO create 'space for grace'. Their actions become 'signs' to the people they serve of the gospel.

However, of course, these signs are pointless if they do not work. Sometimes CNGO work has been characterised as 'all head and no heart' and certainly very motivated people serve in CNGOs in the belief that 'doing something is better than doing nothing'. Our experience is that this may not be always be true, and that some CNGOs do struggle with building objective learning into their organisational cultures. Therefore, first we look at the capacities before legitimacy and accountability.

It is perhaps Christian responses to HIV/AIDS and people affected by AIDS that is most widely seen as exemplary (if not uniquely so). The feeling is caught in the non-Christian context of India: "You are our star players. You are doing wonderful service in the fight against AIDS," said Ms Sujata Rao, head of India's National AIDS Control Organisation to a national gathering of the Christian response to AIDS. In Africa, the World Health Organisation in 2007 released a study of Zambia and Lesotho that showed that two-fifths and one-third, respectively, of HIV services were provided by faith-based organisations (FBOs). This supported the UNICEF / Religions for Peace study (Foster 2004) showing the huge and increasing scale of faith-based responses to children affected by AIDS ('orphans and vulnerable children', OVCs) and illustrates the huge pull of 'the church' to donors, for example, the World Bank:

> The role of African faith-based organisations in combating HIV and AIDS is widely recognised as having growing significance but, at the same time, one which is not fully exploited, given the influence and reach of FBOs in African societies. Their impact at the community and household levels and their well-developed on-the-ground networks make them uniquely positioned to influence values and behaviours and to mobilise communities – World Bank 2004.

There are many other examples of the work of CNGOs in holistic mission that stand out. The following illustrate some important trends.

First is work on child protection, in the relatively recent realization that every child must be considered vulnerable to abuse. In the background, a partnership of secular and Christian agencies, the Keeping Child Safe Coalition (KCS), has worked to create appropriate guidance, policies and training to make NGOs as safe as possible for children. Christian agencies such as Tearfund UK, Viva and World Vision have been at the forefront of this process both in terms of creating the material but also in terms of disseminating it through appropriate networks. It may seem strange to reference a mixed coalition here, but as child protection has such wide statutory and other implications, it is impossible and unhelpful for CNGOs to 'go it alone'.

Networks such as Chab Dai in Cambodia then have been able to work with churches and CNGOs and communities in child protection. Chab Dai is a coalition of 45 Christian agencies that enjoys government recognition because it has paid careful attention to ensuring all members have the highest possible standards of child protection, as well as grass-roots reach analogous to that of FBOs and AIDS above.

Second, increasing numbers of Christian organizations who appreciate that strategy, research, evaluation and responsible management of people are integral to good stewardship of the resources God has given to them. Tearfund[3] have made many of these techniques accessible to churches and FBOs and carefully develop them ensuring that they are theologically sound and useful on a practical level through careful piloting. Their publications are widely translated and contextualized.[4]

However, there remain many areas where great improvement needs to be made. One piece of research suggested that women 'rescued' from commercial sexual exploitation were in fact less empowered after their rescues than before, as their practical life choices were in fact reduced (Adams 2009).

This brings us to the next area of consideration, about being accountable for what we do. Results are another contentious area for several reasons. First, is how is it possible to measure spiritual transformation? Second, who are the results for and who is the accountability to? And third, what kind of results can be measured?

Woolnough (2008) explains that in its essence, a CNGO need not care about results too much as it is the practice – obeying the command to love our neighbours – that ultimately counts, both because Christians are called to obedience, and because God works in all sorts of strange and unpredictable ways, over time periods that NGO measurement rarely can consider. One CNGO project illustrate this point. The MST project[5] seeks to challenge and reach out to male clients of prostitutes. It is relational in nature and the 'results' are difficult to quantify because whether someone's heart has been changed by the conversations held, may be only known between him and God. If results were measured by verbal responses then it might be disappointing, but believing that significant things are happening in the spiritual realm is significant makes it worthwhile. It might be helpful to many CNGOs to develop a theology of 'success' that encompasses this.

Another CNGO, Servants to Asia's Urban Poor models another approach helpful to this discussion. They spend considerable time immersed in the community (described as an 'incarnational' approach) and it may take months of prayer and listening before they understand the slum community enough to work with them in finding local solutions for poverty. However, once established, some have become experts advising government and UN agencies in a way that other CNGOs can only envy as they interface directly with poverty in the slums.

However, understanding results still counts. In much development, accountability is nominally about learning and listening, but evaluation as it is practised is frequently about showcasing success and achieving the next grant award in an extremely competitive market place. Most practitioners are wise to this and vigorous debate goes on between the implementers and the marketers

[3] www.tearfund.org.

[4] For example, Tearfund UK's www.tilz.org.

[5] www.MSTProject.org.

within agencies at all levels. It affects small CBOs and large INGOs, as in the following example.

One Cambodian NGO we know runs excellent programmes, innovative and very responsive, with a dynamic experienced leader who is able to speak very little English. He is inventive and has lots of excellent ideas that are appropriate to the context but he has struggled often to find a suitable funder, even though they could see the great work, because they all required that he write his proposal in English and he was unable to do so. After several years of watching others get funds for unsustainable projects and westerners spending large amounts of money on projects inappropriate to the context, he finally found a donor who allows him to write the proposal in his own language and then get it translated into English. He now will need the same support to write his reports against the plan. This case study illustrates that whilst western donors hold the 'purse strings', finding appropriate local leaders and projects in context may require more creative solutions than are used by most.

The key for CNGOs is to identify the pressures of learning and then seek the greatest possible integrity in identifying and learning from successes and failures, in particular as interpreted by the poor and vulnerable they seek to serve. The practitioners have access to the tools to do this, but the leadership needs to ensure they are used appropriately. It also requires pragmatic responses, such as budgeting time and money for that kind of evaluation, as well as the value-based commitment to let the poor interpret the results of an intervention.

CNGOs and 'Development'

First, it is clear that secular observers see something in Christian holistic mission that is quite remarkable to them. Two British atheists, journalist Matthew Parris and senior politician Roy Hattersley, are unequivocal.

Parris first makes a comment on transformation affecting social and spiritual goals: "Now a confirmed atheist, I've become convinced of the enormous contribution that Christian evangelism makes in Africa: sharply distinct from the work of secular NGOs, government projects and international aid efforts. These alone will not do. Education and training alone will not do. In Africa Christianity changes people's hearts. It brings a spiritual transformation. The rebirth is real. The change is good."

Hattersley (2005) observed Christian responses to Hurricane Katrina in the south of the United States, and noted that, "it is impossible to doubt that faith and charity go hand in hand" because he saw that good works "are most likely to be performed by people who believe that heaven exists."

Secular development agendas are often big news in a globalised age of terror and poverty. Christians must recognise that despite such instruments as the Millennium Development Goals making it appear as if there is a secular development agenda that is pro-poor, this is of itself is highly contested. A whole post-development school of thought considers the concept of development to be little but intellectual wreckage, ameliorating the damage to the islands of the rich caused by the surrounding oceans of poverty (Rahnema 1997). Other schools continue to prescribe development agendas that mitigate the worst effects of neo-liberal capitalist growth – this is probably the general position of the World Bank and DAC countries. And others – such as Jeffrey Sach's (2005) influential *The End of Poverty* – return to a material development agenda that assumes the poor are poor because of lack of material infrastructures etc.

There is much helpful insight here – the key is that there is no monolith, but development is a highly contested and dynamic arena into which voices with legitimacy and credibility have much to contribute. Even more important to note is that development, beside that which is done by development agencies, is primarily a process that is always going on: change, creativity and destruction, and growth. Some of this development is beneficial for some people, some is harmful, but very little is beneficial for all. Development agencies do have a task of recognising this and both ameliorating and shaping such change and it provides CNGOs a clear mandate for advocacy into social policy at all levels[6], as well as a rationale for working with CBOs and churches to enhance capacities within communities. In particular, funding streams appear to dry up once certain indications of poverty reduction are achieved, assuming the job is done. Yet we know that although poverty increases vulnerability, sexual exploitation, for example, occurs in even wealthy contexts. We might say that poverty is part of sin but the effects of sin are more far-reaching than simply alleviating poverty and the need for integral mission remains.

Secular development is currently very focused on the notion of 'good governance'. Crudely, good governance is the focus on the behaviours and processes of the institutions of government, from corruption to efficiency. If government can be made accountable and effective, and not corrupt, then development that helps the poor can occur. Good governance is no doubt good for the citizens of a nation, but the prescription for a Scandinavian style state in the heart of Africa rings hollow without obvious next steps: see Karl Popper's 'utopian social engineering'. This is important in aid, because the World Bank and other development agencies make good governance reform a condition of aid.

---

[6] Interestingly, Majid Rahnema, an influential post-development writer, implicitly invites Christian inputs, saying, "The end of development should not be seen as an end to the search for new possibilities of change, for a relational world of friendship, or for genuine processes of regeneration able to give birth to new forms of solidarity. It should only mean that the binary, the mechanistic, the reductionist, the inhumane and the ultimately self-destructive approach to change is over. It should represent a call to the 'good people' everywhere to think and work together." M. Rahnema, 'Towards Post-Development: Searching for Signposts, a New Language and New Paradigms', in M. Rahnema and V. Bawtree (eds.), *The Post Development Reader* (London: Zed Books, 1997), 391.

Much careful thought by CNGOs has been put into the use of other humanitarian tools such as the United Nations Convention on the Rights of the Child, which is the most ratified UN document in history, not signed by only the United States and Somalia. Whilst some have criticized it, this is usually by people who have not read or understood it. Although it does have limitations, after 20 years it continues to provide a very useful bench-mark against which children's rights can be sought by all governments who have signed the document (i.e. most of the world's countries). It also provides a common language between governments, humanitarian and faith based organizations, not to be underestimated in a complex global array of organizations with different agendas. Indeed some organizations such as World Vision and Tearfund have carefully critiqued in with a biblical approach and concluded that it is something that FBOs should seek to use because it provides a great way for Christians to be engaged in and influence those debates.

CNGOs and the Future

Finally, some thoughts on the challenges of the future.

First, the legitimacy of the work of CNGOs will long continue to be a question as they walk careful tightropes: always potentially compromised by their dependence on funding from the rich, largely of the north; and the tie of the social goals to spiritual goals. As a generalisation, institutional funding (i.e. governmental overseas development aid) is increasingly tied to non-discrimination on the grounds of religion. But for CNGOs, Padilla is clear that there remains, "the witness to Jesus Christ as the Lord of all humankind and the whole creation — the witness that gives meaning to our own struggle for justice and peace." Legitimacy comes from that witness in the context of the poor.

Second is balancing 'good development' with a Christian understanding of people as created with dignity, in God's image. On the one hand, good development requires an enhanced focus on advocacy and a renewed focus on holistic mission that is demonstrably both effective and efficient. Christians are to be wise. But on the other hand, the testimonies of Mother Theresa and the many saints that serve humbly those beyond human hope remind us that Christian holistic mission that truly believes in the God-given dignity of the other, may sometimes not be strategic or efficient, and maybe not even effective (by certain measurements). In Christianity, the individual matters. The Millennium Development Goals, eight goals for improving the lives of the world's poor promoted by the United Nations and a primary agenda of international aid and development,[7] are currently valued as being strategic and effective at generating momentum. But, arguably, they create a terrible triage dividing the poor of the world into those worthy of receiving help and those not (MDG 1 is "Halve, between 1990 and 2015, the proportion of people whose

[7] Chambers (1975) suggested this as a practical (if very incomplete) understanding of development.

income is less than $1 a day" – for which half of the poor?). A belief that every person is loved by God, be they degraded, destitute or degenerate ('the least of these'?), compels service to them because of who they are, not because of what development goals may be achieved. This pushes CNGOs to be at the forefront of speaking up for the rights of those that cannot speak for themselves and facilitating those who are disempowered to have a voice. It has led many organizations to believe that helping just one vulnerable child or person is of significance to God in a context of hundreds or thousands of similar stories where humanly speaking it seems it is a waste of time.

For CNGOs to survive and succeed in the future, creative ways of untying the knots of holistic mission must be achieved. Whilst the fullness of holistic mission remains to be celebrated, it is critical to remember that CNGOs cannot take responsibility for this fullness. In one sense, only the local church can do that, but even then it is the church across the world that is responsible for obeying the God-given mandate to holistic mission. Therefore this is a call to partnership according to kingdom values. The local church that is of and closest to the poor must take on a principal duty of care to its community. This can then be served by other Christians, churches and CNGOs around the world. Each needs to play its part without taking on an unbiblical responsibility. The questions of accountability and legitimacy can only be addressed if money and size are allowed to be servants, and not masters.

Conclusions

Much more has been said and could be considered in understanding effective Christian development work and its connections to holistic mission – the references included and other chapters in this book being very fruitful sources of questions and ideas. However, we offer these as some tentative proposals that can enable CNGOs to truly maintain a meaningful Christian identity; to partner the poor, the churches and other change-agents in the world, to effectively make signs of the coming kingdom as they serve the poor and vulnerable of the world.

1. The Christian identity of CNGOs comes from 'being Christian' – that is, accepting Christ's Lordship over them, their work and the people they serve and developing a spirituality where Christ is expected to be the author of change, not clever programming nor greater grants.
2. CNGOs must continually work to achieve their legitimacy, accountability and capacity by first, learning to improve their practice; second, by listening actively to the poor and vulnerable whom they claim to serve; and third by explicitly recognising the power asymmetries between donors and poor.
3. The primary role of CNGOs that have valid social or development goals in holistic mission is provoking questions; their work bears witness to Christ and his kingdom, it does not have to explain

Christ. This does not take away from, but complements, the necessity of proclamation of the gospel. Holistic mission requires partnership between congregations, CNGOs, CBOs and values the roles played by government and private sectors.

4. CNGOs recognise that the secular development agenda is dynamic, and so place themselves into the creation of that agenda, in order to influence secular development in kingdom ways that give voice to the voiceless and advocates for their rights.

DEVELOPMENT AS HOLISTIC MISSION

Deborah Ajulu

Introduction

This chapter introduces *stewardship* as a concept that defines Christian development. Development understood this way befits the church (in its wider sense) as part and parcel of its holistic mission in the world. Development is, therefore, construed as the very first great commission given to human beings (male and female). Made in the image of God, this commission gave them the unfathomable privilege of being co-creators (Gen. 1:28) with God, in a stewardship role, through which they were to bring forth the full potential of creation and develop the earth, being accountable to God, who owns it. God's story of development starts in a garden (rural primitive state) and ends in a city (urban, all built up, with technological constructions of a developed state). However, the fall severed the good relationships human beings had with God and creation and distorted the stewardship role. God, whose purposes for his world cannot be thwarted, however, remedies the distorted stewardship through the gospel enacted in Jesus Christ, who became the model of the new stewardship. A new stage is set for stewardship, which now becomes a role for only those who respond to the gospel by faith and thus graciously are brought into a stewardship of God's grace that is fulfilled in Jesus, God's chief steward.[1] The church, as the body of Christ (all believers both men and women), is sent into the world through the New Testament's great commission, which provides the mandate for it to execute its stewardship role under God's authority empowered by the Holy Spirit. Holism in development must be viewed as part of the church's overall holistic mission in the world to which it is sent through this commission. The church as the true steward is charged with responsibility by God through Jesus and is empowered by the Holy Spirit to effectively deliver holistic development for the transformation of individuals and their communities, by alleviating poverty and other social and environmental problems.

---

[1] Douglas John Hall, *The Steward: A Biblical Symbol Come of Age* (Grand Rapids, MI: Eerdmans, 1990), 44.

A Snapshot of the Secular Development Process

The trend from WW II

Development is the conventional or traditional understanding of a process of socio-economic advancement pursued by countries, *for flourishing the lives of citizens*. However, over the whole of the twentieth century plus a decade into the twenty-first century, the story is a mixture of both good and bad results. Development experience can be traced from the end of World War II, which was the period that sparked off concerted efforts in the western countries to rescue their devastated economies. Through the Marshall Plan (1948-1952), economic development theories and strategies were developed that helped these economies to achieve high growth rates through which they attained rapid industrialisation, which ultimately lifted them to developmental levels that defined them as developed countries (DCs).

In the 1950s and 1960s, when most of the undeveloped world realised the need to follow suit, they became categorised as the under- or less-developed countries (LDCs). With great enthusiasm, these countries jumped onto the bandwagon of development and indeed, in many ways and in many countries, development made things better than, say 50 years ago. Todaro and Griffin both corroborate this view that results were quite impressive as indicated by increased growth rates of per capita incomes and improvements in several major social indicators like life expectancy and literacy.[2]

In the twentieth century, this good news was highlighted by the breakthrough of four Asian tigers entering into the category of NICs.[3] Following that, the up-to-date situation at the turn of the new century has seen more countries added into High HDI[4] Countries in Latin America, Asia and Island Countries.

However, the situation in Sub-Saharan Africa (SSA) is still bad news, where the bulk of the countries are in the low HDI category, the rest falling into the medium category. In the LDCs Report 2008, the Secretary-General of UNCTAD makes a comment that, "Poverty reduction has been faster in Asian LDCs than in Africa, where the absolute number of extremely poor people continues to rise."[5]

The story today, in the twenty-first century, is more of worsening world poverty, with high costs in human suffering, environmental degradation and

---

[2] Michael P. Todaro, *Economic Development in the Third World* (New York and London: Longman, 1977/89), 87; Keith B. Griffin, *Alternative Strategies for Economic Development* (London: Macmillan, 1989), 4-10.

[3] NICs stands for Newly Industrialised Countries.

[4] HDI stands for Human Development Index.

[5] Supachai Panitchpakdi, 'Trends in Poverty and Progress towards the Millennium Development Goals', in United Nnations, *The Least Developed Countries Report 2008*, v.

climate change. The World Bank's (WB) *World Development Report* (WDR) of 2000/2001 reported that, "at the start of the century, poverty remains a global problem of huge proportions. Of the 6 billion people, 2.8bn live on less than $2 a day, and 1.2bn live on less than $1 a day." Infant and child mortalities are at 6% and 8% respectively; and of school-going age, 9% boys and 14% girls are out of school.[6] The report of the *2010 WDR,* a decade into the century, is still of continuing severe poverty in developing countries.[7]

The UNCTAD Secretary-General attributes this scenario especially of "the recent period of rapid growth… associated with a slow rate of poverty reduction and progress towards" the MDGs, to "the type of economic growth occurring and the development model in place in the LDCs."[8]

A summary of the characteristics of world development initial model

- First, it equated economic growth with 'progress' and modernisation measured quantitatively by per capita gross national product. This overlooked important socio-cultural factors and the existing inequalities among people, regions of countries and countries.
- Second, it was, viewed as a linear process with successive stages through which countries passed to achieve development.
- Third, it employed a philosophy of mechanistic positivism, which sought to solve LDCs' development problems through rationalistic approaches, treating those problems with predetermined universalism, i.e. uniformity or little distinction. Hettne argues it involved "mechanical application of the main body of theory of whatever discipline to LDCs with the assumption that any difference in problems was one of degree rather than of kind."[9]
- Fourth, it was, considered transferrable, involving the transfer of not only capital and other resources, but also of knowledge, skills, information and technology. These were not bad in themselves, but the process created a role of 'the expert' or 'technocrat' as the only person to mediate the transfer. Other transfers included the superimposition of western cultural values; institutional structures and standards; socio-economic and political administrative systems, organisations, styles, procedures etc. on LDCs.
- Fifth, overemphasis was placed on the state as main actor in development, which employed bureaucracies that promoted

[6] World Bank, *World Development Report 2000/2001* (Oxford and New York: Oxford University Press), vi.
[7] World Bank, *World Development Report 2010*, xx.
[8] Panitchpakdi, *The Least Developed Countries Report 2008*, v.
[9] Todaro, *Economic Development in the Third World*, 63; Michael T. Martin and Terry R. Kandal, *Studies of Development and Change in the Modern World* (New York: Oxford University Press, 1989), 6; Bjorn Hettne, *Development Theory and the Three Worlds* (London: Longman Scientific and Technical, Longman, 1990), 1, 5.

technocratic approaches that required efficient controls. These were aimed at organising society into efficient production units and controlling people's lives and their access to sources of livelihoods with limited opportunities for creative individual initiatives both in the public and private spheres which favoured urban-biased top-down and trickle-down[10] macro approaches, hence ignoring rural people's development needs, and agricultural production that produced exports.

- Sixth, growth-centric models required production-centred systems that employed methods geared towards exploitation, manipulation and plunder of natural resources, while ignoring the stewardship aspect of resource utilisation, in order to produce an endless flow of standardised goods and services to satisfy the unending cravings of a mass consumerist society in DCs. The result was to condemn LDCs not only to primary commodity production and export, but also to economic and trade dependency on the monopolistic dominance of DCs.
- Seventh, it employed planning and project processes that had been developed for the construction of physical structures that required methods and procedures of engineering and economic statistical analysis, blue-printing and pre-planning solutions to problems. These procedures suited the construction of physical 'things' in the hands of the western world's private corporation, rather than the development of people.[11]

A Brief Review of World Development Experience To Date

In the twentieth century to the first decade in the twenty-first century development experienced successes and failures with attempts made to redress faults. However, by the 1970s and 1980s, despite some successes, there arose an increased disenchantment with the development process taking place and this led to re-thinking. This triggered off a number of studies[12] that revealed basic weaknesses like the failure to alleviate mass poverty, an overemphasis on rapid cumulative growth, urban bias, and a single-minded pursuit of industrialisation, including some of the characteristics already covered above.

---

[10] Todaro, *Economic Development in the Third World*, 87.

[11] Denis A. Rondinelli, *Development Projects as Policy Experiments: An Adaptive Approach to Development Administration* (London: Methuen, 1983), 5; Robert Chambers, 'Normal Professionalism and Early Project Process Problems and Solutions', in *Agricultural and Rural Problems* (Institute of Development Studies, 1988), 3.

[12] Most notable of these studies include Todaro, *Economic Development in the Third World*, 31; Hollis Burney Chenery with Monteks Ahluwalia and Nicholas G. Carter, *Growth and Poverty in Developing Countries* (London and New York: Oxford University Press, 1974), 8-9.

Other studies compiled by Seligson et al. 2003[13] analyse, among other topics, the income gap between the rich and the poor countries. The World Bank also commissioned studies to evaluate the economic growth of low and high incomes in countries for the period 1950-1975. The findings revealed that rapid growth had been achieved but the gap between the poor and the rich, measured by per capita GNP, was growing wider. The report gives the events responsible for this scenario and they included firstly, the two oil shocks of 1974 and 1979, which altered the character of world economic growth. Secondly, the extended world recession of 1979-1982 that was, followed, thirdly, by the debt crisis among poor countries of the 1980s and 1990s. The World Bank and IMF in response to the debt crisis instituted Structural Adjustment Programmes (SAPs) with austerity measures as efforts to assist debtor countries to remain creditworthy, but the effects were disastrous for the poor and the environment.[14]

Economic growth became further discredited as a strategy for poverty alleviation by analysts who viewed LDCs as never catching up,[15] within a development model which binds these countries to a blind economic growth rat race that ignored the more pressing development needs.

The re-thinking among economists and policy-makers in the 1970s and 1980s led to the search for strategies that would ensure what Todaro called the *dethronement of GNP* through direct attacks on widespread absolute poverty, increasing inequitable income distribution, rising unemployment, and dependency of LDCs on industrialised countries, as well as a rejection of modernisation's dominance in further development processes.

In the 1980s and 1990s, realising that economic growth was still dominant in the process, the search turned to new strategies, models and approaches that laid more emphasis on people. Thus, concepts like people-centredness, poverty-focus, basic needs, participation and self-reliance, sustainability and others entered the centre stage, especially with the NGO involvement.

The 1990s saw the greatest intention and 'resources' committed to what became a war or attack mounted against world poverty from the world development bodies and agencies, including IFAD and World Bank, who threw their total weight behind it. The World Bank's 1990s annual development reports declared a commitment of effort and resources by the Bank to address different aspects of development directed towards the reduction of poverty, which culminated in 2000/2001 with a more aggressive title of *Attacking Poverty* with a foreword note given by the then director stating,

> Poverty amid plenty is the world's greatest challenge. We at the Bank have made it our mission to fight poverty with passion and professionalism, putting it at the

---

[13] Mitchell A. Seligson and John T. Passē-Smith, *Development and Underdevelopment: The Political Economy of Inequality* (Boulder, CO and London: Lynne Rienner, 2003).
[14] Friedmann, *Empowerment*, 5.
[15] Seligson and Passē-Smith, *Development and Underdevelopment*, 4.

centre of all the work we do. And we have recognised the successful development requires a comprehensive, multifaceted, and properly integrated mandate.[16]

This report too had a difference, after an exclusive focus on poverty measured only by income and consumption, to include other dimensions of human deprivation, including "low achievement in education, poor health and nutrition and other areas of human development." This was only after conducting a study on *Voices of the Poor* in order to hear, for the first time in the Bank's development history, the truth about poverty from the poor. Through this study, factors like powerlessness, voicelessness, vulnerability and fear emerged, that then resulted in an identification of three areas of action, and a defining of five key actions that would determine the Bank's commitment.[17] Furthermore, the results aided in the formulation of the Millennium Development Goals (MDGs), the implementation of which leave most nations floundering.

In addition, some of the most notable current approaches that are in vogue in the twenty-first century, include Sen's Entitlement and Capability, and Development as Freedom Approaches, which have assumed central positions in the UNDP Human Development Report (HDR) series and have influenced the World Bank policy. These approaches are a response to the failure made in the economic growth that measured only monetary activity but ignored aspects of human well-being, thereby concealing extreme human deprivation for large populations, especially in low-income countries.[18] The main thesis of these approaches is that development is about human development, defined as the improvement of well-being leading to human flourishing. People are recognised as the principal ends of a development process, not to be viewed simply as labour inputs, which are means (human capital) of production, i.e. economic development is a means to human development, not vice versa.[19]

These approaches have contributed a new quantitative measure of development necessary for comparative studies, developed by Meier and Rauch. This new measure is the Human Development Index (HDI), which replaces GNP as a more suitable measure, and has received popular support. UNDP uses HDI in its HDRs and is a summary of human development, which measures the average achievement of a country in three basic dimensions of human development namely:

- A decent standard of living as measured by a country's per capita income in terms of purchasing power.
- A long and healthy life measured by life expectancy at birth; and

---

[16] Wolfensohn, in *World Development Report 2000/2001*, v. Up until now that mandate was a missing link in the Bank's development process.

[17] Wolfensohn, in *World Development Report 2000/2001*, vi-vii.

[18] UNDP, *Human Development Report 1996*, 56-7, identifies aspects and influences of human well-being to include household work, family life, leisure and freedom.

[19] Sudhir Anand and Amartya K. Sen, *Human Development Index: Methodology and Measurement* (New York: United Nations Development Programme, 2009), 9, 10.

- Knowledge (or educational attainment and effort) as measured by adult literacy combined with primary, secondary and tertiary enrolment ratios.

Current Challenges of World Development:

The *World Report 2010* admits there are serious challenges that remain core priorities in global development. The development experts need to come to terms with the fact that poverty has not only increased and become more multifaceted and complex, but also it seems to have developed a mutative character with deeper roots. Poverty is becoming immune to secular world strategies that offer only half measures of development that are constantly falling short of the development goal with a human face. The world with majority populations in poverty is crying for a development that can bring sustainable transformation through economic justice that will lift masses of these populations out of their inhumane existence.

What is true is that the basic fallen nature of humanity is the underlying factor that renders all human effort tainted with selfish goals that fall far too short of attaining the ultimate good for all as intended by a Sovereign God. Where God is recognised in all that is done, truth and justice and equitable distribution of resources become guiding principles that ensure a development that generates both the progress and the conservation necessary for human flourishing.

This leads us to examine Christian holistic development.

Christian Holistic Development

Holism in development

Holism recognises the integral wholeness of reality and observes this in a development process, addressing whole needs within whole situations as the effective way that brings the desirable impact of human flourishing, community viability and environmental sustainability.

Biblical foundations of Christian holistic development

What then is Christian holism in development, and what makes it distinct?

Christian holistic development is viewed as part of the holistic mission of the church. Holistic mission in general is God's mission or *missio dei* which involves everything God does in establishing his kingdom in the whole world in all its fullness. This mission starts at creation when God makes human beings in his own image and likeness, and assigns them, both male and female, the role of co-workers with him. Creation begins in perfect harmony under the lordship of God, with human beings in relation to their creator as stewards of his creation.[20] This role of stewardship given to human beings (men and women) was a responsibility to care for the whole of creation. To develop it as co-creators, from its raw state into which the creator brought it out of the formless void. Humanity reflects the divine craftsmanship skills in a progressively tilling, shaping, naming, organising, beautifying, multiplying, subduing and caring dominion. According to these activities, development here is understood as stewardship, which God intended to maintain a dynamic tension between conserving and progressing.[21] This is considered the first great commission to human beings, given as development, to continue the 'work of cosmic development',[22] originated by the great developer, God, whose vision for development was from planting the garden to the building of a city. In other words, this vision is both for the present world, and has an eschatological dimension.

The creation account, despite the fall, provides a foundational framework for a model of Christian holistic development, which focuses on stewardship as its defining concept. Underpinning the biblical stewardship is a right relationship that the steward has with God. The implication is that Christian holistic development recognises God's lordship over all aspects of life as well as his ultimate ownership over all creation and resources.[23] Human beings, in responding to their stewardship role, are to extend holistic development to encompass the whole world, enshrining both the temporal/transient and spiritual/eternal dimensions with accountability to God. Stewardship, therefore, becomes a central concept, through which development is defined for Christian holism in development and makes it distinct from secular and other religious views and practices of development.

Effects of the fall on stewardship and its restoration

Through the fall (Gen. 3) sin entered and corrupted the world. It disrupted the original harmonious relationships, which God had with human beings and his good creation. The stewardship role for human beings became distorted and compromised and they usurped God's position of ultimate ownership with catastrophic results. Development that was meant to be a cooperative team effort for the common good, turned into competition and rivalry over resources leading to murder (e.g. Cain and Abel Gen. 4:1-16), and self-seeking ambition (e.g. the Babel story Gen. 11:1-9). Since then, development has continued to be a field dominated by fallen human selfish inclinations with production ceasing to be just for essential goods and services, but for insatiable appetites of consumer societies and exorbitant profits for private corporations, involving the

---

[20] Douglas McConnell, 'Holistic Mission', in A Scott Moreau (ed.), *Evangelical Dictionary of World Mission* (Carlisle, UK: Paternoster Press, 2000), 448-449.

[21] Miller, *Discipling Nations*, 232.

[22] Sinclair in Miller, *Dicipling Nations*, 181.

[23] John Steward, *Biblical Holism: Where God, People and Deeds Meet* (Melbourne: World Vision Australia, 1994), 12.

ruthless exploitation and plunder of natural and economic resources.[24] The inevitable results have become poverty for the masses, inequality and dehumanisation, death, exploitation, environmental degradation and pollution linked to climate change.

God, however, as sovereign creator, whose world mission cannot be hijacked, remedied the situation and restored the stewardship role of human beings through the death and resurrection of his Son Jesus Christ. Through Christ's redemptive work, God has been able to create a new force for stewardship, the church, whom he sends as a special community of his redeemed people (1 Pet.2:9), to continue his mission, which he renewed and modelled through Jesus. It is in the renewed sense that the concept of stewardship is treated in defining and understanding Christian holistic development as church mission.

Stewardship: a Central Biblical Concept for Christian Holistic Development

Stewardship and biblical understanding of development

While the term development does not appear in the bible, stewardship on the other hand, "is a major theme in the bible."[25] The term refers to the management of the affairs of a household, properly administering its resources to ensure the needs of the members are adequately met. The biblical usage of the concept of *household* conveys a meaning that the entire world and its resources are God's household or family. "Stewardship, thus, implies the ordering of life in the world with proper management of all God-given resources (natural resources, all human natural gifts, talents and spiritual gifts, land and environmental resources), not merely in relation to money budgeting, finances, or ordering of affairs of only one family unit."[26]

Old Testament usage of stewardship

In the Old Testament (OT), the usage of the stewardship concept applied to Israel as God's chosen race and the basic resource that called for its diligent exercise was land. Land was a dominant factor in God's dealings with Israel through the covenant's promises to the patriarchs enshrined in the Pentateuch and historical books. For ancient Israel, land was a physical source of viability and life, a place for gathering the hopes of the covenant people, and a vibrant

---

[24] Donald Hay, *Economics Today: A Christian Critique* (Leicester: Apollos, InterVarsity Press, 1989), 21.

[25] Miller, *Discipling Nations*, 221.

[26] Deborah Ajulu, *Holism in Development; An African Perspective on Empowering Communities* (Monrovia, CA: MARC, 2001), 46.

theological symbol. Historically, land for the Jewish people meant a future both secure and without anxiety. Land was not for one's own security, but rather for providing for the family and the entire community and provided the viability of each family unit, which was based on the ownership of a piece of land as an inheritance (1 Kings 21:1-3), and land also meant satiation (Deut. 8:7-10). Leviticus 25:23 gives a twin perspective of the divine largesse and divine ownership of land which implied both rights and responsibilities for Israel, which were to be underpinned by strong moral commitments (like those given in Deut. 7:7f; 8:17f; 9:5) and the maintenance of a good relationship with Israel's God. This relationship required a dependence on God's faithfulness and reliability and called for a strict observance of economic justice, which the prophets enforced, while God's ownership of the land implied a responsibility to God, to one's family and to one's neighbour.[27]

Stewardship in the OT as well as applying to individuals, also defined the role of the king or ruler, setting limits and responsibilities (Deut. 17:16-17) with regard to the handling of resources, especially land. As a steward, the king was not to control or possess land but to manage the land entrusted to him. Rulers were to manage the land properly and to enhance it for the good of the people of God to whom they were bound by common loyalties, knowledge, memories and experience of their history. The use and distribution of land had to be ordered by moral principles. God also gave stipulations for a king (see Deut. 17:14-20), one of which included a proviso that he be one of the children of Israel. The king and the people were to read and be subjected to the Torah as it was the fundamental affirmation that Israel's resources were founded in Yahweh's graciousness. Keeping the Torah would keep Israel in the land whereas neglect of the Torah would lead to a loss of their land. The king was continually warned against the temptation to regard land as a possession handled apart from its spiritual significance.

Generally then, the OT usage of the term *stewardship* has had to do with the management of domestic affairs, the rule or realm of a person in authority, or the dominion of a monarch. In this sense, stewardship is the responsibility of both individuals at the personal and family level, and for authority and management committed to an official or king.

New Testament usage of stewardship

Application in the Gospels

The New Testament (NT) deals with stewardship in two different perspectives – physical/material and spiritual.

---

[27] Chris J.H. Wright, *Living as the People of God: The Relevance of the Old Testament Ethics* (Leicester: Inter-Varsity Press, 1983), 51-59.

In the Gospels, stewardship is used figuratively in a physical/material sense, as found in a number of passages (Mt. 20:8; Lk. 8:3; 12:42-48; 16:1-4; and Jn. 2:8). These verses refer to a steward as a servant-manager of something or someone not belonging to himself. The master is not an earthly king as in the OT, but implicitly is God in Christ. Christ's followers during his absence from the earth are charged with a stewardship responsibility for Christ's household, which is the world. The passages given here record Jesus' teaching about stewards, referring to some as faithful, thrifty, caring and wise but to others as dishonest, unproductive and even cruel. Jesus addressed many of his teachings on stewardship to the leaders of the Jews, urging them to exercise proper stewardship for the welfare of God's people. Miller estimates that '100 percent of Christ's teaching deals with stewardship of life, while just 20 percent focuses specifically on money and material possessions.[28]

Three distinct aspects of stewardship are presented. Firstly, the steward is portrayed as occupying an important and superior position in which he identifies closely with the master. Secondly, Lk. 12:42-48 expresses the obligation on stewardship of the need to both understand and constantly remember that no ultimate ownership or authority over what is managed is retained, because all belongs to God alone. In other words, though superior, the steward is still a servant who is "strictly accountable to [the] master and will be deprived of [that position] unless he upholds in his actions and attitudes the character and true wishes of this other one [God] whom he is allowed and commanded to represent."[29] If the steward forgets this and begins to assume autonomy and liberty to behave as he pleases, as though unambiguously in charge and hence not accountable, this steward shall be most severely punished.

Thirdly, Lk. 12:48b emphasises the unavoidability of responsibility and accountability, first where superior authority involves greater responsibility, and second, in Mt. 25:14-30 where the higher the value added to what is managed (an expectation of good stewards) the greater the rewards.

Jesus' teaching on stewardship, emphasises *wholeness* in all areas that make development transformational, and refers to principle characteristics like obedience and faithfulness, thrift and wisdom, justice and fairness, integrity and truthfulness, respect, care and nurture of human dignity, equity and equality, servant-hood and humility, enhancement and preservation.

Application in the Epistles

The Epistles in the NT add a spiritual dimension to the usage of the term. In 1 Cor. 4:1-2, Paul says that all believers are called to be servants of Christ and stewards of God's mysteries enshrined within the gospel. Paul is applying the concept of stewardship explicitly to himself as an apostle and implicitly to the

[28] Miller, *Discipling Nations*, 221.

[29] Douglas John Hall, *The Steward: A Biblical Symbol Come of Age* (Grand Rapids, MI, Eerdmans, 1990), 34.

church at large. He argues that believers exist not to serve themselves but as servants of God's mysteries to serve the interests of those to whom God sends them.

In Ephesians 2:19-3:11, Paul regards stewards not as hired hands or outsiders of the household but as partners and members of God's household in which they live and participate in different responsibilities. Participation allows stewards to share the bounteous grace of God with others and to bring them into God's household. Here, reference is to a stewardship of grace rather than a stewardship of material things, but stewardship continues to be based on the idea of trustworthiness for the purpose, and of sharing.

The Epistles, influenced by the Jerusalem tradition that was deeply conscious of an imminent end, stressed the eschatological aspect of stewardship. 1 Peter 4:7-11, for instance, expresses the stewardship theme in apocalyptic terms as an awareness of the nearness of the end that ought to reinforce good stewardship of the varied gifts of God's grace for the ultimate glory of the master, God, who comes to demand an account from each of his stewards. This teaching was an attempt to reduce or eliminate the temptation for individuals to isolate themselves and their talents in a proud manner and to seek to create a fuller recognition of the human transience faced by all humanity, which calls for human creaturely solidarity and compassion as God intended.

The NT Great Commission and Holism in Development

Christian holistic development as part of the holistic mission of the church falls within the mandate of the NT great commission.

In the NT, God's mission is renewed for human beings through the great commission given to the church but directed to the whole world. The church is commissioned by Jesus after the redemption event of his death and resurrection, which was necessary for redeeming from the fall a new brand of stewards with a right relationship with God as an essential condition. In Mt. 28:18-20, Mk. 16:15-16, Lk. 24:46-49, Jn. 17:18, Jn. 20:21 and Acts 1:8, Jesus commissions his disciples to continue the world mission he had inaugurated and modelled. These passages convey three crucial facts enshrined within the commission mandate that must guide stewardship in mission, both then and now, for the churches to be effective.

These three facts are namely *the authority* behind the mission, *the model* of the mission, and the *motive power* for the mission.

The first fact refers to the divine authority bestowed on the risen Jesus (Dan. 7; Phil. 2:9-11) is the authority by which he commissions the church.

The second fact is that the model of the mission is Jesus. The church is sent the same way the Father had sent him. In his mission, Jesus was holistic, making his words and deeds complementary. He not only preached the good news of the kingdom, but also performed works that were visible signs of the kingdom with love and compassion.[30]

The third fact is the motive power to propel the mission. The Holy Spirit comes upon the disciples to live inside the formerly fearful and provides power from within.[31] The Holy Spirit made them bold to declare the good news, work miracles and signs with varying gifts and empowered them to live godly lives as witnesses.

Part of their witness was in the obedient working out of the great commandment to love God and the neighbour.

Stott sees in this commandment a vision of the neighbour as a being who is both social and psycho-somatic:

> God created man, who is my neighbour, a body-soul-in-community. Therefore, if we love our neighbour... [we must show concern] for his total welfare, the good of his soul, his body and his community.[32]

This vision of the neighbour is the focal emphasis of holistic development and should be reflected in all development work.

Conclusion

Today in the twenty-first century, billions of people in the two thirds world are still facing worsening poverty, especially in the Sub-Saharan African countries exacerbated by a number of factors beyond the capacity of development communities, like frequent and intensive natural and environmental disasters. What needs to be reckoned with is that development efforts that leave God and his moral ethical agenda out of their development equation render themselves incapable of providing sustainable solutions. The results bring small measures of success against tsunami-size waves of human problems.

Under this magnitude of problems, it is obvious that only God through his power can renew all things, not only through his stewards, the churches, but also through his overarching divine work that transcends the churches' scope. He is able to do this in anticipation of the final renewal for the new earth. It is, therefore, high time that the churches,[33] including the Christian NGOs, in the twenty-first century rethink their biblical stewardship mandate and enter the centre stage of development to counteract negative development, or as Goulet calls it, 'anti-development',[34] due to its costs in immense human suffering and the loss of meaning. They can do this as they recognise God's moral, ethical

---

[30] John Stott, *Christian Mission in the World Mission* (London: Falcon, 1975), 26, 27.

[31] Paul Mumo Kisau, 'Commentary on Acts of the Apostles', in Tonkunboh Adeyemo (ed.), *African Bible Commentary* (Nairobi: WordAlive, Zondervan, 2006), 1300.

[32] Stott, *Christian Mission in the Modern World*, 29-30.

[33] The churches here includes all denominations, Christian academics, professionals and practitioners involved in what contributes to development as well as the para-church institutions and organisations in development.

[34] Denis Goulet, *The Cruel Choice: A New Concept in the Theory of Development* (New York: University press of America, 1971), 216-225.

values as important, even at the top levels of development thinking. Goulet's argument is relevant that "development needs to be redefined, demystified, and thrust into the arena of moral debate."[35] Therefore, the churches can effectively play an active role in world development through their resource endowments, especially those human resources essential to the development process at various levels involving reflection, application, and practice.

The churches worldwide, including Christian development NGOs, are well equipped to engage with the world development community and move towards a paradigm shift that will reverse the consequences of the fall, influenced and guided by biblical principles like light to disperse darkness and salt to salvage and preserve from corruption. Such engagement is likely to promote the positive and minimise the negative impact, thus to bring about the critical transformation, for lifting communities out of the poverty trap and the rest of creation out of its bondage. Churches need constantly to view poverty as a scourge of human life, for the bible condemns it as a scandalous condition demanding justice, and emphasises that God wants an end to it.[36]

The challenge of the twenty-first century churches worldwide is the recovery of "a vision of the wide diversity of ministries to which God calls his people,"[37] to work in unity and commitment to strengthen links between the international and national, through the churches of the rich nations with the national/local churches in poor countries. To apply Jesus' model of holistic ministry to the whole needs of poor people and their communities requires well-resourced development-oriented local resident churches. This will guarantee long-term holistic development strategies along with resource mobilisation undergirded by a stewardship commitment towards proper management and distribution. The individual contexts of the marginalised poor are likely to receive attention, so enhancing poor people's own capacity with boosted human dignity for full participation in and control of their own sustainable development for transformation. The local churches present among the poor cease to stand aloof but become active in their legitimate calling as stewards and agents of socio-economic and political justice, peace and reconciliation (in increasingly conflicting relationships) and act with compassion by reaching out to the

---

[35] Goulet, *The Cruel Choice*, xix.

[36] Julio de Santa Ana, *Good News to the Poor: The Challenge of the Poor in the History of the Church* (Geneva: WCC Publications, 1977), 19; Deut.15:4-5, 11.

[37] John Stott, *Through the Bible: Through the Year* (Oxford, UK: Candle Books, 2006), 320.

persecuted, the marginalised, and the outcasts (women and PLWAs[38]). Essential to this is the application of the conditions of the commission's Trinitarian mandate, namely the Father's love and divine authority in Jesus and the indwelling Spirit's resourcing and empowerment, beyond all secularist development efforts.

[38] PLWAs is acronym for People Living with Aids who are the present day lepers that are the outcast untouchables.

CONFRONTING THE POWERS

Melba Maggay

Historically, the churches have been lead institutions in doing acts of mercy. Even when Christians were yet a small and powerless minority movement (estimated at 200,000 in a total population of 30 million), funds of the fledgling church were used to buy the freedom of slaves, and believers cared for the children of prostitutes, gladiators and infants who were exposed and abandoned on the rubbish heaps of cities in the Roman Empire.[1] This tradition of compassion continues to this day in the many humanitarian and aid institutions that the churches have established to serve the world's poor.

It is in the field of politics, of making democratic institutions work, that the churches have been reluctant to step out and speak truth to the powers. Yet politics – simply defined as the art of governance – is at the heart of the cultural mandate: 'rule over creation.' The prophets tell us that the doing of justice, or seeing to it that power is used to ensure redress for the aggrieved and fairness for all, is at the centre of God's requirements for his people.[2]

Now and again, there have been some solitary voices raised, like that of Bishop Desmond Tutu in the days of apartheid in South Africa. But by and large, the call to speak prophetically and hold accountable those in power has yet to be grasped by the majority of the churches.

In the following we discuss the importance of politics and what it means to confront the powers in a context of systemic injustice.

The Politics of Poverty

Theologically, Scripture sets forth a number of reasons why it is important to confront the powers if we want to truly help the poor:

Poverty is perpetuated by injustice
that is organized and embedded in structures

[1] Charles Ringma, *Liberation Theologians Speak to Evangelicals: A Theology and Practice of Serving the Poor* (Quezon City, Philippines: OMF Lit., 2008), 20-21, citing the work of Peter C. Phan, 'Social Thought', in Thomas Halton (ed.), *Message of the Fathers of the Church* (Wilmington: Michael Glazier, 1984), 20-23.

[2] "What does the Lord require of you," says Micah, "but to do justice, to love kindness, and to walk humbly with your God?" (Micah 6:8).

"On the side of the oppressor is power," says Ecclesiastes.[3] While power may be used for good, it is often biased against the weak and the poor. Isaiah speaks of princes who are 'companions of thieves' and do not bring justice to the fatherless; the widow's cause does not even come within hearing distance.[4] At best, the powers are described by Jesus as indifferent and could be made to accede to requests by small people only by persistent and relentless importunings.[5]

Much of the poverty in the world today is due not only to the residues of colonial history but to bad governance of the ruling classes. 'Democratization' in many parts of the world is useless in contexts where political rights are meaningless to the poor whose interests do not figure at all in the concerns of those in power.

Compassion fatigue and the experience of futility in responding to what looks like bottomless pits of need should warn us that we can not go on ignoring the structural reasons for why people remain poor.

In the words of Martin Luther King,

> We are called to play the Good Samaritan on life's roadside, but that will only be an initial act…we must come to see that the whole Jericho road must be transformed so that men and women will not be constantly beaten and robbed as they make their journey on life's highway." [6]

Poverty is a sign of dysfunction in the institutions of society

There need not be any poor in Israel, God says, "…if only you will strictly obey the voice of the Lord your God, being careful to do all this commandment that I command you today." [7] Massive poverty is a smoke signal that the institutions – in the context of this passage the legal provision of debt relief during the Sabbatical Year – are not working.

Quite early in their history, Moses was commanded to institute safety nets for the most vulnerable segments of society – the poor, the widow, the orphan and the alien. Structural re-arrangements like the Jubilee Year in Leviticus 25 were meant to prevent social imbalances like undue concentration of wealth in the hands of a few.

Israel failed to obey these laws, which were supposed to distinguish them as a just society among the nations. As a consequence, they lost all their identifying marks as a 'called out' people – the land, the temple, the monarchy – and were scattered about as exiles in strange lands. That once great kingdom of David and Solomon, whose lineage was to be the seed for the Messiah of all

---

[3] Eccs. 4:1.
[4] Is. 1:23.
[5] Lk. 18:1-8.
[6] Charles Ringma, 'Let My People Go', reflection 43, as cited in his lecture, *Liberation Theologians Speak to Evangelicals,*14.
[7] Deuteronomy 15:5.

peoples, disintegrated. Israel as a nation dispersed and disappeared because of two major sins – idolatry and oppression, or the failure to love God and neighbor.

Today, the churches in many nations and the civil societies within them are rising to fill the deficits in justice and social services. It is a cause for celebration. Microfinance, particularly, has proven to be a liberating tool for the vast poor who are ignored by those who make decisions in the formal economy.

Yet the rise of civil society, the emergence of microfinance and a growing corporate social responsibility in the two thirds world can also be signs that something is amiss in the structures that should have been delivering justice and growing the economy.

Almsgiving and the proliferation of welfare agencies cannot substitute for the effective functioning of the institutions mandated to enforce equity and build a sound economy that reduces poverty to a minimum.

It is the core business of government, not civil society, to enforce justice – to "punish those who do evil and to praise those who do good." [8] A strong state can only be made possible, not by repression and curtailing dissent in the name of 'peace and order', but by sending strong signals to high and low that the rule of law shall be enforced without fear or favor. Gunnar Myrdal had long ago diagnosed that 'soft states' – those whose rule-keeping tend to get slippery because the institutions are riddled with corruption and subject to the oily machinations of the powerful – are seedbeds to perpetual poverty.

Likewise, it is business institutions and not NGOs that God has ordained to serve as the engines for growing a nation's economy.

It is work that is meant to sustain people, not charity. History shows that when society relegates the plight of the poor to charity, it can feed rather than alleviate poverty. As in the Middle Ages, it can become spiritualized, making poverty a mystical state. The practice of charity slips into spiritual banking, a way of piling up 'treasures in heaven', securing merit or indulgences for the afterlife or some such return for one's investment, besides creating paternalistic dependencies between giver and receiver.[9]

Advocacy on behalf of the poor is a command, not an option

To serve the poor is to get political; inevitably, we will run into issues of power. In many countries, access to resources is not a right but a thing you fight for. For the poor to even have the minimum conditions for survival, inserting their voices in the public square is necessary.

Central to the transforming role of the church is its obligation to speak with a prophetic voice to abusive powers. It is part of its 'kingly rule' as vice-regent of the God of justice. Our calling to exercise 'dominion' is not to lord it over all

---

[8] 1 Peter 2:13-14.

[9] E.H. Oliver, *The Social Achievements of the Christian Church* (Toronto: Board of Evangelism and Social Service of the United Church of Canada, 1930), 103-104.

the structures of society. Our political role is not primarily to put Christians into office, or even to insert our own interests into political space as a power bloc, like the Moral Majority or the religious rightwing in the US or some such return to a Constantinian understanding of the church vis-à-vis the state.

Our primary task is to see to it that God's original purposes for society are realized for the good of all. The church as an institution is not called to usurp the powers of the state and run its affairs, as has happened in the Middle Ages or in the de facto friocracy that held sway in the many countries that were under Spanish colonization. Its calling is to preach the word in such a way that it is truly a conscience to society, a 'voice for the voiceless.' This is the functional equivalent in our time of this oracular admonition addressed to an ancient king:

> Open your mouth for the mute,
> for the rights of all who are destitute.
> Open your mouth, judge righteously,
> defend the rights of the poor and needy.[10]

Understanding Power Structures

It is not enough to have a critical mass of do-gooding individuals who want change. It is naïve to assume that if we change individuals, we change society. All change begins from the inside, it is true; but for such change to impact society, it needs to have the force and the relative permanence of institutions.

It is easy enough to be prophetic and critique what is wrong in society. What is hard is the task of building alternative structures. Reforming vision needs institutionalization if it is to endure as a forceful critiquing element in society. This requires understanding the nature of power and the institutions that give it form and force.

Walter Wink helps us with the insight that embedded in our institutions are spiritual powers. Social institutions have an "outer, visible structure and an inner, spiritual reality." [11]

One only has to walk, for instance, into the offices of notoriously corrupt bureaucracies to sense that the atmosphere has something preternaturally oppressive about it. Clerks strike you as either stone-cold, impervious to entreaty and heavy with anonymous authority, or silkily shifty, as if a reptile from some dark and slimy pit has crawled on to a chair and now smiles at you with a malignant leer. The air reeks with a foggy, ectoplasmic mist that seems to emanate from somewhere beyond the ceiling and clouds clarity and one's sense of the reality of good and evil.

The language of Paul in Ephesians 6 – "thrones, dominions, principalities and powers" – suggests that the demonic manifests itself not only in personalities, but also in subhuman forces – structures and institutions – that

---

[10] Proverbs 31: 8-9.

[11] Walter Wink, *Engaging the Powers: Discernment and Resistance in a World of Domination* (Minneapolis: Fortress, 1992), 3.

enslave or oppress people. The 'powers' are the "interiority of earthly institutions or structures or systems." [12]

People and institutions are in a dialectical relationship and mutually reinforcing: they either weaken or strengthen each other. "Human misery is caused by institutions, but these institutions are maintained by human beings. We are made evil by our institutions, yes; but our institutions are also made evil by us." [13]

The anthropologist Edward Hall way back in the sixties partly grasped this by the idea that the artifacts around us are human 'extensions.'[14] Following this, our institutions are 'extensions' of who we are collectively as people. This collective identity then gets patterned into systems that soon 'extend' themselves such that the whole is more than the sum of the parts. The institution develops an overwhelming ethos that eventually shapes all the individuals in it.

If we are not careful, even institutions meant for good will develop their own logic, seize control, foil our good intentions and run away from us and our original purposes. They will apotheosize and soon demand that we worship them, as Jesus well knew. Satan's offer to give him all the kingdoms of the world was a Faustian temptation; the desire for power would have enabled him to do good, but it was also a way of diverting his loyalty and focus from God and his own sense of what his mission was about.

Examples abound of many organizations that have drifted away from their original purpose and vision. Principles and core values are sacrificed to the altar of institutional 'growth' or 'sustainability.' In the course of this drivenness, idealistic stakeholders get disillusioned, or are expelled from the very institutions they have had a hand in founding and left wounded on the wayside. Both leader and led burn out, staff out in the field lose their sense of purpose and direction, and all get weary in well doing, for lack of care themselves from the institutions that employ them.

Likewise, our tools, theories and systems so reify that they get unduly universalized. What has worked in one context is quickly held up as a 'model' and slavishly replicated, or elevated to the status of a one-answer system for solving the problems of the world. Multilateral development institutions, for instance, come up with one-size-fits-all policies like structural adjustment

---

[12] Wink, *Engaging the Powers*, 65-85.

[13] Wink, *Engaging the Powers*, 75, cf. also Robert C. Linthicum, *Empowering the Poor* (Monrovia CA: MARC), 106.

[14] Hall wrote, "By developing his extensions, man has been able to improve or specialize various functions. The computer is an extension of part of the brain, the telephone extends the voice, the wheel extends the legs and feet. Language extends experience in time and space while writing extends language." Marshall Mcluhan also elaborated on this in his idea of visual and auditory media as 'extensions of man.' See Edward T. Hall, *The Hidden Dimension* (Garden City, NY: Doubleday, 1966), 3; Marshall McLuhan, *Understanding Media: The Extensions of Man* (New York: McGraw Hill, 1964).

programs, which in countries like mine (the Philippines)have caused a great deal of harm.

Globalization is a major example of a process that has reified to the degree that it is heralded in almost Messianic terms as 'lifting all boats', or feared as a mammoth juggernaut driven beyond control by the combined forces of technology and the market.

In each of us is this tendency to absolutize the structural elaborations that grow around the simple substance of an institution's mission. This was at the heart of Jesus' controversy with the legalists of his day: "the Sabbath was made for man, not man for the Sabbath." [15] Edward Hall calls this 'extension transference'; the bible calls it 'idolatry.'

Often unconsciously, our trust, commitment and loyalties shift from the invisible God to the more tangible 'things of God'. Our institutions get invested with overwhelming power and divinity, reducing us all into powerlesss bureaucrats unable to change the system, or cyberslaves willingly overturning normal waking hours to supply the demands of a globalized market for indentured labor.

Whether we are aware of it or not, structures and institutions are as much battlegrounds between good and evil as the human soul. Those who seek to change them must be ready for an intense confrontation with the demonic, however subtly disguised as merely neutral systemic forces. The risks and dangers can be fatal: "He who digs a pit will fall into it, and a serpent will bite him who breaks through a wall." [16]

How then do we dethrone the powers that are degrading human life by systemic injustice and brutality? Or, closer to home, how do we see to it that our own institutions remain servants to the causes for which they were established in the first place?

Simply put, this begins with at least three sensitivities and processes that are spiritual in nature: a) taking seriously the ethic of the cross, b) naming the powers, and c) a conscious refusal to bow the knee. The rest are sociological processes that are best identified, implemented, managed and articulated by social activists and development practitioners themselves within their own organizational contexts. For the task at hand, let me outline what these processes mean.

Towards a Radical Reversal of Power Relations

Genuine transformation requires a radical reversal in the social order. The Magnificat speaks of the coming of the kingdom of God as involving change in power relations: it will mean the "overthrowing of the mighty and the lifting up

---

[15] Mk. 2:23-28.

[16] Eccs. 10:8.

of the lowly." It will also mean the redressing of economic imbalances: the "filling of the hungry and the sending away of the rich empty."[17]

This concern for equitable structures differs from other popular movements, however, in the means by which this reversal could be achieved. Forcible taking of power through revolutionary violence has been tried time and again since the French stormed the Bastille. This has had mixed results. The ensuing reign of terror, disorder and the social trauma that accompanies the collapse of the old order makes the pain of reconstruction almost unending. An alternative to the destructive use of force is the path Jesus had taken: the way of the cross.

Upside down power. The kingdom Jesus inaugurated turns the world upside down, but quietly and no less effectively, inviting those who would be subject to it to become not so much *revolutionaries* as *subversives*. This new social order demands that its citizens cross borders of ethnicity, gender and economic status and demonstrate that in Christ, equality is possible between Jew and Greek, male and female, rich and poor.[18] They are to see to it that in their dealings, the first should be last and the last first. They are to live with the confidence that strength is won out of weakness, and that those who seek authority will find greatness in being servants of all.

Hard pragmatists dismiss this social ethic as unrealistic. Yet recent history shows that even without coercive power, those who possess great moral force could topple despotic regimes. Mahatma Gandhi, that great soul of the Indian struggle for independence, never held office. Yet he galvanized his people by taking a moral high ground that unmasked and disarmed the powers by his very refusal to resort to violence. Part of the paradox of power is that it has most use and force when it is wielded by those who are most disinterested in its use.

The Anabaptist tradition, always suspicious of the use of force, has shown that intransigence can be in the form of 'revolutionary subordination', or, as proposed by Bruce Bradshaw, 'transformative subordination'. One can be subject to governing authorities without always obeying, because one does not relinquish freedom of conscience and the moral choice to "obey God rather than men." Even if one submits to government, John Howard Yoder qualifies this by saying that "the subordinate person in the social order is addressed as a moral agent, and hence responsible for his or her actions."[19]

Submission and not *subservience* characterizes our relationship with the powers, much like the Lord Jesus who submitted to Roman and Jewish laws even as he protested against his treatment before Pilate and challenged the teachings of the religious establishment. The incarnation has both an *affirming* and a *critiquing* element.

We submit to the structures and identify deeply with the people who live within those structures. At the same time, we subvert the structures simply by bearing witness to the reality of another world, a larger story whose transcendent laws take priority and demand our constant allegiance. "In a

[17] Lk. 1:52-53.

[18] Galatians 3:28.

[19] John Howard Yoder, *The Politics of Jesus* (Grand Rapids: Eerdmans, 1972), 163, 174.

transformative relationship with political structures neither the person nor the church ever relinquishes independent moral agency. The person and the church are subordinate to the government for the purposes of social organization, but never for moral or ethical reasons." [20]

Those who have lived under regimes where government instrumentalities have ceased to be servants of the people but instead have turned into their torturers know how important such moral choices are. A soldier, for example, who is under duress to perform duties that violate his sense of right and wrong has the right to refuse and break the chain of command.

Hitler's generals and other functionaries in the ranks of the Third Reich failed to exercise this moral agency. Likewise, the German church of the time got swept by the tidal forces of patriotic hysteria and missed the opportunity to stand decisively against the powers at a catastrophic moment in history.

While many may not be aware of the final import of their actions, it is in making such choices that we confront the powers and turn the tide of history.

This was what I learned in reflecting on Jesus' own choices. For some time, I have been intrigued and puzzled that John Milton's *Paradise Regained* was all about Jesus' temptation in the wilderness. I could not enter at the time into what it was saying – that there in the barren desert, in the inner struggle of that one man against his own vulnerabilities, the fate of the world hung in the balance.

The temptations appealed to the best of what he was and what he was called to do – to ease the hunger of the poor, to establish his promised kingdom so he can do the good he wanted to do. By a flashy display of supernatural power, he could have shown who he was, validated his identity as son of God, and silenced those who continually asked for signs and doubted his credibility.[21] The temptations were attempts to make Jesus perform his Messianic task without having to die on the cross.

People who care for the world go through precisely these same temptations. Impressed by massive feeding programs, like the feeding of a billion Chinese, we embark on a similarly ambitious program and forget that people do not live by bread alone, that the highest and best need even of the poor is still peace with God and neighbor.

In the struggle for political space to champion the cause of the poor, we often end up serving some other cause once entangled in the toils of power. When belittled by critics and challenged to show proof of success, we are sometimes tempted to advertise who we are and what exactly we have done.

But like Tolkien's Gandalf in Lord of the Rings, Jesus refused to 'desire strength in order to do good.' In his willingness to suffer humiliation on the cross, Jesus reversed the pattern by which the world seeks to destroy evil and

---

[20] Bruce Bradshaw, *Change across Cultures: A Narrative Approach to Social Transformation* (Grand Rapids, MI: Baker Academic, 2002), 142.
[20] Lk. 4:1-13.
[21] Lk. 4:1-13.

do good. In a mysterious way, what seemed like an act of supreme weakness and defeat proved to be the disarming of principalities and powers.[22]

To embrace the ethic of the cross is to follow the same pattern. We exercise *dominion*, not primarily by capturing positions of power and influence, but by *servanthood* to the larger society. We become poor in making many rich, accepting the downward mobility that Jesus himself willingly experienced as part of his identification with us. We disarm our enemies and put a stop to violence, not by avenging ourselves with superior arms like Lamech, but by turning the other cheek and praying for them.

The power of this ethic can be seen throughout history. The church had been most powerful when it had been powerless, and most weak when it had been most strong. When Christians were a helpless minority thrown into dungeons or fed to the lions, their numbers swelled and their influence spread like wildfire. When the church sought hegemony and engaged the state in a contest for power, it became most corrupt and lost its spiritual force. Whether by the power of the sword through *conquista* or by the civilizing force of an inflated sense of 'Manifest Destiny', the church does not serve the cause of Christ when its handmaiden is worldly power.

This does not mean that Christians are not to aspire for high office nor exert influence by capturing strategic positions of power. Christians gifted for engagement in the public arena should certainly seek positions where they can be of most good. What this means simply is that power, by its very nature, reifies. The saying that 'power corrupts, and absolute power corrupts absolutely,' is one manifestation of this reification. Power, especially when unbridled by principle or ineffectively leashed by a system of checks and balances, easily turns into a law unto itself unless consciously and inwardly renounced by those who are called to wield it.

Such renunciation is the only way by which revolutions can be other than merely a transfer of power from one oppressor class to another. We have seen how native elites in the two thirds world, post-independence, merely supplanted the old colonial powers, in some cases with greater violence and rapacity. The 'vanguard' of the proletariat in socialist countries had quickly turned into ruthless ruling cliques that perpetuate hegemonic power by annihilating all dissent. The reactionary forces of the failed authoritarian regimes of the '70s and '80s continue to cast their long dark shadows on the precarious democracies that have emerged out of the rubble.

Only the self-denying ethic of the cross can save us from the seductions of the will to power and reverse its corrupting effects.

Naming the Powers

Critical to genuine resistance is when we are able to accurately name whatever it is that ails our organizations and the larger social environment. We need to

[22] Colossians 2:14-15.

ask, '*who*, or *what*, are the powers that truly rule over us?' An NGO may say it is the people, or, if churches, God. But what really drives decisions and shapes our programs?

Let me mention just one.

It is an open secret that part of the ineffectiveness of many programs on the ground is that these originated not from the wishes and desires of the people but from the priority concerns of funders. So-called participatory processes are merely efforts to make the people buy in and own the programs being offered. Very few NGOs are able to resist the inducements of doing something that may be beyond the community's level of preparedness, or, worse, outside the organization's expertise or calling, simply because there is funding.

Many dedicated community workers burn out because of the constant tension of having to mediate between the expectations of funders and the agencies that employ them and the actual condition and pace of where the people are. Faith-based organizations pay lip service to the importance of the inward changes taking place in people's lives, and yet short-circuit the process of winning hearts and minds because of pressure to show visible, tangible progress.[23]

Clearly, a major power to be confronted is the kind of economic determinism that in ancient times was called Mammon. It is not surprising that bible scholars say that Jesus talked more about money than about the kingdom. Perhaps because of all possible rivals to God, money is the most comprehensive in its power to provide sustenance, well-being and a measure of happiness, as well as ensure security, success and sustainability.

This brings us to the next stage, which is the inner resolve to resist being conformed to the image of whatever it is that we hold to be as gods.

The Power of Refusal

As simple as it may seem, change begins when we truly live as if there is another world, another kingdom that compels our allegiance. Daniel and his friends, captive subjects in an alien empire, show us what it means to refuse to capitulate, either to the soft seductions of sophisticated Babylon, or to the coercive power of an arbitrary and despotic king. Before Nebuchadnezzar they boldly declared, "our God whom we serve is able to deliver us from the burning fiery furnace, and he will deliver us out of your hand, O king. But if not, be it known to you, O king, that we will not serve your gods or worship the golden image that you have set up." [24]

Daniel's friends had no doubt that their God is able to deliver, but even if he does not, they will not bow the knee. This loyal intransigence in the face of extreme pressure is what renders the roaring tigers of our fears ultimately

---

[23] For some examples of this kind of tension, see Grant Power's article, 'Let the People Lead, Lessons Learned in African Cities', *Together*, October-December, 1997, 1-4.

[24] Daniel 3:17-18.

toothless. In saying a resounding 'no!' to the powers we declare that even here, in the corridors of power or in the board rooms of those who control what we buy or sell, Jesus is Lord. There is no corner on earth that is outside his rule. And we are called to bear witness to the existence of such a reality, an alternative society that is coming into being as his people remain true to the values and character of their king.

Quite early, I had to learn what this means in our own organization. More than 30 years ago, as a fledgling research and training institution, we have had to survive by doing professional services since contributions were hard to come by. No one of consequence wanted to touch us with a ten-foot pole, since we were young and as yet had no track record and were perceived by a conservative evangelical community to be suspiciously left-wing.

At one point, in a moment of great need, we were offered two research projects by a government think-tank. We rejoiced at the opportunity, until we were told we had to pay a 'finder's fee' of 5% for each of the projects. It was some sort of commission, we were told – it was standard practice for all institutions who wish to do research for the government. I said, "Okay, let's put it in the project budget and have it duly receipted." My friend, who was brokering this, said, "Oh no; actually, the fee goes to my bosses," he said sheepishly. "It is low enough as it is, the usual fee is 15%, as we are aware of the kind of institution that you are."

I must admit I had to pause and think for a while before finally saying, "Sorry, this looks to me to be a bribe, not a commission. We cannot take it." In that inner place where we come face to face with the clarity of our choices, I discerned the boundaries that defined the limits of what we can and cannot do, given who we are and to whom we belong. My friend looked at me askance, quite incredulous. "You can't do this, you know; there is no way you will get any project. This will put you into the mainstream. Besides, even respectable institutions do this. It's just part of the rules around here." It was my turn to look at him in wonder. "You know who we are," I said. "There is no way we can open our mouths again if we do this. We might as well close shop."

It was not an easy decision. Part of me – the more complex, professional part that appreciates the ambiguities of having to make our way into a world that demands some accommodation if we are to be at all serious players in it – wanted to take the job, rationalizing it as a necessary step towards stabilizing the institution until we have had some lead time to develop a reputation. The other part – the more instinctive, primal part – grasped with unerring clarity that acceptance would mean complicity and with it our own inner descent into silent acquiescence and the kind of feckless sufferance that allows corruption in the country to flourish.

My friend went away perplexed, and I was left wondering about the opportunity cost of having refused. Weeks later, I received notice from the Ministry of Education that a research proposal we had submitted months before won a grant out of more than a hundred submissions to a World Bank funded project to restructure the entire educational system. I told my friend he was wrong. It is possible to get a project with the government without playing to their backroom rules. "It cannot be," he said. "That ministry is one of the most corrupt." He could not fathom how it could happen.

A clue presented itself just after we signed the contract. We overheard the top official muttering something under his breath to his project manager just before he left. The staff knit his brow and shook his head. Apparently, the official mistook the name of the head of our research team for someone he knew. We do not know if this had any bearing on the actual research selection. But we came away with a lesson and a confidence that has been our keepsake through the arduous trials of our journey: God is well able to make a way even against all systemic odds for those who prioritize his kingdom and his righteousness.

Through the years, there would be many more incidents that similarly put to us squarely the challenge of simply making choices within the bounds of our identity in Christ.

This simplicity was Mother Teresa's apparently pat remedy for the Catholic psychologist Henri Nouwen, who came to her beset by a host of inner conflicts, doubts and complex uncertainties: "Spend an hour with your Lord every day and do not do anything that you know is wrong and you will be fine." [25]

Who we are and to whom we belong defines the boundaries of what we can and cannot do. At the same time, there are many things in life that are not always black and white. For these we need the guidance and discernment possible only through hearing God in our own daily walk with him.

Walking with God was not always safe, of course. There were moments when dogged loyalty seemed fatal. "Him only you shall serve" kept ringing in my ears every time we tended to go astray, tempted to prioritize the interest of the institution more than the purity and honor of the God that we serve.

I cannot say with certainty if such keeping faith has made any dent on the structures that continue to oppress our people. All that I can say is that it has enabled us to draw a line in the sand and make a stand. It is at least territory that the powers cannot claim.

As we name and dethrone the powers by our refusal to bow the knee, we reclaim God's creation, inch-by-inch, from their grasping hold. We bear witness to the powerful, as Daniel did before Nebuchadnezzar, that "the Most High rules the kingdom of men, and gives it to whom he will." [26]

---

[25] Henry Nouwen, *Here and Now* (New York: Crossroad Publishing, 2001).
[26] Daniel 4:25.

The Evangelical Church's Involvement With National Politics

Martin Allaby

This chapter argues that Christians in low- and middle-income countries who want to maximize their impact on poverty need to get politically involved. Drawing on the experiences of Christian leaders in four countries, it describes common reasons why Christians may not engage in political action, and some pitfalls for those who do. It concludes with the suggestion that evangelicals who want to maximize their contribution to better governance should consider linking believers who hold positions of power in government with Christian groups outside government who can provide them with encouragement, accountability and challenge.

Developing Country Governments Control Far More Resources than Aid Agencies or Charities

The welfare of citizens of poor countries depends more on the accountability and effectiveness of their governments than on the activities of aid agencies or charities, not least because they control far greater resources. For the citizens of nearly all low- and middle-income countries, the resources controlled by their governments exceed official aid monies. There are only six countries (Afghanistan, Central African Republic, Democratic Republic of the Congo, Ethiopia, Madagascar, and Sierra Leone) where, in at least one year since AD 2000, the government received more in the way of official aid than it raised itself as revenue through taxes and fees.[1] In 17 other countries[2] government revenue exceeded official aid by a factor of less than three, but in all other countries with available data official aid was dwarfed by government revenue. We do not have comparable data on the scale of NGO funding or private charitable giving, but it is probably small compared to official aid.

---

[1] The comparison is between net Official Development Assistance and government revenue. The data were sourced from http://data.worldbank.org/data-catalog/world-development-indicators.

[2] Those 17 countries are Benin, Bhutan, Burkina Faso, Cambodia, Cape Verde, Kyrgyz Republic, Lao PDR, Mali, Nepal, Nicaragua, Niger, Togo, Republic of the Congo, Senegal, Tajikistan, Uganda, Zambia.

Good Governance is Vital for Poverty Reduction, but Hard to Achieve

An obvious consequence of the preceding section is that poverty reduction is very dependent on the way that the governments of low- and middle-income countries use the resources they control.[3] At the worst end of the spectrum of governance are 'kleptocracies'. Acemoglu et al. (2003:1) describe a few examples:

> Many developing countries have suffered under the personal rule of 'kleptocrats', who implement highly inefficient economic policies, expropriate the wealth of their citizens, and use the proceeds for their own glorification or consumption.... Many countries in Africa and the Caribbean suffer under 'kleptocratic' regimes, where the state is controlled and run for the benefit of an individual, or a small group, who use their power to transfer a large fraction of society's resources to themselves.... Kleptocratic regimes appear to have been disastrous for economic performance and caused the impoverishment of the citizens.

While kleptocracy represents the extreme end of a spectrum, there are still grounds for doubting whether many governments generally act in the interests of their citizens. North et al. (2006) offer a 'framework for interpreting recorded human history' that distinguishes between 'Limited Access Orders' and 'Open Access Orders', on the basis of the extent to which governments allow aspiring citizens access to political and economic opportunities. All Open Access Orders "have market economies with open competition, competitive multi-party democratic political systems, and a secure government monopoly over violence" (North et al. 2006:4). This contrasts with the norm in Limited Access Orders, where political elites simply divide up control of the economy, each getting some share of the rents,[4] while limiting the access of everyone else to political and economic opportunities. According to their analysis, a country must change from being a Limited Access Order to become an Open Access Order if it is to escape from poverty. North et al. note that such transitions do not occur either frequently or quickly; their estimate of timescale where transitions have occurred is "something of the order of fifty years or less."

---

[3] This is not to deny that factors other than governance are also important. Jeffrey Sachs, *The End of Poverty: How We Can Make it Happen in Our Lifetime* (London: Penguin Books, 2005), 84 lists governance, economic policy, fiscal framework, poverty traps, culture, geopolitics and physical geography as factors to consider when assessing the causes of poverty. Developing country governments have more control over factors at the beginning of the list than those at the end.

[4] In this context 'rent' does not have its commonplace meaning of income from hiring something out. Rather, it refers to 'economic rent', which is defined as 'a payment for the services of an economic resource above what is necessary for it to remain in its current use' (J. Black, N. Hashimzade and G. Myles, *A Dictionary of Economics*, 3rd ed. (Oxford: Oxford University Press, 2009). Examples of economic rents are the profits made by firms that form a cartel to raise prices, and by governments that require producers to pay for licences without providing any useful service.

Recognizing the importance of good governance to poverty reduction, the World Bank has promoted a 'consensus package' of reforms that are intended to improve governance by:

- Improving the capacity, transparency, and accountability of state institutions, in areas such as financial management, public service delivery and the legal system.
- Creating a competitive and responsible private sector.
- Increasing opportunities for participation and oversight by civil society, the media, and communities (World Bank 2007a:47).

Unfortunately, many leading writers on governance see little prospect for success of this sort of strategy. For example, Neild (2002:208-9) identifies several huge obstacles:

> It is hard to see how the international economic agencies and their member governments can introduce incentives that would cause corrupt rulers to say to themselves 'if I do not attack corruption I may be punished so severely that I shall lose power, whereas if I attack it I shall be rewarded so generously that my hold on power will be maintained or enhanced.' Not only are the rich countries and their agencies in this respect impotent, they commonly have been and are accomplices in corruption abroad, encouraging it by their actions rather than impeding it. First, there was the uninhibited use by both sides in the Cold War of corruption and covert operations, including 'destabilization' by arming dissidents, assassination, election rigging and the like, to topple regimes and obstruct the legitimate access to power of political parties perceived to belong to the other side. Secondly, firms from the rich countries have been in the habit of paying bribes to rulers and officials in order to gain export contracts, notably for arms and construction projects... Thirdly, there is the problem of the corruption-inducing effects of the purchase, by the rich countries and their international corporations, of concessions in Third World countries to exploit natural deposits of oil, copper, diamonds and the like.

Protestant Christianity Has Helped to Improve Governance in the Past

Although the task of improving governance is undoubtedly difficult, there is some evidence that Protestants may be able to make a useful contribution. In a quantitative analysis of factors associated with control of corruption (which is a major component of good governance), Treisman (2000:436) found that countries with Protestant traditions tend to have less corruption than others (as do those with more developed economies and long exposure to democracy).[5]

[5] Quite apart from any direct effect of Protestantism in reducing corruption, it can also be argued that Protestantism has also helped to restrain corruption through facilitating both economic development and democracy. Weber's thesis (Max Weber, *The Protestant Ethic and the Spirit of Capitalism* (London: Allen & Unwin, 1930)) is well known. Though controversial, it retains support from some leading academics, such as David Landes, *The Wealth and Poverty of Nations: Why Some are So Rich and Some So Poor* (London: Abacus, 1998), 177 and R.J. Barro and R.M. McCleary, 'Religion and Economic Growth across Countries', *American Sociological Review* 68 (2003), 760-81.

Treisman (2000:427-8) outlines four possible interpretations of the relationship between Protestantism and corruption:

1. Protestant cultures are less understanding toward lapses from grace and press more urgently to institutionalize virtue and cast out the wicked. Other Christian denominations, particularly the Catholic Church, place more emphasis on the inherent weakness of human beings and the need for the church to be forgiving and protecting.
2. Compared with other religious traditions, Protestantism focuses more on the individual rather than on the family, so is less accepting of nepotism.
3. Protestant societies are more likely to discover and punish official abuses, because they are more tolerant of challenges to authority and allow individual dissent, even when threatening to social hierarchies.
4. Protestant traditions — in which the separation of church and state is more pronounced than in, say, Catholicism or Islam — lead to a more vibrant, autonomous civil society that monitors the state more effectively.

The first two interpretations emphasize the moral behaviour of individuals; the second two are more political, focusing on a willingness to challenge abuse of authority, particularly by the state. Each interpretation has different implications for Protestants who are seeking to promote better governance today. The relative importance of the different interpretations is unclear, but it may well be that it is a combination of promoting moral behaviour of individuals and challenging abuse of authority that is most powerful. An example how this can work in practice was given by the Catholic Director of a secular anti-corruption NGO in the Philippines (who had previously commented that "If I were to meet an evangelical in government, my bias would be to tend to believe that these people have their integrity intact"):

> What generally works is partnering with like-minded government officials, those that are already oriented towards reform ... The whole point there is to look over the shoulder of the government, to make sure they're doing their jobs correctly. The reforms that we've tried out to date have always depended on the political will of the person dealing with it. What we want to do is to identify second tier leaders, the Under-Secretaries, and help them stay the course and not give up, because I can imagine to be in that position as a reformer, to be ostracised and persecuted because of what you're trying to do, is a tough thing to experience alone. And while one of the things we do is criticise government where we see fit, we also realise the flipside of that coin is to identify the areas of good, and support that.

As for facilitating democracy, Paul Freston, *Evangelical Christianity and Democracy in Latin America* (Oxford: Oxford University Press, 2009), 2 notes that "of all the major religions, Protestant Christianity has the longest historical links with processes of democratization."

Reasons Why Christians May Not Engage in Political Action

Despite the importance of good governance, and the evidence that Protestants have contributed to good governance in the past, evangelical Protestants are often reluctant to engage in political action. The remainder of this chapter draws on interviews conducted by the author in 2007 and 2008 with Christian leaders (mostly evangelical) in four countries across three continents: the Philippines, Kenya, Zambia and Peru. This section outlines their views on reasons why evangelical Christians may not engage in politics, and the following section describes two potential pitfalls for those who do. (Headings in inverted commas indicate beliefs that the interviewees considered to be false, but widely held.)

Dualism: 'Christianity is only for the soul'

Melba Maggay, Director of the Institute for the Study of Asian Church and Culture in the Philippines said:

> The Philippine church has captured a whole theological tradition that the gospel is for the soul, so we shouldn't have anything to do with politics.

An evangelical who works for a secular anti-corruption NGO in the Philippines said:

> Young people are being taught the theology of 'You can grow as a Christian and not care about the world. God doesn't care whether you're helping the needy people around you; as long as you're not hurting other people, as long as you're doing bible study and praying, that is alright'... You need a pastor who's going to tell the congregation: 'When you do not care about the poor around you and when you don't care about society, you're actually committing sin'. But no pastor would say that.

The leader of a Christian NGO in Kenya said:

> There is a huge dichotomy in this country between being a Christian and being actively involved in social justice issues.... People feel the work of the church is to preach to people on a Sunday, and hope that they will learn a bit about God. Social justice issues are the responsibility of the private sector, or the government, or civil society, or non-government organisations.

According to a pastor in the United Church of Zambia,

> Christian faith is concerned only with issues of spirituality, not so much how you live your Christian life outside the church.

A leader of the evangelical student movement in Peru gave a similar perspective:

> When you go to an evangelical service, in general you're not going to find a message that connects the word to problems of corruption, poverty, injustice, human dignity or problems within the country, because a good part of the church sees that as political discourse, and not as a valid message that comes from the Word of God.

A leader of the Pentecostal Church of Peru summed the situation up succinctly:

> We haven't produced a theological-political discourse, so the two things work very separately – theology on one side, politics on the other.

Conversionism: 'Personal transformation will solve societal problems'

Another perspective is that Christianity *should* be concerned with the material world, but that the Christian response to political, economic or social problems should be limited to the conversion and transformation of individuals. The sociologist David Martin describes this as a general characteristic of evangelicalism:

> Its individualistic approach supposes that political improvement depends on the multiplication of persons of moral integrity; the preferred discourse is through personalized images rather than structural arrangements and forces' (Martin 1999:40).

To give some examples, a leader of the National Council of Churches in Kenya said,

> You would diagnose poverty as a curse, and believe that if your members can come to the Lord and start giving, the poverty will go away.

The leader of a Zambian Christian NGO said:

> The church here sees poverty as a personal problem. Particularly the evangelical church doesn't see poverty as anything to do with the systems that are in place. [They] see poverty as a personal problem of bad decisions, laziness, lack of faith, not having a relationship with Jesus. So they don't see corruption as affecting the level of poverty in the nation.

A leader of the National Evangelical Council of Peru made similar criticisms:

> The problem in our churches is that we are primarily expert in individual formation, and it's assumed that through training and forming people, the systems will change in due course, when what is needed is a greater and heavier public participation. I don't think, like some pastors say, that when Peru is evangelical it'll be paradise ... It's not only the people; it's the systems that the people have produced. The political system is corrupt. So we need to make not moral decisions but political decisions to eliminate a system that's corrupt.

An evangelical church leader in the Philippines expressed similar views:

> You can hardly transform a nation by making everyone goody two shoes. You have to redeem structures that have been used for evil purposes – government fund management, for instance – and evangelicalism hardly addresses those issues.

'Christians should always obey the government'

Some interviewees mentioned interpretations of Rom. 13 which teach that Christians should always obey the government in all circumstances. According to a leader of the evangelical student movement in Peru, neo-Pentecostal leaders used this theology to justify the actions of President Fujimori (which included widespread abuses of human rights as he sought to quash two revolutionary movements in the 1990s):

> They saw him as sent by God: 'We need to obey political authority without criticism, because that's the will of God'.

Father Peter Henriot, Director of the Jesuit Centre for Theological Reflection in Zambia, criticised this theology because:

> It focuses on verses 1 to 2, that speak of authority being put in place by God and that whoever opposes authority opposes God. But it ignores the key phrases of verse 4 that make very clear, very clear indeed, that the one in authority is God's servant 'working for your own good.' In other words, if the ruler is not working for the good of the people... she or he simply loses legitimacy, no longer has authority and should not be obeyed.

'Politics is dirty, so any Christian who get involved in politics will be corrupted'

In the Philippines, an evangelical who works for a secular anti-corruption NGO said,

> The belief that 'politics is evil, Christians should not be involved in that, Christians should just pray about all this evil' – that is a huge problem amongst evangelicals in the country.

David Gitari, a former Anglican Archbishop of Kenya who is well known for his courageous opposition to political oppression under President Moi, described how the theology of the East African Revival movement had discouraged many Christians from political engagement:

> They came up with the very strong idea that a born-again Christian cannot be a politician. In fact a member of the Revival who goes into politics is called a cold, or lukewarm, Christian – because they cannot see how a politician can be a Christian.

An evangelical bishop in Zambia said,

> sometimes the church is aloof, not wanting to get their hands dirty: 'Politics is a dirty game, so let's keep away'.

An evangelical pastor in Peru explained that,

> Many pastors think that politics is like sin. Almost every believer thinks that politics means corruption. If a Christian becomes Mayor they still think he is going to do the same things as the one who is not a Christian.

Succumbing to Bribery by the State

This is more likely to be an issue in countries where evangelicals form a substantial proportion of the population, such as Kenya and Zambia, so that politicians see evangelical leaders as opinion formers whose support is worth cultivating. According to an evangelical lawyer in Kenya this was quite prevalent in his country in 2007:

> Currently we have several church leaders who are being paid by the politicians so that they don't harass them or challenge the government departments, but give high praise to the government.

An evangelical leader in Zambia described his experience of this:

> I personally was offered Kw.150 million[6] to do some campaigning during the election. They said "There are no strings attached. We just feel that people are being misinformed, and we feel that if you, with your deserving reputation – you can correct them and tell them the right thing." I turned it down, I refused. I told them "I'm not available for purchase." But not much later, after I turned it down, I began to see on TV bishops (from the independent Pentecostal churches) who began to campaign and speak the language of the President. They would say "We don't want people who have more than one wife to become President. We don't want smokers for President," and stuff like that. Knowing what I'd been offered, I knew that they'd been paid.

Intimidation by the State

If bribery does not work, intimidation may follow. Paul Collier, former head of research at the World Bank, uses the following words to describe the task faced by reformers in the poorest countries (Collier 2007:180):[7]

> Within the societies of the bottom billion there is an intense struggle between brave people who are trying to achieve change and powerful groups who oppose them. The politics of the bottom billion is not the bland and sedate process of the rich democracies but rather a dangerous contest between moral extremes…

One evangelical leader who was involved in a constitutional review process that sought to limit the powers of the President of his country described his personal experience of this struggle:

> I've been shot at. I was driving home at night. I was just getting home, and a car was trailing me. I would stop and give them an indication that they should pass, they never passed. Then I realised I was in danger. So I quickly turned, facing them, and I tried to rush to the police. As I passed them they fired. I thank God that I'm still alive. In the morning I picked out the cartridge and took it to the police and they said it was one of the police or the military weapons that had been used. What had happened that particular morning makes me certain that it was pre-arranged. Some of my colleagues had a meeting with one of the Commissioners in the Constitution-making process and this man was asking about me and saying 'How well do you know this man? He is hated so much by the

---

[6] This is approximately £20,000 in exchange rate terms, and considerably more in terms of local purchasing power.

[7] The title of his book *The Bottom Billion* refers to the citizens of around fifty states that have the worst governance and who live on less than a dollar a day.

> President.' They told me that in the morning and in the evening the shooting happened.

A pastor in Zambia gave the following account of the intimidation he and colleagues had experienced:

> If all the churches would get together and address these evils, I think our voice would be massive. Many believers in Zambia share my view, but then the problem is we fear the government.... To be singled out as a pastor, to be called to appear before an Intelligence Officer who comes from Lusaka, that can give you a few shivers. There were no direct threats, but they said "If you want to continue, we can prosecute you for defamation of the President." They can even apply some economic embargoes against you. If you are running a firm and you supply to government then they will not buy anything from you. That's how they keep people in line. If your relatives hear that you've been called to appear before these people, they'll tell you to shut up: "You may lose your life."

The next section moves on to consider two common pitfalls encountered by those who have decided to get politically involved.

Pitfalls for Sincere Christians Who Do Engage in Political Action

Naivete about what being a (Christian) politician involves

Some Christians who have sought to reform politics by running for political office have not prepared themselves adequately. A leader of a Christian NGO in Kenya said:

> In the 2002 general elections we had a fellowship of 17 or 18 Christians who wanted to run for office.... A lot of them were new to the whole political game, to involvement in political parties, to developing independent constituencies or support bases etc, to the point of being naïve. When you face off against someone that's not so clean, but has rendered public service for a long time, he has learned in the trenches. So when you just come out and say: "I'm going to get him out because he did this deal," the other side is that he's taken a long time to become the politician he is. It doesn't take only a year, just because you say "I love Jesus."

In 2004 Brother Eddie Villanueva, a prominent evangelical and leader of the Jesus Is Lord Church in the Philippines, ran an unsuccessful campaign for the Presidency. An evangelical businessman who Brother Eddie had sought out, said he had given him the following advice (which was ignored):

> If God called you to be President, he would have prepared you to do that. What kind of equipping have you had for running the government? You've never run a government agency. You've never won an elected post. You've never run a local government. You've not even been a legislator. If you really think that God is calling you to a political career, then you allow him to equip you. Maybe you should run first as you local Congressman, and represent your District in Congress. If God prospers you there, perhaps you should run as a national Senator. And if God prospers you there, then you are prepared for the highest office in the land.

Humberto Lay, a Pentecostal pastor, ran unsuccessfully for the Presidency of Peru in 2006. An observer recalled the reaction of evangelicals to Lay's lack of political experience:

> He said he'd had 25 years' experience of managing a large church. Anyone who's got any kind of political experience knows that that's not enough, but lots of Christians at that meeting said "Yes, we've got to give him a chance, he's better than the rest."

Frederick Chiluba, who made much of his Christian faith, was President of Zambia from 1990 to 2000. After he was found guilty of corruption[8] a former Vice President of Zambia gave the following explanation for the contradictions between his faith and actions:

> I think he was counselled into corruption. The system of government counselled him, "Look, this is the way that things are done. So in order to protect yourself you must do this..." You've got to be strong enough to be able to connect your values and your Christian faith to government. And my conclusion is that my elder brother in the faith failed to practically connect his faith to everyday life of government. The reason could be that it was a new concept, a totally new concept.

The sociologist David Martin (1999:40) points out that evangelical theology provides little help with making these connections:

> As evangelicals experience the intricate dynamics of the political sphere, they have no traditions to use as guides... evangelicals are exposed to the vagaries of circumstance equipped with little more than native good sense and the limited inferences they can draw from the bible.

Co-option of Christian leaders in civil society

Other Christians have sought to influence national politics from outside government, as leaders of civil society. They are at risk of being co-opted by politicians who are seeking religious legitimation of their governments, and a number of interviewees thought they had witnessed examples of this. Bishop Tendero, National Director of the Philippine Council of Evangelical Churches (PCEC), was appointed by President Arroyo to a Commission that was considering amendments to the Constitution. An evangelical who works for a secular anti-corruption NGO said:

> It's good that Bishop Tendero was there in the Constitutional Commission, at least there was a representation for evangelicals. He could probably provide a biblical perspective in crafting the Constitution – but I think it has been too close for him. He's very much identified with the President. If you go a gathering of activists or NGO workers, and they realise that you're an evangelical, they ask you: "So, you're a supporter of the President?" That's the impression that people

---

[8] He was found guilty of stealing $46m of government money in a civil case heard in a London High Court in 2007. A Zambian court in 2009 cleared him of similar charges on the grounds that the funds could not be traced to government money.

> are getting. As a leader representing the evangelical community, I think he has to be more careful.

An evangelical theologian, said:

> The President co-opted him by appointing him as a member of the Commission on Charter Change. From there I could sense that he could not speak, he could not be a prophet.... He has lost his credibility to speak on critical issues, against what the President or her government is doing. So we don't hear from now. NCCP has done its part in speaking out against human rights abuses, but PCEC has not done their part, their voice has not been heard. Silent.

In 2007 Mutava Musyimi, secretary general of the National Council of Churches of Kenya was leading the Steering Committee of the Kenya Anti-Corruption Campaign. A Catholic lawyer thought Musyimi had been co-opted:

> He has been a vocal Christian leader who had built his name as a reliable person, but more recently he's been known as someone who's been co-opted by the state in its political games – he has a very big legitimacy problem. As a result the church is not as vocal and consistent on the anti-corruption crusade as they were in the Kenyatta period and part of the Moi government.

These examples are in no way intended to discourage Christians from getting involved in national politics, but rather to highlight some of the potential pitfalls to avoid.

Conclusion

Better governance is vital for poverty reduction, and Protestant Christianity has contributed to improvements in governance in the past. Strengths that evangelical Protestants brings to this process include an emphasis on moral behaviour and a tendency to reject centralised authority. Weaknesses include a tendency towards theologies that see involvement in the world as irrelevant or even sinful, and an overemphasis on the potential of conversion and transformation of individuals to change society and the state. Having reflected on the experiences of his informants, the author believes that a promising approach for evangelicals who want to maximize their contribution to better governance may be to link believers who hold positions of power in government with Christian groups outside government who can provide them with encouragement, accountability and challenge.

GOD'S GOOD NEWS FOR WOMEN, AND GENDER ISSUES

Beulah Herbert

Introduction

The bible is a primary source for a view of God's good news for women. So we begin with the biblical view.

God's good news was given to both men and women (Gen. 3:14, 15; 12:3; Exo. 3:8; Mk. 1:14, 15; Acts 2: 1-4). The promise of the saviour, the election of a people of God, the preaching of the kingdom of God, the new era of the Holy Spirit and the church , and the life of the community of the redeemed with the vision of the New Heaven and New Earth, belong to both men and women.

Beginning from the historical width of the bible, women have been recipients, retellers and bearers of God's good news and also displayers of faith in the family, church and society. The church through the ages has included women in whatever way and measure that could be. The Protestant Reformation gave greater impetus for women. The modern missionary movement since the eighteenth century has included women. To give a broad sweep, the wives of the missionaries and later single women missionaries formed a large part of the hosts that spread around the globe to bear the good news. [1] The so-called bible women played a key role in being recipients, retellers and bearers of God's good news for women. Women in secluded *zenana*[2] became recipients of God's good news.

---

[1] C.B. Firth, *An Introduction to Indian Church History* (Delhi: ISPCK, 1961),193; for an account of the personal narrative of bible women in China, see Vanessa Wood, 'The Part Played by Chinese Women in the Formation of an Indigenous Church in China: Insights from the Archive of Myfanwy Wood, LMS Missionary', *Women's History Review* 17:4 (Sep. 2008), 599-602; for more information about women missionaries and bible women see the other articles in the same volume.

[2] *Zenana* is the secluded place where the women of the family lived and when women had no freedom to move out, the women missionaries and bible women went into the women to teach them the bible, health, hygiene, basic education. Another example of women receiving the gospel is the Secret Christian of Sivakasi in Tamil Nadu, India. These women of orthodox Hindu families could not openly profess their faith in Christ and hence the name. Many of them have suffered for their hidden faith. The woman teacher would go mostly when the men had gone for work. Bibles were hidden in the storage container for rice.

A hundred years ago the women's suffragette movement was in full swing, and their argument for women's rights had great effect in establishing the legal status of women. But, as we consider the world today, we would find the role of women in many societies far from equal to that of men, far from the biblical one of being 'all one in Christ Jesus'. In many societies, in many Christian societies, despite their enormous strengths and maternal instincts, women are oppressed, over worked, abused and given subservient roles in societies. Even in Christian cultures women are often undervalued, indeed in some cases the church itself reinforces the traditional, cultural dominance of men and allows, encourages, women to be considered as second class citizens to be 'used' at their husband's pleasure.

This issue of gender is an enormous one, too large to be tackled fully here, but examples from recent research, in Asia and in Africa, highlight some of the issues that the church needs to address if its mission is to be holistic.

The first examples consider research done among Tamil Christian Women in south India (Herbert, 2008). This showed women as recipients of the gospel, as retellers of the gospel, as bearers of the gospel, as displayers of faith, as participants in the church and in house groups, and raises specific issues pertaining to gender issues.

Women Recipients of the Gospel

From the earliest days women were central recipients of the gospel. Numerous stories are typified by Hamsa's father's grandmother, who was converted by Ringeltaube of the London Missionary Society (LMS), in the Kanyakumari district of Tamil Nadu, southern India, in the beginning of the nineteenth century. She was one sister with sixteen brothers in the extreme south of India. They lived in houses that formed a circle with a temple for the snake god, the family god, in the middle. Two children of two of the brothers were affected by diarrhoea and were vomiting blood. Their efforts to appease the snake god were of no avail. Then Ringeltaube visited them and prayed, kneeling beside the beds. Not only were the children healed, but the next morning two snakes were also found dead in front of the temple. The brothers, recognising that the snakes were powerless in the presence of Jesus Christ, took two other live snakes, tied them in unbleached new cloth, strangled them and demolished the temple. They vowed to follow Jesus and became Christians, through the influence of these faithful women.[3]

Women Retellers of the Gospel

Women recipients of the gospel also become retellers of the life-transforming Good News. In the Indian sub-continent until the early 1970s Indian indigenous

---

[3] Beulah Herbert, 'Tamil Christian Women at the Turn of the Millennium: Mission Initiatives and Gender Practice', *Women's History Review* 17:4 (Sep. 2008), 616-17.

mission agencies did not generally recruit single Indian women missionaries for cross cultural evangelistic work. But at present every agency recruits single women missionaries.[4] These women have done amazing work, particularly in the areas of evangelism of women and children and also in bible translation to languages and dialects that have not yet been written down.

A particular feature of women retellers of the Good News is itinerary preachers. As early as the nineteenth century the daughter of Thanjai Vedanayagam Sastriar, a Tamil Christian poet, writer and evangelist, was an itinerary preacher both in Tamil and English. She went to Colombo to preach the gospel also through music. Not all women are itinerant preachers. But as it may be seen from the experience of Tamil Christian women, they bring specific gifts and inroads to a community when they are involved in the evangelistic efforts of the church, teaching in the Sunday school and vacation bible school and undertaking their own evangelistic enterprises such as having women's house groups and neighbourhood Sunday classes.

Women Bearers of the Gospel

Women who receive and retell the Good News also bear the gospel in various ways, as seen particularly through their involvement in the life and ministry of the church. A study of the literature shows that women have distinctive feminine issues, the meeting of which emphasises the value of observing Sunday teaching throughout all of the week's activities. Activities such as sharing stories of inner peace and contentment achieved through their involvement in the church or religious activities, making the point that they do their bit humbly, without the need to make tall claims, ennobling women's involvement in community and church based on biblical examples, highlighting the benefits, drawing the contrasts, and boldly claiming a right to be involved, which have led top reports of powerful and active transformation as a result of their active and distinct engagement.

In the research into Tamil women's self-perception of their roles, considering the issue of women preaching and teaching, there are narratives of God's approval in justifying women's preaching and teaching, including claims of personal approval and eulogising. The issue of women's role in church administration, though, is described through a spectrum of responses such as disapproval and approval, from vehement protestation against their involvement to others advocating their contribution as valuable.

Similarly the question of women's ordination also drew very varied responses. Some disapproved, seemingly for the reason of personal objection. Some others brought out arguments concerning pollution, conflict with the supposed role of women, psychological and religious obstacles, and their own

---

[4] Samuel Thambusamy and Beulah Herbert, 'Women and Gender Issues in Christian Missions in India', in Roger E. Hedlund and Paul Joshua Backiaraj (eds.), *Missiology for the 21st Century: South Asian Perspectives* (Delhi: ISPCK/MIIS, 2004), 588-90.

interpretation of Paul's sayings. Others were ambivalent in their opinion. And some approved it, claiming God's approval of the fitness of all to serve in this role regardless of gender. Using biblical texts and rational argument to illustrate the evidence of basic talent, and explaining their theological understanding of scripture, by illustrating God's call to women in this area and the effects of guidance and training, all as arguments in favour.[5]

Women Displayers of Faith

A significant aspect of God's good news for women is the way their faith is displayed in all areas of life. A significant contribution to female empowerment comes from the way the women point to 'faith' being a crucial factor in their lives – in moulding and enabling them, and then carrying them through life, despite a variety of personal and family challenges. Mispah, one of those who have chosen singleness, pointed to faith as the most important ingredient of her spinster life. Jeya, separated from her abusive husband, testified that it is faith and God's grace that have seen her and her two sons through the hard times. Chandramathy was married at the age of fifteen to a widower cousin with small children. She stated that through all the ups and downs of financial loss, sickness and death of her husband, it was faith and prayer that brought her through.

Ester, an orphan, was brought up by a Christian family, but later left to fend for herself. "Though I was an orphan my husband never treats me as one. If it had not been for God's grace, my relatives would have left me nowhere and I would not have been in such a good state with a caring family." On the other hand, special involvement in music has given empowerment to Geethakumari and Bharathamani. They are both part of the Christian Cultural Academy, which has concerts to raise funds for *Utavum Carangkal*. Bharathi says, "Singing God's song makes my hair stand on end. I want to use for God the gift God has given me."[6]

Women Participants in the Church

The participation of women in the life of the church may be seen in the following example of the Kodambakkam church.

Since the beginnings of Kodambakkam church in 1956, the women of the congregation have been actively participating in its life in at least six ways – in the Women's Fellowship and its outreach efforts; Christian outreach efforts among local college students and working women living in a private hostel; a bible study for women on Wednesday evenings; fasting prayer for women every fourth Friday; support for polio victims in Kanchipuram hospital; and

---

[5] Beulah Herbert, *Self Perception of Tamil Christian Women: Narrative Analysis of Gender Practice*, Part II (VDM Verlag Dr. Muller, Mauritius, 2010), 106-7.

[6] Herbert, *Self Perception of Tamil Christian Women*, 117-18.

various sales to raise funds for church building and several mission enterprises. Apart from these activities, the women of the church and several young girls participate actively in regular programmes open to both sexes – village evangelism every third Sunday; visits to the Home for the Aged every second Sunday; weekly Friday evening bible study; prayer for cross-cultural mission work led by the Indian Missionary Society on the first day of the month and for the Friends' Missionary Prayer Band on Thursdays; as well as all-night prayer for both men and women every fifth Friday.

The one-third membership allocation for women on the pastorate committee has been maintained. In fact, they more than fill that requirement, because one committee place is set aside for the representative from the Sunday school, and this is invariably a woman, since the majority of the Sunday school teachers are female. These female committee members actively participate in the pastorate committee's discussions, administration, counting of the collection and various such duties. Other women are zealous in reading the lesson, collecting the offertory and carrying forward the communion elements. Some women are involved in preaching not only in this church but also elsewhere, while a few have been active in the Madras Bible League, Apostolic Christian Assembly and the Evangelical Church of India.

Women in House Groups

In Tamil Nadu another significant feature of female church life is the house groups conducted by some of the women and their outreach efforts. At the time of writing, there were five such women's house groups. The oldest, which has been going on for more than 40 years, is Saguna's which takes place on Tuesday afternoons; one of its special features is learning memory verses. On the first Friday afternoon of the month there is fasting prayer. The women come 'with fasting', having missed their lunch, and after extended prayer for the past and new months, there is a high tea (not a simple snack or a full meal, but sumptuous food) provided. The others met as follows: in Heera's house on Monday afternoons; Bina's house on Tuesday morning; Jeba's house on Wednesday afternoons; and Swarna's house on Friday afternoons, a group which was started only in 2001. When the fieldwork began in 1999, there was another Friday afternoon group in existence, meeting in Viji's house, which was in abeyance in 2001, as she had just moved house. Thus women could presumably find a suitable group to attend, with the choice of any weekday but Thursday.

The women's house group gatherings consist of singing, sharing of the word (biblical message) and prayer for various needs, including the nation and mission work. Quite often special speakers are invited. At the end a high tea or meal is served. Saguna, Heera and Jeba have a day-long retreat once a year. Some of the women attend more than one of these groups. Jeba has a ministry of house-visiting and prayer among non-Christian women. Her daughter Hepsibah wants to have a prayer ministry career when she grows up. Several young girls have indicated a desire for a service-oriented career that will help in mission by giving opportunities for showing by word and deed the love and compassion of Jesus Christ.

Outreach efforts are a special feature of Saguna's group. In the past she had led a day-long evangelistic venture of tract distribution and evangelism by visiting houses in any random area. By 2001, she had changed the pattern to concentrate on just one area, a nearby poorer locality, Rajapillai Thottam. Two young women workers of the COME (Christian Outreach for Mission and Evangelism) ministry visit the houses in that locality all day long on Wednesdays. In the evening they conduct a bible class for children while Saguna teaches teenagers and visits more houses. On Thursday afternoons Saguna visits nearby Nallankuppam to conduct a house group for the women in that poorer locality.

Jeyavathy, who is actively involved in the outreach efforts of the Women's Fellowship and the house group in Bina's house, has a 'Sunday school' in her home for women and children of the neighbourhood on Saturday afternoons. She is also a Jesus Calls evangelist.[7]

Women and Gender Issues

God's good news for women transforms their whole life and gender issues are also addressed by the prophetic voice of the gospel. In a variety of ways and in myriad issues God's good news has changed the life of women. However there is a long way to go to see the abundant life promised by Jesus himself. So we consider the following gender issues that have been and need to be addressed by God's good news.

Female Child

The issue of the female child comprises of many other issues such as preference for a male child, female foeticide, female infanticide, child marriage, discrimination in treatment, health and education, teenage pregnancy and child labour. Some studies and academic feminist discourse found in text books discuss these issues.

Ujvala Rajadhyaksha and Swati Smita discuss gender inegalitarian culture and the low status accorded to women.[8] Niranjan Pant's book deals with issues about a girl child.[9] Sarada Natarajan also has her study in a book form about female infanticide in Tamil Nadu.[10] K. S. Sunanda's title of her book is

---

[7] Herbert, *Self Perception of Tamil Christian Women*, 115-16.

[8] Ujvala Rajadhyaksha and Swati Smita, 'Tracing a Timeline for Work and Family Research in India', *Economic and Political Weekly*, April 24-30, 2004, 1674.

[9] Niranjan Pant, *Status of Girl Child and Women in India* (New Delhi: APH Publishing, 1995).

[10] Sarada Natarajan, *Watering the Neighbour's Plant: Media Perspectives on Female Infanticide in Tamil Nadu* (Chennai: M.S. Swaminathan Research Foundation, 1997).

provocative.[11] A girl child is not valued or welcomed. She is disposed of either before or after birth by the use of female feticide or female infanticide.[12] In many situations the girl child is discriminated against by not being given proper nutrition, health care, education and opportunities for holistic development. The causes for imbalance are both economic and social. She is considered a burden and a liability.[13] She is vulnerable and looked upon as a threat to the sexual purity and morality of men. She is to be married off as soon as possible. She is perceived as a temptress and a seductress. She is attributed impurity and pollution. Further there is no problem in the minds of sexists to use her as a piece of convenience. This devaluing of a girl child that leads to discrimination and abuse is an issue responded to by the members of the focus groups.[14]

However, the responses of the women of Kodambakkam church taken for the field work of the study of self perception of Tamil Christian women are quite different. The narrators themselves, women (adults grown up from being girl children!) construct stories of positive valuing of a girl child. Some would go even further and hold that girls are better.

Some stories are responses to the issue of female infanticide and feticide.[15] Everyone is against it. It may be asked whether anyone would be for it. It has been explained [with economic and other social reasons], why some communities and some parents would resort to female infanticide and female feticide. Jeyavathy, Mariam, Saral, Swarna and Jeyam construct stories of outright condemnation rooting their narratives in God's work and biblical theology. It is God who gives the child and it is not right for humans to destroy what God gives. Amar and Gem bemoan the practices of female infanticide and feticide. They narrate stories with their perception of how it may be avoided by finding ways of making a girl child useful and beneficial.[16]

These responses show how God's good news has been for women in applying that good news in various areas of life. Many governmental, non-governmental and faith based organisations raise awareness about the issues of the girl child and work out remedial measures. Abandoned children are given homes. Ms. Jeyalalitha, the former Chief Minister of Tamil Nadu set up a program 'Cradle' to find place in children's homes for abandoned girl babies. Sex determination and selection, abortion, child marriage are banned. Some agencies offer to take care of the child born of teenage pregnancy without the

---

[11] K.S. Sunanda, *Girl Child Born to Die in Killing Fields?* (Madras: Alternative for India Development, 1995), cited in Herbert, *Self Perception*, Part II, 114.

[12] Batra and Dangwal note that because of desire for a male child the female foetus is aborted. G.S. Batra and R.C. Dangwal, *Globalisation and Liberalisation: New Developments* (New Delhi: Deep & Deep Publications, 2000), 115.

[13] Batra and Dangwal, *Globalisation and Liberalisation*, 107.

[14] Herbert, *Self Perception*, Part II, 114-17.

[15] See Vibhuti Patel, 'Sex Determination and Sex Preselection Tests: Abuse of Advanced Technology', in Rehana Ghadially (ed.), *Women in Indian Society: A Reader* (New Delhi: Sage Publications, 1988), 178-185.

[16] Herbert, *Self Perception*, Part II, 127-28.

teenager having to resort to abortion. However, the prophetic voice of God's good news has to be sounded more adequately and appropriately.

Widowhood and sati

In south Asia particularly, a widow is nobody.[17] "It may be noted that widowhood brings about much deprivation."[18] "This is stated in the study of Alka Ranjan that widowhood brings about severe social, economic and cultural deprivations."[19] Tamil Christian women's discussion of widowhood brought out responses of positive compassion recognising the difficulties and needs of widows. The contrast between the different treatments of widows in different communities is brought out. While angry disapproval of mean or ill-treatment is displayed, the biblical pattern of God's concern and care for the widow is also highlighted. The positive value of freedom and opportunity for greater service is also recognised. Single status is accepted. Any victimisation or faulting or accusing or denigration is disapproved with defence of the position of the single ones.[20]

God's good news for the widowed women is that God cares for them and has a place for them among the people of God. Though *sati*, widow burning, is banned it is found that it is not completely removed. Stringent action has to be taken and total abolition of *sati* will become a reality only when God's good news is real for the widow.

Single parenthood

This issue, just as some other issues presented in some of the following sections, may not be considered as a gender issue. But, as shown below, because women are socially and economically more vulnerable and weaker, it becomes a significant gender issue. The issue of single parenthood was also discussed in the focus groups. The term 'single parenthood' was used to cover any type of single parenthood, the parent being a single person unmarried, married, separated, divorced or deserted, or a widow or a widower. The narrators in their story construction did not make a fine distinction among these categories. They focused mainly on a parent having to carry on life single-handedly.[21] All the narrators who construct their stories about single parenthood have spoken about divorcees. They construct their perceptions of defence

---

[17] See Nagamani Rao, 'Widowhood', in J.B. Tellis-Nayak (ed.), *Indian Women: Then And Now. Situation, Efforts, Profiles* (Indore: Satprakashan Sanchar Kendra), 83-86.

[18] This is supported by Fay Fransella and Kay Frost, *On Being a Woma:. A Review of Research on How Women see Themselves* (London and New York: Tavistock Publications, 1977), 114.

[19] Alka Ranjan, 'Determinants of Well-Being among Widows: An Exploratory Study in Varanasi', *Economic and Political Weekly*, Oct 27, 2001, 4088.

[20] Herbert, *Self Perception*, Part II, 206-7.

[21] Herbert, *Self Perception*, Part II, 176.

against victimisation and advocacy to help. They bring in assertions, claims, religious or biblical points to construct their perceptions. No single narrator has any negative perception or accusation. In their perception, single parenthood has to be responded to with compassion and help. This is different from the dire situation, victimisation and helplessness of the single women, including divorcees portrayed in N. S. Krishnakumari's book.[22] [23]

Dowry

Kanakalatha Mukund[24] shows how women's property rights have changed over time, resulting in inequality and discrimination when women lost much of their property rights. She also discusses how the value of a woman has been eroded as the practice of *sridhanam*[25] has degenerated to dowry. *Sridhanam* was originally the jewellery, things and property the parents of the bride gave her for her own use, especially in communities in which the married daughter had no claim to the ancestral or parental property. This has degenerated into a dowry that is demanded and received by the parents of the bridegroom, with no claim for the daughter for the use of or authority over the dowry.[26] The practice of dowry, being the cash given by the parents of the bride to the parents of the bridegroom, is prevalent in many communities especially in south India. Many of the Tamil Christians also follow this custom. Many do not approve of this. The members of the focus group respond to this issue in various ways. Shashi Jain notes that even the educated have accepted dowry as part of the system.[27] [28] Whatever explanation may be given, the practice of dowry demeans the person. The practice of bride price has also degenerated and become demeaning. So God's good news has to be applied to this area too.. The Indian Government legally prohibits the practice of dowry. But it is not strictly applied. One way of combating this evil practice is for God's people to take a stand against this. This is seen among some of the people of God.

---

[22] N.S. Krishnakumari, *Status of Single Women in India* (New Delhi: Uppal Publishing House, 1987).

[23] Herbert, *Self Perception*, Part II, 183.

[24] Kanakalatha Mukund, 'Women's Property Rights in South India: A Review', *Economic and Political Weekly*, May 29, 1999, 1352-58.

[25] *Sridhanam* is the gift in cash or kind or both given to the woman by her parents when she is married.

[26] Herbert, *Self Perception*, Part II, 114-15.

[27] Shashi Jain, *Status and Role Perception of Middle Class Women* (New Delhi: Puja Publishers, 1988), 99. Caplan notes that the Brahmins take dowry, Patricia Caplan, *Class and Gender in India* (London: Tavistock Publications, 1985), 45.

[28] Herbert, *Self Perception*, Part II, 141.

Domestic violence

Domestic violence is mentioned separately though it may be considered as one form of violence against women. There is awareness-raising by various agencies in the area of domestic violence. There are efforts taken to raise awareness also as seen from the article of Nisha Srivastava. This is based on the collection of stories about the efforts of Vanagana, a women's group in Uttar Pradesh. This group organised a campaign for awareness of domestic violence by putting on a street play based on a real life incident and having a discussion.[29] Neera Desai and Maithreyi Krishnaraj note that there is growing violence against women such as rape, wife beating, family violence, dowry deaths and prostitution. They also note that these women are considered as victims to be saved or as objects of welfare and not as equal participants. Domestic violence brings out two types of response. One is that of laying the burden at the feet of the woman, requiring her to be patient and not provocative, and to keep the peace of the house while resorting to counselling and praying. The other view displays outright disapproval and condemnation of any type of domestic violence, physical, emotional and psychological.[30] Given the facts that both men and women have been created by God in God's image and likeness, and that both are offered new life by the saving work of Jesus Christ, any type of domestic violence is out of place. It is not justified by the reconciling work of Jesus Christ.

Sex work

Sex work includes commercial sex work, call girls and the *devadasi* system of temple prostitution. The issue of sex work also draws a variety of responses. For some there is a positive acceptance with the recognition to help the sex workers come out of their situation. The causal reasons, such as being forced into it because of deception, lack of love in the family, and economic need are also pointed out. However, positive attitudes of compassion and understanding are displayed. Some show disapproval, probably of sex work and not the sex worker. Biblical examples of compassion and forgiveness are upheld.[31]

Quite a few government, non-government and faith based agencies are working for the betterment of the life of the commercial sex workers. In Asia it is found that women are forced into sex work. Apart from the effort to liberate them from the sex work, there is an effort taken to care for their health and hygiene, teach them income generation work, and take care of their children.

---

[29] Nisha Srivastava, 'Exposing Violence against Women', *EPW* 34 (6 Feb., 1999), 453-54. Neetha has studied women domestics in Delhi. She has examined the role of the women in migration, job search and social networking. However she has also discovered social control by males, patriarchal relations and wife beating. N. Neetha, 'Making of Female Breadwinners', *EPW* (April 24-30, 2004), 1681-88.

[30] Herbert, *Self Perception*, Part II, 207.

[31] Herbert, *Self Perception*, Part II, 208.

Sex work includes both young girls and boys. While God's good news is to help them come out of this work, God's people who look for a new heaven and new earth have to address the systemic evil, and pray and work for the routing out of this systemic evil. A lot has still to be done to work out practical ways in which former sex workers may truly become members of the people of God, the redeemed community, celebrating the abundant life Jesus Christ gives.

HIV and AIDS

Why is the issue of HIV and AIDS a gender issue? As in the case of many other similar issues, HIV and AIDS becomes a gender issue because women are affected more. For no reason on their part, women are infected by a sex partner or a mother. This becomes quite important particularly in the case of sex workers and their children. Women in non-western and not-developed countries become more vulnerable. If the man, the bread winner, wastes or dies of AIDS, the destitute woman faces numerous challenges for survival of herself and her family. In these countries where those who live below the poverty line are numerous, an epidemic such as HIV and AIDS devastates those, especially those who struggle without education, employment and life skills. Vast effort is undertaken on behalf on those affected by HIV and AIDS. But this is not enough. Awareness, prevention, medical help, care, support and long term strategic planning and action are necessary. Women are particularly vulnerable in those societies where men demand 'their sexual rights', whenever and however they want, and thus transfer the HIV/AIDS that they have to their wives. However, it is imperative that God's good news becomes real for these persons. By not merely announcing forgiveness of sin, but also including them in the community of God's redeemed, true dignity, respect , love and care will be shown.

Practices such as female foot binding and female circumcision

There are practices such as foot binding in the Far East Asia and female circumcision in some African tribal cultures. These show the underlying attitude and notion that women are commodities and sex objects. Just as *sati* has been banned in India, these have been banned. However, these practices have not completely disappeared. God's good news for women needs to critique and challenge any practice that diminishes the personhood and true humanity of people. In south India the 'upper cloth' controversy, fighting for the right of the lower caste women to wear blouses to cover the upper portion of their bodies, was a significant one. The work of Dhonavur Fellowship in rescuing abandoned children and *devadasis* and the forming of orders of widows are also noteworthy.[32] At present indigenous Indian missions are also

[32] Thambusamy and Herbert, 'Women and Gender Issues', 587-89.

following the lead in providing habits of proper clothing to the tribals who are not used to clothing. Thus God's good news becomes concretised for women.

Violence against women

This topic is huge. Apart from the ones dealt with already, there are numerous issues such as rape, pornography, media violence, militarism, globalisation, sex tourism, surrogate mother or hired womb, family planning methods, infertility clinics, unethical development projects, caste, unethical biotechnological methods and so on. It may be questioned how some of these issues are gender issues. Women are more vulnerable. A friend said that it was a pain to go to the infertility clinic and finally she refused. After 11 years the couple with prayer had the opportunity of having a girl child. At the time of writing, the Indian media focuses on a German couple who are not able to take home the twins they have had hiring an Indian womb. Globalisation and development displace populations and, in societies that make the woman responsible for domestic duties, fetching firewood, water and essential commodities becomes a struggle for women. Militarism not only produces atrocities in the armed forces but also kills the male soldiers, leaving women widows most affected. It is imperative that God's good news becomes real in the lives of those affected by these issues.

Environmental issues

God's creation is good and the humans are to take care of it. If we hope for a new heaven and new earth we should live in such a way that the present world is not destroyed by our greed and irresponsible use of the resources God has provided. Once again the question may arise how environmental issues become gender issues. It has been explained how women are more vulnerable. When there is depletion of essential resources and natural catastrophes caused or aggravated by human input, women suffer and struggle more. Water scarcity – who walks miles to bring home water? Pollution – who is responsible for house cleaning and taking care of those who fall sick? Lack of nutritional food – who takes care? This is also a vast subject. But when and how will God's good news sound its clarion call of prophetic voice?

A Christian Response to Gender Abuses

Increasingly, churches around the world are responding to such unscriptural practices by sound bible study on the role of women, first through pastors and then through local churches. But, it should be reiterated that many churches still reinforce the male domination roles of traditional, tribal cultures and thus miss out on the God-given strengths and qualities of their sisters in Christ. Some still hold a judgemental attitude to those suffering from HIV/AIDS. Some cast them out from the fellowship with the only advice that they should pray for God's healing and trust that he will heal them, not recognising that God also works through medical and physical means.

To develop gender issues positively, the two genders can be considered separately. Some issues are related to women, their self image and potential, others to men and their attitudes and, often, entrenched practices.

Women have enormous creative instincts, and so many of the best development and relief work is focussed on, and builds upon, women's materialistic instincts. It has been said that "if you educate a boy you educate a man, but if you educate a girl you educate a woman and a family and a community." The scandal of girls' under-education is shameful, to Christians especially.

Many examples of women's leadership could be given. In Kenya some of the best community work is headed up by a woman in the CCS (Church Communities Services) of ACK (the Anglican Church of Kenya). In Zimbabwe, some excellent HIV/AIDS work with a rapidly increasing network of church based projects looking after HIV/AIDS orphans has been done in ZOE (Zimbabwe Orphans Endeavour), and this is lead by a woman. In India, thousands on lives have been transformed in the slum communities of Delhi, by the ASHA community health and development society, founded and headed up by a woman empowering hundreds of local women Community Health Volunteers. And at the local level it is the women who 'naturally' take prime care of the sick, the elderly, the young and the hungry.

Addressing the attitudes, actions and prejudices of men is more difficult, but it is being tackled. It can only be tackled by local male leaders, which means the male leaders of the local churches, as only they will have influence over other local men. One of the most encouraging programmes on changing men's attitudes to gender issues has been developed in Zimbabwe and in Bukina Faso[33] (Marshall 2009, Marshall and Taylor 2006). Their work, developed through Tearfund and their partners, is written up as a case study called 'Gender, HIV, and the Church'. Working with groups of local pastors, bible studies have been developed with a series of activities for workshops in the local churches. These are based around biblical passages outlining God's view of the role of women, and real life case studies of sex and gender incidents. They have been very effective at changing people's attitudes and thus behaviour. The most significant changes reported in both urban and rural area included increased testing for HIV, changed behaviour in both men and women, including a reduction in multiple and concurrent partners, and increased discussion within relationships about love and sexuality. In urban

---

[33] This work has been written up in M. Marshall and N. Taylor, 'Tackling HIV and AIDS with faith-based communities: learning from attitudes on gender relations, and sexual rights within local evangelical churches in Bukina Faso, Zimbabwe and South Africa', *Gender and Development* 14:3 (November 2006), and also in Tearfund's publication, *Gender, HIV and the Church: A Case Study*, available from www.tearfund.org.

areas, groups reported increased condom use. Young people said they no longer saw HIV as a death sentence, but spoke of increased hope for the future.

All is based on a biblical perspective of gender which recognises that "we are all unique human beings, and that men and women are both created with equal value, in the image of God" (Gen. 1:27). Gender inequalities and socially-constructed 'roles' can restrict both men and women from fully using their skills and talent, and damage relationships between them. They can prevent people from realising their full potential as individuals, and growing as men and women into the fullness of life in Christ. Every individual, males and females of all ages, should be encouraged and enabled to reach their potential and so be able to contribute positively to the home, church and society as a whole. (Marshall 2009).

Such a vision for the role of men and women must be developed if our gospel, our mission, is to be holistic and the kingdom of God expressed in all of God's creations.

STORM CLOUDS AND MISSION: CREATION CARE AND ENVIRONMENTAL CRISIS

Margot R. Hodson

Introduction

The 1910 missionary conference would have expected mission to include medical care, education and agriculture. Care for the environment, however, would not have been seen as a focus of mission. In 2010 there is still a mixed reaction to the place of environment within a mission agenda, but there are now significant voices speaking for environmental mission and many examples of good practice. This chapter traces the development of care for the environment as a focus of holistic mission worldwide. It considers contemporary environmental challenges and Christian responses to them. Christian organisations such as A Rocha, Au Sable and the John Ray Initiative (JRI) are examined, and the rise of environmental concern amongst American evangelicals. The interaction between environment and development is investigated, leading to a consideration of the relationship between poverty and environmental degradation. Finally the chapter considers environmental missiology and its importance for the twenty-first century.

Four major environmental challenges

As we enter the second decade of the twenty-first century it has become clear that we face four major environmental challenges: climate change, biodiversity loss, human population and resource depletion.

Climate change

Despite the very ambivalent coverage in the popular media, there is a firm consensus among serious climate scientists that our global climate is changing as a result of human activity.[1] The projections for change this century are very serious and have significant implications for mission. Globally there is an

[1] The Royal Society, 'Climate Change Controversies', http://royalsociety.org/Policy-Publications (accessed 24.2.2010). The Society is currently reviewing their coverage of climate change and will publish their conclusions on the Royal Society website.

increase in frequency and severity of weather events. A warmer atmosphere is more vigorous and provides conditions for more extreme weather events. Examples of floods have been Jakata in February 2007, and Burma in 2008 following hurricane Nargis. Bangladesh has seven million people living below one metre above sea level and annual floods are already making many environmental refugees. Other regions are affected by severe drought – northern Kenya is experiencing an ongoing drought that is leading to famine, and Australia has had ten years of drought and this has had a severe impact on agriculture in some areas.

Global warming causes ice melt and the warming of seas. The Intergovernmental Panel on Climate Change (IPCC) predicted a 0.4 metre rise in sea level this century from thermal expansion. They did not give figures for ice melt as it is too unpredictable. In terms of temperature change there will be uneven impacts across the globe with very high latitudes and low latitudes being the worst affected. These latitudes contain some of the poorest people of the world and for low latitudes some of the richest biodiversity.

Overall the impact of climate change will mean less land available for agriculture and a need to adopt new farming practices in many areas. There are likely to be a significant number of environmental refugees – possibly as many as 200 million by the middle of the century.[2] These pressures could well lead to conflict and war.

Biodiversity loss

The Millennium Ecosystem Assessment concluded that "Changes in biodiversity due to human activities were more rapid in the past 50 years than at any time in human history."[3] Though individuals have benefited from the loss of biodiversity to create human dominated ecosystems, the cost to society has often been far greater than any benefit. In tropical areas, benefit from clearing forest may also be short term as the soils are not suitable for agriculture after a few bumper years. One of the problems is that current economic measures do not give a value to natural resources. A country could clear its forests and heavily over-fish its inland seas leaving very degraded environments, but the GDP would show a net benefit as the 'environmental capital' loss would not be recorded. Biodiversity loss also impacts on climate, and the carbon emitted from the burning of tropical forest is a significant component of global carbon output.[4] This pattern is being repeated in many

---

[2] N. Myers, 'Environmental Refugees: A Growing Phenomenon of the 21st Century', *Philosophical Transactions of the Royal Society of London, Series B*, 357 (2002), 609-613.

[3] Millennium Ecosystem Assessment, *Ecosystems and Human Well-being: Biodiversity Synthesis* (Washington DC: World Resources Institute, 2005).

[4] A. Campbell, V. Kapos, I. Lysenko, J.P.W. Scharlemann, B. Dickson, H.K. Gibbs, M. Hansen, and L. Miles, *Carbon Emissions from Forest Loss in Protected Areas* (UNEP World Conservation Monitoring Centre, 2008).

parts of the developing world and the long term implications for those nations and global environmental stability are severe.[5]

Human population

In 1910 global human population was approximately 1.7 billion. By 2010 it is four times this size at 6.8 billion. The rate of increase is now slowing and population is predicted to stabilise at 9 billion by the middle of this century. This is a major cause of our current global problems.[6] Increased population has placed strain on finite resources and caused direct competition between human needs for food and other resources and space for biodiversity. It is a well-established trend that population increase is associated with poverty, and family size decreases as people move out of subsistence. The challenge for this century is to see whether the rate of stabilisation of world population happens fast enough to slow the increasing rate of destruction of our global environment. What is the upper 'carrying capacity' of human population for our planet? Given the current level of human poverty and environmental degradation, have we reached it already?

Resource depletion

Finally resource depletion is the fourth major factor with water and oil being key resources.

Water: Of the world's water 97% is salty and 2% of fresh water is locked in snow and ice. Humanity survives on the 1% left and the changes in biodiversity and climate change are likely to reduce the availability of fresh water. For example, the Himalayan glaciers are melting, and although it is difficult to assess the rate of change, 40% are predicted to be gone by 2050.[7] The loss of these glaciers will be devastating for water supply to the Indian subcontinent. Globally, by 2025, 1.8 billion people are likely to be living in areas of water scarcity.[8]

Oil: Popular thinking about fossil fuels has been to believe that there are many decades of these resources left to us. The question, however, is not to ask how long it will be until these resources run out, but to ask when will demand outstrip supply? With finite reserves of oil and gas we are likely to reach peak production levels in the near future.[9] Once we are past 'peak oil' the price will

---

[5] L.M. Curran, S.N. Trigg, A.K. McDonald, D. Astiani, Y.M. Hardiono, P. Siregar, I. Caniago, and E. Kasischke, 'Lowland Forest Loss in Protected Areas of Indonesian Borneo', *Science* 13, vol. 303. no. 5660 (February 2004), 1000-1003.

[6] J. Collodi and F. M'Cormack, 'Population Growth, Environment and Food Security: What Does the Future Hold?', *Horizon: Future Issues for Development*, pilot issue (July 2009).

[7] B. Larmer, 'The big melt', *National Geographic* 217:4 (April 2010), 68.

[8] C. Johns, 'Editorial', *National Geographic* 217:4 (April 2010), 2.

[9] S. Sorrell, J. Speirs, R. Bentley, A. Brandt, R. Miller, 'UK Energy Research Centre,

increase dramatically. When this is combined with the fact that our economy and culture is oil based, we face a very uncertain future. Oil is not simply used for fuel: most aspects of our modern culture require oil, from clothing to computers. Furthermore, nitrogen fertilizers require fossil fuels for their production and so our current methods of food production for our large global population depends on this rapidly disappearing resource. As economic development comes to countries of high populations, the impact of peak oil will be even more severe. One might hope that at least this will reduce carbon output – however, it is possible to produce oil by a very expensive and inefficient processing of coal, which remains abundant. So peak oil may ironically mean increased carbon emissions.

There are many other resources, including valuable rare metals, which are equally under pressure with our fast developing world. During this century we will need to learn to live with the impact of resource depletion and this is likely to have the greatest impact on the poorest populations of the world.

Conclusion on environmental factors

From this brief summary of environmental challenges facing humanity in 2010, it is clear that the overall situation is very serious indeed and the rate of change is unprecedented in human history. If the church has neglected creation care in the past, the current rate of change demands a fresh look at our responsibility. Any society without leadership is vulnerable to anarchy. Humanity has been given leadership over creation (Gen. 1:28).[10] This is the first command from God to humankind and it has been demonstrably ignored. At this time of crisis, it should be a foundational mission call for all who take God's commands seriously.

The Rise of Environmental Concern in the Twentieth Century

During the first half of the twentieth century there was a rise in concern for local and regional conservation and a growth in the understanding of the historical impact humans have had on changing the face of the Earth. In 1949 Aldo Leopold proposed a 'Land Ethic' that considered the needs of the non-human elements of an ecosystem, and this formed the beginnings of environmental ethics as a discipline.[11] In 1962, Rachel Carsen wrote her iconic book *Silent Spring* and raised the profile of the damage that humans were inflicting on the natural world.[12]

Global Oil Depletion, An assessment of the evidence for a near-term peak in global oil production', http://www.ukerc.ac.uk/support/Global%20Oil%20Depletion (August 2009, accessed 28.5.10).

[10] *Rada*, the Hebrew word to rule in Gen. 1:28, is also used in connection with Solomon in his command to rule wisely over the Israelite people.

[11] A. Leopold, *A Sand County Almanac* (New York: Oxford University Press, 1949).

[12] R. Carson, *Silent Spring* (Boston: Houghton Miflin, 1962).

During the second half of the century the emphasis shifted from seeking to combat local and regional pollution to understanding the global problems that were resulting from human development. It was within this context that the Gaia hypothesis was developed by James Lovelock. In 1972 Lovelock proposed that the Earth could be understood in a similar way to a living organism and that there were feed back mechanisms that kept the Earth's processes in balance.[13] Environmental ethics developed as a discipline during the second part of the twentieth century, with theories such as Deep Ecology, proposed by Arne Næss.[14]

The global understanding of the negative human impact on the world also led to the development of bodies such as the World Wildlife Fund (WWF) in 1961, and the IPCC which was formed in 1988 by the World Meteorological Organisation and the United Nations Environment Programme. The IPCC issued reports in 1990, 1995, 2001 and 2007.

In 1992, 1,500 scientists, including several Nobel Prize winners, issued a 'Warning to Humanity' that the planet was in environmental crisis. Later that year the United Nations Conference on Environment and Development held an 'Earth Summit' in Rio de Janeiro, which marked the beginnings of global action on climate change. This led to the Kyoto Protocol in 1997, which aimed to bring carbon emissions to 5% below 1990 levels by 2012. The developing world including China was not included in this agreement and this led to opposition by the United States. The Protocol finally came into force in 2005. In 2009 world leaders again met in Copenhagen. By this time the 2007 IPCC report and the 2005 Millennium Ecosystem Assessment provided evidence for the size of environmental crisis. Sadly, world economic recession, the rise of the Chinese economy and the relatively new Obama administration all led to a very disappointing result. This was possibly also fuelled by a campaign to undermine the scientific consensus by those whose economic interests were tied to continued exploitation of fossil fuels.

Christianity challenged for being the cause of the problem

In 1967, Lynn White published a paper in *Science* entitled "The historical roots of our ecologic crisis".[15] In this paper he described Christianity as the "most anthropocentric religion the world has seen." He found the roots to the contemporary environmental crisis in medieval Christian Europe and an aggressive interpretation of 'dominion' in Gen. 1. In seeing a spiritual cause to the problem, he also proposed a spiritual solution and believed that for western

---

[13] J.E. Lovelock, 'Gaia as Seen through the Atmosphere', *Atmospheric Environment* 6 (1972), 579-580.

[14] A. Næss, 'The Basics of Deep Ecology', *The Trumpeter Journal of Ecosophy* 21:1 (2005). This paper is a revised version of one given in a lecture in Canberra, Australia, in 1986.

[15] L. White, 'The Historical Roots of Our Ecologic Crisis', *Science* 155 (1967), 1203-1207.

cultures it would need to come from a rethinking of the Christian faith. Subsequent writers have firmly refuted White's view of Christianity as the primary source of the crisis and have provided more positive examples of Christian approaches to the environment, including Celtic Christians, Benedictines, Franciscans and the natural theology of English Protestants in the seventeenth to nineteenth centuries. [16] If there are examples of positive approaches to the Earth, the church still has to grapple with a very mixed and, at times, ambivalent approach to nature. Paul Santmire identified a Spiritual Motive and an Ecological Motive that he traced through Christian history.[17] The Spiritual Motive was especially influenced by Greek philosophical ideas of a good spiritual world contrasted with a perception of an evil physical world. In this view God is transcendent and our aim is to escape this world. This outlook contrasts strongly with the Ecological Motive, which took a more Hebraic approach to the Earth seeing it described in Genesis as fundamentally good. In this model God is immanent and is actively involved in the world he has created. The Spiritual Motive leads to a 'proclamation only' approach to mission, whereas the ecological motive provides theological underpinning for a holistic approach where the whole of life is seen as God's concern. This does not undermine the call for a proclamation of the gospel but gives a fuller understanding of the scope of the gospel for our world. Wright proposes the true relationship between God, humanity and the Earth as an ethical triangle.[18]

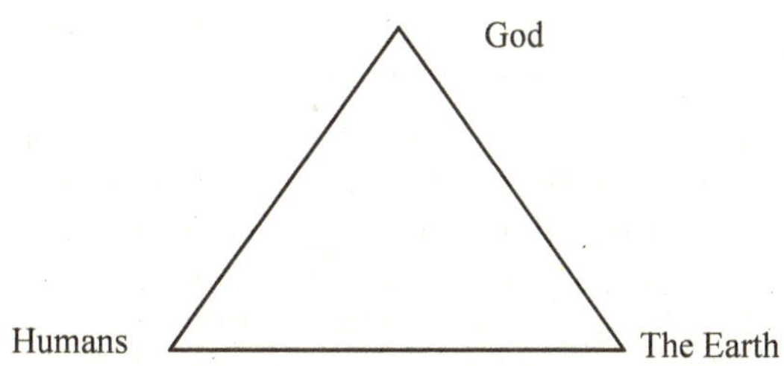

All too often the church has concentrated on the relationships between humanity and God, and humans with each other in the light of faith. The relationships between humans and the Earth and God's concern for his creation have often been ignored. It is as we regain a positive theology of our material world that we will regain our true call to holistic mission to our whole Earth.

If Lynn White gave a biased picture of the Christian approach to the environment, sadly, Christians have frequently ignored the environment and this has significant implications for mission and for the future direction of holistic mission.

---

[16] M.J. Hodson and M.R. Hodson, *Cherishing the Earth: How to Care for God's Creation* (Oxford: Monarch, 2008), 93.

[17] H. Paul Santmire, *The Travail of Nature: The Ambiguous Ecological Promise of Christian Theology* (Philadelphia, PA: Fortress Press, 1986).

[18] C.J.H. Wright, *Living as the People of God* (Leicester: IVP, 1983), 19.

Christian Responses to Contemporary Environmental Challenges

Church councils

As concern for the environment began to rise in the secular world, so the number of voices within the church gradually increased. In 1986 WWF held a conference in Assisi leading to the 'Assisi Declaration'.[19] This called on world religions to make a response to the current environmental crisis. The conference was called by Prince Phillip who also founded the Alliance of Ecology and Religions in 1995. In the mission world, the World Council of Churches (WCC) at their 1983 Vancouver conference, added the 'Integrity of Creation' to the remit of the Peace and Justice group. This group held a World Convention in Seoul, in 1990. A dispute arose because the conference document did not distinguish humanity from the rest of creation as uniquely created in God's image. Ronald Sider suggested an amendment, which was voted down. This led to a meeting of evangelicals with ecological concern at the Au Sable Institute in Michigan in 1992. The conference report, 'Evangelical Christianity and the Environment' led to the formation of the Evangelical Environmental Network (EEN). One of its first publications was 'An Evangelical Declaration on the Care of Creation', released in 1994.[20]

Church mission statements

As WCC began to debate environment as part of mission, so denominations began to include an environmental strand in their mission statements. In 1984 the Anglican Consultative Council met in Nigeria and defined Four Marks of Mission, which did not include environment.[21] In 1990 the Council met in Cardiff and agreed a fifth mark: "To strive to safeguard the integrity of creation and sustain and renew the life of the Earth."[22] In 1993, the Methodist Church of Ireland had as one of its four core features: "wholeness – God's creative purpose and active compassion inspire concern for the whole of human life and the environment." Significantly in the current vision statement, environment

---

[19] L. Serrini, 'The Assisi Declarations', http://www.nyo.unep.org/eaf/eafadec.pdf (accessed 30.4.10).

[20] R.J. Berry, *The Care of Creation* (Leicester: IVP, 2000), 14.

[21] Anglican Consultative Council, *Bonds of Affection: Proceedings of ACC-6, Badagry, Nigeria, 1984* (London: Anglican Consultative Council, 1984), 49.

The Four Marks of Mission agreed were:

1) To proclaim the Good News of the kingdom
2) To teach, baptise and nurture new believers
3) To respond to human need by loving service
4) To seek to transform unjust structures of society.

[22] Anglican Consultative Council, *Mission in a Broken World: Report of ACC-8, Wales 1990* (London: Anglican Consultative Council, 1990), 101.

has been moved from 'wholeness' to the 'witness' section, 'caring for the Earth its people and its resources'.[23]

The Church of North India also included care of creation in its mission statement, which has a focus on justice and restoring the integrity of God's creation by: "breaking down the barriers of caste, class, gender, economic inequality and exploitation of nature."[24] In the last 10 years many more denominations have added an environmental strand to their mission statement. There has been a shift toward seeing environmental care as mission and an increasing urgency in the resolutions on action.

Missions and movements

As environment became a more visible issue, Christian organisations responded. Some specialist Christian environmental organisations began to emerge and missions and denominations have implemented environmental programmes.

A Rocha: conservation, education and lifestyle

In 1983, Peter and Miranda Harris, mission partners with Crosslinks, set up an environmental field station 'Cruzinha', on the Alvor estuary in the Algarve, Portugal. This was the starting point of the environmental mission 'A Rocha'. Cruzinha developed to become an important ecological centre in Portugal and has made a significant contribution to conservation in that country. In the 1990s A Rocha began to found centres in other countries and now has field centres or teams in 18 countries including: Lebanon, Kenya, France, Czech Republic, USA, Canada, India and the UK. A Rocha works in partnership with other Christian organisations, environmental agencies and local authorities. It has had a major environmental influence on Christian mission.

The John Ray Initiative: education, advocacy and research

JRI was founded in 1997 by Sir John Houghton, former co-chair of the IPCC. He sought to gather scientists, policy makers, theologians and church leaders to create a think-tank style of organisation that could provide the research base for the education and advocacy that was needed to tackle global environmental problems. JRI provides a specialist knowledge base for other Christian organisations and has been particularly known for its high quality conferences, courses and publications.[25] Its current projects include a distance learning

---

[23] The Methodist Church in Ireland, 'Witness', http://www.irishmethodist.org/about/witness.php (accessed 30.4.10).

[24] The Church of North India, 'CNI Mission Statement', http://www.cnisynod.org (accessed 30.4.10).

[25] JRI authors include R.J. Berry, P. Carruthers, M.J and M.R. Hodson, J.T. Houghton,

course, Christian Rural and Environmental Studies (CRES); and a research initiative, the Agriculture and Theology Project (ATP). JRI members provide consultancy and education to other organisations and are increasingly being called on by mission agencies to advise on the environmental dimension of holistic mission.

Au Sable Institute for Environmental Studies

In 1979 the Au Sable Institute was established in Michigan by Calvin DeWitt, to provide Christian environmental education for college and high school students. The overall aim is, "the integration of knowledge of the Creation with biblical principles for the purpose of bringing the Christian community and the general public to a better understanding of the creator and the stewardship of God's Creation."[26] In addition to Au Sable's original campus in the Great Lakes it now has locations in the Pacific Rim, south Florida and Tamil Nadu in south India.

The Church of south India, Seven Year Plan to Protect the Living Planet

In 2008 the The Church of South India (CSI) Synod Ecological Concerns Committee held a conference on environment and eco-leadership. From this the province has adopted a seven year plan, which was approved to protect the living planet as part of the mission strategy of CSI. The programme promotes inclusion of creation care in management structures, awards for good practice, integration into worship and biblical study, practical projects and work in schools. Bishop Thomas Samuel[27] in his presidential address at the 2008 conference, called upon all Christians to work in this world as God's partner.[28]

Rural Extension with Africa's Poor

In Kenya, Rural Extension with Africa's Poor (REAP) works to provide practical, accessible technology for the rural poor. Their stewardship of the environment programme teaches sustainable agriculture and promotes tree planting.[29]

H. Marlow, C. Russell, J. Weaver and R. S. White.

[26] Au Sable, 'Our Mission', http://www.ausable.org/au.ourmission.cfm (accessed 15.4.10).

[27] Rt. Rev. Thomas Samuel, Bishop of CSI Madhya Kerala Diocese.

[28] Church of South India, 'A Seven Year Plan to Protect the Living Planet', http://www.arcworld.org/downloads/Christian-CSI-7YP.pdf (accessed 30.4.10).

[29] REAP, 'A Biblical teaching to motivate farmers to maintain a living soil', http://reap-eastafrica.org/ (accessed 30.4.10).

The American evangelical story: concern and opposition

In July 2002 JRI and Au Sable Institute jointly held a symposium in Oxford entitled 'Climate Forum 2002'. They invited scientists, church leaders and climate policy makers with the aim of raising the profile of climate change among evangelical Christians. One of the delegates was Richard Cizik, then Vice-President of the National Association of Evangelicals in America. Cizik responded to the conference by changing his lifestyle and convening a series of conferences in the States to bring this cause before the leaders of the evangelical movement there. This culminated in 86 US evangelical leaders signing an 'Evangelical Call to Action' on climate change, which challenged the Bush administration.[30] American Christians with a concern to take action on climate change have faced considerable opposition. The 'Cornwall Alliance for the Stewardship of Creation' and 'Focus on the Family' have both opposed taking action on climate change.

Mission education

As churches and missions have begun to address the need to have environment as a focus for mission, a need has grown for education in this area and especially for an integration of environment, theology and mission. Overall colleges have been a little slow in responding.[31] Four approaches have been identified: ignore the environment altogether; have a few lectures on environmental theology within a whole course; have one or more whole modules included in a course; or, integrate environmental theology across the whole syllabus.

Given that vocational courses are becoming increasingly packed, an integration of environmental thinking is a productive approach to encourage, though specialist modules are also essential if environment is to become established as a legitimate Christian concern. The International Baptist Theological College in Prague and Redcliffe College, Gloucester UK, both have environmental modules in their masters programmes and an overall priority for environment. Ripon College Cuddesdon, Oxford UK, offers a complete distance learning course (Christian Rural and Environmental Studies, CRES). Both Regent College in Vancouver and Wheaton College, Illinois integrate an environmental perspective into a number of their theological courses as do Trinity College, Bristol, UK and South Wales Baptist College, Cardiff UK. In the US, Au Sable offers a wide range of courses and modules

---

[30] J.A. Wardekker, A.C.Petersen, J.P.van der Sluijs, 'Ethics and public perception of climate change: Exploring the Christian voices in the US public debate', *Global Environmental Change* 19 (2009), 512-521.

[31] M.J. Hodson, 'Environmental Theology Courses in Europe: Where are we now?', in J. Weaver, and M.R. Hodson, (eds.), *The Place of Environmental Theology: A Guide for Seminaries, Colleges and Universities* (Oxford, Whitley Trust and Prague, International Baptist Seminary 2007), 107-120.

with a large number of participating colleges. By being flexible in approach they can provide an ecological element to many US students from Christian colleges and universities. For specifically mission education, Au Sable teach courses on 'Tropical Agriculture and Missions' at their Florida Campus, and 'Global Development and Ecological Sustainability' at their Great Lakes Campus.

The Asian Rural Institute in Tochigi-ken, Japan runs practical courses on sustainable agriculture, leadership and community development. [32] Their courses are aimed at rural leaders from Asia and Africa, with an emphasis on poor and oppressed peoples who wish to return to their own communities when they have completed training. In India CSI Madras and Medak Dioceses are running pastors programmes on creation care. In Trichy Tanjavore Diocese, Bishop Heber College has become the base for Heber Au Sable Institute of Environmental Studies.

This survey of mission education is far from comprehensive, but it is clear that environment is not yet established in the mission curriculum of many colleges. Modern mission demands a holistic curriculum with current affairs, economics, globalisation, poverty, development and environment as core subjects taught within a biblical theological framework.

Environment and Development

Environment and development have been seen as competing issues. The reality is that human poverty cannot be alleviated without taking environmental care seriously and care of the environment is ineffective if human concerns are not also addressed. There is a direct relationship between poverty and environmental degradation, and both need to be improved together if a future is to be found for the poorest of the world and for the planet. The United Nations Environment Programme (UNEP) seeks to: "provide leadership and encourage partnership in caring for the environment by inspiring, informing, and enabling nations and peoples to improve their quality of life without compromising that of future generations."[33]

One positive example of a joint environment and development project is the tree planting scheme in the Diocese of Mara, Tanzania. The Bishop of Mara saw the suffering that had been brought about by deforestation. Women were having to walk increasing distances to fetch water and firewood. He decided to promote tree planting around homesteads, where the women would protect the trees and benefit from them.[34]

---

[32] ARI, 'ARI: that we may live together', http://www.ari-edu.org (accessed 30.4.10).

[33] UNEP, 'United Nations Environment Programme, environment for development', http://www.unep.org/Documents.Multilingual/Default.asp?DocumentID=43 (accessed on 7.5.10).

[34] M.J. Hodson and M.R. Hodson, *Cherishing the Earth: How to Care for God's Creation* (Oxford: Monarch, 2008), 157.

Tearfund

Tearfund became involved in environmental mission as they saw the impacts of climate change and other environmental problems on the poorest in the world. They are involved in campaigning and advocacy to raise awareness, especially of the interaction between environmental problems and human suffering. They seek to have an integrated approach to their practical projects to take account of the environmental dimension alongside human needs. One project they partner with is 'Goodwill for Development' in Lahore, Pakistan.[35] This project is seeking to integrate environment and development programmes as it works at grass roots to provide sustainable development for the poorest in society. An example is the promotion of low cost fuel efficient smokeless stoves for local women. Black carbon from open stoves contributes to global warming both from the carbon released and from the soot that absorbs the suns rays. The introduction of smokeless stoves therefore reduces global warming and significantly benefits human health.

Tearfund also has extensive education programmes. The Hope for Planet Earth tour ran in the UK for seven weeks in the spring of 2008 and 2009 to raise awareness of climate change. It was a collaborative project with A Rocha, JRI and Share Jesus International, and was attended by thousands of school children and adults.

Africa Inland Mission

The work of Africa Inland Mission (AIM) in Lesotho has expanded to include environment and development.[36] Mission partners who arrived 'to preach' discovered food shortages caused by unsustainable farming practices. Part of the problem has been the poor status of farmers and farming in the country. AIM staff are working to teach sustainable farming practices alongside a biblical understanding of God's heart for the land.

Interserve

Interserve has an operating principle that all their ministries should be integrated and lead towards wholeness. Interserve take a stewardship approach to the environment and are involved in training and practical environmental projects, including A Rocha Lebanon.[37]

---

[35] 'Activities', http://www.goodwill4humandevelopment.org (accessed 7.5.10).

[36] M. Delorenzo, 'God is a Farmer', http://www.aimint.org/usa/stories/god_is_a_farmer.html (accessed 8.5.10).

[37] Interserve, 'Christian missions in Asia, the Middle East and the UK', http://www.interserve.org.uk (accessed on 15.4.10).

Toward an Environmental Missiology

In 2007, the UK Environment Agency asked a panel of 25 experts to give the most important things needed to save the planet. Of their priorities the second highest was that, "Religious leaders need to make the planet their priority."[38] While being wise about responding to secular appeals, Christians need to take seriously this call to provide a spiritual and moral lead. A firm basis of the doctrines of creation, salvation and eschatological hope should make caring for the Earth a mission priority. One of the important issues is to understand their inter-relationship. Creation is not simply a stage on which the missiological drama of human salvation is worked out. God's creation and his care for it is an expression of his character. Christ, in becoming human, hallowed our material world and his death and resurrection were in response to the sin of the world. All creation groans, waiting for the glory of God to be revealed and for a liberation from its bondage to decay (Rom. 8:18-25). This indicates that the salvation won by Christ has an impact on the whole cosmos. As we look toward the renewed heaven and Earth in Revelation 21 and 22, we see God, humanity and creation reconciled and freed from the negative forces of sin and death. Therefore the work of the cross has cosmic implications and our gospel is greater than some of previous generations may have imagined.

Alongside an environmental missiology, we need a strong global ecclesiology. Internationally, churches have well developed communities at grass roots in both rich and poor nations. In many places there is also high level influence with governments and institutions. Humanity needs to make a transition from living or aspiring to live a high carbon lifestyle to a sustainable pattern of low carbon usage; and from living at the expense of the rest of biodiversity to living sustainably within the limits of our Earth. This shift can only happen as governments change direction and as local communities work together to live in a different way. Churches therefore could play a strategic role at different levels of society across large parts of the world. This action finds a biblical foundation in the salvation narratives of Romans 8:18-21 and the Christology of Colossians 1:15-20. Inspiration can also be found in the Old Testament teaching on the relationship between God, people and land found in books such as Leviticus and Deuteronomy. Sustainable Christian communities could thus model what being 'in Christ' means for both people and planet.

Holistic sustainable missiology does not have to have a static 'hands-off' model of the natural world. God placed Adam in the garden to work it and give life to it (Gen. 2:15). In many places in the Old Testament the people of God were encouraged to farm and adapt the natural ecology (Deut. 28, Is. 65:21). The imperative is not to preserve nature untouched but to enable nature to flourish alongside human flourishing. This is an expression of resurrection hope and is beautifully illustrated in the resurrection scene in John's gospel where

---

[38] The UK Environment Agency, 'The 50 Things that will Save the Planet', *Your Environment Extra* 17 (2007), 17.

Mary mistakes Jesus for the gardener (Jn. 20:15).[39] How can we authentically preach the resurrection if we live lives that indirectly bring suffering to the poor and death to many of our global ecosystems? To be a gospel people we need to seek to be life giving to all. Table 1 gives a broad summary of the biblical underpinnings for environmental holistic mission.

Table 1: A biblical basis for environmental mission	
Genesis and Isaiah	Interactive: not afraid to use technology but in a sensitive way to benefit both people and planet
Leviticus and Deuteronomy	Rooted in communities
Colossians	Holistic in approach seeing human and environmental needs as interconnected
Gospels	Seeking to be life-giving to all. Demonstrating the intrinsic value of creation and our respect for all that God has made.
Revelation and Isaiah	Bringing hope for the future

Conclusion

We face a very difficult century for humanity's relationship with the environment. If there is an Edinburgh conference in 2110, it is likely that the major focus will be environment as the impacts of our over-use of the world's resources will by then have impacted so severely that all people will have environmental care as their highest concern for human survival.

As a church we have a responsibility to respond to the needs of God's creation and this provides us with a mission opportunity. We need to have a strong biblical and theological basis for this by connecting our biblical understanding of creation to mission. We need to make holistic mission work and this will only come as we connect human and environmental concerns. Our mission involvement needs to lead to a positive transformation of human living conditions but also provide sensitive management of nature and protect the natural world. Overall our gospel message must provide hope in an effective way for both people and planet. We are partners with Christ in revealing his

[39] P. Carruthers, 'Creation and the Gospels', in S. Tillett (ed.), *Caring for Creation: Biblical and Theological Perspectives* (Oxford: Bible Reading Fellowship, 2005), 75-76.

salvation to the cosmos, and we have a crucial task to bring good news to all creation (Mk. 16:15).

PART E

THE WAY AHEAD WITH HOLISTIC MISSION

IMPLICATIONS FOR THE CHURCH OF TOMORROW

Brian E Woolnough

In this book we have sought to bring together insights to aspects of holistic mission, celebrating what has been achieved since 1910 and raising outstanding issues. At the end of this process we brought together a group of 65 church leaders, practitioners and scholars to discuss what had been achieved and highlight opportunities and challenges for holistic mission in six specific areas of the church – the individual Christian, the local church, the denominations, missionary societies, Christian NGOs, and theological training institutions. Professor Ron Sider gave the lead address, the names of the 65 contributors to the discussion are listed in Appendix B. The following sections summarise those discussions, and insights from the writings. There then follows specific conclusions and recommendations, and final thoughts.

Implications for Different Parts of the Church

Individual Christians

Achievements

The church of God is primarily the company of believers, worldwide. It is the family of God. With two billion Christians, approximately a third of the world, it is the prime mechanism for demonstrating and proclaiming the whole gospel of Christ around the world. We can celebrate the growth of this Christian family over the last century, especially in the majority world,[1] and see much growth in the spread of the holistic gospel through the daily love and compassion of individual Christians. Even in churches where a more limited gospel is preached, individual Christians will often be showing the love of God to their neighbours in whatever way is appropriate to the place where God has placed them. Whether those individuals are as celebrated as Bishop Desmond

[1] David Kilingray uses the phrase 'gossiping the gospel' as the prime reason for the remarkable spread of Christianity in Africa over the last century, see D. Killingray, 'Gossiping the Gospel: Indigenous Mission in Africa', *Transformation* (2010, forthcoming).

Tuto, Mother Teressa or Rev Martin Luther King, or the unsung millions showing care and love for their sick and needy neighbour and looking after children and the elderly around them, they are exhibiting holistic mission in the way most appropriate to them.

There has been a growing awareness of the needs of the world as the means of global communication have brought the world, in all its needs and suffering, into the lives of everyone. Many have responded with much personal commitment as well as financial support. Many have been able to experience and serve the needy through relatively easy travel and the opportunity for short term, as well as long term, ministry. In most case folk return from such experiences totally transformed, both by the experience gained and the lives shared with faithful, joyful, poor and needy fellow Christians.

Limitations

Of course many Christians fall short of the example of Christ and, as fallen, selfish individuals, too often tend to look after themselves rather than the needy around them. Especially, but not exclusively, western Christians have often been seduced by the materialistic consumerism of the secular world around them, and tend to concentrate on their own welfare (spiritual and physical). Even the church services, the worship and the published literature and conferences tend to concentrate on 'personal piety' and focus on the individual (the inglorious trinity of I, myself and me!). Selfishness, the prosperity gospel, and undue emphasis on personal salvation can also lead to individual self-centredness and away from the need to serve others. Too much emphasis is often placed on being saved *from* rather than being saved *for*.

Opportunities and challenges

The challenge for the individual Christian is to stay close to their saviour, to read their bibles faithfully, and to heed the example and the exhortation of Jesus. Parables such as the good Samaritan, the sheep and the goats, and the rich man and Lazarus, all give strong exhortations for holist mission, as well as strong judgement for those who are indifferent to the poor. All can heed this in their local communities, where the needs may be material, spiritual or emotional. Many are now able to serve further a field as opportunities arise.

Another challenge for well meaning western Christians is how to find ways of genuinely helping the poor in the majority world in such a way that it meets *their* local needs, and does not just meet the personal needs of the donor, which may well be paternalist and patronising. Corbett and Fikkert, in their challenging book *When Helping Hurts*[2] illustrate ways where well-intentioned charity can cause dependency in the receiver and a God-complex in the donor.

---

[2] S. Corbett and B. Fikkert, *When Helping Hurts: How to Alleviate Poverty without Hurting the Poor and Yourself* (Chicago: Moody Publishers, 2009). An important, if

In a world with so many differing needs, and filled by individuals to each of whom God has given different gifts and commitments, holistic mission provides the opportunity for individual Christians to develop their faith according to those particular giftings and personal situation. Sometimes we are tempted just to pray that our faith may be strengthened, whereas in practice it is in obedience and in service to others that we find our faith being renewed.

The Local Church

Achievements

God's organisation of his people into local churches was one of his most inspired decisions! It brings together his people, not only to learn of and worship him, but also to encourage and train his people to look out and serve the community in which they are placed. When, for instance, a benefactor wishes to help the needy in, say, a poorer part of Africa, some organisation, some structure will be necessary to enable that help to get to the needy. But, in fact, such a structure already exists within the Christian world – it is the network of local churches. And in this, each church already has as its core commission the desire to serve those around, and the love of God to motivate and strengthen them. In many cases, especially in the majority world, the church itself will be part of the poor and so have a particular rapport and empathy with those in need. Over the years, many churches have formed the hub of humanitarian provision for the community, delivering holistic mission as part of their work.

In affluent countries, the nation state has tended to take over the provision of health, education and many other social services, provision which was originally provided by the church. In many of the poorer countries of the majority world the church itself, both at the local and the denominational level, is still the provider of health clinics, schools and social care. In all countries, there are needs that the state will not, cannot, meet and here the local church has, in many cases, been meeting the needs, holistically, in a magnificent way. There are many examples – my mind immediately springs to cases in Zimbabwe, Zambia and Moldova, where the local churches are meeting the physical, as well as the spiritual, needs of the local community, where no other organisation can. In Zimbabwe, for instance, where the politics of the national government have prevented other external forms of aid from getting through to those suffering dreadful poverty, the local church has been the only group helping the poor and needy there. And because their mission is holistic, the deeper, more fundamental spiritual needs are being met alongside the material needs.

There are two models for the church, that of 'an ark' and that of 'salt and

---

disturbing, book for anyone who seeks and enjoys helping the poor.

light.' An ark sees the local community as sinful, Godless, and seeks to draw outsiders away from it into the safety of the church, an ark. The 'salt and light' model sees the local community as part of Gods world, fallen and imperfect, but in which God is working and wishes His people to be involved in it too, being salt and light to flavour and enlighten the whole. Do we seek to take people out of the world and into the church, or do we take the church into the world, and thus transform it? A holistic gospel more readily does the latter. There are local churches in all denominations and traditions which fall into both camps.

In the UK evangelical churches, where churches are often very self-centred, some are starting to look outwards, from being 'arks' to being 'salt and light' in the world. Notable examples can be seen in St Andrew's, Chorley Wood, a powerful but previously introverted charismatic church which has changed from a 'come to us' to a 'go to them' attitude through the development of Mission Shaped Communities,[3] and Steve Chalke's Church.Co.UK[4] serving the community in Waterloo, East London.

As the churches have grown throughout the world, many of the communities in which they are grounded have been transformed remarkably.

A powerful, and surprising, affirmation of the power of holistic mission to change society came from Matthew Parris, a leading journalist in the UK and a convinced atheist. He wrote an article in The Times newspaper recounting his experience as he revisited Malawi to study the effectiveness of some development charity work. "Now as a confirmed atheist, I've become convinced of the enormous contribution that Christian evangelism makes in Africa: sharply distinct from the work of secular NGOs, government projects and international aid efforts. These alone will not do. Education and training alone will not do. In Africa Christianity changes peoples heart. It brings spiritual transformation. The rebirth is real. The change is good." [5] No-one could accuse Matthew Parrish of being a biased reporter with vested interests!

Limitations

Having said which, there are still many churches which seem indifferent to the needs of those around them, and seem only concerned with the members of their own 'club'. Bill Hybels described the local church as 'the hope of the world', and so it should and can be. But in many areas the church seems irrelevant to the concerns of the real world, and the claim that the church is the hope of the world would be met by a derisive laugh. Whether it is an affluent, self-centred church in Europe, or a vast, charismatic, prosperity gospel-preaching church in Africa, many churches still leave the problems of the world

---

[3] Written up in Mark Stibbs and Andrew Williams, *Breakout* (Carlisle, UK: Authentic 2009).

[4] See Steve Chalke's book *Intelligent Church: A Journey towards Christ-Centred Community* (Grand Rapids: Zondervan, 2006).

[5] From *The Times*, 27 Dec., 2008.

untouched. Though worship, disciplining, and spiritual strengthening are important, indeed vital, roles for a church, where this leads to a self-centredness of focus it can miss out on the equally vital role of looking out to, and caring for, the community around.

We have seen, and rejoiced in, much wonderful church growth over the last century. But we have also learnt that numerical growth in itself is not adequate. We have seen some forms of Christianity that have proved superficial, where the mind only and not the heart have been affected, where Christ has not been allowed to transform the whole of one's life, where width has been substituted for depth. 'One mile wide and one inch deep' has been a jibe about some of African Christianity. The example of the Rwandan genocide is often used to illustrate this, where great church growth and even 'spiritual revival' was quickly followed by deeds of horrendous brutality. Yet such a jibe can be applied much more widely – the two great (sic!) European wars were fought between Christian countries, many Christian leaders become involved with corruption, and even more affluent Christians are indifferent to the detrimental effect their lifestyles have on the poor. It is only as the gospel is preached and accepted holistically, with body, mind and spirit all affected, that the churches will fully represent the life and example of Jesus.

Challenges and opportunities

The challenge for the local churches now is to find the best ways, the most appropriate ways, to be salt and light in their own communities. Perhaps in the west, there is more appeal, more romance, in seeking to meet the needs of those in other countries, the other side of the world. The fact that such can be indifferent to the less romantic, more demanding, needs of the poor on their own doorsteps, raises worrying questions about underlying motives.

Why so many local churches do not change, do not accept the holistic mission, is largely due to personal self-centredness and too much focus on personal salvation by the church leaders, especially in evangelical churches. But that can be changed in two ways – intellectually (by being convinced by the biblical arguments outlined such as those in this book), and experientially. Any person who has experienced the work of Christians and churches serving their poor community for themselves, possibly in having experience of short term mission in Africa, Asia or South America, cannot fail but to be transformed and convinced of holistic mission.

The challenge again for church leaders is to give a strong lead, through preaching and example, about the holistic nature of Jesus' mission. With all of us having a natural propensity to be selfish, we need positive encouragement to be less self-centred and to look out for our neighbour.

The concept of *Missio Dei*, the realisation that God is at work throughout the world, and that we are privileged to be a small, humble part of that work, has important implications for Christians, churches and missionary societies. It is his world, it is his power and will which will prevail, whether or not we comprehend it. Our task is not to pretend that we can do his work – God is able to do that himself, even at times working his unfathomable will through non-Christians! Our task is just to obey his commands, and follow his example.

The Denominations, and Church Groupings

Achievements

All the major denominations, Protestant and Catholic, have had a commitment to social action and have set up departments and activities to further them. Some needs throughout the world are too large and too expensive to be met by individual Christians or local churches, and in such cases denominations and church organisations have stepped in to address those needs. Schools and hospitals have been built – in Africa, more than half of the schools and hospitals have been built and run by faith-based, largely Christian, organisations. In some countries, e.g. Uganda and Nepal, the church denominations have taken responsibility for providing clean drinking water and hygiene systems in the rural areas. In most countries the different denominational organisations have been increasingly active in campaigning and working for relief of poverty and fighting injustices.

Whilst making a distinction here between local churches and denominations, in practice some of the very large churches, the mega churches in America or Korea, often feel big enough to act as denominations by themselves, and their leadership becomes all powerful.

Limitations

There is a danger that such big projects may not be the most appropriate to the local countries. Big, expensive, hospitals in the towns of Africa, now run down through lack of funding and underused, may be less appropriate than local clinics and itinerant medics in the rural areas.

The proliferation of different denominations and church grouping, an inevitable result of Protestantism (where if we do not like our church we protest and set up our own), is that it is difficult for the churches to speak with a single voice and to give a clear Christian lead in a secular world, thus weakening the prophetic, campaigning voice of the church.

Within a particular denomination there will be a central organisation, which can be both a strength and a weakness. The denominational organisation can organise on an appropriate scale for large projects, but will have all the petty organisational problems that belong to any other structure, secular or religious. The problem for the denominations is to be a facilitator for the local church and individual Christians, not an inhibiting straight jacket. At their worst the denominations can become competitive rather than co-operative. Even ecumenical discussions between denominations can emphasise more the differences and distinctions between them, rather than what they have in common. Paradoxically, churches working together in holistic mission, specifically when working together in relief and development projects, find that their denominational differences are irrelevant as they work out the love of God in the service of others – an organic ecumenicalism has developed, without trying!

Challenges and opportunities

The challenge for the denominations is to prioritise and see what ways they can most effectively serve their community. Should it be more pro-active in getting involved with the national debate, taking religion into the market place, which in Europe especially has become highjacked by the secular world? This is an area where there is a growing intellectual debate, with the churches fighting back.[6]

In the UK there is a growing renewal from the church denominations, e.g. the Anglican churches and OASIS, to take responsibility for new, faith-based schools, and the government has been encouraging this. The church based schools, Protestant and Catholic, have always been very popular and oversubscribed because of the quality of their education – despite opposition from the more vociferous, secular wing of society. In the majority world this opportunity is much greater, and being well taken up.

Missionary Societies

Achievements

The story of the development of the missionary societies since 1910 is a long, varied and often glorious one. It is too long to tell here. For an excellent recent analysis we would commend *Edinburgh 2010: Mission Then and Now* by Kerr and Ross, specifically prepared for Edinburgh 2010.[7] The traditional missionary society then was sent from the prosperous Christian west to the under-developed, non-Christian countries to preach the gospel, gain conversions, educate and heal, and set up churches. There have also been national, indigenous Christian evangelistic missions active in Africa, Sout America and Asia, though these are less well documented or fully celebrated.[8] Even when

---

[6] See writings of the Christian philosopher, Professor Roger Trigg, such as *Religion in the Public Life: Must Religion Be Privatised?* (Oxford: Oxford University Press, 2007).

[7] David Kerr and Kenneth Ross, *Edinburgh 2010: Mission Then and Now* (Oxford: Regnum Press, 2009).

[8] See, however, Kwame Bediako, *Jesus in Africa: The Christian Gospel in African History and Experience* (Carlisle, UK: Regnum, 2000); L. Pirouet, *Black Evangelists: The Spread of Christianity in Uganda 1891-1964* (London, 1978); and Ogbu Kalu, *African Christianity: An African Story* (Pretoria, 2005).

the stories of European missionaries are told, the enormous importance of the African agents working as intermediary was rarely given credit – in 1910, for instance it was reckoned that there were 4,500 European missionaries working through 26,470 African agents[9] – the Africans were 'gossiping the gospel' to their own communities and thus the church grew.

Since then, the activities and goals of many, but not all, mission societies have become more holistic, partly because of a change of understanding about the nature of mission and partly for more pragmatic reasons as non-Christian countries, hostile to Christianity, would not allow missionaries in, except as 'tent-makers'. Many more specialist, inter-denominational, and international missionary societies have been developed over the century, as the missionary activities of the main line denominations has decreased. At the beginning of the century mainline denominations in America supplied 80% of the North American missionary force. At its end, they supplied no more than 6% of it[10].

Typically, CMS now has five holistic principles of mission.[11] Similar changes have developed in other societies such as the BMS (the Baptist Missionary Society, one of the oldest Protestant missionary societies founded by William Carey, the father of modern mission, in 1752). In 2010 BMS stated on its website that "BMS believes in holistic mission, an approach that stays true to the Christian call to evangelism without neglecting the duty to take care of the physical needs of the poor." Their work now involves church planting, development, disaster relief, education, health, and advocacy. This brings them very close in aims and approach to many of the CNGOs, such as Tearfund. For such missionary societies the divide between evangelism and social concern has been overcome, mission has become more holistic. Evidently, the achievements of missionary societies have been significant and dramatic both in changed lives and transformed communities.

One of the greatest achievements of missionary societies has been the translation of the bible into the local language, through organisations like the Wycliffe Bible Translators. Many in the majority world, who had felt dominated and disempowered by the western, English-based, form of Christianity, speak of the freedom, independence and self respect that came when they were able to read the bible in their own language. Such personal empowerment, and the ability to read the scriptures in and according to their own culture, has been particularly influential in the growth of the African, AIC, churches.

---

[9] From J.S. Dennis *et al*, *World Atlas of Christian Missions* (New York: Student Volunteer Movement for Foreign Mission, 1911).

[10] A S. Moream, quoted by D.J. Hesselgrove, 'Will We Correct the Edinburgh Error? Future Mission in Historical Perspective', *Southern Jornal of Thheology* 49:2 (2007), 126.

[11] CMS five marks of mission as expressed by the Anglican Communion: to proclaim the good news of the kingdom, to teach, baptize and nurture new believers, to respond to human need by loving service, to seek to transform unjust structures of society, to strive to safeguard the integrity of creation and to sustain the life of the earth.

One of the most dramatic changes, alongside the shift of Christianity's centre of gravity from the north to the south, has been the growth of missionary societies from the south who now send missionaries around the world. New sending countries, such as Korea, Africa, Brazil and India, are now active around the world in 'cross-cultural' mission. Ugandans are coming to the UK as missionaries, Koreans are sending missionaries all around the world. Currently Korea sends over 12,000 missionaries abroad, second only in numbers to the United States! It is reckoned that India has now 44,000 cross-cultural missionaries, though many of them work cross-culturally in their own country. A recent study (2010) is entitled *Reverse in Ministry and Missions: Africans in the Dark Continent of Europe.*[12] This presents a study of African churches in Europe, part of the African diaspora, a product of globalisation.

Missionary societies clearly had, and have, organisational structures which can promote individual missionaries and harness financial, technical and prayer support whilst they are away from home, and this can be very supportive for their work and for the receiving countries.

Limitations

As the church, and the cultures, of previously 'sent to' countries have grown so dramatically, so the need for western missionaries has become less necessary or appropriate. If the role of the western missionary societies is merely to maintain, or seek to promote, a western type of Christianity, it is very questionable whether that is necessary or helpful. The local churches around the world are increasingly, and rightly, able to meet the spiritual and physical needs of their communities, as the AICs (the African Initiated Churches) are showing so well.

It is not difficult to travel around Africa or Asia and find large churches identical in architectural style, and form of worship, to that of nineteenth century England. The services, the liturgy, replicate that of the Church of England in a way that separates the gospel from the local culture. Furthermore, it makes the local Christians dependent on outside support, with theology, church buildings and even hospitals, which need external support for their maintenance. Similarly, many well-intentioned American missionaries have achieved the promotion of a very American form of Christianity which does not always correspond to the local culture and its needs, and is not accountable to the local communities. The 'prosperity gospel' approach, apart from being unscriptural, can be particularly unhelpful in that it takes away personal responsibility for caring for the poor and needy.

Throughout the twentieth century, it should be recognised that much western missionary activity to the majority world, though well intentioned, has been paternalistic and often racist. It has been ineffective because it was often

---

[12] Israel Olofinjana's *Reverse in Ministry and Missions: Africans in the Dark Continent of Europe* (Milton Keynes: Author House, 2010).

associated with colonialism and the business and political interests of the west, and the missionaries often did not understand, or even seek to understand, the culture and the language of those they sought to convert.

Many missionary societies in the west are finding a shortage of funds, which limit their ability to do what they would like. This is partly due to a lack of vision for mission, evangelistic or holistic, and partly due to churches 'doing their own thing' independent of the denominational societies. Some churches are not mission minded, and thus do not support missionary societies. Other churches are very mission minded but tend to support their own missionaries through independent and personal contact, or support some of the many non-denominational specialist charities or CNGOs.

Such independent action can be inefficient due to lack of experience, expertise and cultural awareness, and a reliance on emotional enthusiasm of a few, transient, individuals. It does, however, allow for individual, short term visits to the communities which can build up relationships and mutual understanding. It will also inspire and motivate giving and support.

Opportunities and challenges

Missionary societies, particularly missionary societies based in the affluent north, are at the moment in an ambivalent position towards the majority world. Clearly, for many Christians, there is a real desire to help, save and transform those in other countries, and this is a laudable response to Jesus' great command and great commission. But, for reasons of the current strength of the local churches and the past history of colonialisation, many in the majority world do not want that help! They have their own churches and their own church leaders, often much more spiritually strong than the rich Christians of the north. This is particularly so when previous relationships have been paternalistic, if not imperialistic.

And yet we are a global Christian family, we have different strengths and a love one for another. Experience has shown that relationships between the missionaries and the incipient churches have often been tremendously loving and supporting. The challenge now is to find ways of developing these relationships so that they will be of mutual benefit, with the missionary societies, showing genuine humility to listen and to learn. All societies need to learn much about the different cultures they seek to serve. And money, the one thing that the north has more than the south, may not always be a blessing if it separates the recipient away from his or her community.

Christian NGOs

Achievements

One of the great successes in the second half of the twentieth century has been the introduction and growth of the CNGOs (Christian Non-Governmental Organisations) dealing with relief and development. This has been part of the national and international relief and development movement.[13] With the growth of international communication and global media making the needs in the majority world known to those in the affluent west – with stories of drought and starvation, of war refugees, of one billion people living on less than $1 per day, of disease and of sexual exploitation – the consciences of rich Christians has been stirred. CNGOs have proliferated around the world, ranging from small personal charities to larger ones such as Tearfund,[14] WorldVision and Cafod.

Such CNGOs have had an enormous effect in bringing relief and development in many countries, and many have built up an impressive degree of expertise in areas such as health, water and sanitation, food security, HIV/AIDS, climate change, disability, children at risk, and the elderly, all being used in the service of God. At the same time they have been able to change the attitude of Christians through their churches in such areas as child and disabled welfare, and HIV/AIDS and gender relationships.

They have responded quickly and generously to national disasters such as earthquakes and tsunamis and, perhaps more importantly, have produced ongoing development and mitigation schemes. In all of these ways Christians, either personally or vicariously through giving and praying, have been able to show God's love to those in need. Often, they have brought holistic transformation as well as physical relief, especially when they have worked through the local churches.

CNGOs are also often involved in campaigning at the national and the international level, seeking to tackle the more fundamental causes of poverty, and they have had real success in so doing in many countries. Issues such as FairTrade, governments' international aid, environmental issues, and human trafficking have been tackled in this way, even if not they have not (yet!) been solved.

---

[13] It is estimated that there are about 40,000 NGOs working internationally, with India having over a million NGOs working in their country! The number of Christian NGOs is much smaller, but not insignificant, working with Christians both in the home country and the receiving countries.

[14] Mike Hollow, *A Future and a Hope: The Story of Tearfund and Why God Wants the Church to Change the World* (Oxford: Monach, 2008), gives a splendid description of Tearfund's development through from the 1960s to the present day.

CNGOs, because of the acceptance of the quality of their work, have been able to gain access to countries closed to traditional Christian ministries, and hence demonstrate God's love to many who would otherwise not hear of it.

Limitations

At times CNGOs have been accused of simply adopting the secular agenda and bringing a purely physical relief to the needy which, though good in itself, lacks the fuller transformation that a more holistic mission tackling the spiritual as well as the physical needs of the community would provide. Such limitations, whilst appropriate in places, are obviated by those CNGOs who work with and through the local churches, and who have a holistic agenda through all they do.

Other criticisms focus on the tendency for the donor relief organisations to work to their own priorities and bring a paternalistic attitude to those in need. Whilst this was undoubtedly true in the early days, increasingly CNGOs are now working along side those whom they serve, and seek to listen well to the needs and preferences of the local communities. That this criticism has still not been fully heard is illustrated in the book *When Helping Hurts*.[15] The easy way of 'helping' is to provide money, but this can easily distort values at the recipient end, cause dependence, and separate the person receiving the money from their poorer community. There are dangers that well intentioned Christians will leap in 'where angels fear to tread' and, without the appropriate knowledge, skills, and wisdom, will do more harm than good.

There is also a danger that Christians see the CNGOs as their way of showing the love of God abroad, and fail to recognise the poor and needy in their own communities. CNGOs can salve the conscience of Christians and leave their own Christian service to their own communities as far from holistic

Increasingly CNGOs have introduced strict accountability systems to measure the impact that the projects they are supporting have produced. In this they have followed the secular system of quantitative measure in log frames (or logical frameworks) etc. But this has real dangers of measuring, and thus prioritising, only those things that can be easily measured and leaves aside the really important Christian objectives in holistic, transformational work. It may be easy to get quantitative measures of toilets built and food supplied; it is much more difficult (it is impossible!) to get quantitative measures of communities transformed and individual lives made more Christ-like. Perhaps the evaluation of the projects should be more in the hands of the recipients than the donors.[16]

---

[15] This book, by Steve Corbett and Brian Fikkert, published by Moody Publishers 2009, argues that giving aid can cause dependency and reduced self-confidence in the recipients and cause a 'God complex' – *we know best* – in the givers.

[16] This argument is expanded in Brian Woolnough, 'But How Do We Know We Are Making a Difference? Issues Relating to the Evaluation of Christian Development Work', *Transformation* 25:2 and 25:3 (2008), and Roche's *Impact Assessment for Development Agencies: Learning to Value Change* (Oxfam, 2004).

Opportunities and challenges

Perhaps one of the biggest challenges facing CNGOs is to maintain a fully holistic mission in the face of dealing with such enormous physical needs in the context of 'equal treatment to all' and in the company of other secular NGOs. It is easy to let the spiritual issues go by default. Many of the secular organisations are (and certainly were) very suspicious of CNGOs' 'preaching and proselytizing'. And CNGOs also are wary of creating 'rice Christians'. However, there has more recently become a recognition by governmental and cross-governmental organisations that faith-based organisations do appropriately meet the whole personal needs, of individuals and communities.

CNGOs, along with other aid providing organisations, do need to listen carefully to the recipient communities to find out what they really need, and respond appropriately in long term planning as well as short term action. The donor organisation does need to go in as a partner, and as a servant, even when accountability systems tend to make uncomfortable power relationships. The saying that 'he who pays the piper calls the tune' is one which presents a challenge to many CNGOs, but one which must be addressed. The leadership and management of all CNGOs should be 'listening, learning and loving' – and that love should be unconditional, responsive to the guidance of the Holy Spirit rather than pre-determined objectives. The donor, the CNGO, needs great humility, and must recognise that the western values are often quite different, and inferior, to the values within the recipient community. Often the recipient community has a far greater Christian faith, and a far greater trust that their God will provide, than the more affluent, donor, Christians who more readily put their trust in money!

At the heart of all relief and development work lies the question of what we mean by development, and what is development for? The Commission for Africa[17] asked this question and stated that different cultures would give different answers. "Many in western countries see it as being about places in Africa 'catching up' with the developed world. In Africa, by contrast, you will be more likely to be told something to do with well-being, happiness and membership of a community." A much more holistic message. It is easy for the two approaches to be counter-productive, and too much emphasis on the materialistic can be destructive to the community. Even the splendid micro-credit schemes can finish up concentrating on the entrepreneurial poor and ignoring the 'poorest of the poor'. This is especially true when using targets derived from the commercial banking system. These targets can give precedence to the successful over the really poor, and cut out the Christian objectives of helping the weak and the disadvantaged that had been its original goal.

[17] Commission for Africa, *Our Common Interest* (London: Penguin Books, 2005).

Theological Training Institutions

Achievements

The future of the church is, humanly speaking, in the hands of its leaders, and because most church leaders receive their theological training just once in their life, the theological college, whether by extension or in residence, has an enormous potential to influence the church of the future. If the ministerial training is based on a dualist, fragmented, theological approach, and in many western (and western-modelled) colleges that is so, then those ministers so trained will preach and encourage such an approach to mission for all of their working lives. If the ministerial training involves more practical situations and focuses on a holistic approach to ministry, and an increasing number of colleges and TEE (Theological Education by Extension) courses are doing so, then those so trained will be inspired to teach and practice holistic mission throughout their ministry. In India, for instance, at UBS (Union Biblical Seminary) the theological training not only contains a serious biblical foundation for holistic mission, but many students are given the opportunity of a one term placement with a CNGO working among the poor in the local slum communities. Many students change their professional orientation completely after that, having been inspired to serve among the poor rather than in a traditional ministerial role in one of the established churches.

There has been an increasing emphasis on practical teaching in many theological institutions and seminaries throughout the world. The teaching of applied theology, of holistic mission, has been combined with short term mission opportunities and 'tent-maker' models, ensuring that the students are grounded holistically in the real world. Many staff too have long experience of, and continuing commitment to, the work of the church through CNGOs and personal involvement in Christian activism in their society. This increasingly has influenced the 'flavour' of their institutions.

The growing number of TEE courses also provide the opportunity for students to learn their trade whilst still living among their local poor, thus ensuring that their training is continually grounded in the real world that God is calling them to serve.

Limitations

There is still the feeling that too many theology courses are far too academic and removed from the real world that the trainees are being prepared to serve. Too many of the courses are traditional and academic, and are based on knowledge rather than experience. They follow the western academic, dualistic model of learning. They do not readily engage with the real world, the world in which the students will be living and working. The theological colleges should be the servants of the church, and too many theologians are experts in small, esoteric, fragmented areas which do not readily engage with the problems of the poor and needy in contemporary society.

Many theological colleges in the majority world have followed the same model as is used in the west, and some would suggest that this model is even more inappropriate in the majority world where the students, and also those they will serve, think and act much more holistically. There is the danger that this type of training will have a debilitating, deskilling effect on the learners who will have to reject their more natural holistic way of thinking, and try and learn the western way of thinking – a double, and inhibiting problem for potential church leaders. There is a need for more theological trainers in the majority world to confidently build on their own Christian lives and experience, and develop their own rigorous but more local training courses.

Opportunities and Challenges

Perhaps the greatest challenge for theological colleges is to rethink their courses holistically, to ensure that they serve their local churches rather than frighten and over-power them. This will need serious, and genuine, consultation with local church leaders to ensure the courses and experience of the students are grounded in church life. The experience of the trainee students should also be shared in a genuine partnership between academia and the churches, through out the whole period of training. The training will need to be shared, in a relationship of mutual respect, between the scholar in academia and the practitioner in the church.[18] When the curriculum and ethos of theological training is holistic, rather than fragmented, it will be more natural for holistic mission to be integrated within it.

The culture of a TTI (theological training institution) depends to a large extent on the people working within it, and it is this permeating culture which has a greater influence on students than the explicit curriculum. That being so, the challenge that TTIs have is to ensure that they employ, and use influentially, staff with practical, holistic experience of, and commitment to, working with the poor and needy. Increasingly this is being done, but it should not be seen as an 'add on' to an otherwise dominant culture of academic colleagues

We have stressed the need for Christians to experience holistic mission in practice before they are personally convinced of its virtues. Theological

---

[18] The shift of training pattern that has occurred in teacher education in the UK over the last few decades forms an ideal model for theological education. Where previously the trainee teacher was taught the theories of education, psychology, sociology, and philosophy in academic institutions and then left to learn how, if at all, to apply it for themselves when faced with classrooms of real kids in real schools, now the training is shared between academic and classroom teacher, in schools as well as academia, through out the course. The experience at Oxford University, which pioneered such an approach, is described in Peter Benton's *The Oxford Internship Scheme, Integration and Partnership in Initial Teacher Education* (London: Gulbenkian Foundation, 1990).

colleges can provide opportunity for this initially through the initial training course, but there is even more opportunity for first hand practical work in serving the poor to be the project for Masters and Doctoral research work, and within TEE courses. Such practical experience must be given equal, or greater, status to the more academic studies.

Too often theological colleges 're-invent their own wheels' when developing their curriculum, and this practice *does* have some advantages in giving the staff ownership of the course. But the opportunity for sharing resources between institutions must also make sense, and with the advent of the internet, it is unacceptable for colleges not to share resources and build on best practice.

Conclusions and Recommendations

Having covered such a wide and important area as holistic mission, it is appropriate to try to draw together some of the more important conclusions and implications for the church today.

1. We would reiterate the Lausanne (1974)[19] principle 5 on Christian Social Responsibility as our starting point,

> We affirm that God is both the creator and the judge of all men. We therefore should share his concern for justice and reconciliation throughout human society and for the liberation of men from every kind of oppression. Because mankind is made in the image of God, every person, regardless of race, religion, color, culture, class, sex or age, has an intrinsic dignity because of which he should be respected and served, not exploited. Here too we express penitence both for our neglect and for having sometimes regarded evangelism and social concern as mutually exclusive. Although reconciliation with man is not reconciliation with God, nor is social action evangelism, nor is political liberation salvation, nevertheless we affirm that evangelism and socio-political involvement are both part of our Christian duty. For both are necessary expressions of our doctrines of God and man, our love for our neighbor and our obedience to Jesus Christ. The message of salvation implies also a message of judgment upon every form of alienation, oppression and discrimination, and we should not be afraid to denounce evil and injustice wherever they exist. When people receive Christ they are born again into his kingdom and must seek not only to exhibit but also to spread its righteousness in the midst of an unrighteous world. The salvation we claim should be transforming us in the totality of our personal and social responsibilities. Faith without works is dead.
>
> We express penitence both for our neglect of our Christian social responsibility and for our naive polarization in having sometimes regarded evangelism and social concern as mutually exclusive. We affirm that evangelism and socio-political involvement are both part of our Christian duty.

---

[19] The International Congress on World Evangelization was held in Lausanne, Switzerland in 1974. The gathering was called by a committee headed by Rev. Billy Graham and drew more than 2,300 evangelical leaders, from 150 countries.

2. We mean by holistic mission what the Oxford Conference (2001)[20] called integral mission and affirm it to encompass both,

> the proclamation and demonstration of the gospel. It is not simply that evangelism and social involvement are to be done alongside each other. Rather, in integral mission our proclamation has social consequences as we call people to love and repentance in all areas of life. And our social involvement has evangelistic consequences as we bear witness to the transforming grace of Jesus Christ. If we ignore the world we betray the word of God which sends us out to serve the world. If we ignore the word of God we have nothing to bring to the world. Justice and justification by faith, worship and political action, the spiritual and the material, personal change and structural change belong together.

3. We welcome and celebrate the way that,

a) an increasing number of churches, including evangelical churches, share this vision and are serving their communities both in evangelism and in meeting their practical needs;
b) the growing church in the majority world is addressing the needs of many of the poorest in society, and demonstrating the love of God holistically;
c) the growth of Christian NGOs are addressing the needs and development of the poor around the world;
d) the way many CNGOs are now working through, and in support of, the local churches who are addressing the whole needs of their communities in their physical, social, emotional, and spiritual needs;
e) an increasing number of individual Christians, denominations, churches and CNGOs are tackling the injustices around the world through advocacy and involvement in direct political action;
f) the involvement of individual Christians and the growth of CNGOs, such as A Rocha, are sensitising the church to their responsibilities to maintain and restore God's creation.

4. We regret and repent the way that,

a) many Christian churches still see that evangelism as independent of (and preferable to) addressing the social needs of the communities, and ignore those aspects of social responsibility inherent in holistic mission;
b) many Christian churches still see the social gospel as the whole means of addressing the needs of the suffering world, and ignore the need for evangelism and tackling the fundamental problem of sin, selfishness and greed, and thus miss the opportunity for holistic transformation of society and individuals;
c) many churches and Christians align themselves with the rich, the successful, and the powerful in society and avoid tackling the

---

[20] The World Evangelical Fellowship met with 140 leaders of Christian organisations from 50 countries and the newly formed Micah Network ratified this in its Declaration on integral mission.

injustices in society which so oppress the poor, and misuse the environment;

d) many churches and church leaders still undervalue and oppress women and hold them in a subservient role without tackling the inherent sexism in many homes and communities;

e) some theologies, relating to the prosperity gospel and pre-millennialism, lead the church away from the potential of the kingdom of God on earth, and avoid tackling the abuses and injustices in today's society.

5. We would encourage all theological training of ministers and Christian workers to review their theology of the gospel so that the students might fully appreciate, and experience, the holistic gospel in its fullness. Also, that all theological training should include some period of placement where the student spends time experiencing and working alongside those working with the poor and oppressed. We would encourage all churches, church leaders. colleges, and trainees to question whether the western model of theology is really appropriate to the more holistic approach of the majority world, and to consider how the relative strengths of the dualist and the holistic approaches, the theoretical, the practical and the experiential approaches, may be build upon in all ministerial training.

6. We would encourage all churches, missions and evangelists to emphasise not only what people are saved *from* but also what they are saved *for* – to follow the example of Jesus their saviour and to serve the poor and needy in their community.

7. We would encourage all Christian NGOs working in relief and development, tackling the needs of the poor, the needy, and the oppressed, to do so by working through the local churches, to enable the holistic aspects of the gospel to be addressed naturally and sustainably.

8. We recognise that the church is the body of Christ and, as such, has many different parts (eg 1 Cor. 12 vv 12-31), each of which is important and worthy of mutual respect and encouragement. Different parts might concentrate on evangelism, or church planting, or worship, or teaching, or social and political activity. Different people might well concentrate on one of these functions, but the church as a whole should ensure a holistic coverage of all. We would encourage all local churches, church denominations, and theological colleges, and all individual Christians, to do an audit of their activities to ensure that their mission, as a whole, is holistic.

9. We recognise the impressive work being done by many CNGOs working in relief and development, usually in a secular environment where the Christian aspect of transformation work has been down-played and unappreciated by the international donors. We believe that it is now time for CNGOs to be more self-confident and assert that genuine transformation of societies can only be obtained where the underlying spiritual and religious aspects are addressed.

10. We recognise the splendid work being done by many missionary societies, their increasingly holistic approach, and the changing world and

changing conditions in which they now work, especially the missionary societies based traditionally in the north. We would encourage them, especially those working out of their own country, to continue re-examining how they can best, and most appropriately, work in partnership with Christians in the majority world, and in humility recognise the strengths and God-given independence of the church in the majority world, and ensure that all they do builds up that local strength and does not create unhealthy dependency. We would encourage all missionaries to ensure that the gospel they preach is holistic, is grounded in the local culture and their needs, and is seeking to address all the needs of the community.

We started this book with a question, "Is holistic mission good news for the poor and the oppressed?" The answer is a clear "Yes" – but only when and where it is being applied. There are still too many cases in the church where the holistic gospel is not being promoted. Some years ago, soon after soap was invented, a soap salesman was challenged that it did not seem to be working on the scruffy and dirty poor in the slums of London. "It is not that it doesn't work," responded the salesman, "it is just that it is not being used!" In Chesterton's words, "The Christian ideal has not been tried and found wanting. It has been found difficult and left untried."[21]

Above all, Christian mission is not a matter of either one type of gospel or another – holistic, integrated, evangelistic or social. Jesus is our example in all we do, and in him we see holism at its fullest. He came that we all 'might have life and life to the full.' By word and by example we should show the love of God as expressed in the life of Jesus, and follow his example as the perfect holistic man. We should seek to show God's unconditional love to those in need,

This is not a new message, God's plan for God's people has always been that his church follows the great commission *and* the great commands: "Go and make disciples of all nations… teaching them to obey everything I commanded you", and, "Love the Lord your God… and love your neighbour as yourself." As we follow this, and the example of Jesus, we will find that God's plan for God's people through holistic mission is *the* way to bring his kingdom closer "on earth as it is in heaven."

---

[21] G.K. Chesterton (1874-1936), an English Christian writer.

Selected Bibliography

Acemoglu, D., J.A. Robinson and T. Verdier. 'Kleptocracy and Divide-and-Rule: A model of personal rule'. National Bureau for Economic Research Working Paper Number 10136. Cambridge MA, 2003.

Adams, N. et al. '*Religious Conviction and Human Trafficking: Motive Matters*'. Paper presented at First Annual Interdisciplinary Conference on Human Trafficking, 2009 University of Nebraska – Lincoln. 2009.

Ajulu, Deborah. *Holism in Development: An African Perspective on Empowering Communities.* Monrovia, CA: MARC, 2001.

Algorta, R. *El Renacimiento*. Enero, 1936.

Alkire, S. *Valuing Freedoms: Sen's Capability Approach and Poverty Reduction.* New York: OUP, 2002.

Amoah, E.D., Akintunde and D. Akoto (Eds.). *Cultural Practices and HIV/AIDS: African Women's Voice.* Inbadan: Sefer, 2005.

Anand, Sudhir and Amartya K. Sen. *Human Development Index: Methodology and Measurement.* New York: United Nations Development Programme, 2009.

Anglican Consultative Council. *Mission in a Broken World: Report of ACC-8, Wales 1990.* London: Anglican Consultative Council, 1990.

Anglican Consultative Council. *Bonds of Affection: Proceedings of ACC-6, Badagry, Nigeria, 1984.* London: Anglican Consultative Council, 1984.

Asian Rural Institute. 'ARI: that we may live together'. http://www.ari-edu.org, 2010.

Au Sable Institute of Environmental Studies. 'Our Mission'. http://www.ausable.org/au.ourmission.cfm.

Barrett, D.B. *Schism and Renewal in Africa: An Analysis of six thousand contemporary Religious Movements*. Oxford: OUP, 1968.

Barro R.J. and R.M. McCleary. 'Religion and Economic Growth across Countries'. *American Sociological Review* 68 (2003), 760-81.

Barth, Karl. *Church Dogmatics.* G.W. Bromiley, T.F. Torrance (eds.). Edinburgh: T. & T. Clark, 1936-1977).

Beek, K A. 'Spirituality: a development taboo'. *Development in Practice* 10:1 (2000), 31-43.

Berry, R.J. *The Care of Creation.* Leicester, UK: IVP, 2000.

Black, J., N. Hashimzade and G. Myles. *A Dictionary of Economics.* 3rd Ed. Oxford: Oxford University Press, 2009.

Boadi, A. 'Engaging Patriarchy: Pentecostal Gender Ideology and Practice in Nigeria'. In J. Korieh Chima and G. Nwokeji Ugo (eds.). *Religion, History and Politics in Nigeria: Essays in Honour of Ogbu U. Kalu.* University Press of America, 2005. 172-186

Bockmuehl, K. *Evangelicals and Social Ethics.* Trans. David T. Priestly. Downers Grove, IL: InterVarsity, 1979.

Bosch, D J. 'In Search of New Evangelical Understanding', in Bruce J. Nicholls (ed.). *In Word and Deed: Evangelism and Social Responsibility.* Grand Rapids, MI: Eerdmans, 1986.

Bosch, D. *Transforming Mission Paradigm Shifts in Theology of Mission.* Maryknoll, NY: Orbis Books. 1993.

Bowerman, A and M. Amuyunzu-Nyamongom. *The Christian distinctiveness in the response to HIV and AIDS in Africa: Lessons for Action.* London: Tearfund, 2006.

Boyd, S. *In the Thick of It: Why the Church Is an Essential Partner for Sustainable Development in the World's Poorest Countries?* London: Tearfund, 2009.

Bradshaw, B. *Change across Cultures: A Narrative Approach to Social Transformation.* Grand Rapids, MI.: Baker Academic, 2002.

Branson, M L. 'Striving for Obedience, Haunted by Dualism', *TSF Bulletin* 6:1 (September/October 1982).

Bremmer, Jan N. *The Social and Religious Capital of the Early Christians.* http://irs.ub.rug.nl/dbi/49d094e147a56, 2007.

Campbell, A., V. Kapos, I. Lysenko, J.P.W. Scharlemann, B. Dickson, H.K. Gibbs, M. Hansen, and L. Miles. *Carbon emissions from forest loss in protected areas*. UNEP World Conservation Monitoring Centre, 2008.

Caplan, P. *Class and Gender in India.* London, Tavistock Publications, 1985.

Carruthers, P. 'Creation and the Gospels', in S. Tillett (ed.). *Caring for Creation, biblical and theological perspectives.* Oxford: Bible Reading Fellowship, 2005.

Carson, R. *Silent Spring.* Boston: Houghton Miflin, 1962.

CDE. *Dormant Capital: Pentecostalism and its Potential and Social Economic Role.* Johannesburg: Centre for Development and Enterprise, 2008.

Chambers, Robert, 'Normal Professionalism and Early Project Process Problems and Solutions'. In *Agricultural and Rural Problems.* Institute of Development Studies, 1988.

Chenery, Hollis Burney, with Monteks Ahluwalia and Nicholas G. Carter, *Growth and Poverty in Developing Countries.* London and New York: Oxford University Press, 1974.

Chester, T. (ed.). *Justice, Mercy and Humility: Integral Mission and the Poor.* Carlisle, UK: Paternoster, 2002.

Chilson, E H. *Ambassador for the King.* Wichita, KS, 1943.

Church of North India. 'CNI Mission Statement'. *The Church of North India.* http://www.cnisynod.org.

Church of South India. 'A Seven Year Plan to Protect the Living Planet'. *Alliance of religions and conservation.* http://www.arcworld.org/downloads/Christian-CSI-7YP.pdf.

Collier, Paul. *The Bottom Billion: Why the Poorest Countries Are Failing and What Can Be Done About It.* New York: Oxford University Press, 2007.

Collodi, J. and F. M'Cormack. 'Population Growth, Environment and Food Security: What Does the Future Hold?' *Horizon: Future issues for development.* Pilot Issue (July 2009).

Costas, O. 'Proclaiming Christ in the Two Thirds World'. In Vinay Samuel and Chris Sugden (eds.) *Sharing Jesus in the Two Thirds World.* Grand Rapids, MI: Eerdmans, 1984.

Costas, O. 'Report on Thailand '80'. *TSF Bulletin* 4:1 (October 1980).

Curran, I.M., S.N. Trigg, A.K. McDonald, D. Astiani, Y.M. Hardiono, P. Siregar, I. Caniago, and E. Kasischke. 'Lowland Forest Loss in Protected Areas of Indonesian Borneo'. *Science* 13, vol. 303. no. 5660 (February 2004).

Daleep, M. 'Christian Development agencies and mission: A Christian Aid perspective'. *Connections* 1 (2003), 22-24.

Dangwal, R C. *Globalisation and liberalization: New Developments.* New Delhi: Deep & Deep Publications, 2000.

De Santa Ana, Julio. *Good News to the Poor: The Challenge of the Poor in the History of the Church.* Geneva: WCC Publications, 1977.

Deiros, Pablo Alberto. *Historia del Cristianismo en América Latina*, Publicado por Fraternidad Teológica Latinoamericana (FTL). Buenos Aires, Argentina. Primera Edición, 1992.

Delorenzo, M. 'God Is a Farmer'. Africa Inland Mission, www.aimint.org/usa/stories/god_is_a_farmer.html.

Dempster, M.W., B.D. Klaus, and D. Petersen (eds.). *Called and Empowered: Global Mission in Pentecostal Perspective* (Peabody, MA: Hendrickson, 1991).

Deneulin, Séverine, and Masooda Bano. *Religion in Development: Rewriting the Secular Script.* London: Zed, 2009.

Easterly, William. *The White Man's Burden: Why the West's Efforts to Aid the Rest Have Done So Much Ill and So Little Good.* New York: Penguin Press, 2006.

Ecumenical News International, 'Indian churches praised for role in HIV-AIDS struggle'. http://www.ekklesia.co.uk/node/5068, 18 April 2007.

Escobar, Samuel. 'El avance evangélico en América Latina'. In *La Fe Evangélica y las teologías de la Liberación.* Casa Bautista de Publicaciones, 1987. 49–50.

_____. 'El Legado Misionero de Juan A. Mackay'. In *El Otro Cristo Español*, Edición Especial de 1992, Casa Unida de Publicaciones S.A. de C.V: (CUPSA), México y Asociación de Ediciones La Aurora, Argentina y Ediciones Semilla, Guatemala. Tercera Edición, 1991. Edición Especial de Celebración de Bodas de Diamante del Colegio San Andrés (antes Anglo-Peruano). Impreso en Perú, Noviembre 1991.

Evans, C.H. *The Social Gospel Today.* Louisville, KY: Westminster/John Knox, 2001.

Firth, C.B. *An Introduction to Indian Church History.* Delhi: ISPCK, 1961.

Fonseca, Juan. 'Secularización y Tolerancia: cementerios, muerte y protestantismo en el Perú (1890–1930)'. In *Protestantismo y Vida Cotidiana en América Latina: un estudio desde la cotidianidad de los sujetos.* Pablo Moreno (Copilador), CEHILA, Fundación Universitaria Seminario Teológico Bautista Internacional, Cali, Colombia, 2007. 57–80.

Foster, G. 'Study of the response by faith-based organisations to orphans and vulnerable children'. UNICEF and World Conference of Religions for Peace, January 2004, www.wcrp.org.

France, Richard, *The Gospel according to Matthew: An Introduction and Commentary.* Leicester, UK: Inter-Varsity Press, 1985/7).

Fransella, F. and K. Frost. *On Being a Woman: A review of research on how women see themselves.* London and New York: Tavistock Publications, 1977.

Freston, Paul. *Evangelical Christianity and Democracy in Latin America.* Oxford: Oxford University Press, 2009.

Friedmann, John, *Empowerment: The Politics of Alternative Development.* Cambridge, MA: Blackwell, 1992.

Galloway, K. *Starting Where We Are: Liberation Theology in Practice.* Glasgow: Wild Goose Publications, 1998.

Gärtner, B. *The Temple and the Community.* Cambridge: Cambridge University Press, 1965.

Gideon. Githega. *The Church as the Bulwark against Authoritarianism.* Oxford, Regnum, 2002.

Gifford, P. *Christianity, Politics and Public Life in Kenya.* Columbia University Press, 2009.

Gill, A. 'Christian Social Responsibility'. In C. Rene Padilla (ed.). *The New Face of Evangelicalism: An International Symposium on the Lausanne Covenant.* Downers Grove, IL: InterVarsity, 1976.

Good Will for Human Development. 'Activities'. http://www.goodwill4humandevelopment.org.

Goulet, Denis. *The Cruel Choice: A New Concept in the Theory of Development.* New York: University Press of America, 1971.

Graham, B. 'Why Lausanne?' In James D. Douglas (ed.). *Let the Earth Hear His Voice: International Congress on World Evangelization.* Minneapolis, MN: World Wide Publications, 1975.

Gramby-Sobukwe, S. and Tim Hoiland. 'The Rise of Mega Churches'. *Transformation* 26:2 (April, 2009).

Griffin, Keith B. *Alternative Strategies for Economic Development.* London: Macmillan, 1989.

Gutierrez Sanchez, Tomas. *Los Evangélicos en Perú y América Latina: ensayos sobre su historia.* Chhila: Ediciones AHP, 1997.

_____. *Desafíos a la Fe Cristiana: una Perspectiva Evangélica.* Lima, Perú: Ediciones AHP, 2002.

Gweini, *Faith in Wales: counting for communities*. Evangelical Alliance Wales, 2008.

Hall, Douglas John. *The Steward: A Biblical Symbol Come of Age.* Grand Rapids, MI: Eerdmans, 1990.

Hall, E.T. *The Hidden Dimension*. Garden City, NY: Doubleday, 1966.

Hattersley, R. 'Faith does breed charity'. *The Guardian*, 12 September 2005.

Hay, Donald. *Economics Today: A Christian Critique.* Leicester: Apollos, 1989.

Hedlund, R. *Roots of the Great Debate in Mission.* Bangalore, India: Theological Book Trust, 1997.

_____.'The Witness of New Christian Movements in India'. Unpublished paper, IAMS Assembly, Malaysia, 2004.

_____ (ed.). *Christianity Is Indian: The Emergence of an Indigenous Christianity.* Delhi: ISPCK, 2000.

Hempton, David, 'Evangelicalism and Reform'. In J. Wolffe (ed.). *Evangelical Faith and Public Zeal.* London: SPCK, 1995.

Henry, C.F.H. *Evangelical Responsibility in Contemporary Theology.* Grand Rapids, MI: Eerdmans, 1957.

_____. *The Uneasy Conscience of Modern Fundamentalism.* Grand Rapids, MI: Eerdmans, 1947.

Herbert, B. *Self Perception of Tamil Christian Women: Narrative Analysis of Gender Practice.* Part II. VDM Verlag Dr. Muller, Mauritius, 2010.

Herbert, H. 'Tamil Christian Women at the Turn of the Millennium: mission initiatives and gender practice'. *WHR* 17:4 (Sep. 2008). 616-17.

Hertzke, Allen. *Freeing God's Children: The Unlikely Alliance for Global Human Rights*. New York: Rowman & Littlefield, 2004.

Hettne, Bjorn, *Development Theory and the Three Worlds.* London: Longman Scientific and Technical, 1990.

Hobsbawn, E.J. *Age of Extremes: The Short History of the Twentieth century 1914-1991* (London: Abacus, 1995)

Hodson M.J. 'Environmental Theology Courses in Europe: Where are we now?' In J. Weaver and M.R. Hodson (eds.). *The Place of Environmental Theology, A guide for seminaries, colleges and universities.* Oxford: Whitley Trust; Prague: International Baptist Seminary, 2007.

Hodson, M.J. and M.R. Hodson. *Cherishing the Earth, how to care for God's creation.* Oxford: Monarch, 2008.

Hoek, M. and J. Thacker. *Michah's Challenge.* Milton Keynes: Paternoster, 2009.

Howard, D.M. *The Dream That Would Not Die: The Birth and Growth of the World Evangelical Fellowship, 1846-1986.* Exeter, UK: Paternoster, 1986.

Hughes, Dewi. *Power and Poverty: Divine and Human Rule in a World of Need.* Nottingham/Downers Grove: InterVarsity Press, 2008.

Hunsinger, George. 'Karl Barth's Christology'. In John Webster (ed.). *The Cambridge Companion to Karl Barth.* Cambridge: Cambridge University Press, 2000.

Hylsom-Smith, K.. *To the Ends of the Earth: The Globalisation of Christianity.* London: Paternoster, 2007.

Interserve. 'Christian missions in Asia, the Middle East and the UK'. http://www.interserve.org.uk.

Jain, S. *Status and Role Perception of Middle Class Women.* New Delhi: Puja Publishers, 1988.

James, D. and J.D. Douglas (eds.). *Let the Earth His Voice.* Minneapolis; MN: World Wide Publications, 1975.

James, R. *Creating Space for Grace: God's power in organisational change.* Sundbyberg: Swedish Mission Council, 2004.

Jayakumar, Samuel. *Dalit Consciousness and Christian Conversion: Historical Resources for a Contemporary Debate.* Oxford: Regnum; Delhi: ISPCK, 1999.

_____. *Mission Reader: Historical Models for Wholistic Mission in the Indian Context.* Oxford: Regnum; Delhi: ISPCK, 2002.

_____. *Renewal of Mission in India: A Historical Perspective.* Chennai: Mission Educational Books, 2008.

_____ and Ponraj Jayakumar (eds.). *Mission as Transforming Service.* Chennai: Mission Educational Books, 2004.

Jenkins, Philip. *The New Faces of Christianity: Believing the Bible in the Global South.* New York: OUP, 2006.

Johns, C. 'Editorial'. *National Geographic*, vol. 217, no.4 (April, 2010).

Kairos, Ediciones. 'Christian Reflection from the Latino South'. *Journal of Latin American Theology* 2:2 (2007).

Kalu, W. 'Soul Care in Nigeria: Constructing Pentecostal Models in Pastoral and Counseling'. In G. Korieh, J. Chima and Ugo Nwokeji (eds.). *Religion, History and Politics in Nigeria: Essays in Honour of Ogbu U. Kalu.* New York: University Press of America, 2005.

Kerr, D.A, and K.R. Ross. *Edinburgh 2010: Mission Then and Now.* Oxford: Regnum Books, 2009.

Kessler, J.B.A., Jr. 'Early Protestant Efforts in Peru and Chile'. In *A Study of the Older Protestant Missions and Churches in Peru and Chile: with special reference to the problems of division, nationalism and native ministry.* Oosterbaan and Le Cointre N.V., Goes, 1967. 19-23.

_____. 'The Establishment of Protestantism in Peru'. In *A Study of the Older Protestant Missions and Churches in Peru and Chile: with special reference to the problems of division, nationalism and native ministry.* Oosterbaan and Le Cointre N.V., Goes, 1967. 37-38.

Kisau, Paul Mumo. 'Commentary on Acts of the Apostles'. In Tonkunboh Adeyemo (ed.). *African Bible Commentary.* Nairobi: Word Alive, 2006.

Landes, David. *The Wealth and Poverty of Nations: Why some are so rich and some so poor.* London: Abacus, 1998.

Larmer, B. 'The Big Melt'. *National Geographic* 217: 4 (April 2010).

Leopold, A. *A Sand County Almanac*. New York: Oxford University Press, 1946.

'Letters: A Report of Visits to the Churches during the Ecumenical Decade-Churches in Solidarity with Women'. Geneva: WCC, 1997.

Linthicum, R.C. *Empowering the Poor*. Monrovia CA: MARC, 1991.

Lovelock, J.E. 'Gaia as seen through the atmosphere'. *Atmospheric Environment* 6 (1972).

Lumsdaine, D. *Evangelical Christianity and Democracy in Asia*. New York: Oxford University Press, 2009.

MacPherson, John M. 'School and Nation: Roots Entwining'. In *At the Roots of a Nation: The Story of Colegio San Andrés, a Christian School in Lima, Peru.* Edinburgh: Knox Press, 1993. 4–6.

Maluleke, T.S. 'Christian Mission in Africa in the 21st Century'. Conference paper cited in E. Eliot Kendal. *The end of an Era: Africa and the Missionary*. London: SPCK, 1978.

Marshall, M. and N. Taylor. 'Tackling HIV and AIDS with faith-based communities: learning from attitudes on gender relations, and sexual rights within local evangelical churches in Bukina Faso, Zimbabwe and South Africa'. *Gender and Development* 14:3 (2006),

Marshall, M, *Gender, HIV and the Church, a Case Study*. London: Tearfund (available from www.tearfund.org)

Martin, David. 'The Evangelical Upsurge and Its Political Implications'. In Peter Berger (ed.). *The Desecularization of the World: Resurgent religion and world politics.* Grand Rapids: Eerdmans, 1999. 37-49.

Martin, Michael T. and Terry R. Kandal. *Studies of Development and Change in the Modern World.* New York: Oxford University Press, 1989.

McAlpine, Thomas H. *By Word, Work and Wonder.* Monrovia, CA: MARC, 1995.

McConnell, Douglas. 'Holistic Mission'. In A. Scott Moreau (ed.). *Evangelical Dictionary of World Mission.* Carlisle: Paternoster Press, 2000.

McLuhan, M. *Understanding Media: The Extensions of Man.* New York: McGraw Hill, 1964.

Meier, Gerald M. and James E. Rauch. *Leading Issues in Economic Development*. New York, Oxford University Press, 2005.

Methodist Church in Ireland. 'Witness'. *The Methodist Church in Ireland.* http://www.irishmethodist.org/about/witness.php.

Millennium Ecosystem Assessment, *Ecosystems and Human Well-being: Biodiversity Synthesis*. Washington DC: World Resources Institute, 2005.

Miller, D.E. and T. Yamamori. *Global Pentecostalism: The New Face of Christian Social Engagement*. Berkeley: University of California Press, 2007.

Miller, Darrow L. *Disciplining Nations: The Power of Truth to Transform Cultures*, 2nd ed. Seattle: YWAM Publishing, 2001.

Moberg, D.O. *The Great Reversal: Evangelism versus Social Concern.* Philadelphia, PA and New York: Lippincot, 1972),

Moule, C.F.D. 'The Significance of the message of the Resurrection for Faith in Jesus Christ'. *Studies in Biblical Theology* 8 (1968).

_____. 'Fulfilment-Words in the New Testament'. *New Testament Studies* 14 (1968). 293-320.

Mukund, K. 'Women's Property Rights in South India: A Review'. *Economic and Political Weekly.* May29, 1999.

Myers, B.L. *Walking with the Poor: Principles and Practices of Transformational Development.* Maryknoll, NY: Orbis Books, 1999.

_____. 'The Church and Transformational Development'. *Transformation* 17:2 (2000). 64-67.

_____. 'What Makes Development Christian? Recovering from the Impact of Modernity'. *Missiology* 26:2 (1998). 143-153.

Myers, N. 'Environmental refugees: a growing phenomenon of the 21st century'. *Philosophical Transactions of the Royal Society of London, Series B* 357, 2002.

Næss, A. 'The Basics of Deep Ecology'. *The Trumpeter Journal of Ecosophy* 21:1 (2005).

Narayan-Parker, Deepa, Robert Chambers, Meera Shaw, and Patti Petesch. *Voices of the Poor: Crying out for Change.* New York: Oxford University Press for the World Bank, 2000.

Natarajan, S. *Watering the Neighbour's Plant: Media Perspectives on Female Infanticide in Tamil Nadu.* Chennai: M.S. Swaminathan Research Foundation, 1997.

Nazir-Ali, M. *From Everywhere to Everywhere: A Worldview of Christian Mission.* London: Harper, 1990.

Neild, Robert. *Public Corruption: The dark side of social evolution.* London: Anthem Press, 2002.

Nicholls, B.J. (ed.). *Word and Deed: Evangelism and Social Responsibility.* Grand Rapids, MI: Eerdmans, 1986.

North, D.C., J.J. Wallis and B.R. Weingast. 'A Conceptual Framework for Interpreting Recorded Human History'. National Bureau for Economic Research Working Paper 12795, Cambridge, MA, 2006.

Nouwen, H. *Here and Now.* New York: Crossroad Publishing, 2001.

Nunez, Emilio Antonio. *Teología de la Liberación: una perspectiva evangélica.* Miami: Editorial Caribe, Tercera Ediciόn, 1988.

Nussbaum S. (ed.). *The Contribution of Christian Congregations to the Battle with HIV/AIDS at the Community Level: A seven-country research report prepared for the Summer Mission Briefing at the Oxford Centre for Mission Studies 7-9 June 2005.* Oxford: Global Mapping International, 2003.

Oduyoye, M.A. and E. Amoah (eds.). *People of Faith and the Challenge of HIV/AIDS.* Ibadan: Sefer, 2004.

Oliver, E H. *The Social Achievements of the Christian Church.* Toronto: Board of Evangelism and Social Service of the United Church of Canada, 1930.

Padilla, C.R. 'Holistic Mission'. In John Corrie (ed.). *Dictionary of Mission Theology.* Downers Grove, IL: IVP, 2007.

_____. 'Evangelism and Social Responsibility: From Wheaton '66 to Wheaton '83'. *Transformation* 2:3 (April/June 1985).

_____. 'La contextualización del evangelio'. In *Misión Integral: Ensayos sobre el Reino y la Iglesia.* Buenos Aires: Nueva Creación, 1986.

_____. 'Hacia una Cristología Evangélica Contextual'. *Boletín Teológico* 30 (June 1998).

_____. 'Evangelism and the World'. Lausanne 1974 documents. www.lausanne.org

_____. 'Holistic Mission'. Lausanne Occasional Paper 33. Pattaya: LCWE, 2005.

_____ and Chris E. Sugden (eds.). *Texts on Evangelical Social Ethics, 1974-1983.* Nottingham, UK: Grove Books, 1985.

Panitchpakdi, Supachai. 'Trends in Poverty and Progress towards the Millennium Development Goals'. In *UN The Least Developed Countries Report 2008.*

Pant, N. *Status of Girl Child and Women in India.* New Delhi: APH Publishing, 1995.

Paredes, Ruben. 'The Protestant Movement in Ecuador and Peru: A Comparative Socio-Anthropological Study of the Establishment and Diffusion of Protestantism in Two Central Highland Regions'. Ph.D. dissertation, University of California, Los Angeles, 1980.

_____. 'Indigenous Peoples'. In John Corrie (ed.). *Dictionary of Mission Theology: Evangelical Foundations.* Downer Grove: Inter-Varsity Press, 2007.

Parris, M. 'As an atheist, I truly believe Africa needs God'. *The Times*, 27 December 2008.

Patel, V. 'Sex Determination and Sex Preselection Tests: Abuse of Advanced Technology'. In R. Ghadially (ed.). *Women in Indian Society: A Reader.* New Delhi: Sage Publications, 1988.

Penzotti, F. 'Apuntes Autobiografía y Notas del Rev. F. Penzotti en Centro y Sud America'. In Daniel Hall (ed.). *Llanos y Montañas*. London, 1913.

Peskett, H. and V. Ramachandra. *The Message of Mission.* Leicester: IVP, 2003.

Phiri, A.I., B. Haddad and M. Masenya. *African Women, HIV and AIDS and Faith Communities.* Pietmaritzburg: Cluster, 2003.

_____. *Grant Me Justice: HIV/AIDS and Gender Readings of the Bible.* Pietmaritzburg: Cluster, 2004.

Phiri, A.I. and S. Nadar. (eds.). *African Women, Religion and Health: Essays in Honor of Mercy Amba Ewudziwa Oduyoye.* Maryknoll: Orbis, 2006.

Picket, J.W. *Christ's Way to India's Heart.* Lucknow: Lucknow Publishing, 1938.

Piper, John J. *Love Your Enemies.* Cambridge: Cambridge University Press, 1979.

Prilleltensky, Isaac. 'Poverty and Power'. In S.C. Carr and T.S. Sloan (eds.). *Poverty and Psychology: From Global Perspective to Local Practice.* New York: Plenum Publishers, 2003.

Quebedeaux, R. *The Young Evangelicals.* New York: Harper and Row, 1974.

Rahnema, M. 'Towards post-development: searching for signposts, a new language and new paradigms'. In M. Rahnema and V. Bawtree (eds.). *The Post Development Reader.* London: Zed Books, 1997.

Rajadhyaksha, U. and S. Smita. 'Tracing a Timeline for Work and Family Research in India'. *Economic and Political Weekly*, April 24–30, 2004.

REAP. 'A Biblical teaching to motivate farmers to maintain a living soil'. *Rural Extension with Africa's Poor.* http://reap-eastafrica.org.

Ringma, C. *Liberation Theologians Speak to Evangelicals: A Theology and Practice of Serving the Poor The Church and Poverty in Asia.* Quezon City, Philippines: OMF Lit., 2008.

Ritchie, J. 'El Renacimiento'. *Enero* 1936, 10.

Ro, B.R. 'The Perspectives of Church History from New Testament Times to 1960'. In Bruce J. Nicholls (ed.). *In Word and Deed: Evangelism and Social Responsibility.* Grand Rapids, MI: Eerdmans, 1986.

Rondinelli, Denis A. *Development Projects as Policy Experiments: An Adaptive Approach to Development Administration.* London: Methuen, 1983.

Rooy, Sidney. 'Our story'. www.ftl-al.org, 2010.

Rostow, Walt Whitman. *The Stages of Economic Growth.* Cambridge: Cambridge University Press, 1960.

Royal Society. 'Climate Change Controversies: Policy Publications'. *The Royal Society* http://royalsociety.org/Policy-Publications.

Sachs, Jeffrey. *The End of Poverty: Economic Possibilities for Our Time.* New York: Penguin Press, 2005.

_____. *The End of Poverty: How we can make it happen in our lifetime.* London: Penguin Books, 2005.

Sachs, W. 'Introduction'. In W. Sachs (ed.). *The Development Dictionary: a guide to knowledge as power.* London: Zed Books, 1992.

Samuel, C.B. Spirituality and Social Transformation'. In B.J. Nicholls and B.R. Wood (eds.) *Sharing the good news with the poor.* Carlisle: Paternoster/World Evangelical Fellowship, 1996.

Samuel, V. 'Mission as Transformation'. *Transformation* 19:4 (2002).

Samuel, V. and C. Sugden. *The Church in Response to Human Need.* Grand Rapids, MI: Eerdmans, 1987.

_____ (eds.). *Mission as Transformation.* Oxford: Regnum, 1999.

_____. 'Introduction'. In V. Samuel and C. Sugden (eds.). *The Church in Response to Human Need.* Grand Rapids, MI: Eerdmans, 1987.

Sanneh. L. *Translating the Message: The missionary impact on culture.* Maryknoll, NY: Orbis Books, 1989.

Santmire, H.P. *The Travail of Nature: The Ambiguous Ecological Promise of Christian Theology*. Philadelphia, PA: Fortress Press, 1986.
Sargunam, Ezra. *Christian Contribution to Nation Building*. Chennai, Mission Educational Books, 2006.
Schweizer, E. *The Good News according to Matthew*. Atlanta: John Knox, 1975.
Seligson, Mitchell A. and John T. Passē-Smith. *Development and Underdevelopment: The Political Economy of Inequality*. Boulder, CO: Lynne Rienner, 2003.
Sen, Amartya. *Development as Freedom*. New York: Knopf, 1999.
Serrini, L. 'The Assisi Declarations'. In *The United Nations Environment Programme*. http://www.nyo.unep.org/eaf/eafadec.pdf.
Shah, T. 'The Political Witness of African Churches: separating Sheep from the Goats'. Paper presented at the Workshop on Church and Society in Africa, Yale University, World Christianity Initiative, March, 2010.
Sider, R.J. 'Introduction'. In Ronald J. Sider (ed.). *Evangelicals and Development: Toward a Theology of Social Change*. Exeter, UK: Paternoster, 1981.
_____. *Rich Christians in an age of hunger*. London: Hodder and Stoughton, 1977.
_____. 'An Historic Moment for Biblical Social Concern'. In Ronald J. Sider (ed.). *The Chicago Declaration*. Carol Stream, IL: Creation House, 1974.
_____. 'What Is the Gospel?'. *Transformation* 16 (1999).
_____. *Good News and Good Works: A Theology for the Whole Gospel*. Grand Rapids: Baker, 1999.
_____. *The Scandal of the Evangelical Conscience: Why Are Christians Living Just Like the Rest of the World?* Grand Rapids: Baker Books, 2005.
_____ (ed.). *Lifestyle in the Eighties: An Evangelical Commitment to Simple Lifestyle*. Philadelphia, PA: Westminster, 1982.
Sinclair, Maurice. *Green Finger of God*. Exeter: Paternoster Press, 1980.
Sine, Tom, Wayne Bragg, Maurice Sinclair, Waldron Scott, David Bosch and Edward Dayton, *The Church in Response to Human Need*. Monrovia, CA: MARC, 1983.
Smidt, C.E., et al. *Pews, Prayers: Participation and Civic Responsibility in America*. George Town University Press, 2008.
Smith, L. 'Recent Historical Perspectives of the Evangelical Tradition'. In Edgar J. Elliston (ed.). *Christian Relief and Development: Developing Workers for Effective Ministry*. Dallas, TX: Word, 1989.
Snyder, H. *Liberating the Church*. Downers Grove, IL: Inter-Varsity, 1983.
So, Damon W.K., *Jesus' Revelation of His Father: A Narrative-Conceptual Study of the Trinity with Special Reference to Karl Barth*. Milton Keynes: Paternoster, 2006.
_____. *The Forgotten Jesus and the Trinity You Never Knew*. Eugene: Wipf and Stock, 2010.

Sorrell, S., J. Speirs, R. Bentley, A. Brandt, and R. Miller. 'UK Energy Research Centre, Global Oil Depletion, An assessment of the evidence for a near-term peak in global oil production'. *UK Energy Research Centre.* http://www.ukerc.ac.uk/support/Global%20Oil%20Depletion, 2009.

Spector, M. and J. Kitsuse. *Constructing Social Problems*. New Brunswick, NJ: Transaction Publishers, 1987.

Srivastava, N. 'Exposing Violence against Women'. *Economic and Political Weekly* 34:6 (Feb., 1999).

Stackhouse. J. *Making the best of it: Following Christ in the Real World.* New York: OUP 2008.

Stanley, B. *The Bible and the Flag: Protestant missions and British imperialism in the nineteenth and twentieth centuries.* Leicester: Apollo's, 1990.

_____. *The World Missionary Conference, Edinburgh 1910.* Grand Rapids, Eerdmans, 2009.

'Status of Global Mission, 2010, in Context of 20th and 21st Centuries'. *International Bulletin of Missionary Research* 34:1 (2010).

Steuernagel, V.R. 'The Theology of Mission in Its Relation to Social Responsibility within the Lausanne Movement'. ThD thesis, Lutheran School of Theology, Chicago, 1988.

Steward, John. *Biblical Holism: Where God, People and Deeds Meet.* Melbourne: World Vision Australia, 1994.

Stott, J.R.W. *The Lausanne Covenant: An Exposition and Commentary.* Minneapolis, MN: World Wide Publications, 1975.

_____. *Christian Mission in the World Mission.* London: Falcon, 1975.

_____. *Through the Bible: Through the Year.* Oxford: Candle Books, 2006.

_____ (ed.). *Making Christ Known: Historic Mission Documents from the Lausanne Movement, 1974-1989.* Grand Rapids, MI: Eerdmans, 1996.

_____ (ed.). *The Grand Rapids Report: Making Christ Known.* Grand Rapids, MI: Eerdmans, 1996.

Sugden, C. 'Evangelicals and Wholistic Evangelism'. In V. Samuel and A. Hauser (eds.). *Proclaiming Christ in Christ's Way.* Oxford: Regnum, 1989.

_____. 'Transformational Development: Current State of Understanding and Practice'. *Transformation* 20:2 (April 2003).

_____. 'Death, Injustice, Resurrection and Transformation'. *Transformation* 22:2 (2005).

_____. 'Identity and Transformation: The Oxford Lectures of Vinay Samuel'. *Transformation* 24:4 (2007).

_____. 'What is Good about Good News to the Poor?'. In V. Samuel and C. Sugden (eds.). *AD 2000 and Beyond.* Oxford: Regnum, 1991.

_____. *Seeking the Asian Face of Jesus.* Oxford: Regnum, 1997.

Sunanda, K.S. *Girl Child Born To Die In Killing Fields?* Madras: Alternative for India Development, 1995.

Thambusamy, S. and B. Herbert. 'Women and Gender Issues in Christian Missions in India'. In E. Roger Hedlund and Paul Joshua Backiaraj (eds.). *Missiology for The 21st Century: South Asian Perspectives.* Delhi: ISPCK/MIIS, 2004.

Thiongo, N.W. *Moving the Centre: The struggle for Cultural Freedom.* London: Heinemann, 1993.

Tizon, Al. *Transformation after Lausanne: Radical Evangelical Mission in Global-Local Perspective*. Oxford, Regnum, 2008.

Todaro, Michael P. *Economic Development in the Third World.* New York and London: Longman, 1977.

Treisman, Daniel. 'The Causes of Corruption: A cross-national study'. *Journal of Public Economics* 76:3 (2000), 399-457

Tucker, A. *Eighteen Years in Uganda*. London: Edward Arnold, 1908.

UK Environment Agency. 'The 50 things that will save the planet'. *Your Environment Extra* 17 (2007).

UNDP. *Human Development Report 1996.*

_____. 'What are the Millennium Development Goals?'. http://www.undp.org/mdg/basics.shtml.

UNEP. 'Environment for development'. *United Nations Environment Programme.* http://www.unep.org/Documents.Multilingual/Default.asp?DocumentID=43.

Utuk, E.S. 'From Wheaton to Lausanne'. In James A. Scherer and Stephen B. Bevans (eds.). *New Directions in Mission and Evangelization 2: Theological Foundations*. Maryknoll, NY: Orbis, 1994.

Wagner, C.P. 'Lausanne's Consultation on World Evangelization: A Personal Assessment'. *TSF Bulletin* 4:1 (October 1980).

_____. 'Lausanne Twelve Months Later'. *Christianity Today*, 4 July 1975.

Wallis, J. *A Call to Conversion.* Tring: Lion, 1981.

Wanyoike, E.N. *An African Pastor.* Nairobi. East Africa Publishing House, 1974.

Wardekker, J.A., A.C. Petersen, and J.P. van der Sluijs. 'Ethics and public perception of climate change: Exploring the Christian voices in the US public debate'. *Global Environmental Change* 19 (2009), 512-521.

Weber, Max. *The Protestant Ethic and the Spirit of Capitalism.* London: Allen & Unwin, 1930.

White, L. 'The historical roots of our ecologic crisis'. *Science* 155 (1967), 1203-1207.

Wink, W. *Engaging the Powers: Discernment and Resistance in a World of Domination*. Minneapolis: Fortress, 1992.

Winter, R. 'The Future of Evangelicals in Mission'. *Mission Frontiers*, September–October, 2007.

Wood V. 'The Part Played by Chinese Women in the Formation of an Indigenous Church in China: Insights from the archive of Myfanwy Wood, LMS Missionary'l *Women's History Review* 17:4 (Sep. 2008).

Woolnough, B E. *Life on the Streets, and by the Sea: reflections on visits to India with Tearfund.* Abingdon, UK: Larkhill Publishers, 2006.

_____. *Life on the Streets: reflections on visits to India with Tearfund.* Abingdon, UK: Larkhill Publishers, 2001.

_____. 'But How Do We Know We Are Making a Difference? Issues relating to the evaluation of Christian development work'. *Transformation* 25 (2008).

World Bank. *World Development Report 2000/2001.*

_____. *World Development Report 2010.*

_____. 'Strengthening Bank Group Engagement on Governance and Anticorruption'. http://siteresources.worldbank.org/DEVCOMMINT/Documentation/21046515/DC2006-0017(E)-Governance.pdf, 2007.

Wright, Chris J.H. *Living as the People of God: The Relevance of the Old Testament Ethics.* Leicester: Inter-Varsity Press, 1983.

Wright, N.T. *Jesus and the Victory of God.* London: SPCK, 1996.

Yamamori, T., Bryant L. Myers and David Conner. *Serving with the Poor in Asia.* Monrovia, CA: MARC, 1995.

Yamamori, T., Bryant L. Myers, and Kenneth Luscombe. *Serving with the Urban Poo:, Cases in Holistic Ministry.* Monrovia, CA: MARC, 1998.

Yamamori, T., Bryant L.Myers, Kwame Bediako, and Larry Reed. *Serving with the Poor in Africa: Cases in Holistic Ministry.* Monrovia, CA: MARC. 1996.

Yamamori, T., Bryant L.Myers, René Padilla, and Greg Rake. *Serving with the Poor in Latin America: Cases in Holistic Ministry.* Monrovia, CA: MARC, 1997.

Yoder, J.H. *Politics of Jesus.* Grand Rapids: Eerdmans, 1972.

Index

'in this generation', 94, 95
'Upside down power', 181
A Rocha, 212, 219, 223, 245, 270
Accountability, 152
Advocacy, 177
African culture, 41, 78
African Instituted Churches, 41, 76
AIC, 236
AIDS, 32, 36, 45, 84, 141, 143, 145, 150, 153, 208, 210, 239,
Anglican Church, 90, 210,
ASHA, 8
Au Sable, 212, 218, 220, 221, 222
Awareness, 208
Azariah, 87, 89, 90, 91, 92, 93
Barth,, 48, 49, 52, 248
Bearers, 200
BFBS, 105
BFSS, 105
Bible, 40, 45, 94, 95, 100, 105, 107, 108, 172, 173, 202, 225, 236
Biodiversity loss, 213
Blasphemer, 25
BMS, 11, 236
Bribery, 193
Chicago Declaration, 65
Christ, 4, 5, 7, 9, 11, 20, 23, 25, 26, 27, 28, 29, 30, 31, 32, 33, 34, 36, 37, 38, 40, 43, 44, 45, 46, 47, 48, 49, 52, 55, 56, 57, 58, 62, 63, 68, 70, 71, 72, 73, 78, 79, 87, 88, 89, 90, 91, 93, 95, 96, 97, 98, 99, 100, 101, 114, 115, 119, 122, 129, 132, 133, 135, 136, 138, 139, 140, 149, 152, 157, 158, 160, 168, 170, 181, 183, 186, 198, 199, 203, 207, 208, 209, 211, 224, 225, 229, 230, 232, 233, 240, 244, 245, 246
Christian NGOs, 11, 14, 144, 146, 147, 149, 151, 172, 229, 239, 245, 246
Christian Social Responsibility, 5, 66, 67, 244
Church, 9, 11, 12, 26, 28, 47, 48, 63, 66, 70, 74, 76, 77, 83, 84, 87, 91, 92, 94, 97, 99, 108, 110, 111, 112, 116, 128, 130, 131, 134, 137, 142, 145, 173, 175, 177, 187, 190, 191, 192, 195, 198, 201, 202, 210, 218, 219, 220, 229, 231, 232, 234, 237, 239
Church - as hope of the world, 232
Church leaders, 9, 145
Church planting, 131
Climate Change, 212, 213
CMS, 11, 236
CNGOs (Christian Non-Governmental Organisations), 8, 149, 150, 151, 152, 153, 154, 241, 242
Collier, Paul, 123, 194
Community, 54, 78, 137, 141, 210, 232
Compassion, 97, 98, 176
Condescension, 48
Conservative, 9, 47, 56, 69, 70, 96, 106, 112, 113, 119, 185
Context, 93
Conversion, 139, 253
Corrupt, 133
Corruption, 197
Costas, 71, 72, 128
Creation Care, 212
Culture, 89, 132, 134, 191
Dalit Christians, 92, 93
Death, 54, 259
Deneulin, Severine, 126
Denominations, 234
Development, 6, 10, 31, 40, 66, 74, 75, 79, 81, 89, 93, 110, 119, 126, 139, 142, 155, 156, 157, 160, 161, 162, 163, 164, 165, 166, 167, 168, 171, 172, 187, 204, 210, 214, 222, 223, 240
Discernment, 178
Discipleship Centre, 8
Domestic violence, 207
Dornakal mission, 87
Dowry, 206
Dualism, 73, 191
EAM, 13
Easterly, William, 123
ECI, 87, 94, 97

Ecumenical, 45, 64
Ecumenism, 12
Education, 69, 92, 95, 96, 105, 109, 110, 155, 185, 232, 242, 243
EFICOR, 8, 10, 97
Environment, 214, 216, 218, 222, 224
Environment and Development, 216, 222
Environmental ethics, 216
Escobar, Samuel, 2, 33, 67, 70, 110, 113, 116, 119, 128
Evaluation, 125, 240
Evangelical, Evangelicals, 28, 61, 62, 64, 65, 66, 70, 71, 73, 74, 87, 94, 96, 97, 110, 114, 116, 120, 130, 131, 138, 143, 144, 167, 187, 190, 192, 196, 202, 218, 221, 245
Evangelism, 4, 38, 62, 63, 64, 67, 68, 70, 72, 73, 74, 94, 97, 120, 128, 129, 177, 203
Exaltation, 47, 56
Experience, 163, 235, 238
Failure, 41
Faith, xiv, 23, 45, 92, 94, 140, 143, 184, 201, 244
Family, 203, 221
Father, 12, 20, 21, 24, 47, 50, 51, 52, 53, 54, 55, 57, 58, 96, 116, 171, 174, 193
FMPB, 87, 94, 95, 97, 98
Forgiveness, 6, 17, 18, 19, 20, 21, 25, 26, 27, 28, 29, 30, 50, 55, 58, 78, 207, 208
freedom, 27, 40, 43, 48, 51, 52, 58, 93, 99, 104, 106, 108, 135, 165, 175, 181, 198, 205, 236
Gender, 45, 78, 198, 199, 200, 201, 203, 206, 208, 209, 210, 211
Gitari, 12, 130, 193
Global warming, 213
Globalization, 123, 180
God complex, 240
Gospel, 17, 25, 33, 54, 94, 99, 199, 200, 229, 235
Gospel/good news 17, 25, 33, 54, 94, 99, 199, 200, 229, 235
Governance, 188, 189, 261
Government, 187, 206
Great Commission, 94, 95, 96, 171
Great Reversal, 62, 63, 64
Greek dualism, 5
HBI, xiv, 95
Healing, 85
Health, 45, 153, 210
Hertzke, Alan, 120
HIV/AIDS, 13, 36, 45, 141, 143, 153, 208, 209, 210, 239
Holism, 4, 98, 122, 160, 166, 167, 168, 171
Holistic, 4, 6, 9, 15, 37, 43, 44, 46, 59, 61, 76, 87, 90, 94, 102, 103, 104, 106, 110, 114, 117, 119, 122, 133, 138, 149, 159, 160, 166, 167, 168, 224, 225, 227
Holy Spirit, 21, 26, 29, 31, 33, 34, 39, 51, 55, 76, 77, 79, 85, 96, 114, 116, 133, 138, 139, 160, 172, 198, 241
Home-coming, 55, 58
Hope, 8, 223, 239
Huddleston, Trevor, 12
Human, 66, 74, 132, 161, 165, 167, 179, 213, 214
Hybels, Bill, 232
Identity, 149
Individual Christian, 229
Injustice, 259
Institutions, 7, 130, 131, 132, 135, 242
Integral mission, 1, 6, 137
Integrity, 218
Intimidation, 194
Israel, 19, 49, 50, 139, 168, 169, 176, 237
Jesus, 3, 4, 5, 8, 11, 13, 17, 18, 19, 20, 21, 22, 23, 24, 25, 26, 27, 28, 29, 30, 31, 35, 37, 43, 44, 47, 48, 49, 50, 51, 52, 53, 54, 55, 56, 57, 71, 72, 78, 79, 85, 87, 88, 89, 91, 96, 97, 98, 99, 114, 115, 119, 123, 133, 138, 139, 147, 157, 160, 168, 170, 171, 173, 176, 179, 180, 181, 182, 183, 184, 185, 192, 195, 199, 203, 207, 208, 223, 225, 230, 233, 235, 238, 244, 245, 246
Jubilee 2000, 12
Justice, 5, 45, 67, 97, 137, 138, 218, 245
Land, 168, 215
Lausanne, 4, 10, 13, 31, 33, 47, 61, 63, 65, 66, 67, 68, 69, 70, 71, 72, 73, 74, 110, 116, 119, 120, 128, 129,

144, 244
Lausanne Conference, 4, 10, 128
Lausanne Covenant, 1, 4, 10, 33, 66, 67, 70, 72, 116, 119
LDCs, 161, 162, 163, 164
liberal, 9, 47, 48, 62, 63, 91, 96, 104, 106, 156
Liberation, 12, 40, 57, 58, 68, 75, 77, 85, 90, 96, 104, 106, 111, 112, 113, 114, 116, 141, 224, 244
Local church, 141, 142
Local community, 124
LTF, 112, 113, 114, 116
Malto people, 97
Manifesto, 52
Martin Luther King, 12, 176, 230
Marxism, 32, 98, 104, 112
Mau Mau, 77
McGavran, 68, 87, 94, 96
mega-churches, 99, 100
Micah Challenge, 5, 6
Micah Network/Declaration, 1, 137, 245
Microfinance, 177
missio dei, 37, 166
Mission, 11, 31, 32, 33, 37, 39, 40, 41, 42, 43, 44, 45, 61, 63, 64, 67, 69, 70, 71, 72, 74, 77, 79, 88, 90, 92, 94, 95, 96, 97, 98, 100, 110, 114, 120, 128, 129, 130, 131, 132, 134, 137, 139, 141, 149, 150, 152, 167, 172, 199, 203, 212, 218, 219, 220, 221, 223, 229, 232, 235, 236
Mission as transformation, 32
Missionaries, 88, 89, 98
Missionary journey, 52
Missionary Societies, 235
Missioners, 85
Modernity, 121, 124, 255
Mott, 94, 95, 96
MTM, 128, 131, 132, 133, 134, 136
Myers, Bryant, 6, 13, 99, 119, 121, 122, 139, 140, 144, 152, 213
Nationalist churches, 77, 78
Networks, 153
Newbegin, Leslie, 132
Non-Catholic, 104
Oil, 214, 215, 259
OMF, 175, 257
Padilla, Rene, 12, 33, 61, 64, 66, 67, 68, 71, 112, 116, 119, 128, 137, 150, 157
Participation, 84, 171
Pentecostal churches, 76, 79, 80, 194
Pentecostalism, 10, 78, 79
Pentecostals, 33, 79, 80, 87, 98, 99
Penzotti, 106, 107, 108, 109
Physical, 3, 4, 5, 6, 8, 12, 29, 47, 49, 52, 53, 56, 57, 81, 93, 102, 140, 144, 145, 146, 150, 151, 163, 168, 169, 170, 188, 207, 210, 217, 230, 231, 236, 237, 239, 240, 241, 245
Pitfalls, 195
Politics, 24, 78, 85, 175, 181, 187, 193
Poor, 3, 6, 137, 139, 140, 144, 154, 165, 173, 175, 179, 189, 220, 230, 249, 250, 254, 255, 257, 259, 261, 271
Population, 214
Poverty, 12, 13, 67, 93, 123, 135, 156, 161, 163, 164, 166, 175, 176, 188, 189, 230
Power, 2, 93, 178, 180, 183, 184
Prilleltensky, 126
Protestant Church, 40, 41, 42, 61, 63, 94, 102, 103, 104, 105, 106, 107, 108, 109, 112, 113, 114, 116, 189, 190, 197, 198, 234, 235, 236
Radical, 68, 69, 180
Recipients, 199
Relationships, 148
Relief, xiv, 10, 66, 120, 132
Resource depletion, 214
Resources, 187, 213
Resurrection, 23, 26, 54
Ringeltaube, 199
Roho, 77, 78, 79, 80, 81, 83
Roman Catholic Church, 104, 129
Sachs, Jeffrey, 257
Salvation, 13
Samuel, Vinay, 14, 33, 34, 66, 68, 71, 72, 74, 75, 97, 128
Scripture/scriptures, 51, 175
Sen, Isaac Amartya, 126, 165
Sex work, 207, 208
Shalom, 6
Sider, Ron, 3, 13, 17, 65, 70, 71, 74, 120, 138, 218, 229
Single parenthood, 205
Social, 33, 62, 63, 64, 65, 66, 67, 70,

71, 72, 73, 74, 79, 83, 93, 97, 113, 175, 177, 178, 182, 191
Social Ethic, 67, 71
Social Gospel, 62, 64, 66, 67
Society, 11, 90, 94, 105, 107, 108, 112, 130, 199, 202, 204, 212, 213, 236
Spiritual, 3, 4, 5, 6, 18, 29, 33, 38, 39, 41, 42, 47, 53, 56, 57, 73, 75, 76, 78, 79, 81, 82, 91, 96, 97, 99, 120, 121, 122, 123, 124, 125, 129, 133, 140, 144, 146, 150, 151, 152, 154, 155, 157, 167, 168, 169, 170, 177, 178, 180, 183, 216, 224, 230, 231, 232, 233, 237, 240, 241, 245, 246
Spiritual churches, 76, 77
Spirituality, 81, 248, 257
Stackhouse.Max, 123, 124, 132, 135
Steward, 160, 167, 170
Stewardship, 167, 168, 169, 221
Structures, 178
Sustainability, 222
Tafakari, 80
Tearfund, 2, 3, 4, 8, 10, 13, 140, 142, 143, 153, 154, 157, 210, 223, 236, 239
Tension, 71
The John Ray Initiative, 219
Transformation, 17, 31, 33, 34, 64, 75, 95, 97, 99, 128, 129, 130, 131, 133, 134, 182, 229, 240
Transformational development, 144
Tsunami, 8, 13
TTIs (Theological Training Institutions), 243
Tutu, Desmond, 175
UMN, 11
Umoja, 140, 271
Violence against women, 209
Water, 6, 209, 214
Wheaton, 63, 64, 67, 74, 120, 132, 221
Wholistic, 68, 74
Widowhood and *sati*, 90, 205, 208
Women, 23, 44, 45, 198, 199, 200, 201, 202, 203, 204, 205, 206, 207, 208, 209, 210, 22
World Bank, 121, 153, 156, 162, 164, 165, 185, 189, 194
World Vision, 10, 35, 97, 120, 131, 150, 153, 157, 167
Yamamori, Ted, 120
Zenana, 198
ZOE, xvi, 210

Contributors

Deborah Ajulu. Holds a doctorate in Economic Development, previously Dean of Academics at Kumi University, Eastern Uganda and missionary and development and research consultant for a CNGO in Uganda; author of *Holism in Development.*

Martin Allaby. A public health physician, with a particular interest in poverty reduction. He has worked with CNGOs in Nepal, and has researched the churches' involvement with national government, and how that has been affected by corruption and theological issues, in Kenya, Zambia, the Philippines and Peru.

Beulah Herbert. Faculty Lecturer in Lutheran Theological College, Gurukul, India, and visiting professor at Jubilee Memorial Bible College, Chennai; has experience as teacher and first woman cross cultural missionary in the field of Friends Missionary Prayer Band. Her vocation includes wholistic mission along with her husband Herbert, Ministry Director of Scripture Union.

Margot R Hodson. Church Minister, previously Chaplain, Jesus College, Oxford; on the boards of John Ray Initiative and A Rocha; teaches Environmental Ethics at Oxford Brookes University; research is with the Agriculture and Theology Project. Publications include The *Place of Environmental Theology* and *Cherishing the Earth* (co-author with her husband).

Sam Jayakumar. Served as a cross-cultural missionary in North India and later an ordained Minister of the Evangelical Church of India (ECI). Formerly Principal of the ECI Seminary, and currently Professor of Mission and Ministry with TAFTEE, Madras, India. Specializes in history of missions and contextual theologies

Nicta Lubaale. General Secretary of the Organization of African Instituted (OAIC) since January 2007. Served as the Director for Development and HIV/AIDS Programme of the OAIC and as a Pastor with Centre for Evangelism in Uganda for 13 years. Nicta has been involved in mobilizing and training church leadership from OAIC member churches to participate in holistic mission – where the church responds to development issues in the context of mission. He holds an MA in development studies from the University of Reading (UK).

Melba Maggay. President and Founder of the Institute for Studies in Asian Church and Culture (ISACC), Manilla, Philippines, a social anthropologist with

Batchelor, Master and Doctorate degrees from the University of the Philippines. Author of numerous books on Filipino religious culture and three times winner of the Don Carlos Memorial Awards for Literature.

Glenn Miles. Asian Director of Prevention for Love146; Research Advisor for Chab Dai based in Cambodia; previously Celebrating Children Training Facilitator for Viva and Children at Risk Facilitator for Tearfund. Helped to set up Evangelical Fellowship of Cambodia Children's commission. Co-Editor of *Celebrating Children.*

Esther Mombo. Lecturer at St. Paul's University, Limuru, Kenya Faculty of Theology. Lecturer and Researcher in history of mission with special reference to women, the church and society, especially on Christian response to HIV/AIDS. A lay person in the Anglican Church of Kenya. A member of the Circle of Concerned African women theologians.

Bryant Myers. Professor of Transformational Development at Fuller Theological Seminary, California. With a doctorate in Bio-Chemistry from UCLA, and much experience with World Vision International, most recently as Vice President for Develoment and Food Resources, his writings (including *Walking with the Poor,* and *Working with the Poor)* have been particularly influential to those in the Christian development world.

Tito Paredes. Peruvian, currently teaching in the area of Anthropology and Mission at PRODOLA (Programa Doctoral Latinoamericano) and The 'Orlando Costas' MA program in missiology in Lima Peru. General Secretary of the Latin American Theological Fraternity (1992-2004); Board Member of World Vision International (1992-2001); Member of Research Team on Primal Religion as Substructure of Christianity.

Tulo Raistrick. Tulo Raistrick is Tearfund's Church and Development Adviser. He has worked extensively with local churches in Africa, Asia and Latin America, and is the author of *Church, Community and Change* and the co-author of *Umoja*, a series of facilitation guides on church and community mobilisation.

Vinay Samuel. Director of Oxford Centre for Religion and Public Life (OCRPL), Founding Secretary of International Fellowship of Mission Theologians (INFEMIT).

Ronald J Sider. Professor of Theology, Holistic Ministry and Public Policy, Director of the Sider Centre on Ministry and Public Policy, at Palmer Theological Seminary, Eastern University, USA, and President of Evangelicals for Social Action. Prolific speaker and writer, including the seminal book *Rich Christians in an Age of Hunger.*

Damon So. Research Tutor and Stage Leader at OCMS, with doctorates in Mathematics and Theology, Pastor of the Chinese Church in London working with Chinese immigrant families. Having researched the Trinity, he brings a special interest in the presentation of Jesus in gospel narratives and how Jesus serves as a window into the Trinity through his birth, life, ministry, death resurrection and universal reign.

Chris Sugden. Member of founding board of OCMS; Registrar/Director of Academic Affairs/Executive Director 1983-2004; sometime Secretary of Unit on Ethics and Society of World Evangelical Fellowship; Chairman of trustees of Traidcraft; Executive Secretary of Anglican Mainstream; member of General Synod of Church of England, Canon of St Luke's Cathedral, Jos, Nigeria.

Al Tizon. Associate Professor of Holistic Ministry at Palmer Theological Seminary, Eastern University, USA and Director of Evangelicals for Social Action's Word and Deed Network. Author of *Transformation after Lausanne* and co-author of *Linking Arms, Linking Lives.*

Ian de Villiers. Asia Co-ordinator for Viva Network, partnering networks building collaborative responses to children at risk issues in South and South-East Asia. Co-author of "At Risk People" chapter for Lausanne 2004 World Evangelisation Forum.

Brian Woolnough. Research Tutor at Oxford Centre for Mission Studies (OCMS) and Emeritus Fellow of St Cross College, Oxford. Having originally trained as a physicist, spent most of professional life in education as an academic at Oxford University, he then worked with international team of Tearfund, UK, travelling widely in Asia and Africa, before moving to OCMS.

Conference Delegates

Fanen Ade
Deborah Ajulu
Martin Allaby
Bruce Anderson
Deryke Belshaw
Judy Berinai
Gilly Burn
Graham Chipps
Jennie Collins
Corneliu Constantineanu
Bishop Devaryai
Ian DeVilliers
Seringa Dudley
Ian Enticott
Bernard Farr
April Foster
Jerry Foster
Shaha Bahadur Gurung
Hilary Guest
Ralph Hangar
John Harding
Kate Harris
Tom Harvey
Brenda Hoddinot
Margot Hodson
Dewi Hughes
Zoe Jennings
Dong Woo Jung
Jina Kim
Hun Kim
Hun Kim's wife
Habila Kohon
Deborah Lake
Aklilu Lalego
Bawa Leo
Martin Lloyd
Nicta Lubaale
Wonsuk Ma
Julie Ma
Esther Maxton
Anne Moseley
Steve Muneza
Sabine Muri
Reginald Nalugala
Las Newman
Concorde Niyigena
Philippe Ouedraogo
Ky Prevette
Bill Prevette
Caitlin Reilly
Christian Romocea
Cathy Ross
Ronald Sider
Phil Simpson
Damon So
Chris Sugden
Jill Suttie
Noel Taylor
Kantha Thota
Jane Travis
Pehhy Vinden
Francis Waihenya
Robin Wainwright
Brian Woolnough

REGNUM EDINBURGH 2010 SERIES
Series Listing

David A. Kerr, Kenneth R. Ross (eds.)
Edinburgh 2010
Mission Then and Now
2009 / 978-1-870345-73-6 / xiv + 343pp (paperback)
2009 / 978-1-870345-76-7 / xiv + 343pp (hardback)

No one can hope to fully understand the modern Christian missionary movement without engaging substantially with the World Missionary Conference, held at Edinburgh in 1910. As the centenary of the Conference approaches, the time is ripe to examine its meaning in light of the past century and the questions facing Christian witness today. This book is the first to systematically examine the eight Commissions which reported to Edinburgh 1910 and gave the conference much of its substance and enduring value. It will deepen and extend the reflection being stimulated by the upcoming centenary and will kindle the missionary imagination for 2010 and beyond.

Daryl M. Balia, Kirsteen Kim (eds.)
Edinburgh 2010
Witnessing to Christ Today
2010 / 978-1-870345-77-4 / xiv +301pp

This volume, the second in the Edinburgh 2010 series, includes reports of the nine main study groups working on different themes for the celebration of the centenary of the World Missionary Conference, Edinburgh 1910. Their collaborative work brings together perspectives that are as inclusive as possible of contemporary world Christianity and helps readers to grasp what it means in different contexts to be 'witnessing to Christ today'.

Claudia Währisch-Oblau, Fidon Mwombeki (eds.)
Mission Continues
Global Impulses for the 21st Century
2010 / 978-1-870345-82-8 / 271pp

In May 2009, 35 theologians from Asia, Africa and Europe met in Wuppertal, Germany, for a consultation on mission theology organized by the United Evangelical Mission: Communion of 35 Churches in Three Continents. The aim was to participate in the 100th anniversary of the Edinburgh conference through a study process and reflect on the challenges for mission in the 21st century. This book brings together these papers written by experienced practitioners from around the world.

Brian Woolnough and Wonsuk Ma (Eds)
Holistic Mission
God's plan for God's people
2010 / 978-1-870345-85-9

Holistic mission, or integral mission, implies God is concerned with the whole person, the whole community, body, mind and spirit. This book discusses the meaning of the holistic gospel, how it has developed, and implications for the the church. . It takes a global, eclectic approach, with 19 writers, all of whom have much experience in, and commitment to, holistic mission. It addresses critically and honestly one of the most exciting, and challenging, issues facing the church today. To be part of God's plan for God's people, the church must take holistic mission to the world.

REGNUM STUDIES IN GLOBAL CHRISTIANITY

(Previously GLOBAL THEOLOGICAL VOICES series)

Series Listing

David Emmanuuel Singh (ed.)

Jesus and the Cross

Reflections of Christians from Islamic Contexts

2008 / 978-1-870345-65-1 / x + 226pp

The Cross reminds us that the sins of the world are not borne through the exercise of power but through Jesus Christ's submission to the will of the Father. The papers in this volume are organised in three parts: scriptural, contextual and theological. The central question being addressed is: how do Christians living in contexts, where Islam is a majority or minority religion, experience, express or think of the Cross? This is, therefore, an exercise in listening. As the contexts from where these engagements arise are varied, the papers in drawing scriptural, contextual and theological reflections offer a cross-section of Christian thinking about Jesus and the Cross.

Sung-wook Hong

Naming God in Korea

The Case of Protestant Christianity

2008 / 978-1-870345-66-8 / xiv + 170pp

Since Christianity was introduced to Korea more than a century ago, one of the most controversial issue has been the Korean term for the Christian 'God'. This issue is not merely about naming the Christian God in Korean language, but it relates to the question of theological contextualization—the relationship between the gospel and culture—and the question of Korean Christian identity. This book examines the theological contextualization of the concept of 'God' in the contemporary Korean context and applies the translatability of Christianity to that context. It also demonstrates the nature of the gospel in relation to cultures, i.e., the universality of the gospel expressed in all human cultures.

Hubert van Beek (ed.)

Revisioning Christian Unity

The Global Christian Forum

2009 / 978-1-870345-74-3 / xx + 288pp

This book contains the records of the Global Christian Forum gathering held in Limuru near Nairobi, Kenya, on 6 – 9 November 2007 as well as the papers presented at that historic event. Also included are a summary of the Global Christian Forum process from its inception until the 2007 gathering and the reports of the evaluation of the process that was carried out in 2008.

Paul Hang-Sik Cho
Eschatology and Ecology
Experiences of the Korean Church
2010 / 978-1-870345-75-0/ 260pp (approx)

This book raises the question of why Korean people, and Korean Protestant Christians in particular, pay so little attention (in theory or practice) to ecological issues. The author argues that there is an important connection (or elective affinity) between this lack of attention and the other-worldly eschatology that is so dominant within Korean Protestant Christianity. Dispensational premillennialism, originally imported by American missionaries, resonated with traditional religious beliefs in Korea and soon came to dominate much of Korean Protestantism. This book argues that this, of all forms of millennialism, is the most damaging to ecological concerns.

Dietrich Werner, David Esterline, Namsoon Kang, Joshva Raja (eds.)
The Handbook of Theological Education in World Christianity
Theological Perspectives, Ecumenical Trends, Regional Surveys
2010 / 978-1-870345-80-4/ 759pp

This major reference work is the first ever comprehensive study of Theological Education in Christianity of its kind. With contributions from over 90 international scholars and church leaders, it aims to be easily accessible across denominational, cultural, educational, and geographic boundaries. The Handbook will aid international dialogue and networking among theological educators, institutions, and agencies. The major objectives of the text are (1) to provide introductory surveys on selected issues and themes in global theological education; (2) to provide regional surveys on key developments, achievements, and challenges in theological education; (3) to provide an overview of theological education for each of the major denominational / confessional traditions; and (4) to provide a reference section with an up-to-date list of the regional associations of theological institutions and other resources.

David Emmanuel Singh & Bernard C Farr (eds.)
Christianity and Education
Shaping of Christian Context in Thinking
2010 / 978-1-870345-81-1/ 244pp (approx)

Christianity and Education is a collection of papers published in *Transformation: An International Journal of Holistic Mission Studies* over a period of 15 years. It brings to life some of the papers that lay buried in shelves and in disparate volumes of *Transformation,* under a single volume for theological libraries, students and teachers. The articles here represent a spectrum of Christian thinking addressing issues of institutional development for theological education, theological studies in the context of global mission, contextually aware/informed education, and academies which deliver such education, methodologies and personal reflections.

REGNUM STUDIES IN MISSION
Series Listing

Kwame Bediako

Theology and Identity

The Impact of Culture upon Christian Thought in the Second Century and in Modern Africa

1992 / 1-870345-10-X / xviii + 508pp

The author examines the question of Christian identity in the context of the Graeco–Roman culture of the early Roman Empire. He then addresses the modern African predicament of quests for identity and integration.

Christopher Sugden

Seeking the Asian Face of Jesus

The Practice and Theology of Christian Social Witness in Indonesia and India 1974–1996

1997 / 1-870345-26-6 / xx + 496pp

This study focuses on contemporary holistic mission with the poor in India and Indonesia combined with the call to transformation of all life in Christ with micro-credit enterprise schemes. 'The literature on contextual theology now has a new standard to rise to' – Lamin Sanneh (Yale University, USA).

Hwa Yung

Mangoes or Bananas?

The Quest for an Authentic Asian Christian Theology

1997 / 1-870345-25-8 / xii + 274pp

Asian Christian thought remains largely captive to Greek dualism and Enlightenment rationalism because of the overwhelming dominance of Western culture. Authentic contextual Christian theologies will emerge within Asian Christianity with a dual recovery of confidence in culture and the gospel.

Keith E. Eitel

Paradigm Wars

The Southern Baptist International Mission Board Faces the Third Millennium

1999 / 1-870345-12-6 / x + 140pp

The International Mission Board of the Southern Baptist Convention is the largest denominational mission agency in North America. This volume chronicles the historic and contemporary forces that led to the IMB's recent extensive reorganization, providing the most comprehensive case study to date of a historic mission agency restructuring to continue its mission purpose into the twenty-first century more effectively.

Samuel Jayakumar

Dalit Consciousness and Christian Conversion

Historical Resources for a Contemporary Debate

1999 / 81-7214-497-0 / xxiv + 434pp

(Published jointly with ISPCK)

The main focus of this historical study is social change and transformation among the Dalit Christian communities in India. Historiography tests the evidence in the light of the conclusions of the modern Dalit liberation theologians.

Vinay Samuel and Christopher Sugden (eds.)

Mission as Transformation

A Theology of the Whole Gospel

1999 / 0870345133/ 522pp

This book brings together in one volume twenty five years of biblical reflection on mission practice with the poor from around the world. The approach of holistic mission, which integrates proclamation, evangelism, church planting and social transformation seamlessly as a whole, has been adopted since 1983 by most evangelical development agencies, most indigenous mission agencies and many Pentecostal churches. This volume helps anyone understand how evangelicals, struggling to unite evangelism and social action, found their way in the last twenty five years to the biblical view of mission in which God calls all human beings to love God and their neighbour; never creating a separation between the two.

Christopher Sugden

Gospel, Culture and Transformation

2000 / 1-870345-32-0 / viii + 152pp

A Reprint, with a New Introduction, of Part Two of Seeking the Asian Face of Jesus

Gospel, Culture and Transformation explores the practice of mission especially in relation to transforming cultures and communities. - 'Transformation is to enable God's vision of society to be actualised in all relationships: social, economic and spiritual, so that God's will may be reflected in human society and his love experienced by all communities, especially the poor.'

Bernhard Ott

Beyond Fragmentation: Integrating Mission and Theological Education

A Critical Assessment of some Recent Developments in Evangelical Theological Education

2001 / 1-870345-14-2 / xxviii + 382pp

Beyond Fragmentation is an enquiry into the development of Mission Studies in evangelical theological education in Germany and German-speaking Switzerland between 1960 and 1995. The author undertakes a detailed examination of the paradigm shifts which have taken place in recent years in both the theology of mission and the understanding of theological education.

Gideon Githiga

The Church as the Bulwark against Authoritarianism

Development of Church and State Relations in Kenya, with Particular Reference to the Years after Political Independence 1963-1992

2002 / 1-870345-38-x / xviii + 218pp

'All who care for love, peace and unity in Kenyan society will want to read this careful history by Bishop Githiga of how Kenyan Christians, drawing on the Bible, have sought to share the love of God, bring his peace and build up the unity of the nation, often in the face of great difficulties and opposition.' Canon Dr Chris Sugden, Oxford Centre for Mission Studies.

Myung Sung-Hoon, Hong Young-Gi (eds.)

Charis and Charisma

David Yonggi Cho and the Growth of Yoido Full Gospel Church

2003 / 1-870345-45-2 / xxii + 218pp

This book discusses the factors responsible for the growth of the world's largest church. It expounds the role of the Holy Spirit, the leadership, prayer, preaching, cell groups and creativity in promoting church growth. It focuses on God's grace (charis) and inspiring leadership (charisma) as the two essential factors and the book's purpose is to present a model for church growth worldwide.

Samuel Jayakumar

Mission Reader

Historical Models for Wholistic Mission in the Indian Context

2003 / 1-870345-42-8 / x + 250pp

(Published jointly with ISPCK)

This book is written from an evangelical point of view revalidating and reaffirming the Christian commitment to wholistic mission. The roots of the 'wholistic mission' combining 'evangelism and social concerns' are to be located in the history and tradition of Christian evangelism in the past; and the civilizing purpose of evangelism is compatible with modernity as an instrument in nation building.

Bob Robinson

Christians Meeting Hindus

An Analysis and Theological Critique of the Hindu-Christian Encounter in India

2004 / 1-870345-39-8 / xviii + 392pp

This book focuses on the Hindu-Christian encounter, especially the intentional meeting called dialogue, mainly during the last four decades of the twentieth century, and specifically in India itself.

Gene Early

Leadership Expectations

How Executive Expectations are Created and Used in a Non-Profit Setting

2005 / 1-870345-30-4 / xxiv + 276pp

The author creates an Expectation Enactment Analysis to study the role of the Chancellor of the University of the Nations-Kona, Hawaii. This study is grounded in the field of managerial work, jobs, and behaviour and draws on symbolic interactionism, role theory, role identity theory and enactment theory. The result is a conceptual framework for developing an understanding of managerial roles.

Tharcisse Gatwa

The Churches and Ethnic Ideology in the Rwandan Crises 1900-1994

2005 / 1-870345-24-X / approx 300pp

Since the early years of the twentieth century Christianity has become a new factor in Rwandan society. This book investigates the role Christian churches played in the formulation and development of the racial ideology that culminated in the 1994 genocide.

Julie Ma

Mission Possible

Biblical Strategies for Reaching the Lost

2005 / 1-870345-37-1 / xvi + 142pp

This is a missiology book for the church which liberates missiology from the specialists for the benefit of every believer. It also serves as a textbook that is simple and friendly, and yet solid in biblical interpretation. This book links the biblical teaching to the actual and contemporary missiological settings with examples, making the Bible come alive to the reader.

Allan Anderson, Edmond Tang (eds.)

Asian and Pentecostal

The Charismatic Face of Christianity in Asia

2005 / 1-870345-43-6 / xiv + 596pp

(Published jointly with APTS Press)

This book provides a thematic discussion and pioneering case studies on the history and development of Pentecostal and Charismatic churches in the countries of South Asia, South East Asia and East Asia.

I. Mark Beaumont

Christology in Dialogue with Muslims

A Critical Analysis of Christian Presentations of Christ for Muslims from the Ninth and Twentieth Centuries

2005 / 1-870345-46-0 / xxvi + 228pp

This book analyses Christian presentations of Christ for Muslims in the most creative periods of Christian-Muslim dialogue, the first half of the ninth century and the second half of the twentieth century. In these two periods, Christians made serious attempts to present their faith in Christ in terms that take into account Muslim perceptions of him, with a view to bridging the gap between Muslim and Christian convictions.

Thomas Czövek,

Three Seasons of Charismatic Leadership

A Literary-Critical and Theological Interpretation of the Narrative of Saul, David and Solomon

2006 / 978-1-870345484 / 272pp

This book investigates the charismatic leadership of Saul, David and Solomon. It suggests that charismatic leaders emerge in crisis situations in order to resolve the crisis by the charisma granted by God. Czovek argues that Saul proved himself as a charismatic leader as long as he acted resolutely and independently from his mentor Samuel. In the author's eyes, Saul's failure to establish himself as a charismatic leader is caused by his inability to step out from Samuel's shadow.

Jemima Atieno Oluoch

The Christian Political Theology of Dr. John Henry Okullu

2006 / 1-870345-51-7 / xx + 137pp

This book reconstructs the Christian political theology of Bishop John Henry Okullu, DD, through establishing what motivated him and the biblical basis for his socio-political activities. It also attempts to reconstruct the socio-political environment that nurtured Dr Okullu's prophetic ministry.

Richard Burgess

Nigeria's Christian Revolution

The Civil War Revival and Its Pentecostal Progeny (1967-2006)

2008 / 978-1-870345-63-7 / xxii + 347pp

This book describes the revival that occurred among the Igbo people of Eastern Nigeria and the new Pentecostal churches it generated, and documents the changes that have occurred as the movement has responded to global flows and local demands. As such, it explores the nature of revivalist and Pentecostal experience, but does so against the backdrop of local socio-political and economic developments, such as decolonisation and civil war, as well as broader processes, such as modernisation and globalisation.

David Emmanuel Singh & Bernard C Farr (eds.)
Christianity and Cultures
Shaping Christian Thinking in Context
2008 / 978-1-870345-69-9 / x + 260pp

This volume marks an important milestone, the 25th anniversary of the Oxford Centre for Mission Studies (OCMS). The papers here have been exclusively sourced from Transformation, a quarterly journal of OCMS, and seek to provide a tripartite view of Christianity's engagement with cultures by focusing on the question: how is Christian thinking being formed or reformed through its interaction with the varied contexts it encounters? The subject matters include different strands of theological-missiological thinking, socio-political engagements and forms of family relationships in interaction with the host cultures.

Tormod Engelsviken, Ernst Harbakk, Rolv Olsen, Thor Strandenæs (eds.)
Mission to the World
Communicating the Gospel in the 21st Century:
Essays in Honour of Knud Jørgensen
2008 / 978-1-870345-64-4 / 472pp

Knud Jørgensen is Director of Areopagos and Associate Professor of Missiology at MF Norwegian School of Theology. This book reflects on the main areas of Jørgensen's commitment to mission. At the same time it focuses on the main frontier of mission, the world, the content of mission, the Gospel, the fact that the Gospel has to be communicated, and the context of contemporary mission in the 21st century.

Al Tizon
Transformation after Lausanne
Radical Evangelical Mission in Global-Local Perspective
2008 / 978-1-870345-68-2 / xx + 281pp

After Lausanne '74, a worldwide network of radical evangelical mission theologians and practitioners use the notion of "Mission as Transformation" to integrate evangelism and social concern together, thus lifting theological voices from the Two Thirds World to places of prominence. This book documents the definitive gatherings, theological tensions, and social forces within and without evangelicalism that led up to Mission as Transformation. And it does so through a global-local grid that points the way toward greater holistic mission in the 21st century.

Bambang Budijanto

Values and Participation

Development in Rural Indonesia

2009 / 978-1-870345-70-5 / x + 237pp

Socio-religious values and socio-economic development are inter-dependant, inter-related and are constantly changing in the context of macro political structures, economic policy, religious organizations and globalization; and micro influences such as local affinities, identity, politics, leadership and beliefs. The three Lopait communities in Central Java, Indonesia provide an excellent model of the rich and complex negotiations and interactions among all the above factors. The book argues that the comprehensive approach in understanding the socio-religious values of each local community is essential to accurately describing their respective identity which will help institutions and agencies, both governmental and non-governmental, to relate to these communities with dignity and respect.

Young-hoon Lee

The Holy Spirit Movement in Korea

Its Historical and Theological Development

2009 / 978-1-870345-67-5 / x + 174pp

This book traces the historical and theological development of the Holy Spirit Movement in Korea through six successive periods (from 1900 to the present time). These periods are characterized by repentance and revival (1900-20), persecution and suffering under Japanese occupation (1920-40), confusion and division (1940-60), explosive revival in which the Pentecostal movement played a major role in the rapid growth of Korean churches (1960-80), the movement reaching out to all denominations (1980-2000), and the new context demanding the Holy Spirit movement to open new horizons in its mission engagement (2000-). The volume also discusses the relationship between this movement and other religions such as shamanism, and looks forward to further engagement with issues of concern in wider society.

Alan R. Johnson

Leadership in a Slum

A Bangkok Case Study

2009 / 978-1-870345-71-2 xx + 238pp

This book looks at leadership in the social context of a slum in Bangkok from an angle different from traditional studies which measure well educated Thais on leadership scales derived in the West. Using both systematic data collection and participant observation, it develops a culturally preferred model as well as a set of models based in Thai concepts that reflect on-the-ground realities. This work challenges the dominance of the patron-client rubric for understanding all forms of Thai leadership and offers a view for understanding leadership rooted in local social systems, contrary to approaches that assume the universal applicability of leadership research findings across all cultural settings. It concludes by looking at the implications of the anthropological approach for those who are involved in leadership training in Thai settings and beyond.

Titre Ande

Leadership and Authority

Bula Matari and Life - Community Ecclesiology in Congo

2010 / 978-1-870345-72-9 xvii + 189pp

This book proposes that Christian theology in Africa can make significant developments if a critical understanding of the socio-political context in contemporary Africa is taken seriously. The Christian leadership in post-colonial Africa has cloned its understanding and use of authority on the Bula Matari model, which was issued from the brutality of colonialism and political absolutism in post-colonial Africa. This model has caused many problems in churches, including dysfunction, conflicts, divisions and a lack of prophetic ministry. Titre proposes a Life-Community ecclesiology for liberating authority, where leadership is a function, not a status, and 'apostolic succession' belongs to all the people of God.

Frank Kwesi Adams

Odwira and the Gospel

A Study of the Asante Odwira Festival and its Significance for Christianity in Ghana

2010 /978-1-870345-59-0

The study of the Odwira festival is the key to the understanding of Asante religious and political life in Ghana. The book explores the nature of the Odwira festival longitudinally - in pre-colonial, colonial and post-independence Ghana - and examines the Odwira ideology and its implications for understanding the Asante self-identity. The book also discusses how some elements of faith portrayed in the Odwira festival could provide a framework for Christianity to engage with Asante culture at a greater depth. Theological themes in Asante belief that have emerged from this study include the theology of sacrament, ecclesiology, eschatology, Christology and a complex concept of time. The author argues that Asante cultural identity lies at the heart of the process by which the Asante Christian faith is carried forward.

Bruce Carlton

Strategy Coordinator

Changing the Course of Southern Baptist Missions

2010 / 978-1-870345-78-1 xvii + 268pp

In 1976, the Southern Baptist Convention adopted its Bold New Thrusts in Foreign Missions with the overarching goal of sharing the gospel with every person in the world by the year 2000. The formation of Cooperative Services International (CSI) in 1985 and the assigning of the first non-residential missionary (NRM) in 1987 demonstrated the Foreign Mission Board's (now International Mission Board) commitment to take the gospel message to countries that restricted traditional missionary presence and to people groups identified as having little or no access to the gospel. Carlton traces the historical development along with an analysis of the key components of the paradigm and its significant impact on Southern Baptists' missiology.

Julie Ma & Wonsuk Ma
Mission in the Spirit:
Towards a Pentecostal/Charismatic Missiology
2010 / 978-1-870345-84-2 xx + 312pp

The book explores the unique contribution of Pentecostal/Charismatic mission from the beginning of the twentieth century. The first part considers the theological basis of Pentecostal/Charismatic mission thinking and practice. Special attention is paid to the Old Testament, which has been regularly overlooked by the modern Pentecostal/Charismatic movements. The second part discusses major mission topics with contributions and challenges unique to Pentecostal/Charismatic mission. The book concludes with a reflection on the future of this powerful missionary movement. As the authors served as Korean missionaries in Asia, often their missionary experiences in Asia are reflected in their discussions.

GENERAL REGNUM TITLES

Vinay Samuel, Chris Sugden (eds.)
The Church in Response to Human Need
1987 / 1870345045 / xii+268pp

Philip Sampson, Vinay Samuel, Chris Sugden (eds.)
Faith and Modernity
Essays in modernity and post-modernity
1994 / 1870345177 / 352pp

Klaus Fiedler
The Story of Faith Missions
1994 / 0745926878 / 428pp

Douglas Peterson
Not by Might nor by Power
A Pentecostal Theology of Social Concern in Latin America
1996 / 1870345207 / xvi+260pp

David Gitari
In Season and Out of Season
Sermons to a Nation
1996 / 1870345118 / 155pp

David. W. Virtue
A Vision of Hope
The Story of Samuel Habib
1996 / 1870345169 / xiv+137pp

Everett A Wilson
Strategy of the Spirit
J.Philip Hogan and the Growth of the Assemblies of God Worldwide, 1960 - 1990
1997 /1870345231/214

Murray Dempster, Byron Klaus, Douglas Petersen (eds.)
The Globalization of Pentecostalism
A Religion Made to Travel
1999 / 1870345290 / xvii+406pp

Peter Johnson, Chris Sugden (eds.)
Markets, Fair Trade and the Kingdom of God
Essays to Celebrate Traidcraft's 21st Birthday
2001 / 1870345193 / xii+155pp

Robert Hillman, Coral Chamberlain, Linda Harding
Healing & Wholeness
Reflections on the Healing Ministry
2002 / 978-1- 870345-35- 4 / xvii+283pp

David Bussau, Russell Mask
Christian Microenterprise Development
An Introduction
2003 / 1870345282 / xiii+142pp

David Singh
Sainthood and Revelatory Discourse
An Examination of the Basis for the Authority of Bayan in Mahdawi Islam
2003 / 8172147285 / xxiv+485pp

For the up-to-date listing of the Regnum books see www.ocms.ac.uk/regnum

regnum

Regnum Books International

Regnum is an Imprint of The Oxford Centre for Mission Studies
St. Philip and St. James Church
Woodstock Road
Oxford, OX2 6HR
Web: www.ocms.ac.uk/regnum